Forgotten Books

Marie Bashkirtseff

The Journal of a Young Artist, 1860-1884

By

Marie Bashkirtseff

Published by Forgotten Books 2012
Originally Published 1884

PIBN 1000211209

MARIE BASHKIRTSEFF

THE JOURNAL OF A YOUNG ARTIST

1860-1884

TRANSLATED BY

MARY J. SERRANO

AUTHOR OF " DESTINY AND OTHER POEMS,"
TRANSLATOR OF " DRAGON'S TEETH," " PEPITA XIMENEZ," ETC.

ILLUSTRATED

CASSELL & COMPANY, LIMITED

104-106 FOURTH AVENUE, NEW YORK

·

Press of W. L. Mershon & C<

Rahway, N . J.

TO

JOSEPHINE LAZARUS

THIS TRANSLATION IS DEDICATED, IN ACKNOWLEDGMENT OF HER APPRECIATION
OF THE AUTHOR OF THIS JOURNAL, AND HER GENEROUS CRITICISM
OF THE WORK OF THE TRANSLATOR.

TRANSLATOR'S PREFACE.

HERE is the record of an extraordinary life—' a book without a parallel,' as Gladstone has called it. In these pages, science, art, literature, social questions, love, are treated with all the cynicism of a Machiavelli and the *naïveté* of an ardent and enthusiastic girl. On a background solemn and somber as the steppes of her native land are traced pictures that reflect the vivid hues, the luminous atmosphere, the life, the movement, the variety, of France, Spain, Italy. With a nature that was profoundly religious, and a spirit that was essentially skeptical, with ambition to conquer the universe, and a heart that yearned with a passionate longing for affection, demanding all things for herself, yet capable of the most utter self-abnegation. "hoping all things," and fearing all things alternately, clinging to life with an eagerness that is pathetic in its intensity, wishing for death with an eagerness no less pathetic, regarding herself by turns as the superior of kings, and as less than the least of created beings, Marie Bashkirtseff has left us as her contribution to the literature of humanity these confessions, which no one who has a mind to think or a heart to feel can read unmoved. Certain portions of the Journal, which in its entirety might seem diffuse to American readers, have been omitted in the translation.

M. J. S.

AUTHOR'S PREFACE.

OF what use were pretense or affectation? Yes, it is evident that I have the desire, if not the hope, of living upon this earth by any means in my power. If I do not die young I hope to live as a great artist; but if I die young, I intend to have my journal, which cannot fail to be interesting, published. Perhaps this idea of publication has already detracted from, if not destroyed, the chief merit that such a work may be said to possess? But, no! for in the first place I had written for a long time without any thought of being read, and then it is precisely because I hope to be read that I am altogether sincere. If this book is not the *exact*, the *absolute*, the *strict* truth, it has no *raison d'etre*. Not only do I always write what I think, but I have not even dreamed, for a single instant, of disguising anything that was to my disadvantage, or that might make me appear ridiculous. Besides, I think myself too admirable for censure. You may be very certain, then, charitable readers, that I exhibit myself in these pages *just as I am*. As a subject of interest for you *I* may appear to you of little consequence ; but forget that it is *I;* think simply that a fellow-being is recounting to you her impressions from her infancy. Such a document is very interesting from a human standpoint. Ask M. Zola if this be not so, or even M. de Goncourt, or Maupassant himself ! My journal commences at my twelfth year, but begins to possess some value only from after my fifteenth or sixteenth year. There is in it, therefore, a blank to be filled up ; so that I shall write a sort of preface in order to render this monument of human and literary interest intelligible.

Assume, then, that I am of noble birth, and let us begin :

I was born on the 11th of November, 1860. Only to write it down is frightful. But then I console myself by thinking that I shall be of no age at all when you read my journal.

My father was the son of General Paul Gregorievitch Bashkirtseff, a provincial nobleman who was of a brave, obstinate, severe, and even ferocious nature. My grandfather was raised to the grade of General after the Crimean war, I think. He married a young girl—the adopted daughter of a *grand seigneur;* she died at the age of thirty-eight, leaving five children—my father and four daughters.

Mamma was married at the age of twenty-one, after having rejected several very good *partis.* She was a Babanine. On the side of the Babanines we belong to an old noble family of the provinces ; and grandpapa has always boasted of being of Tartar origin (his ancestors having come to Russia at the time of the first invasion). Baba Nina are two Tartar words—for my part I laugh at all this. Grandpapa was the contemporary of Lermontoff, Poushkine, etc. He was an admirer of Byron, a poet, a soldier, and a man of letters. He married, while quite young, Mademoiselle Julie Cornelius, a girl of fifteen, very sweet and very pretty. They had nine children—if you will pardon the smallness of the number !

After two years of marriage mamma went, with her two children, to live with her parents. I was always with grandmamma, who idolized me. Besides grandmama to adore me, there was my aunt, when mamma did not carry her off with her—my aunt, who was younger than mamma, but not so pretty ; who sacrificed herself to and was sacrificed by everybody.

In May, 1870, we set out to travel. The dream so long

cherished by mamma was realized. We remained a month in Vienna, making ourselves dizzy with novelties of every description—fine shops, theaters, etc. We arrived at Baden-Baden in June, at the height of the season, and found ourselves in the midst of a luxury truly Parisian. Our party consisted of grandpapa, mamma, my aunt Romanoff, Dina (my cousin-german) my brother Paul, and myself; and we had with us a doctor, the angelic, the incomparable Walitsky. He was a Pole, but without any exaggerated patriotism, of a sweet nature, and very winning manners. He spent all his income on his profession. At Achtirka he was the physician of the district. He attended the University with mamma's brother, and was always treated as one of the family at our house. At the time of our setting out on our travels a physician was needed for grandpapa, and for that reason we took Walitsky with us. It was at Baden that I first became acquainted with the world, and with the refinements of polite society, and that I suffered the tortures of vanity.

But I have not said enough about Russia, and about myself, which is the principal thing. I had two governesses, one a Russian, the other a French woman. The former, whom I remember very well, was a certain Madame Melnikoff, a woman of elegant manners, well educated, romantic, and who was separated from her husband. She became a governess on a sudden impulse, after reading a great many romances. She was regarded by the family as a friend, and treated by them as an equal. All the men paid court to her, and one fine morning, after a certain romantic adventure, she disappeared. She might have bade us good-by and gone away quite naturally, but the Slav nature, with French civilization grafted on to it and influenced by romantic reading, is a curious compound. In her character of unhappy wife this lady had at once set herself to adore the little girl confided to her care. I had returned her adoration through an instinctive feeling of dramatic fitness, and my family, *poseuse* and simple-minded, thought her departure ought to make me ill ; they all regarded me with compassionate looks that day, and I remember that grandmamma ordered a certain soup—a soup for invalids—to be made expressly for me. I felt myself grow quite pale before this exhibition of sensibility. I was, indeed, sickly looking, fragile, and not at all pretty—all which did not prevent every one's regarding me as a being destined to become one day beautiful, brilliant, and magnificent. Mamma once went to a Jew who told fortunes.

"You have two children," he said to her ; " your son will be like everybody else, but your daughter will be a star ! "

One evening at the theater a gentleman said to me, laughingly :

"Show me your hand, mademoiselle. Ah, by the style in which you are gloved, there is not the slightest doubt but that you will one day be a terrible coquette."

I was for a long time very proud of this. Since I have been able to think, since I was three years old (I was not weaned until I was three and a half), I have always had aspirations toward greatness of some kind. My dolls were always kings or queens ; all my thoughts, everything I heard from those who surrounded mamma, always bore some reference to this greatness which must one day inevitably come to me.

When I was about five years old I dressed myself one day in mamma's laces, put flowers in my hair, and went to the drawing-room, to dance. I was the great *danseuse*. Petipa, and all the household were there to look at me. Paul was nobody beside me, and Dina, although the daughter of the dearly beloved Georges, did not put me in the shade. One more incident : When Dina was born, grandmamma took her from her mother, and kept her from that time forth with herself. This was before I was born.

After Mme. Melnikoff I had for a governess Mdlle. Sophie Dolgikoff, a girl of sixteen—blessed Russia!—and another, a Frenchwoman called Mme. Brenne, who wore her hair in the style of the Restoration, had pale blue eyes, and was a sorrowful looking creature with her fifty years, and her consumption. I was very fond of her. She taught me how to draw. I drew a little church under her instructions. I drew at other times also. While the grown-up people played cards I would often draw on the green cloth.

All this brings us back to Baden in 1870. War having been declared, we had betaken ourselves to Geneva, I with my heart filled with bitterness, and cherishing projects of revenge. Every evening on going to bed I recited in my own mind the following supplementary prayer :

"My God, grant that I may never have the small-pox ; that I may grow up pretty ; that I may have a beautiful voice ; that I may be happily married ; and that mamma may live for a long time to come !

At Geneva we put up at the Hotel de la Couronne on the borders of the lake. There I had a professor of drawing who brought designs with him for me to copy—little chalets in which the windows were like trunks of trees, and did not at all resemble the windows of real chalets, so I refused to draw them. The good man then told me to copy them from nature, just as they appeared to me. Just then we left the hotel to live in a family boarding-house, with Mont Blanc in front of us. I therefore copied scrupulously all that was visible of Geneva and the lake.

When I am dead, my life, which appears to me a remarkable one, will be read. (The only thing wanting is that it should have been different.) But I detest prefaces (they have kept me from reading a great many excellent books), as well as the notices of editors. For this reason I write my own preface. It might have been omitted if I had published the whole of my journal, but I limited myself to beginning at my twelfth year; to give what precedes would render the book too long. Besides, I give you glimpses enough into it in the course of the journal. I go back to the past very often, apropos of anything or nothing.

What if, seized without warning by a fatal illness, I should happen to die suddenly! I should not know, perhaps, of my danger; my family would hide it from me; and after my death they would rummage among my papers; they would find my journal, and destroy it after having read it, and soon nothing would be left of me—nothing—nothing— nothing! This is the thought that has always terrified me. To live, to have so much ambition, to suffer, to weep, to struggle, and in the end to be forgotten;—as if I had never existed. If I should not live long enough to become famous, this journal will be interesting to the psychologist. The record of a woman's life, written down day by day, without any attempt at concealment, as if no one in the world were ever to read it, yet with the purpose of being read, is always interesting; for I am certain that I shall be found sympathetic. and I write down everything, every- thing, everything. Otherwise why should I write? Be- sides, it will very soon be seen that I have concealed nothing.

PARIS, May 1, 1884.

MARIE BASHKIRTSEFF;

THE JOURNAL OF A YOUNG ARTIST.

1873.

VILLA ACQUA-VIVA,   ⎫
PROMENADE DES ANGLAIS, NICE. ⎰

January (at the age of twelve years).—Aunt Sophie is playing some of the national airs of Little Russia on the piano, and this recalls our country to me. I am transported in fancy, and what recollections can I have of that life that are not associated with poor grandmamma? The tears are coming to my eyes; they are there now, and in another instant they will fall; they are falling already. Poor grandmamma! How unfortunate I am to have you no longer beside me! How tenderly you loved me, and I you! But I was too young to love you as you deserved to be loved! I am deeply moved by these memories. The memory of grandmamma is a respected, a sacred, a beloved one, but it is not a living one. O my God! grant me happiness in this life, and I will be grateful! But what am I saying? It appears to me that I have been placed in this world in order to be happy; make me happy, O my God!

Aunt Sophie is still playing. The sounds of the piano reach me at intervals, and penetrate my soul. I have no lessons to learn for to-morrow, for it is Aunt Sophie's fete-day. God grant that the Duke of H—— may be mine! I will love him and make him happy! I will be happy too.

I will do good to the poor. It is a sin to think that one can purchase the favor of God by good works, but I know not how otherwise to express myself.

I love the Duke of H   , but I cannot tell him that I love him ; and even if I were to tell him so, he would pay no attention to it. When he was here I had some object in going out, in dressing myself, but now !— I used to go to the terrace in the hope of seeing him for even a single instant, at a distance. My God, assuage my grief ! I can pray no more; hear my prayer. Thy grace is infinite; Thy mercy great ! Thou hast granted me so many blessings ! It grieves me to see him no longer on the promenade. His face was easily distinguishable among the vulgar faces of Nice.

Mrs. Howard invited us yesterday to spend the day with her children. We were on the point of setting out, when she returned to say that she had asked mamma's permission to keep us till evening. We remained, and after dinner we all went to the great drawing-room, which was dark, and the girls begged me so much to sing ; they went on their knees to me—the children as well; we laughed a great deal ; I sang " Santa Lucia," " The Sun is Risen," and some *roulades.* They were so delighted that they all embraced me frantically. If I could produce the same effect upon the public I would go on the stage this very day.

It causes so profound an emotion to be admired for something more than one's dress ! Truly, I am transported by these words of praise from children. What would it be, then, if I were admired by *others ?*

I was made for triumphs and emotions ; the best thing I can do, therefore, is to become a singer. If the good God would only *preserve, strengthen,* and *develop* my voice, then I should enjoy the triumph for which I long. Then I should enjoy the happiness of being celebrated, and admired ; and in that way the one I love might be mine. If I remain as I am, I have but little hope of his loving me; he is ignorant even of my existence. But when he sees me surrounded by glory, in the midst of triumphs! Men are so ambitious! And I shall be received in society, for I shall not be a celebrity out of a tobacco-shop or a filthy street. I am of noble birth; I have no need to make use of my talents—my fortune does not exact it—so that I shall have all the greater glory for elevating myself, and it will be all the easier for me to do so. In that way my life would be perfect. I dream of glory, of fame, of being known throughout the world!

To see thousands of persons, when you appear upon the stage, await with beating hearts the moment when you shall begin to sing; to know as you look at them that a single note of your voice will bring them all to your feet; to look at them with a haughty glance (for I can do anything)—that is my dream, that is my life, that is my happiness, that is my desire. And then, in the midst of all this, Monsignor le Duc de H—— will come with the others to throw himself at my feet, but he shall not meet with the same reception as the others. Dear, you will be dazzled by my splendor, and you will love me! You will behold me in all my glory, it is true—you deserve for a wife only such a woman as I hope to become. I am not ugly; I am even pretty—yes, rather pretty than ugly. I am extremely well-formed, with all the perfection of a statue; I have tolerably fine hair; I have a coquettish manner that is very becoming, and I know how to conduct myself toward men.

I am a modest girl, and I would never give a kiss to any other man than my husband; I can boast of something that not every girl of twelve or fourteen years can say, that is, of never having been kissed, and of never having kissed anyone. Then, to see a young girl at the highest point of glory to which a woman can attain, who has loved him from her childhood with a constant love, simple and modest—all this will astonish him ; he will want to marry me at any cost, and he will do so through pride. But what do I say? Why should I not admit that he may love me? Ah, yes, with the help of God ; God has made me discover the means by which I may possess him I love. I thank Thee, O my God, I thank Thee !

Friday, March 14.—This morning I heard a noise of car-riages in the Rue de France ; I looked out and saw the Duke of H—— driving with four horses on the Promenade. Ah, if he is here, he will take part in the pigeon-shooting match in April ; I will be there at any cost !

To-day I saw the Duke of H—— again. No one bears himself as he does ; he has the air of a king when he is driving in his carriage.

I shall be happy with my husband, for I will not neglect myself ; I will adorn myself to please him, as I adorned my-self when I wished to please him for the first time. Besides, I cannot understand how a man and a woman can love each other tenderly, and endeavor to please each other unceas-ingly, and then neglect themselves after marriage. Why believe that with the word marriage love must pass away, and that only cold and reserved friendship remains ; why profane marriage by representing the wife in curl-papers and a wrapper, with cold-cream on her nose, trying to get money from her husband for dresses ; why should a woman be careless of her appearance before the man for whom she should adorn herself the most? I do not see why one should treat one's husband like a domestic animal, and yet so long as one is not married, why one should wish to please this man. Why not always retain something of coquetry with one's husband, and treat him as a stranger whom one desires to please? Is it because one need not conceal one's love, because it is not a crime to love, and because marriage has received God's benediction? Is it because that which is not forbidden possesses no value in our eyes, and that one can find pleasure only in secret and forbidden things ? This ought not to be.

I have strained my voice in singing and injured it, so that I have made a promise to God to sing no more (a resolution that I have since broken a hundred times) until I take lessons ; I have prayed to Him in the mean time to purify, strengthen and develop it. And in order that I may not be tempted to break my vow, I have even besought Him to take it from me, should I do so. This is frightful, but I will do all I can to keep my vow.

Friday, December 30.—To-day I have on an antediluvian dress, my little petticoat and black velvet coat, over it the tunic and sleeveless jacket of Dina, and it all looks very well. I think it is because I know how to wear the dress, and carry myself well. (I looked like a little old woman.) I was very much noticed. I should like to know why they all look at me, and whether it is because I appear ridiculous, or because I am pretty. I would reward well any one who would tell me the truth. I have a mind to ask some one (some young man) if I am pretty. I always like to believe things that are good, and I should prefer to believe that it is because I am pretty. Perhaps I deceive myself, but if it be a delusion I would rather keep it, because it is a flattering one. What would you have ? In this world it is necessary to look at things in their best possible light. Life is so beautiful and so short !

I have been thinking of what my brother Paul will do when he is a man. What profession will he choose ? For he cannot spend his life as so many people spend theirs— first saunter idly about, and then throw himself into the world of gamblers and *cocottes ;* no ! Besides, he has not the means of doing this. I write sensible letters to him every Sunday—not sermons, no ! but letters such as a comrade might write him.   Well, I shall know what to do, and, with God's help, I shall exert some influence over him, for he must be a man.

I was so preoccupied that I had almost forgotten (what a shame !) the absence of the Duke !   It seems as if so great a gulf separate us, especially if we go to Russia in the summer.   They are talking seriously of that.   How can I imagine that he should ever be mine ?   He no more thinks of me than he does of last year's snow.   I do not exist for him.   If we remain in Nice for the winter, I may still hope ; but it seems to me that with our departure for Russia all my hopes will vanish ; everything that I had thought possible is disappearing from my gaze.   I am passing through a period of supreme anguish—a change in my whole nature is taking place.   How strange it is !   .

I am overwhelmed by my thoughts.   O my God, at the thought that he will never love me I am ready to die of grief !   I have no longer any hope.   I was mad to desire things so impossible.   I wished to possess what was too beautiful.   Ah, but no ! I must not allow myself to be thus carried away.   What ! I dare despair thus !   Is there not a God to whom all things are possible, who protects me ?   What ! I dare entertain these thoughts ?   Is He not everywhere always, watching over us ?   He can do all things ; He is all-powerful ; for Him there is neither time nor space.   I may be in Peru, and the Duke in Africa, and if He wishes He can bring us together.   How can I have entertained for a single moment a despairing thought ?   How can I have forgotten for an instant His divine goodness ?   Is it because He does not give me everything that I desire at once that I dare to deny Him?   No, no, He is more merciful ; He will not allow a soul as innocent as mine to be torn apart by these sinful doubts.

This morning I pointed out a coal-vender to Mlle. Colignon (my governess) saying : "See how much that man

resembles the Duke of H   ." She replied, smiling:
" What nonsense!" It gave me an indescribable pleasure to
pronounce his name. But I notice that if we never speak of
the man we love, our love grows stronger; but if we speak
continually of him, our love diminishes. It is like a vial of
some essence ; if it be corked, the perfume remains strong,
while if it be open, the perfume evaporates. This is precisely the case with my love ; it remains strong because I
never hear him I love spoken of. I never speak of him, I
keep him entirely for myself.

I am very sad. I have no positive ideas regarding my
future ; that is to say, I know what I would like to have,
but not what I shall have. How gay I was last winter !
Everything smiled on me ; I had hope. I love a shadow
which perhaps I shall never possess. I am in despair about
my gowns ; they have cost me many tears. I went with my
aunt to two dressmakers ; but they were both unsatisfactory.
I shall write to Paris ; I cannot bear the gowns here.

This evening we spent at church ; it is the first day of
our Holy Week, and I performed my devotions. I must
say that there are many things about our religion which I
do not like ; but it is not for me to reform them ; I believe
in God, in Christ, and in the Holy Virgin. I pray to God
every night, and I have no wish to trouble myself about a
few trifles that have nothing to do with true religion—with
true faith. I believe in God, and He is good to me ; He
gives me more than I need. Oh, if He would only give me
what I desire so much ! The good God will have pity on
me, although I might do without what I ask. I should be
so happy if the Duke would only take notice of me, and I
would bless God.

I must write his name, for if I neither mentioned it to
any one nor even wrote it down here I could no longer
live. . . . It is some slight consolation only to write it.
On the Promenade I saw with joy a carriage containing a

young man,* tall, slender, and dark. I thought I recognized some one. I gave a cry of surprise : " Oh, *caro*—!"
They asked me what was the matter ; I answered that Mlle.
Colignon had stepped on my foot. He resembles his brother
in nothing. Nevertheless, it makes me happy to see him.
Ah, if I could only make his acquaintance, at least ; for
through him I might come to know the Duke ! I love this
one as if he were my brother ; I love him because he is *his*
brother. At dinner Walitsky said suddenly, "H   ." I
blushed ; I was confused, and I walked toward the cup-
board. Mamma reproved me for this, saying that it was
very wrong. I think she divines something, because every
time any one mentions the name H—— I blush or leave the
room abruptly. She does not scold me for it, however.

They are all sitting in the dining-room, chatting together
quietly, and thinking me occupied with my studies. They
are ignorant of what is passing within me, and they do not
know what my thoughts are now. I must be either the
Duchess of H   , and that is what I most desire (for God
knows how ardently I love him), or become famous on the
stage ; but this career does not attract me so much as the
other. It is doubtless flattering to receive the homage of
the entire world, from the lowest to the sovereigns of the
earth, but the other !—Yes, I will have him I love ; that is
altogether another kind of happiness, and I prefer it. A
great lady—a duchess—I would rather be this in society,
than be the first among the celebrities of the world, for that
would not be my world.

May 6.—Mamma is up, and Mlle. C—— also, for she has
been ill. It was so delightful after the rain ! so fresh, and
the trees looked so beautiful with the sun shining on them,
that I could not study. I went into the garden and placed
my chair beside the fountain, and had before me a magnifi-

---

* The Duke's brother.

cent picture, for this fountain is surrounded by large trees, that completely shut out the prospect. All that is to be seen is a brook, and rocks covered with moss, and on every side trees of different kinds, their foliage lighted up by the sun. And the soft, green turf ! Truly I was tempted to roll on it. All this made a sort of grove, so fresh, so soft, so green, so beautiful that I should try in vain to give you an idea of it ; I cannot. If the villa and the garden do not change, I will bring him here to show him the spot where I have so often thought of him. Yesterday evening I prayed to God, and when I came to the part where I asked that I might know the Duke, that God would grant me this happiness, I shed tears. Three times already has God listened to me, and granted my prayer : the first time I asked Him for a set of croquet, and my aunt brought me one from Geneva ; the second time I asked Him to help me to learn English. I prayed and wept so much, and my imagination was so excited, that I thought I beheld an image of the Virgin in a corner of the room, who promised what I asked for. I could even recognize the face, if I should see it again.

I don't want any one to think that, when I have done with studying, I shall do nothing but dance and dress myself ; no, having finished the studies of childhood, I shall devote myself seriously to painting, music, and singing. I have talent for all this, and a great deal of it ! What a consolation it is to write this ! I am already calmer. Not only do the annoyances I suffer injure my health, but they injure my disposition and my appearance. This flush that overspreads my face makes my cheeks burn as with fire, and when calmness returns they are no longer either fresh or rosy. This color which I am condemned to have always in my face will make me pale and faded, and that is Mlle. C 's fault, for the agitation she causes me produces it. I even have slight headaches after my face has burned like this. Mamma scolds me ; she says it is my fault that I do not speak English.   How indignant that makes me !

I think, if he should ever read this journal, that he will find it stupid,—above all, my confessions of love.   I have repeated them so often that they have lost all their force. Ah, when one thinks what a miserable creature man is ! Every other animal can, at his will, wear on his face the expression he pleases.   He is not obliged to smile if he has a mind to weep.   When he does not wish to see his fellows he does not see them.   While man is the slave of everything and everybody !   And yet I draw this very fate upon myself.   I love to visit, and I love to see visitors.

Last night I had a horrible dream.   We were in a house that I had never seen before; when suddenly I, or some one, I do not remember who, looked out of the window.   The sun had increased in size until it covered almost half of the sky, but it did not shine, and it gave forth no heat.   Then it separated into parts, and a quarter of it disappeared ; the remainder separated again into parts, changing color as it did so, and casting a glow all around ; then a cloud over-spread one half of the sun, and everybody cried out, "The sun has stopped moving."   It remained for some moments immovable, but pallid ; then something strange happened to the earth ; it was not that it trembled ; I can-not describe what it was.   There are no words to express what we do not comprehend.   Then the sun began to move again, like two wheels, one within the other ; that is to say, that part of the sun which remained shining was covered at intervals by a cloud round like itself.   Every one was troubled.   Mamma was not with us ; she came afterward in a kind of omnibus, and seemed to be not at all frightened. Everything was strange ; this omnibus was not like other omnibuses.   Then I began to examine my dresses ; we were packing our things into a little trunk.   But at that instant everything began over again.   "It is the end of the world," I thought, and I asked myself how it was that God had not warned me of it, and how it was that I was thought worthy to be present in the flesh, on this day. Every one was afraid, and we got into the vehicle with mamma, and returned, I know not where.

What is the meaning of this dream? Is it sent by God to forewarn me of some great event? or is it simply the result of nervousness?

Mlle. C—— goes away to-morrow. All the same it is a little sad. It is painful to part from even a dog with which one has lived. It matters not whether the existing relations were pleasant or not, I have a worm gnawing at my heart.

Time passes swift as an arrow. In the morning I study a little—the piano for two hours. The Apollo Belvidere which I am going to copy bears some slight resemblance to the Duke. In the expression, especially, the likeness is very strong—the same manner of carrying the head, and the same shaped nose.

Manote, my music teacher, was very much pleased with me this morning. I played a passage in Mendelssohn's concerto in G-minor without a single mistake. Then we went to the Russian church—the Church of the Trinity. The whole church was decorated with flowers and plants. Prayers were offered up, in which the priest asked pardon for sins, mentioning each one separately. Then he knelt down and prayed again. Everything he said was so applicable to me that I remained motionless, listening to and echoing his prayer. This is the second time that I have prayed with so much fervor in church. The first time was on New Year's Day. The service has become so hackneyed, and then the things spoken of are not those of everyday life—things that concern every one. I go to mass, but I do not pray. The prayers and the hymns they sing find no response either in my heart or in my soul. They prevent me from praying with freedom, while the *Te Deum*, in which the priest prays for every one (where every one finds something applicable to himself) penetrates my soul.

Paris—At last I have found what I longed for without knowing what it was! Life, that is Paris! Paris, that is life! I tormented myself because I did not know what I desired ; now I see before me—I know—what I desire. To go from Nice to Paris ; to have an apartment, to furnish it ; to have horses, as we have at Nice ; to have the *entree* to society through the medium of the Russian Ambassador— this, this is what I desire. How happy it makes one to know what one desires ! But there is one thought that tortures me—it is, that I am ugly ! This is horrible !

Nice—I regard Nice as an exile. I must, before every- thing, make an order of exercises for each day, including the hours of my different professors. On Monday I begin again my studies, which were cut so diabolically short by Mlle. Colignon. With the winter people will come to the city, and with people, gayety. It will then be no longer Nice, but a little Paris. And the races ! Nice has its good side. All the same, the six or seven months we are to spend here seem to me like a sea that is to be crossed without once removing my eyes from the beacon that guides me. I do not hope to stand upon its shore, I only hope to see land, and the sight of it alone will endow me with force of character, and give me strength to endure life until next year. And then ? And then ! Upon my word I know nothing about it, but I hope. I believe in God and in His divine goodness—that is why I do not lose courage.

" He that dwelleth in the secret place of the Most High shall abide in the shadow of the Almighty. He shall cover thee with his feathers, and under his wings shalt thou trust ; his truth shall be thy shield and buckler. Thou shalt not be afraid for the terror by night ; nor for the arrow that flieth by day." I cannot express what I feel, nor my grati- tude to God for his goodness toward me.

June 9.—I have begun to study drawing. I feel tired, weak, unable to work. The summers in Nice are killing me ; no one is here ; I am ready to cry ; in a word, I am unhappy. We live only once. To spend a summer at Nice is to lose half one's life. I am crying now, a tear has fallen on the paper. Oh, if mamma and the others knew what it costs me to remain here, they would not keep me in this FRIGHTFUL desert ! Nothing diverts my thoughts from *him.* It is so long since I have heard his name mentioned. It seems to me as if he were dead. And then, I am enveloped in darkness ; the past I can scarcely recall, the present is hideous ; I am completely changed ; my voice is hoarse ; I have grown ugly ; formerly on awaking in the morning I was fresh and rosy. But what is it that tortures me thus? What has happened to me ? What is going to happen ?

We have hired the Villa Bacchi. To tell the truth, it is very distressing to have to live there ; for the *bourgeois* it is well enough, but for us ! As for me I am an aristocrat ; I prefer a ruined gentleman to a rich *bourgeois.* I find a greater charm in old satin, or in the gilding, blackened by time, of old-fashioned columns and ornaments, than in rich and tasteless furniture that obtrudes itself upon the eye. A true gentleman will not base his pride on having shining boots and well-fitting gloves. Not that one should be careless as to one's appearance, no ; but between the carelessness of the nobleman and the carelessness of the plebeian there is such a difference !

We are going to leave this lodging, and I am sorry for it ; not because it is convenient or handsome, but because it is like an old friend, and I am accustomed to it. When I think that I shall never again see my beloved study ! I have thought so often of him here ! This table on which I am leaning, and on which I have written day by day all that was sweetest and most sacred in my soul ; those walls over which my glances wander, seeking to pierce them and

fly far, far away! In each flower of the wall-paper I behold him! How many scenes have I pictured to myself in
this study, in each of which he played the principal *role!*
It seems to me there is not a single thing in the world of
which I have not thought in this little room, from the simplest to the most fantastic.

In the evening Paul, Dina, and I remained for a while
together; then they left me alone. The moon shone into
my chamber, and I did not light the candles. I went out
on the terrace, and listened to the distant sounds of a vio-
lin, guitar, and flute. I returned quickly to my room and
sat down by the window in order to listen more at my ease.
It was a charming *trio*. It is long since I have listened to
music with so much pleasure. In a concert one's attention
is engaged more by the audience than by the music, but
this evening, seated all alone by the light of the moon, I
devoured, if I may use the expression, this serenade, for
such it was, given us by the young men of Nice. They
could not be more gallant. Unfortunately the fashionable
young men do not like these amusements; they prefer to
spend their time in the *cafés chantants*, but as for music—
What can be nobler than to take part in a serenade, as in
Spain in olden times!. Upon my word, after riding, I
should choose to spend my time under my mistress's window, and afterward at her feet.

I should so much like to have a horse! Mamma has
promised that I shall have one, and my aunt also. This
evening, in mamma's room, I asked her to give me one, in
my airy, enthusiastic way, and she promised it to me seriously. I shall go to bed quite happy to-night. Every one
tells me I am pretty, but in truth, in my own mind I don't
think so. My pen refuses to write the word; I am graceful only—and occasionally pretty. How happy I am!

I am to have a horse! Did any one ever see a little girl
like me with a race-horse? I shall make a *furore*. What

colors shall my jockey wear? Gray and parti-colored? No, green and pale rose. A horse, for me! How happy I am! What a creature I am! Why not give something from my overflowing cup to the poor, who have nothing? Mamma gives me money; I will give half of it to the poor.

I have altered the arrangement of my room; it is prettier without the table in the middle. I have put in it several trifles—an inkstand, a pen, and two old traveling candle-sticks which had lain hidden away for a long time in the box in which things out of use are kept. The world, that is my life; it calls me, it waits for me, I long to run to meet it, but I am not old enough yet to go into society. But I long to be old enough, not for the sake of marrying, but because I want to see mamma and my aunt shake off their laziness. Not the world of Nice, but the world of St. Petersburg, of London, of Paris; there it is that I could breathe freely, for the constraints of society are freedom for me.

Paul has no taste, as yet; he understands nothing about woman's beauty. I have heard him say: "Beauties, such ugly creatures as those!" I must form his manners and his tastes. So far, indeed, I do not exercise a great deal of influence over him, but I hope to do so in time. For the present, I try to communicate my own views of things to him, but without his suspecting it; I convey sentiments of the severest morality to him under a frivolous guise.

Tuesday, July 29.—Here we are on our way to Vienna; our departure was, on the whole, a cheerful one. I was, as usual, the soul of the party.

September 2.—The drawing-master has come; I gave him a list of subjects I wished to study, the other day, that he might send me some professors from the Lyceum. At last

I shall set to work ! On Mlle. Colignon's account I have lost four months, which is monstrous. Binsa went to the censor, who asked him for a day's time. Seeing my note he inquired, "How old is the young girl who wants to study all this ; and who makes out such a programme for herself ?" The stupid Binsa answered, "Fifteen years old." I scolded him severely for doing so ; I was furious, enraged. Why should he say I am fifteen ? It is not true. He excused himself by saying that, judging from my reasoning powers, I was twenty ; that he thought he did very well in saying that I was only two years older than I am, etc. I exacted from him to-day at dinner a promise that he should tell the censor how old I am ; I *exacted it.*

Friday, September 19.—I try to be cheerful under all circumstances ; one ought not to sadden one's-self by grieving. Life is so short, one should laugh while one can. Tears will come of themselves, those at least we can avoid. but there are sorrows which we cannot escape, such as death and absence ; yet even this last has its charms, so long as one has the hope of being reunited to the absent one. But to spoil one's life with petty worries is a shame. I pay no heed to such trifles ; I have a horror of trivial, every-day annoyances, so I let them pass with a smile.

Monday, October 13.—I was looking up my lesson to-day when little Heder, my English governess, said to me : "Do you know that the Duke is going to marry the Duchess M   ?" I put the book closer to my face, for I was as red as fire. I felt as if a sharp knife had pierced my heart. I began to tremble so violently that I could scarcely hold the volume. I was afraid I was going to faint, but the book saved me. I pretended to be looking for the place for a few moments, until I grew calmer. I said my lesson in a voice that trembled with emotion. I summoned all my courage—as I had done on a former occasion, when I wished to throw myself over the bridge—and told myself that I must control myself. I wrote a dictation so as not to have to speak. I was rejoiced when I went to the piano ; I tried to play, but my fingers were cold and stiff. The Princess came to ask me to teach her to play croquet. "With pleasure," I responded gayly ; but my voice still trembled. I ran to dress myself. In a green gown—my hair is the color of gold, and my complexion white and red—I looked as pretty as an angel or a woman. I kept thinking continually, " He is going to marry ! Can it be possible ? How unhappy I am ! "—not unhappy, as formerly, on account of the paper of one room, or the furniture of another, but really unhappy !

I'did not know how to tell the Princess that he was going to be married (for they will all know it some day), and it is better I should tell it myself. I chose a moment when she was seated in an arm-chair ; the light was behind me so that she could not see my face. " Do you know the news, Princess ? " I said (we spoke in Russian), " the Duke of H is going to be married." At last ! I had said the words. I did not grow red ; I was calm ; but what passed within me, in the depths of my soul, no one shall ever know !

We went out for a walk, but Nice is no longer Nice. The only thing that bound me to Nice was he. I detest Nice ! I can scarcely endure the thought of remaining here. I am weary ! ah, how weary I am !

My God, save me from despair ! My God, pardon me my sins ; do not punish me for them ! All is ended !—ended !

To-day I am happy ; I am gay at the thought that perhaps it is not true, for the terrible news has not been confirmed, and I prefer ignorance to the certainty of the crushing truth.

Friday, October 17.—I was playing on the piano when the newspapers were brought in. I took up *Galignani's Messenger*, and the first words on which my eyes fell related to the marriage of the Duke of H   . The paper did not fall from my hands ; on the contrary it remained tight in my grasp. I had not the strength to stand ; I sat down and re-read the blighting lines a dozen times over to assure myself that I was not dreaming. O Divine charity! what have I read ! My God, what have I read ! I could not write in the evening, I threw myself on my knees and wept. Mamma came into the room, and in order that she might not see me in this state I pretended I was going to inquire if tea was ready. And I have to take a Latin lesson ! Oh, torture ! Oh, anguish ! I can do nothing, I cannot remain quiet. There are no words to express what I feel ; but what makes me desperate, what enrages me, what kills me, is jealousy—jealousy and envy ; they rend my soul apart, they make me furious, mad ! If I could only let my feelings be seen ! But I must hide them and seem calm, and that makes me all the more miserable.

I shall learn to forget in time, no doubt. To say that my grief will be eternal would be ridiculous—nothing is eternal. But the fact is that, for the present, I can think of nothing else. He does not marry ; they marry him. It is all owing to the machinations of his mother. (1880.—*All this on account of a man whom I had seen a dozen times in the street,— whom I did not know, and who did not know that I was in existence.*) Oh, I detest him ! I want to see them together. They are at Baden-Baden that I loved so much ! Those walks where I used to see him, those kiosks, those shops ! .

(*All this re-read in* 1880 *produces no effect on me whatever.*)

To-day I will alter in my prayer all that relates to him. I will no longer pray to God that I may become his wife ! To give up this prayer seems to me impossible, killing ! I shed tears like a fool! Come, come, my child, let us be reasonable.

It is ended! yes, it is ended! Ah, I see now that our wishes are not always granted. Let me make ready for the torture of altering the prayer. Ah, that is the cruelest of all suffering—it is the end of everything. *Amen.*

Saturday, October 18.—I have altered my prayer. I have omitted the prayer for him. I felt as if my heart were being torn out—as if I saw them carrying away the coffin of one dear to me. While the coffin is still there, one is unhappy indeed, but not so unhappy as when one feels a void on every side. I am a strange creature ; no one suffers as I do, yet I live, I sing, I write. How changed I am since the thirteenth of October,—that fatal day! Suffering is depicted on my countenance. His name is no longer the source of a beneficent warmth. It is fire ; it is a reproach to me, it awakens jealousy and grief within me. This is the greatest misfortune that can happen to a woman ; and I have experienced it ! Bitter mockery !

I begin to think seriously about my voice. I should so much like to sing. To what end, now ? He was as a lamp within my soul, and now this lamp is extinguished. All there is dark, gloomy, sorrowful. I know not which way to turn. Before, in my little troubles I had something to lean upon—a light that guided and strengthened me. And now I may seek in vain, I shall find nothing but a dark and dreary void. It is horrible ! horrible ! when there is only a void in the depths of the soul.

Saturday, October 25.—Yesterday a knock came to my door, and they told me that mamma was very ill. I went down stairs, half asleep, and found her sitting in the dining-room in a dreadful state. She wished to see me, she said, before her death. I was seized with horror, but I did not

allow this feeling to appear.   Every one was in despair.   Dr.
Reberg and Dr. Macari were sent for.   Servants were hurried off in all directions for remedies.   Never could I give
an idea of this terrible night.   I spent it seated in an arm-
chair near the window.   There were enough persons present
to do all that was necessary, and besides, I am not a good
nurse.   Never have I suffered so much!   Yes, on the
thirteenth of October I suffered as much, but in a different
way.

Tuesday, October 28.—Poor mamma is no better ; those
brutes of doctors have blistered her, which has made her
suffer horribly.   The best medicines are cold water or tea ;
those are natural and simple.   If a man is to die, he will die
even though he has the attendance of all the doctors in the
world ; if, on the contrary, he is not to die, then he will not
die, even if he have no assistance at all.   Reasoning calmly,
it appears to me that it is better to dispense with all those
pharmaceutic horrors.

Paul will do nothing ; he does not study ; he is not serious enough ; he does not understand that it is his duty to
study, and this grieves me.   My God, inspire him with
wisdom ; make him understand that he ought to study ; inspire him with a little ambition—a little, just enough to
make him desire to be something.   My God, hear my
prayer, direct him, guard him against all those miscreants
who seek to turn him from the right path !

Never could a man beneath me in station succeed in
pleasing me.   Common people *disgust* me ; they sicken me.
A poor man loses half his manhood.   He looks small, miserable, and has the air of a beggar, while the rich and independent man carries himself haughtily, and has a certain
comfortable air.   Self-confidence gives one a victorious look.
And I love in H— – this self-confident, capricious, vain,
and cruel air.   He has something of the Nero in him.

Saturday, November 8.—We should never give too much of our society even to those who love us. It is well not to stay too long in any company so as to leave regrets and illusions behind us when we depart. One will thus appear to better advantage, and seem to be worth more. People will then desire to see you return ; but do not gratify that desire immediately ; make them wait for you, but not too long, however. Anything that costs too much loses by the difficulty with which it is obtained. Something better was anticipated. Or, on the other hand, make them wait a very long time for you—then you will be a queen.

I think I must have a fever ; I suffer, and I try to disguise my feelings by talking. No one would suspect it ; I sing, I laugh, I jest. The more unhappy I am the gayer I seem to be.

All that I could write would never express what I feel ; I am stupid, mad ; I feel myself deeply aggrieved. It seems to me that in marrying the Duke they are robbing me of him. It is, in truth, as if they had taken something from me that was my own. What a wretched state ! I do not know how to express myself, but I feel that I am too weak ; for a mere nothing I make use of the strongest expressions, and when I wish to speak seriously I find there is nothing left.

It is only now that looking at mamma as if she were a stranger, I find that she is charming, beautiful as the day ; although she is worn out with all sorts of troubles and maladies. When she speaks her voice is so sweet—not high, but vibrating and sweet—and her manners, although natural and simple, are agreeable.

Saturday, November 29.—I am tortured by jealousy, love, envy, deceit, wounded vanity, by every hideous feeling in the world. Above all, I feel his loss. I love him !

One thing tortures me especially ; it is that in a few years I shall laugh at myself, that I shall have forgotten all this! (1875.—*It is two years since that time, yet I do not laugh at myself, and I have not forgotten.*)   All these sorrows will seem to me childishness and affectation—but, no, I conjure you, do not forget!   When you read these lines go back to the past, think that you are again thirteen years old; that you are at Nice; that all this is taking place now!   Think that the past lives now!   You will understand!   You will be happy!

Sunday, November 30.—I wish he would marry at once. It is always thus with me; when anything disagreeable is to be done, instead of wanting to put it off, I wish to have it over.   When we left Paris, I made them hasten the hour of our departure; I knew that pill must be swallowed.   The expectation of an unpleasantness is more terrible than the thing itself.

1874.

Sunday, January 4.—How sweet it is to awaken naturally from sleep!   My alarm has not yet sounded, and my eyes have unclosed of themselves!   It is as if one were gliding on in a boat: one sinks into a revery, and when one wakens out of it one has already arrived at one's destination.

Friday, January 9.—On returning from a walk to-day I said to myself that I would not be like some girls, who are comparatively serious and reserved.   I do not understand how this seriousness comes; how from childhood one passes to the state of girlhood.   I asked myself, "How does this happen?   Little by little, or in a single day?"   Love, or a misfortune, is what develops, ripens, or alters the character. If I were a *bel esprit* I should say they were synonymous terms; but I do not say so, for love is the most beautiful thing in the whole world.   I compare myself to a piece of water that is frozen in its depths, and has motion only on the surface, for nothing amuses or interests me in my DEPTHS.

Thursday, January 24.—All last winter I could not sing a note. I was in despair; I thought I had lost my voice, and I blushed and remained silent when I was spoken to. Now it has come back again, my voice, my treasure, my fortune! I receive it with tears in my eyes, and I thank God for it on my knees. I said nothing, but I was cruelly grieved. I did not dare to speak of it. I prayed to God, and He has heard me! What happiness? What a pleasure it is to sing well! One feels as if one were all-powerful, one thinks one's-self a queen! How happy one is! happy in one's own worth. It is not like the pride that springs from the possession of wealth or a title. One is more than woman; one feels one's self immortal. One is freed from earth; one soars into heaven! And all the people who hang upon your notes, who listen to your song as to a voice from heaven, who are electrified, carried away by enthusiasm, ravished—you hold sway over them all. After real sovereignty comes the sovereignty of song. The sovereignty of beauty comes after this, because its sway is not a universal one; but song lifts man above the earth; his soul soars above it in a cloud like that in which Venus appeared to Æneas.

Tuesday, July 6.—Nothing in the world is lost. If we cease to love one individual, this affection is immediately transferred to another, even without our being conscious of it; and if we fancy we love no one, we deceive ourselves. If one does not love a man, one loves a dog or a piece of furniture; and with the same ardor, only in a different fashion. If I loved a man, I would want him to love me as I loved him. I would allow nothing—not even a single word—for another.   Such a love is not to be found ; therefore I will never love, for I should never be loved as I desire to be loved.

July 14.—They have been talking of Latin, of the Lyceum, of the examination ; all this has given me an intense desire to study, and when Brunet came to-day, I did not keep him waiting.   I asked him about the examination ; the information he gave me was such that I feel myself capable, after a year's preparation, of presenting myself for the degree of bachelor of arts and sciences.   I will speak to him further about it.

July 15.—Last night I said to the moon, after leaving the Sapogenikoff's : "Moon, O beautiful moon, show me the person I shall marry before I die ! "

If you say these words to the moon, without speaking afterward until you fall asleep, they say the person you dream of is the one you are to marry.

It is all nonsense.   I dreamed of S. and A.—two impossibilities.   I am in a bad humor ; I fail in everything I attempt ; nothing succeeds with me.   I shall be punished for my pride and my stupid arrogance.   Read this, good people, and profit by it !   This journal is the most useful and the most instructive of all the books that ever were or ever will be written.   It is the transcript of a woman's life—her thoughts and hopes, her deceptions, meannesses, good qualities, sorrows and joys.   I am not yet altogether a woman, but I shall be.   One may follow me here from childhood to death.   For the life of any one—one's entire life, without any concealment or disguise—is always a grand and interesting spectacle.

Friday, July 16.—In regard to the transference of love, all I possess at present is concentrated on Victor, one of my dogs.   I breakfast with him sitting opposite to me, his fine, large head resting on the table.   Let us love dogs ; let us love only dogs. Men and cats are unworthy creatures. And yet a dog is a filthy animal! He looks at you with hungry eyes while you eat ; he follows you about for the sake of his dinner. Still I never feed my dogs and they love me, and Prater, through jealousy of Victor, has left me and gone over to mamma! And men—do not they ask to be fed? Are not they voracious and mercenary?

We do not return to Russia. . . .

I am going to say once more to the moon : " Moon, O beautiful moon, show me in my sleep the person I am to marry before I die!"

My hair, fastened in a Pysche knot, is redder than ever. In a woolen gown of a peculiar white, well-fitting and graceful, and a lace handkerchief around my neck, I look like one of the portraits of the First Empire ; in order to make the picture complete I should be seated under a tree, holding a book in my hand. I love to be alone before a looking-glass, and admire my hands, so fine and white, and faintly rosy in the palms.

Perhaps it is stupid to praise one's-self in this way, but people who write always describe their heroine, and I am my heroine. And it would be ridiculous for me to lower or belittle myself through false modesty. One makes little of one's-self in conversation, because one is sure of being contradicted, but if I were to do so in writing, every one would believe I was speaking the truth, and that I was ugly and stupid, and that would be absurd!

Fortunately or unfortunately, I esteem myself so great a treasure that I think there is no one worthy of me, and those who raise their eyes to this treasure are regarded by me as hardly worthy of pity. I think myself a divinity, and I cannot conceive how a man like S. should fancy he could please me. I could scarcely treat a king as an equal. I think that is as it should be. I look down on men from such a height that they find me charming, for it is not becoming to despise those who are so far beneath us. I regard them as a hare would regard a mouse.

Monday, August 2.—After a day spent with seamstresses and dressmakers, in shopping, promenading, and coqueting, I put on my wrapper and sat down to read my good friend Plutarch.

Tuesday, August 17.—Last night I dreamed of the Fronde : I had entered the service of Anne of Austria, I thought, and she doubted my loyalty, so I led her into the midst of the rebellious people, crying *"Vive la Reine !"* and the people cried after me, *" Vive la Reine !"*

Wednesday, August 18.—To-day has been spent in admiring me. Mamma admired me, and the Princess S. admired me. The Princess is always saying that I look either like mamma or like her daughter ; and that is the greatest compliment she could pay me. One never thinks better of others than of one's own. The fact is, that I am really pretty. The picture on the ceiling of the great saloon of the Ducal Palace at Venice, by Paul Veronese, represents Venus as a tall woman, blonde and fresh-colored. I resemble that picture. My photographs are never like me. Color is wanting in them, and the unequaled freshness and whiteness of my skin are my chief charm. But let any one put me in a bad humor ; let me be dissatisfied with anything ; let me be tired,—and adieu to my beauty! There is nothing more fragile than I. It is only when I am happy and tranquil that I am charming.

PARIS, *Wednesday, August* 24.—I begin now to live, and to try to realize my dreams of becoming famous. I am already known to many people. I look at myself in the glass, and I find that I am beautiful. I am beautiful ; what more do I want? Can I not accomplish anything with that? My God, in giving me the little beauty I possess (I say little through modesty) you have already given me too much. O my God! I feel myself to be beautiful; it seems to me that I shall succeed in all that I undertake. Everything smiles upon me, and I am happy, happy, happy!

The noise of Paris, this hotel, as large as a city, with people always walking, talking, reading, smoking, looking, confuse me. I love Paris, and it makes my heart beat with emotion to be here. I want to live faster, faster, faster! ("I never saw such a fever of life," D. says, looking at me.) It is true; I fear that this desire to live always at high pressure is the presage of a short existence. Who knows? Come, I am growing melancholy. No, I will have nothing to do with melancholy.

Sunday, September 6.—There were so many people from Nice in the Bois that I thought for a moment I was at Nice. Nice is so beautiful in September! I recall the morning walks I took last year with my dogs, the sky so pure, the sea so silvery. Here there is neither morning nor evening. In the morning they are sweeping; in the evening the innumerable lights irritate my nerves. I lose my bearings here—I cannot distinguish the east from the west. While at Nice one is comfortable! It is as if one were in a nest surrounded by mountains, not too high nor too bare. One is sheltered on three sides as if by a graceful and easy mantle, and in front there is a boundless horizon, always the same, and always new. I love Nice. Nice is my country. Nice has seen me grow up; Nice has given me health and a fresh color. It is so beautiful! One rises with the dawn and sees the sun appear yonder to the left, behind the mountains which stand out boldly from a silvery blue sky, so soft and vaporous that one can scarcely speak for joy. Toward noon the sun faces me; it is a warm day, but it does not

seem warm ; there is that delightful breeze that always keeps
the atmosphere cool.   Everything seems asleep.   There is
not a soul to be seen on the promenade save two or three of the
town's-people dozing on the benches.   Then I can breathe
freely ; then I can admire nature.   In the evening the same
sea, the same sky, the same mountains.   But at night all is
black or deep blue.   And when the moon shines, leaving a
silvery track upon the waters that looks like an enormous fish
with diamond scales, and I am seated at my window, peaceful and alone, a mirror and two wax tapers in front, I ask for
nothing more, and I bow down in thankfulness before God.
Oh, no, what I desire to express will not be understood ; it
will not be understood because it has not been experienced.
No, it is not that !   It is that I grow desperate every time I
try to express what I feel !   It is as when one is in a night-
mare and has not the strength to cry out !

Besides, one can never give by words the least idea of
real life.   How describe the freshness, the perfume of memory ?   One may invent, one may create, but one cannot
copy.   It is of no avail to feel what one writes ; commonplace
words only are the result ; woods, mountains, sky, moon,
everybody uses these words.   And then, why write all this?
What does it matter to others ?   Others will never understand it, since it is not they, but I, who have felt it.   I alone
understand and remember.   And then, men are not worth
the trouble of trying to make them understand.   Every one
feels for himself, as I do.   I should like to see others feel as
I feel, through my means ; but that would be impossible ; to
do so they must be *I*.   My child, my child, leave all this
alone ; you lose yourself in subtleties of thought.   You will
become crazy if you excite yourself about those things as
you did before about your DEPTHS.   There are so many
people of intelligence—well, not that.   I mean to say that
it is their part to understand you.   Well, no !   They can
create, but understand—no, no, a hundred thousand times,

no! In all this what is very evident is, that I am homesick for Nice.

Monday, September 6.—Though I am in a state of depression and constant suffering, I do not curse life ; on the contrary, I love it, and I find it good.   Will it be believed, I find everything, even tears, even grief, good and pleasant.   I love to weep ; I love to give myself up to despair ; I love to be troubled and sorrowful.   I regard these feelings as so many diversions, and I love life, notwithstanding them all.   I wish to live.   It would be cruel to make me die when I am so accommodating.   I weep, I complain, and I take pleasure in doing so.   No, not that ; I don't know how to express myself.   In a word, everything in life pleases me ; I find everything agreeable ; and while I ask for happiness I find myself happy in being miserable ; my body suffers and cries out, but something within me, above me, rejoices at everything.   It is not that I prefer tears to joy, but far from cursing life in my moments of despair, I bless it ; I say to myself that I am unhappy, I pity myself, but I find life so beautiful that everything seems to me beautiful, and I feel I must live !   Apparently this *some one* who is above me, who rejoices at so much weeping, has gone out this evening, for I feel very unhappy.

Thursday, September 9.—We are at Marseilles, and are to leave this ill-smelling city at one o'clock.

At last I behold it, the Mediterranean, for which I have sighed.   How black the trees are !   And the moon casts a track of silvery light across the waters.

The silence is complete ; there is not a sound, either of carriage-wheels or footsteps, to be heard.   I enter my dressing-room and throw open the window to look out upon the chateau, which is unchanged.   And the clock strikes—what hour I know not—and my heart is oppressed with sadness,

Ah, I might well call this year the year of sighs! I am tired, but I love Nice!—I love Nice!

Friday, September 10 (Journey to Florence).—The mosquitoes awakened me a dozen times during the night, but, notwithstanding this, I woke up in the morning with a sense of well-being, though I was still a little fatigued.

Sunday, September 13.—We drove through the city *en toilette,* in a landau. Ah, how I admire these somber edifices, these porticos, these columns, this grand and massive architecture! Blush for shame, ye architects of England, France, and Russia! Hide yourselves under the earth; sink into the ground, ye cardboard palaces of Paris! Not the Louvre—that is above criticism—but all the others. They will never bear comparison with the superb magnificence of the Italians. I was struck with amazement on seeing the huge stones of the Palazzo Pitti. The city is dirty, almost squalid, but how many beauties it possesses! O city of Dante, of the Medici, of Savonarola, how full of splendid memorials for those who think, who feel, who know! What masterpieces! What ruins! O puppet-king! Ah, if I were only queen!

I adore painting, sculpture, art, in short, wherever it is to be found. I could spend entire days in those galleries, but my aunt is not well; she has difficulty in keeping up with me, and I sacrifice myself to her comfort. Besides, life is all before me; I shall have time enough to see all this afterward.

At the Pitti Palace I did not find a single costume to copy, but what beauty, what art? Must I say it? I dare not. Every one will cry "Shame, shame!" Come then, in confidence—Well, I don't like the *Madonna della Sedia,* of Raphael. The countenance of the Virgin is pale, the color is not natural, the expression is that of a waiting-maid

rather than that of a Madonna. Ah, but there is a Magdalen of Titian that enchanted me. Only—there is always
an only—her wrists are too thick, and her hands are too
plump—beautiful hands they would be in a woman of fifty.
There are things of Rubens and Vandyke that are ravishing.
The " Mensonge," of Salvator Rosa is very natural. I do
not speak as a connoisseur ; what most resembles nature
pleases me most. Is it not the aim of painting to copy
nature ? I like very much the full, fresh countenance of
the wife of Paul Veronese, painted by him. I like the style
of his faces. I adore Titian and Vandyke ; but that poor
Raphael ! Provided only no one knows what I write ! people would take me for a fool. I do not criticise Raphael,
I don't understand him ; in time I shall no doubt learn to
appreciate his beauties. The portrait of Pope Leo—Tenth,
I think it is—is admirable, however. A " Virgin with the
Infant Jesus," of Murillo, attracted my attention ; it is fresh
and natural. To my great satisfaction I found the picture
gallery smaller than I had thought it to be. Those galleries
without end—those labyrinths more intricate than that of
Crete—are killing.

I spent two hours in the palace without sitting down for
an instant, yet I am not tired. That is because the things
one loves do not tire one. So long as there are paintings,
and, better still, statues, to be seen, I am made of iron.
Ah, if I were compelled to walk through the shops of the
Louvre, or the Bon Marche, or even through the establishment of Worth, I should be ready to cry at the end of three-
quarters of an hour. No journey ever pleased me so much
as this one has done. I find an endless number of things
that are worth being seen ; I adore those somber Strozzi
palaces. And I adore those immense doors, those superb
courts, those galleries, those colonnades. They are majestic, grand, beautiful ! Ah, the world is degenerating ; one
would like to sink into the earth when one compares our

modern buildings with those structures of gigantic stones, piled one upon another, and mounting up to the sky. One passes under bridges that connect palaces at a prodigious height.

Oh, my child, be careful of your expressions! What then, will you say of Rome?

————

1875.

Friday, October 1.—God has not done what I asked Him to do; I am resigned; (not at all, I am only waiting). Oh, how tiresome it is to wait, to do nothing but wait!

Disorder in the house is a source of great annoyance to me. The swallow builds her nest, the lion makes his lair; why, then, should not man, so superior to the other animals, follow this example.

When I say "so superior," I do not mean that I esteem man more than the other animals. No; I despise men profoundly and from conviction. I expect nothing good from them. I should be satisfied after all my waiting to find one good and perfect soul. Those who are good are stupid, and those who are intelligent are either too false or too self-conceited to be good. Besides, every human being is by nature selfish, and find goodness for me if you can in an egotist! Self-interest, deceit, intrigue, envy, rather. Happy are they who possess ambition—that is a noble passion; through vanity or through ambition one seeks to appear well in the eyes of others sometimes, and that is better than not at all. Well, my child, have you come to the end of your philosophy? For the moment, yes. In this way, at least, I shall suffer fewer disappointments. No meanness will grieve me, no base action surprise me. The day will doubtless come when I shall think I have found a man, but, if so, I shall deceive myself wofully. I can **very** well foresee that day ; I shall then be blind. I say this now while I can see clearly. But in that case why live ; since there is nothing but meanness and wickedness in the world ? Why ? Because I am reconciled to the knowledge that this is so ; because, whatever people may say, life is very beautiful. And because, if one does not analyze too deeply, one may live happily. To count neither on friendship nor gratitude, nor loyalty nor honesty ; to elevate one's-self courageously above the meannesses of humanity, and take one's stand between them and God ; to get all one can out of life, and that quickly ; to do no injury to one's fellow-beings ; to make one's life luxurious and magnificent; to be independent, so far as it be possible, of others ; to possess power !—yes, power !—no matter by what means !— this is to be feared and respected ; this is to be strong. and that is the height of human felicity, because one's fellow-beings are then muzzled, and either through cowardice or for other reasons will not seek to tear one to pieces.

Is it not strange to hear me reason in this way ? Yes, but this manner of reasoning in a young creature like me is but another proof of how bad the world is ; it must be thoroughly saturated with wickedness to have so saddened me in so short a time. I am only fifteen.

And this proves the divine mercy of God ; for, when I shall be completely initiated into all the baseness of the world, I shall see that there is only He above in the heavens, and I here below on earth. This conviction will give me greater strength ; I shall take note of vulgar things only in order to elevate myself, and I shall be happy when I am no longer disheartened by the meannesses around which men's lives revolve, and which make them fight with each other, devour each other, and tear each other to pieces, like hungry dogs.

Here are words enough ! And to what am I going to elevate myself ? And how ? Oh, dreams !

I elevate myself intellectually for the present; my soul is great, I am capable of great things; but of what use will all that be to me, since I live in an obscure corner, unknown to all?

There, you see that I do set some store by my worthless fellow-beings; that I have never disdained them; on the contrary, I seek them; without them there is nothing in the world. Only—only that I value them at their worth, and I desire to make use of them.

The multitude, that is everything. What matter to me a few superior beings? I need everybody—I need *eclat,* fame!

Why can one never speak without exaggeration? . . . There are peaceful souls, there are beautiful actions and honest hearts, but they are so rarely to be met with that one must not confound them with the rest of the world.

Saturday, October 9.—If I had been born Princess of Bourbon, like Madame de Longueville; if I had counts for servitors, kings for relations and friends; if, since my first step in life, I had met only with bowed heads and courtiers eager to please me; if I had trodden only on heraldic devices, and slept only under regal canopies, and had had a succession of ancestors each one more glorious and haughtier than all the rest, it seems to me I should be neither prouder nor more arrogant than I am.

O my God, how I bless thee! These thoughts with which you inspire me will keep me in the right path, and will prevent me from turning away my gaze even for an instant from the luminous star toward which I move. I think that, at present, I do not move at all; but I shall move; and for so slight a cause it is not worth while to alter so fine a sentence. Ah, how weary I am of my obscurity! I am consumed by inaction; I am growing moldy in this darkness. Oh, for the light, the light, the light!

From what side will it come to me? When? Where? How? I desire to know nothing, provided only that it come!

In my moments of wild longing for greatness common objects appear to me unworthy of my attention; my pen refuses to write a commonplace word; I look with supreme disdain on everything that surrounds me, and I say to myself with a sigh, "Come, courage! this stage of existence is but the passage to that in which I shall be happy."

Monday, December 27.—All my life is contained in this diary; my calmest moments are those in which I write; they are perhaps my only calm moments.

If I should die young, I will burn these pages; but if I live to be old, this diary will be given to the public. I believe there is no photograph yet, if I may so express myself, of the whole life of a woman—of all her thoughts, of everything, everything. It will be curious.

If I die young, and it should chance that my journal is not burned, people will say, "Poor child; she has loved, and all her despair comes from that!"

Let them say so, I shall not try to prove the contrary, for the more I should try to do so the less would I be believed.

What can there be more stupid, more cowardly, more vile, than humanity? Nothing. Humanity was created for the perdition of—good! I was going to say, of humanity.

It is three o'clock in the morning, and, as my aunt says, I shall gain nothing by losing my sleep.

Oh, how impatient I am! I wish to believe that my time will come, but something tells me that it will never come; that I shall spend my life in waiting—always waiting.

Tuesday, December 28.—I am so nervous that every piece of music that is not a galop makes me shed tears.

The most commonplace words of any opera I chance to come across touch me to the heart.

Such a condition of things would do honor to a woman of thirty. But to have nerves at fifteen, to cry like a fool at every stupid, sentimental phrase I meet, is pitiable.

Just now I fell on my knees, sobbing, and praying to God with outstretched arms, and eyes fixed straight before me, just as if He were there in my room. It appears that God does not hear me. Yet I cry to Him loudly enough.

Shall I ever find a dog on the streets, famished, and beaten by boys; a horse that drags behind him from morning till night a load beyond his strength; a miller's ass, a church mouse, a professor of mathematics without pupils, an unfrocked priest, a—poor devil of any kind sufficiently crushed, sufficiently miserable, sufficiently sorrowful, sufficiently humiliated, sufficiently depressed, to be compared to me? The most dreadful thing with me is that humiliations, when they are past, do not glide from my heart, but leave there their hideous traces. To be compelled to lead a life like mine, with a character such as mine! I have not even the pleasures proper to my age! I have not even the resource that every American girl has, I do not even dance!

Wednesday, December 29.—My God, if you will make my life what I wish it to be, I make a vow, if you will but take pity upon me, to go from Kharkoff to Kieff, on foot, like the pilgrims. If, along with this, you will satisfy my ambition and render me completely happy, I will take a vow to make a journey to Jerusalem, and to go a tenth part of the way on foot. Is it not a sin to say what I am saying? Saints have made vows; true, but I seem to be setting conditions. No; God sees that my intention is good, and if I am doing wrong He will pardon me, for I desire to do right.

My God, pardon me and take pity on me; ordain that my vows may be fulfilled!

Holy Mary, it is perhaps stupid of me, but it seems to me that you, as a woman, are more merciful, more indulgent ; take me under your protection, and I will make a vow to devote a tenth of my revenue to all manner of good works. If I do wrong, it is without meaning it.   Pardon !

1876.

ROME, *Saturday, January* 1.—Oh, Nice, Nice!   Is there, after Paris, a more beautiful city than Nice?   Paris and Nice, Nice and Paris.   France, nothing but France.   In France only does one live.

The question now is to study, since that is what I am in Rome for.   Rome does not produce on me the effect of Rome.   Is Rome an agreeable place?   May I not deceive myself?   Is it possible to live in any other city than Nice? To pass through other cities, to visit them, yes; but to live in them, no!

Bah! I shall become accustomed to it.

I am here like a poor transplanted flower.   I look out of the window, and instead of the Mediterranean I see grimy houses; I look out of the other window, and instead of the chateau I see the corridor of the hotel.

It is a bad thing to acquire habits, and to hate change.

Wednesday, January 9.—I have seen the facade of St. Peter's; it is superb.   I was enchanted with it, especially with the colonnade to the left, because there no other building intercepts the view, and these columns, with the sky for a background, produce the most ravishing effect. One might fancy one's-self in ancient Greece.

The bridge and fort of St. Angelo are also after my own ideas.

And the Coliseum!

What remains for *me* to say of it, after Byron?

Friday, January 14.—At eleven o'clock my painting-master, Katorbinsky, a young Pole, came, bringing with him a model—a real Christ-face, if the lines and the shadows were a little softened. Katorbinsky told me he always took him for his model when he wished to paint a Christ.

I must confess that I was a little frightened when I was told to draw from nature, all at once, in this way, without any previous preparation. I took the charcoal and bravely drew the outlines: "Very good," said my master. "Now do the same thing with the brush." I took the brush and did as he told me.

"Good," said he once more; "now work it up."

And I worked it up, and at the end of an hour and a half it was all finished.

My unhappy model had not budged, and, as for me, I could not believe my eyes. With Binsa two or three lessons were necessary to draw the outlines and copy a picture, and here was the whole thing done at once, after nature—outline, coloring, and background. I am satisfied with myself, and, if I say this it is because I deserve it. I am severe and hard to please, especially where I myself am concerned.

Nothing is lost in the world. Where, then, does love go? Every created being, every individual, is endowed with an equal portion of this force or fluid at his birth; only that he seems to have more or less of it according to his constitution, his character, and his circumstances. Every human being loves always, but not always the same object; when he seems to love no one, the force goes toward God, or toward nature, in words, in writings, or simply in sighs or thoughts.

Now there are persons who eat, drink, laugh, and do nothing else: with these the force is either absorbed by the animal instinct, or dissipated among men and things in general; and these are the persons who are called good-natured, and who, generally speaking, are incapable of the passion of love.   There are persons who love no one, it is sometimes said.   This is not true; they always love some one, but in a different manner from others—in a manner peculiarly their own.   But there are still other unhappy persons, who really love no one, because they have loved, and love no longer? Another error!   They love no longer, it is said.   Why, then, do they suffer?   Because they still love, and think they love no longer, either because of disappointed affection, or the loss of the beloved object.

Thursday, January 20.—To-day Facciotti made me sing all my notes.   He was struck with admiration.   As for me, I don't know what to do with myself for joy; my voice, my treasure, my dream, that is to cover me with glory on the stage!   This is for me as great a destiny as to become a princess.

Tuesday, February 15.— . . . Rossi came to see us to-day.   My mother asked him who A—— was.   "He is Count A——," replied Rossi; "a nephew of the Cardinal."

"I asked you who he was," said my mother, "because he reminds me very much of my son."

"He is a charming fellow," returned Rossi; "he is a little *passarello;* sprightly and full of intelligence, and he is very handsome."

Friday, February 18.—There was a grand masked ball at the Capitol to-night.   Dina, my mother, and I went there at eleven o'clock.   I wore no domino: I was dressed in a close-fitting gown of black silk, with a train, a tunic of black gauze trimmed with silver lace, light gloves, a rose and some lilies of the valley in my corsage.   It was charming; consequently our entrance produced an immense effect.

A—— has a perfectly beautiful countenance; he has a pale complexion, black eyes, a long and regular nose, beautiful ears, a small mouth, very passable teeth, and the mustache of a young man of twenty-three. I treated him by turns as a young fqp, as a deceitful fellow, as unhappy, as audacious; and he told me in return, in the most serious manner in the world, how he had run away from home at nineteen; how he had thrown himself head-foremost into the pleasures of life; how *blasé* he is; how he has never loved, etc.

"How many times have you been in love?" he asked me.

"Twice."

"Oh! oh!"

"Perhaps even oftener."

"I should like to be the *oftener*"

"Presumptuous man! Tell me, why has every one taken me for that lady there in white?"

"Because you resemble her. That is why I am with you. I am madly in love with her."

"It is not very amiable of you to say so."

"What would you have! It is the truth."

"You look at her enough. She is evidently pleased by it, for she is posing."

"Never! She never poses; you may say anything else of her but that!"

"It is easily seen that you are in love."

"I am—with you; you resemble her."

"Oh! I have a much better figure."

"No matter. Give me a flower."

I gave him a flower, and he gave me a spray of ivy in return. His accent and his languishing air irritated me.

"You have the air of a priest. It it true that you are going to be ordained?" I said.

He laughed.

"I detest priests; I have been a soldier."

"You! you have never been anywhere but at the seminary."

"I hate the Jesuits; that is why I am always at odds with my family."

"My dear friend, you are ambitious, you would like to have people kiss your slipper."

"What an adorable little hand!" he cried, kissing my hand—an operation he repeated several times in the course of the evening.

"Why did you begin so badly with me?" I asked.

"Because I took you for a Roman, and I hate that kind of woman."

Wednesday, February 23.—Looking down from the balcony, I saw A——, who saluted me. Dina threw him a bouquet, and a dozen arms were stretched out to seize it as it fell. One man succeeded in catching it; but A——, with the utmost *sang froid*, caught him by the throat, and held him in his strong grasp until the wretch let go his prey. It was so beautifully done that A—— looked almost sublime. I was carried away by my enthusiasm, and forgetting my blushes, and blushing anew, I threw him a camellia; he caught it, put it in his pocket, and disappeared.

You will laugh, perhaps, at what I am going to tell you, but I will tell it to you all the same.

Well, then, by an action like this a man might make himself loved by a woman at once. His air was so calm while he was strangling the villain that it took my breath away.

Monday, February 28.—On going out into the balcony on the Corso I found all our neighbors at their posts, and the Carnival going on with great animation. . . .

. . . "But what do you do with yourself?" said A——, with his calm, sweet air. "You do not go to the theater."

"I was ill; I have a sore finger."

" Where ? " (and he wanted to take my hand.)   " Do you know that I went every evening to the Apollo, and remained only for five minutes or so ? "

" Why ? "

" Why ? " he repeated, looking me straight in the eyes.

" Yes, why ? "

"Because I went there to see you, and you were not there."

He said a great many other things of the same kind, accompanied with tender glances, to my great amusement.

He has adorable eyes, especially where he does not open them too wide.   His eyelids, covering a quarter of the pupil, give his eyes an expression that makes my heart beat, and my head grow dizzy.

March.—At three o'clock we were at the Porta del Popolo.   Debeck, Plowden, and A—— met us there, and A—— helped me to mount my horse, and we set off.

My riding-habit is of black cloth, and made in a single piece by Laferriere, so that it has nothing of the English stiffness, nor of the scantiness of riding-habits in general. It is a princesse robe, closely fitting—everywhere.

"How *chic* you are on horseback," said A   .

Plowden annoyed me by wanting to be continually at my side.

Once alone with the Cardinalino the conversation naturally turned on love.

" Eternal love is the tomb of love," said he ; "one should love for a day, then make a change."

" A charming idea !   It is from your uncle the Cardinal you have learned it, I suppose."

" Yes," he answered, laughing.

Tuesday, March 8.—I put on my riding-habit, and at five o'clock we were at the Porta del Popolo, where the Cardinalino was waiting for us with two horses. Mamma and Dina followed in a carriage.

" Let us ride in this direction," said my cavalier.

" Let us do so."

And we entered a sort of field—a green and pretty place called *La Farnesina.* He began his declarations again, saying :

" I am in despair."

" What is despair ? "

"It is when a man desires a thing and cannot have it."

" You desire the moon ? "

" No, the sun."

" Where is it?" I said, looking around the horizon. "It has set, I think."

" No, it is shining upon me now ; you are it."

" Bah ! bah ! "

" I have never loved before, I hate women—"

" And as soon as you saw me you loved me ? "

" Yes, that very instant—the first evening I saw you, at the theater."

" You told me that had passed away."

" I was jesting."   •   .

" How can I tell when you are jesting, and when you are in earnest? "

" That is easy to be seen."

" True ; one can almost always tell when a person is speaking the truth, but you inspire me with no confidence, and your fine ideas regarding love with still less."

" What are my ideas? I love you and you will not believe it. Ah," said he, biting his lips, and giving me a side glance, " then I am nothing, I can do nothing."

" Yes, play the hypocrite," said I, laughing.

" The hypocrite ! " he cried, growing furious. "Always the hypocrite ; that is what you think of me ! "

" How can one help admiring you ? " he said, looking at

me fixedly, a little further on ; " You are beautiful, only I think you have no heart."

"On the contrary, I assure you I have an excellent heart."

" You have an excellent heart, and you don't want to fall in love."

" That depends."

" You are a spoiled child ; am I not right ? "

" Why should I not be spoiled ?   I am not ignorant ; I am good ; the only thing is I have a bad temper."

" I have a bad temper, too : I am passionate ; I can get furiously angry ; I want to correct these faults.—Shall we jump that ditch ? "

" No."

And I rode across the little bridge, while he jumped the ditch.

" Let us canter toward the carriage," he said, " we have finished the descent."

I put my horse into a trot, but a few paces from the carriage he began to gallop.   I turned to the right.   A——— followed me, my horse galloping rapidly.   I tried to hold him in, but he dashed forward madly ; I had lost control of him ; there was an open space in front ; my hair fell down on my shoulders, my hat dropped on the ground.   I could hear A——— behind me ; I felt what they must be suffering in the carriage.   I had a mind to jump to the ground, but the horse flew on like an arrow.   " It is stupid to be killed in this way," I thought—I had no longer any strength. " They must save me ! "

" Hold him in ! " cried A.——— who could not catch up with me.

" I cannot," I answered in a low voice.

My arms trembled ; an instant more and I should have lost consciousness ; just then he came close to me and gave my horse a blow across the head with his whip ; I seized his arm, as much to touch him as to stop myself.

I looked at him ; he was pale as death ; never had I seen a countenance so full of emotion !

" God ! " he said, " how you have made me suffer ! "

" Ah, yes, but for you I should have fallen ; I could hold the reins no longer. Now it is over—well, that is good." I added, trying to laugh. " Let some one give me my hat ! "

Dina had got out of the carriage, which we now approached. Mamma was beside herself with terror, but she said nothing to me. She knew that something was the matter, and did not wish to annoy me.

" We will return slowly, step by step, to the Porta del Popolo," he said.

" Yes, yes ! "

" How you frightened me ! And you—were you not afraid ? "

" No, I assure you, no."

" Oh, but you were—I could see it."

" It was nothing—nothing at all."

And in a second more we were declining the verb " to love," in all its moods and tenses ; he told me everything, from the first evening he had seen me at the opera, when, observing Rossi leaving our box, he left his own to go meet him.

When we returned home I took off my habit, threw on a wrapper, and lay down on the sofa, tired, charmed, confused. I could remember nothing clearly at first, of all that had taken place ; it took me a couple of hours to get together what you have just read. I should be at the height of joy if I believed him, but notwithstanding his air of sincerity, of candor even, I doubt him. This is what it is to be " canaille" one's-self. And besides it is better that it should be so.

Tuesday, March 4.— . . . To-day we leave the Hotel de Londres ; we have taken a large and handsome apartment on the first floor, in the Hotel della via Babuina—consisting of an ante-chamber, a large drawing-room, a small drawing-room, four bed-rooms, a studio, and servants' rooms.

Saturday, March 18.—I have never yet had a moment's *tete-a tete* with Pietro A——; this vexes me. I love to hear him tell me that he loves me. When he has told it to me over and over again, I rest my elbows on the table and think with my head between my hands. Perhaps I am in love with him. It is when I am tired and half-asleep that I think I love Pietro. Why am I vain? Why am I ambitious? Why do I reason coldly about my emotions? I cannot make up my mind to sacrifice to a moment's happiness whole years of greatness and satisfied ambition.

" Yes," say the romance-writers, "but that moment's happiness is sufficient to brighten by its splendor an entire life-time." Oh, no; to-day I am cold, and in love; to-morrow I shall be warm, and in love no longer. See on what changes of temperature the destinies of men depend.

When he was going A—— kept my hand in his while he said good-night, and asked me a dozen questions, afterward, to defer the moment of our parting.

I told all this immediately to mamma. I tell her every-thing.

Friday, March 24; *Saturday, March* 25.—A—— came a quarter of an hour earlier than usual to-day; he looked pale, interesting, sorrowful, and calm. When Fortune an-nounced him, I clothed myself at once from head to foot in an armor of cold politeness such as a woman uses when she wishes to make a man in his position angry.

I let him spend ten minutes with mamma before going in. Poor fellow! he is jealous of Plowden! What an ugly thing it is to be in love!

" I had sworn not to come again to see you," he said.

" Why have you come, then ? "

" I thought it would be rude toward your mother, who is so amiable to me, if I stayed away."

" If that is the reason, you may go away now, and not come back again. Good-by."

" No, no, no, it is on your account."

" Well, that is different."

" Mademoiselle, I have committed a great mistake," he said, " and I know it."

" What mistake ? "

" That of giving you to understand—of telling you—"

" What ? "

" That I love you," he said, with a contraction of the lips, as if he found it hard to keep from crying.

" That was not a mistake."

" It was a great—a very great—mistake ; because you play with me as if I were a ball or a doll."

" What an idea ! "

" Oh, I am well aware that that is your character. You love to amuse yourself ; well, then, amuse yourself ; it is my own fault."

" Let us amuse ourselves together."

" Then it was not to dismiss me that you told me at the theater to leave you ? "

" No."

" It was not to get rid of me ? "

" I have no need to make use of a stratagem, Monsieur, when I want to get rid of any one. I do it quite simply, as I did with B——."

" Ah, and you told me that was not true."

" Let us speak of something else.'

He rested his cheek against my hand.

" Do you love me ? " he asked.

" No, not the least bit in the world."

He did not believe a word of it. At this moment Dina

and mamma entered the room, and at the end of a few minutes he left.

Monday, March 27.—In the evening we had visitors, among others A   . I think he has spoken to his father, and that his communication has not been well received. I cannot decide upon anything. I am entirely ignorant of the condition of affairs, and I would not for anything in all the world consent to go live in another family. Am I not extremely sensible for a girl of my age?

"I will follow you wherever you go," he said to me the other evening.

"Come to Nice," I said to him to-day. He remained with bent head, without answering, which proves to me that he has spoken to his father. I do not understand it; I love him and I do not love him.

Monday, March 30.—To-day Visconti spoke to mamma about A——'s attentions.   .   .

"Pietro A—— is a charming young man," he ended, "and will be very rich, but the Pope interferes in all the affairs of the A——'s, and the Pope will make difficulties."

"But why do you say all that?" mamma answered; "there is no question of marriage. I love the young man like a son, but not as a future son-in-law."

It would be well to leave Rome, the more so as nothing will be lost by putting off the matter till next winter. . . .

What irritates me is that the opposition does not come from our side but from the side of the A   's. This is hateful, and my pride revolts against it.

Let us leave Rome.

In the evening Pietro A—— came. We received him very coldly in consequence of the Baron Visconti's words, and our own suspicions; for, except the words of Visconti, all the rest is only suspicion.

"To-morrow," said Pietro, after a few moments, "I leave Rome."

"And where are you going?" I asked.

"To Terracina. I shall remain there a week, I think."

"They are sending him away," said mamma to me in Russian.

I had said the same thing to myself, but what a humiliation! I was ready to cry with rage.

"Yes, it is disagreeable," I replied in the same language.

When we were alone I attacked the question bravely, though with some nervousness.

"Why are you leaving Rome? Where are you going?"

Well, if you think he answered those questions as plainly as I put them, you are mistaken.

I continued to question him, and he evaded answering.

. . . I wanted to know all, at any cost. This state of disquiet and suspicion made me too miserable.

"Well, monsieur," I said, "you wish me to love a man of whom I know nothing, who conceals everything from me! Speak, and I will believe you! Speak, and I promise to give you an answer. Listen well to what I say: after you have spoken, I promise to give you an answer."

"But you will laugh at me, mademoiselle, if I tell you. It is so great a secret that if I tell it to you there will be nothing left for me to conceal. There are things that one can tell no one."

"Speak, I am waiting."

"I will tell it to you, but you will laugh at me."

"I swear to you I will not."

After many promises not to laugh, and not to betray it to any one, he at last told me the secret.

It seems that last year, when he was a soldier at Vicenza, he contracted debts to the amount of thirty-four thousand francs. When he returned home ten months later he had a quarrel with his father, who refused to pay them. At last, a few days ago, he pretended he was going to leave the house, saying that he was badly treated at home. Then his mother told him that his father would pay his debts, on condition that he would promise to lead a sensible life. "And to begin," she said, "and before being reconciled with your parent, you must be reconciled with God." He had not confessed himself for a long time past.

In short, he is going to retire for a week to the convent of San Giovanni and Paolo, Monte Coelio, near the Coliseum.

I found it hard enough to remain serious, I can assure you. To us all this seems odd, but it is natural enough to the Catholics of Rome.

This, then, is his secret. . . .

Next Sunday, at two in the afternoon, I am to be in front of the convent, and he will show himself at the window, pressing a white handkerchief to his lips.

After he went away I ran to soothe mamma's wounded pride, by telling her all this ; but with a smile, so as not to appear as if I were in love with him.

Friday, March 31.— . . . . Poor Pietro in a cassock, shut up in a cell, with four sermons a day, a mass, vespers, matins— I cannot accustom myself to so strange an idea.

My God, do not punish me for my vanity. I swear to you that I am good at heart, incapable of cowardice or baseness. I am ambitious—that is my greatest fault ! The beauties and the ruins of Rome make me dizzy. I should like to be Cæsar, Augustus, Marcus Aurelius, Nero, Caracalla, Satan, the Pope ! I should like to be all these—and I am nothing.

But I am always myself ; you may convince yourself of that by reading my diary. The details and the shading of the picture change, but the outlines are always the same.

Wednesday, April 5.— . . . . I paint and I read, but that is not enough. For a vain creature like me it is best to

devote one's-self entirely to painting, because that is im-
perishable.   .

I shall be neither a poet nor a philosopher, nor a *savante*.
I can be nothing more than a singer and a painter. But
that is always something. And then I want to be talked of
by everybody, which is the principal thing. Stern moralists,
do not shrug your shoulders and censure me with an affected
indifference for worldly things because I speak in this way.
If you were more just you would confess that you yourselves
are the same at heart! You take very good care not to let
it be seen, but that does not prevent you from knowing in
your inmost souls that I speak the truth.

Vanity! Vanity! Vanity!

The beginning and the end of all things, and the eternal
and sole cause of all things. That which does not spring
from vanity springs from passion. Vanity and passion are
the sole masters of the world.   .

Friday, April 7.—I live in torture! Oh, how expressive
is the Russian saying, " To have a cat in one's heart "! I
have a cat hidden in my heart. It makes me suffer incredi-
bly to think it possible that a man I care for should not
love me.

Pietro has not come ; he left the convent only this evening. I saw his clerical and hypocritical brother, Paul
A   , to-day. There is a creature to be crushed under
foot—little, black, sallow, vile, hypocritical Jesuit !

If the affair of the monastery be true he must know of it,
and how he must laugh with his mean, cunning air as he
relates it to his friends! Pietro and Paul cannot abide
each other.

Sunday, April 9.—I have been to confession and received
absolution, and now I fly into a passion and swear. A certain amount of sin is as necessary to a man's existence, as

a certain volume of air is to sustain life. Why are men attached to this earth? Because the weight of their conscience drags them down. If their conscience were pure, men would be too light to keep their footing on this planet, and would soar up to the skies like little red balloons.

There is a fantastic theory for you! No matter!

And Pietro does not come.

Monday, April 10.—They have shut him up forever. No, only for the time I am to remain in Rome.

To-morrow I go to Naples; they cannot have foreseen this trick. Besides, once he is released, he will come in search of me. . . .

I don't know whether to think him a worthless fellow, a coward, or a child whom they tyrannize over. I am quite calm, but sad. It is only necessary to look at things from a certain point of view, mamma says, in order to see that nothing in the world is of any consequence. I am in complete accord with madame, my mother, as to this, but to be able to judge what that point of view is in the present instance, I must first know the exact truth. All that I now know is that this is a strange adventure.

Tuesday, April 18.—At noon to-day we set out for Pompeii; we are to make the journey in a carriage, as we pass through a beautiful country and can thus enjoy the view of Vesuvius and of the cities of Castellamare and Sorrento.

I overheard mamma speaking of marriage.

"Woman is made to suffer," she said, "even if she has the best of husbands."

"Woman before marriage," I said, "is Pompeii before the eruption; and woman after marriage is Pompeii after the eruption."

It may be that I am right!

Wednesday, April 19.—See at what a disadvantage I am placed! Pietro, without me, has his club, society, his friends—everything, in a word, except me ; while I, without Pietro, have nothing.

His love for me is only the occupation of his idle moments, while mine for him is everything to me. He made me forget my ambition to play an active part in the world ; I had ceased to think of it, I thought only of him, too happy to escape thus from my anxieties. Whatever I may become in the future, I bequeath my journal to the world. I offer you here what no one has ever yet seen. All the memories, the journals, the letters, which are given to the public are only inventions glossed over, and intended to deceive the world. I have no interest in deceiving any one ; I have neither any political action to gloss over, nor any unworthy action to conceal. No one troubles himself whether I am in love or not, whether I weep or whether I laugh. My chief anxiety is to express myself with as much exactness as possible. I do not deceive myself in regard to my style or my orthography. I can write letters without mistakes, but in this ocean of words, doubtless, I make a great many. Besides, I am not a Frenchwoman, and I make mistakes in French. Yet if you asked me to express myself in my own language I should do it still worse, perhaps.

ROME, *Monday, April* 24.—I had matter enough to keep me writing all day, but I have no longer a clear idea of anything. I only know that in the Corso we met A   , that he ran up to the carriage, radiant and joyous ; and that he asked if we should be at home in the evening. We said we should be, alas!

He came, and I went into the drawing-room and took part in the conversation quite naturally like the others. He told me he had remained four days in the convent, and that he had then gone to the country ; that he was at present on

good terms with his father and mother ; and that he was now
going to be sensible and to think of his future. Finally,
he said that I had amused myself at Naples ; that I had
been flirting there as usual, and that this showed I did not
love him. He told me also that he had seen me the other
Sunday near the Convent San Giovanni and Paolo ; and to
prove that he spoke the truth he told me how I was dressed
and what I was doing ; and I must confess he was correct.

"Do you love me?" he asked me at last.

"And you?"

"Ah, that is the way with you always ; you are always
laughing at me."

"And what if I should say that I do?"

He is altogether changed ; in twenty days' time he seems
to have become a man of thirty. He speaks quite differently ; he has become surprisingly sensible, and has grown
as diplomatic as a Jesuit.

"You know I play the hypocrite," he said ; "I bow down
before my father, I agree to everything he wishes ; I have
grown very sensible, and I think of my future."

Perhaps I shall be able to write more to-morrow ; to-night
I am so stupid that I cannot.

Tuesday, April 25.—"I will come to-morrow," he said,
to pacify me, "and we will talk over all this seriously."

"It is useless," I said. "I see now how much I can depend upon your fine professions of love. You need not
come back," I added more faintly. "You have vexed me ;
I bid you good-by in anger, and I shall not sleep to-night.
You may boast of having put me in a rage—go!"

"But, mademoiselle, how unjust you are ! To-morrow
I will speak with you when you are calmer."

It is he who complains ; it is he who says I have always
repulsed him ; that I have always laughed at him ; that I
have never loved him. In his place I should have said the

same; nevertheless, I find him very dignified and very self-possessed for a man who is really in love. I know how to love better than that; at any rate I am furious, furious, furious!

It was still raining when the Baron Visconti—who, not-withstanding his age, is both charming and *spirituel*—was announced. Suddenly, while discussing the Odescalchi marriage, the conversation turned on Pietro.

"Well, madame, the boy, as you call him, is not a *parti* to be despised," he said, "for the poor Cardinal may die at any moment, so that one of these days his nephews will be millionnaires, and Pietro, consequently, a millionnaire."

"Do you know, Baron, they tell me the young man is going to enter the convent," said mamma.

"Oh, no, indeed, I assure you; he is thinking of something altogether different."

Then the talk turned on Rome, and I observed that I should be sorry to leave it.

"Remain here, then," said the Baron.

"I should like very much to do so."

"I am glad to see that you are fond of our city."

"Do you know," I said, "that they are going to leave me here in a convent?"

"Oh," said Visconti, "I hope you will stay here from another reason than that. We shall find the means,—I will find them," he said, pressing my hand warmly.

Mamma was radiant,—I was radiant; it was quite an aurora borealis.

This evening, contrary to our expectations, we had a great many visitors, among them A——.

Our visitors were seated at one table; Pietro and I at another. We talked of love in general, and Pietro's love in particular. His principles are deplorable, or rather he is so crazy that he has none. He spoke so lightly of his love for me that I don't know what to think. And then his character is wonderfully like my own.

I don't know how it was, but at the end of five minutes we were good friends again; everything was explained and we agreed to marry; he did, at least; I remained silent for the most part.

" You leave Rome on Thursday ?" he said.

" Yes, and you will forget me."

" Ah, no, indeed ; I am going to Nice."

" When ? "

" As soon as I can ; for the present I cannot."

" Why not ? Tell me,—tell me this instant ! "

" My father will not allow it."

" You have only to tell him the truth."

" Of course I shall tell him that I go there on your account, that I love you, and that I wish to marry you—but not yet. You do not know my father. He has only just forgiven me ; I dare not ask anything more from him for the present."

" Speak to him to-morrow."

" I dare not ; I have not yet gained his confidence. Only think, he had not spoken to me for three years ; we had ceased to speak to each other. In a month I will be at Nice."

" In a month I shall be no longer there."

"And where shall you go?"

"To Russia. I shall go away and you will forget me."

"But I shall be at Nice in a fortnight, and then—and then we will go away together. I love you, I love you," he ended, falling on his knees.

"Are you happy?" I asked, pressing his head between my hands.

"Oh, yes, because I believe in you—I believe your word."

"Come to Nice, now," I said.

"Ah, if I could!"

"What one wants to do, one can do."

Thursday, April 27.— . . . At the railway station I walked up and down the platform with the Cardinalino.

"I love you," he cried, "and I shall always love you, to my misfortune, it may be."

"And you can see me go away with indifference."

"Oh, don't say that. You must not speak so; you do not know what I have suffered. Since I have known you I am completely changed; but you, you always treat me as if I were the most despicable of men. For you I have broken with the past; for you I have endured everything; for you I have made this peace with my family. . . . Will you write to me?"

"Don't ask too much," I said gravely. "It is a great favor if a young girl permits herself to be written to. If you don't know that, I shall teach it to you. But they are entering the car. Let us not lose time in useless discussion. Will you write to me?"

"Yes, and all that you can say is of no avail. I feel that I love you as I can never love again. Do you love me?"

I nodded affirmatively.

"Will you always love me?"

The same sign.

"Good-by, then."

"Till when?"

"Till next year."

"No!"

"Come, come, good-by."

And without giving him my hand I went into the railway coach where our people were already seated.

"You have not shaken hands with me," he said, approaching the car.

I gave him my hand,

"I love you!" he said, very pale.

"*Au revoir,*" I answered softly.

"Think of me sometimes," he said, growing still paler; "as for me, I shall do nothing else but think of you."

"Yes; *au revoir.*"

The train started, and for a few seconds I could still see him looking after me with an expression of deep emotion on his countenance; then he walked a few steps toward the door, but as the train was still in view, he stopped again, mechanically crushed his hat down over his eyes, took a few steps forward, and then—then we were already out of sight.

NICE, *Friday, April* 28.— . . . The house is charmingly furnished; my room is dazzling, all upholstered in sky-blue satin. On opening the window of the balcony and looking out on our pretty little garden, the Promenade, and the sea, I could not help saying aloud:

"They may say what. they will, but there is no place at once so charmingly home-like and so adorably romantic as Nice."

Sunday, May 7.—One finds a miserable satisfaction in having cause to despise everybody. At least one no longer cherishes illusions. If Pietro has forgotten me, I have been grossly insulted, and there is another name to inscribe on the list of those to whom I owe hatred and revenge.

Such as they are, I am satisfied with my fellow-beings and I like them; my interests are the same as theirs; I live among them, and on them depend my fortune and my happiness. All this is stupid enough. But in this world what is not stupid is sad, and what is not sad is stupid.

To-morrow at three o'clock I start for Rome, to enjoy the gayeties there, as well as to show A—— my contempt for him if the occasion should present itself.

ROME, *Thursday, May* 11.— . . . I left Nice yesterday at two o'clock, with my aunt. . . . We arrived here at two. I took my aunt to the Corso. (What a delightful thing it is to see the Corso again after Nice!) Simonetti came over to us. I presented him to Mme. Romanoff, and told him it was by a miraculous chance I was in Rome.

I made a sign to Pietro to come to us; he was radiant, and looked at me with a glance that shows he has taken everything seriously.

He made us laugh a great deal telling us about his sojourn in the monastery. He had consented, he said, to go there for four days, and they kept him for seventeen.

"Why did you tell me a falsehood?" I asked. "Why did you say you were going to Terracina?"

"Because I was ashamed to tell you the truth."

"And do your friends at the club know of it?"

"Yes; at first I said I had gone to Terracina; then they asked me about the monastery, and I ended by telling them all about it; I laughed, and everybody laughed. Only Torlonia was furious."

"Why?"

"Because I did not tell him the truth at first; because I had not confidence in him."

Then he told us how, in order to please his father, he had let a rosary fall, as if by chance, out of his pocket, so that it might be thought he always carried one. I said all sorts of mocking and impertinent things to him, to all of which he responded, I must say, with a good deal of spirit.

Saturday, May 13.—I feel unable to write to-night, and yet something compels me to write. So long as I leave anything unsaid, something within torments me.

I chatted and made tea to the best of my ability till half-past ten. Then Pietro arrived. Simonetti went away soon afterward, and we three were left alone. The talk turned on my diary, that is to say, on the questions I have touched on in it, and A—— asked me to read him some extracts from it on God and the soul. I went to the antechamber, and knelt down beside the famous white box to look up the passages while Pietro held the light. But in doing so I came across others of more general interest, and read them aloud. And this lasted almost half an hour. On returning to the drawing-room A—— began to tell us all sorts of anecdotes of his past life, from the time he was eighteen. I listened to everything he said with something like jealousy and terror.

In the first place, his absolute dependence upon his family freezes my blood. If they were to forbid him to love me, I am certain he would obey.

The thought of the priests, the monks, terrifies me, notwithstanding all he has told me of their piety. It frightens me to hear of the atrocities they perpetrate, of their tyranny.

Yes, they make me afraid, and his two brothers also, but this is not what most troubles me; I am free to accept or to refuse him. All I heard to-night and the conclusions I drew from it, taken in connection with what has passed between us, confuse my mind.

Wednesday, May 17.—I had much to write about yesterday but it was nothing compared to what I have to write about to-night. He spoke to me again of his love. I told him it was useless; that my family would never consent.

"They would be right in not doing so," he said dreamily. "I could not make any woman happy. I have told my mother everything; I spoke to her about you. I said, 'She is so good and so religious, while as for me I believe in nothing, I am only a miserable creature.' See, I remained seventeen days in the monastery, I prayed, I meditated, and I do not believe in God; religion does not exist for me, I believe in nothing."

I looked at him in terror.

"You must believe," I said, taking his hand in mine; "you must correct your faults; you must be good."

"That is impossible; and as I am no· one could love me. Am I not right? I am very unhappy," he continued: "you could never form an idea of my position. I am apparently on good terms with my family, but only apparently. I detest them all—my father, my brothers, my mother herself. I am unhappy; if you ask me why, I cannot tell you. I do not know. Oh, the priests!" he cried, clenching his fists and grinding his teeth as he raised to heaven a face hideous with hatred. "The priests! oh, if you knew what they were!"

It was fully five minutes before he grew calm.

"I love you, however, and you only. When I am with you I am happy," he said at last.

"Give me the proof."

"Speak."

"Come to Nice."

"You put me out of my senses when you say that; you know that I cannot go."

"Why not?"

"Because my father will not give me the money; because my father does not wish me to go to Nice."

"I understand that very well, but if you tell him why you wish to go?"

"He would still refuse his consent; I have spoken to my mother; she does not believe me. They are so accustomed to see me behave badly that they no longer believe in me."

"You must reform; you must come to Nice."

"But you have told me that I shall be refused."

"I have not said you would be refused by me."

"Ah, that would be too much happiness," he said, looking at me intently; "That would be a dream."

"But a beautiful dream; is it not so?"

"Ah, yes!"

" Then you will ask your father to let you go ? "

" Yes, certainly ; but he does not wish me to marry."

" All is ended, then," I said, drawing back. " Farewell !"

" I love you ! "

" I believe you," I said, pressing both his hands in mine,
" and I pity you."

" You will never love me ? "

" When you are free."

" When I am dead."

" I cannot love you at present, for I pity you, and I despise you. If they commanded you not to love me, you
would obey."

" Perhaps ! "

" That is frightful ! "

" I love you," he repeated for the hundredth time, and he
went away, his eyes filled with tears.

He came back once more and I bade him farewell.

"No, not farewell."

" Yes, yes, yes, farewell. I loved you until this conversation." (1881.—*I never loved him ; all this was but the effect
of an excited imagination in search of romance.*)

For the past three days I have had a new idea—it is that
I am going to die. I cough and complain. The day before
yesterday I was seated in the drawing-room at two o'clock
in the morning ; my aunt urged me to retire, but I paid no
heed to her ; I said I was convinced that I was going
to die.

"Ah," said my aunt, " from the way in which you behave
I don't doubt but that you will die."

" So much the better for you ; you will have less to
spend ; you will not have to pay so much to Laferriere ! "

And being seized with a fit of coughing I threw myself
face downward on the sofa, to the terror of my aunt, who
left the room so as to make it appear that she was angry.

Friday, May 19.— . . . I have just been singing, and my chest pains me ; here you see me playing the role of martyr ! It is too stupid ! My hair is dressed in the fashion of the Capitoline Venus : I am in white, like a Beatrice ; and I have a rosary with a mother-of-pearl cross around my neck. Say what you will, there is in man a certain leaning toward idolatry—a necessity for experiencing physical sensations. God, in His simple grandeur, is not enough. One must have images to look at and crosses to kiss. Last night I counted the beads on the rosary ; there were sixty, and I prostrated myself sixty times on the ground, touching the floor with my forehead each time I did so. I was quite out of breath when it was over, but I thought I had performed an act agreeable in the sight of God. It was no doubt absurd, but the intention was there. Does God take intentions into account ! Ah, but I have here the New Testament. Let me see.—As I could not find the good book I read Dumas instead. It is not quite the same thing.

When Count A—— was announced this evening I was alone. . . . My heart beat so violently that I was afraid it would be heard, as they say in novels.

He seated himself beside me and tried to take my hand, which I withdrew immediately.

" I have so many things to say to you," he began.

" Indeed ? " . . .

" But serious things."

" Let us hear them." . . .

" Listen : I have spoken to my mother, and my mother has spoken to my father."

" Well ? "

" I have done right, have I not ? "

" That does not concern me ; whatever you have done you have done to please yourself."

" You no longer love me ? " he asked.

" No."

"And I, I love you madly."

"So much the worse for you," I said, smiling, and allowing him to take my hands in his.

"No, listen," he said; "let us speak seriously; you are never serious; I love you, I have spoken to my mother. Be my wife!"

"At last!" I thought to myself. But I remained silent.

"Well?" he said.

"Well," I answered, smiling.

"You know," he said, encouraged by this, "it is necessary to take some one into our confidence."

"What do you mean?"

"This: I can do nothing myself. We must find some one who will undertake the affair—some one of respectability who is serious and dignified, who will speak to my father and arrange the whole matter, in short. But whom?"

"Visconti," I said, laughing.

"Yes," he replied very seriously, "I had thought of Visconti; he is the man we need. . . Only," he resumed, "I am not rich—not at all rich. Ah, I wish I were a hump-back and had millions."

"You would gain nothing in my eyes by that."

"Oh! oh! oh!" he exclaimed incredulously.

"I believe you wish to insult me," I said, rising.

"No, I don't say that on your account; you are an exception to women."

"Then don't speak to me of money."

"Heavens, what a creature you are! One can never understand what you want. Consent—consent to be my wife!"

He wished to kiss my hand; I held the cross of the rosary before him, which he kissed instead; then raising his head:

"How religious you are!" he said, looking at me.

"And you, you believe in nothing?"

"I? I love you; do you love me?"

"I don't say those things."

"Then, for Heaven's sake, give me to understand it, at least."

After a moment's hesitation I gave him my hand.

"You consent?"

"Not too fast!" I said, rising; "you know there are my father and my grandfather, and they will strongly oppose my marrying a Catholic."

"Ah, there is that, too!"

"Yes, there is that, too."

"He took me by the arm and made me stand beside him before the glass; we looked very handsome standing thus together.

"We will give it in charge to Visconti," said A——.

"Yes."

"He is the man we need. . . . But we are both so young to marry; do you think we shall be happy?"

"You must first get my consent."

"Of course. Well, then, *if* you consent, shall we be happy?"

"*If* I consent, I can swear to you by my head that there will be no happier man in the world than you."

"Then let us be married. Be my wife."

I smiled. . . .

At this moment voices were heard on the staircase, and I sat down quietly to wait for my aunt, who soon entered.

A great weight was lifted from my heart. . . .

At twelve A—— rose, and bade me good-night, with a warm pressure of the hand.

"Good-night," I answered.

Our glances met, I cannot tell how, it was like a flash of lightning.

"Well, aunt," I said, after he had gone, "we leave early to-morrow. You retire, and I will lock the door of your

---

* Marie belonged to the Greek Church, of Russia.

room so that I need not disturb you by my writing, and I will soon go to bed."

"You promise?"

"Certainly."

I locked my aunt's door, and after a glance at the mirror went downstairs, and Pietro glided like a shadow through the half-open door.

"So much may be said without words when one is in love. As for me, at least I love you," he murmured.

I amused myself by imagining this to be a scene from a novel, and thought involuntarily of the novels of Dumas.

"I leave to-morrow," I said, "and we have so many things to talk seriously about, which I had forgotten."

"That is because you no longer think of anything."

"Come," I said, partly closing the door, so that only a ray of light could pass through.

And I sat down on the lowest step of the little stairs at the end of the passage.

He knelt down by my side.

I fancied at every moment that I heard some one coming. I remained motionless, and trembled at every drop of rain that fell on the flags.

"It is nothing," said my impatient lover.

"It is very easy for you to say that, monsieur. If any one should come, it would only flatter your vanity, and I—should be lost."

With head thrown back I looked at him through my half-closed lids.

"Through me?" he said, misunderstanding the meaning of my words. "I love you too much; you are safe with me."

I gave him my hand, on hearing these noble words.

"Have I not always shown my consideration and respect for you?" he said.

"Oh, no; not always. Once you even wanted to kiss me."

"Don't speak of that, I entreat you.   I have begged your forgiveness for it so often.   Be good and forgive me."

"I have forgiven you," I said softly.

I felt so happy !   Is this what it is to be in love, I thought ? Is it serious ?   I thought every moment he was going to laugh, he looked so grave and tender.

I lowered my glance before the extraordinary intensity of his.   .

"But see, we have again forgotten our affairs.   Let us be serious, and talk of them."

"Yes, let us talk of them.

"In the first place, what are we to do if you go away to-morrow ?   Stay !   I entreat you, stay ! "

"Impossible ; my aunt—"

"She is so good !   Oh, stay ! "

"She is good, but she will not consent to that.   Good-by, then, perhaps forever ! "

"No, no ; you have consented to be my wife."

"When ? "

"Toward the end of the month I will be at Nice.   If you consent to my borrowing, I will go to-morrow."

"No, I will not have that ; I would never see you again in that case."   . . .

"Advise me ; you, who reason like a book, advise me what to do."

"Pray to God," I said, holding my cross before him ; ready to laugh if he ridiculed my advice, or to maintain my air of gravity if he took it seriously.   He saw my impassive countenance, pressed the cross against his forehead, and bent his head in prayer.

"I have prayed," he said.

"Truly ? "

"Truly.   But let us continue.   We will entrust the whole affair to Baron Visconti then."

"Very well."

I said "Very well," and thought "CONDITIONALLY."

"But all that cannot be done immediately," I resumed.

"In two months."

"Are you jesting?" I asked, as if what he suggested were the most impossible thing in the world.

"In six months, then?"

"No."

"In a year."

"Yes, in a year; will you wait?"

"If I must—on condition that I shall see you every day."

"Come to Nice, for in a month I go to Russia."

"I will follow you."

"You cannot."

"And why not?"

"My mother would not allow it."

"No one can prevent my traveling."

"Don't say stupid things."

"Oh, how I love you!"

I leaned toward him so as not to lose a single one of his words.

"I shall always love you," he said. "Be my wife." . . . He proposed that we should confide all our secrets to each other.

"Oh, as to yours, they do not interest me."

"Tell me, mademoiselle," he said, "how many times have you been in love?"

"Once."

"And with whom?"

"With a man I do not know, whom I saw ten or twelve times in the street, and who is not even aware of my exist-ence. I was twelve years old at the time, and I had never spoken to him."

"What you tell me is like fiction."

"It is the truth."

"But this is a novel, a fantastic tale. Such a feeling would be impossible ; it would be like loving a shadow."

"Yes, but I feel that I have no reason to blush for having loved him, and he has become for me a species of divinity. I compare him to no one in my thoughts, and there is no one worthy of being compared to him."

"Where is he ?"

"I do not even know. He is married and lives far away."

"What an absurdity ! "

And my good Pietro looked somewhat disdainful and incredulous.

"But it is true : I love you now, but the feeling is an entirely different one."

"I give you the whole of my heart," he answered, "and you give me only the half of yours."

"Do not ask for too much, and be satisfied with what you have."

"But that is not all ? There is something else."

"That is all."

"Forgive me, and allow me to disbelieve you for this once."

(See what depravity !)

"You must believe the truth."

"I cannot."

"So much the worse," I cried, vexed.

"That is beyond my understanding," he said.

"That is because you are very wicked."

"Perhaps."

"You do not believe that I have never allowed any one to kiss my hand ?"

"Pardon me, but I do not believe it."

"Sit down here beside me," I said, "let us talk over our affairs, and tell me everything." . . .

"You will not be angry ?" he asked.

" I shall be angry only if you conceal anything from me."

" Very well, then ; you understand that our family is very well known here ? "

" Yes."

" And that you are strangers in Rome ? "

" Well ? "

" Well, my mother has written to some persons in Paris."

" That is very natural ; and what do they say of me ? "

" Nothing, as yet, but they may say what they choose, I shall always love you."

" I stand in no need of your indulgence—"

" Then," he said, " there is the religion."

" Oh, the religion."

" Ah," he said, with the calmest air imaginable, " become a Catholic."

I cut him short with a *very severe* expression.

" Do you wish me, then, to change my religion ? " asked A——.

" No, because, if you did so, I should despise you." To tell the truth it would have displeased me only on account of the Cardinal.

" How I love you ! How beautiful you are ! How happy we shall be ! "

My only answer was to take his head between my hands and kiss him on the forehead, the eyes, the hair. I did it rather on his account than my own.

" Marie ! Marie ! " cried my aunt from above.

" What is the matter ? " I asked quietly, putting my head through the door at the head of the stairs, that the voice might seem to come from my room.

" You should go to sleep ; it is two o'clock."

" I am asleep."

" Are you undressed ? "

" Yes, let me write."

" Go to bed."

" Yes, yes."

I went down again and found the place empty ; the poor fellow had hidden himself under the staircase.

" Now," said he, resuming his place, "let us speak of the future."

" Yes, let us speak of it."

" Where shall we live ?   Do you like Rome ? "

" Yes."

" Then we will live in Rome, but by ourselves—not with my family."

" No, indeed ; in the first place, mamma would never consent to let me live with the family of my husband."

" She would be right ; and then, my family have such extraordinary ideas !   It would be torture.   We will buy a little house in the new quarter."

" I should prefer a large one."

" Very well, then, a large one."

And we began—he, at least—to make plans for the future.

" We will go into society," I resumed ; "we will keep up a large establishment, shall we not ? "

" Oh, yes ; tell me all you would like."

" Yes, when people decide to spend their lives together, they want to do so as comfortably as possible."

" I understand that.   You know all about my family ; but there is the Cardinal."

" You must make your peace with him."   •

" Of course ; I shall do so decidedly.   The only thing is that I am not rich."

" No matter," I answered, a little displeased, but sufficiently mistress of myself to refrain from making a gesture of contempt ; this was perhaps a trap. . . .

No, this cannot be true love ; in true love there is no room for meanness or vulgarity.

I felt secretly dissatisfied. . . .

Do I love him truly, or is it only that he has turned my head? Who can tell? From the moment doubt exists, however, there is no longer room for doubt.

"Yes, I love you," I said, taking his hands in mine and pressing them tightly.

He did not answer; perhaps he did not understand the importance I attached to my words; perhaps he found them quite natural. . . .

But I began to be afraid, and I told him he must go. "It is time," I said.

"Already? Stay with me a moment longer. How happy we are thus! Dost thou love me?" he cried; "Wilt thou love me always, always?"

This *thou* chilled me and made me feel humiliated.

"Always!" I answered, still dissatisfied, "always; and you, do you love me?"

"Oh, how can you ask me such things? Oh, my darling, I should like to remain here forever!"

"We should die of hunger," I replied, humiliated by this term of endearment, and not knowing what to say.

"But what a beautiful death!—In a year, then," he said, devouring me with his eyes.

"In a year," I repeated, for form's sake rather than for any other reason.

At this moment I heard the voice of my aunt, who, seeing light still in my room, began to grow impatient.

"Do you hear?" I said.

We kissed each other and I fled, without once turning back. It is like a scene out of a novel, that I have read somewhere. I feel humiliated. I am angry with myself! Shall I always be my own critic, or is it because I do not entirely love him that I feel thus?

"It is four o'clock!" cried my aunt.

"In the first place, aunt, it is only ten minutes past two; and in the next place leave me in peace."

"This is frightful! You will die, if you sit up so late," exclaimed my aunt.

"Listen," I said, opening her door, "don't scold, or I shall tell you nothing."

"What is it? Oh, what a girl!"

"In the first place, I was not writing, I was with Pietro."

"Where, miserable child?"

"Downstairs."

"How dreadful!"

"Ah, if you cry out you shall hear nothing."

"You were with A ."

"Yes!"

"Well, then," she said, in a voice that made me tremble, "when I called you just now, I knew it."

"How?"

"I had a dream in which your mother came to me and said, "Do not leave Marie alone with A——.""

A cold shiver passed down my back when I comprehended that I had escaped a real danger. . . .

NICE, *Tuesday, May 23.*—I should like to be certain of one thing—do I love him or do I not love him?

I have allowed my thoughts to dwell so much on grandeur and riches that Pietro appears to me a very insignificant person indeed. Ah, H——! And if I had waited?—waited for what? A millionnaire prince, an H— —? And if no one came? I try to persuade myself that A— — is very *chic,* but when I am with him he seems to me even more insignificant than he really is. . . .

To-night I love him. Should I do well to accept him? So long as love lasted, it would be very well, but afterward?

I greatly fear that I could not endure mediocrity in a husband!

I reason and discuss as if I were mistress of the situation. Ah! misery of miseries!

To wait! To wait for what?

And if nothing comes! Bah! with my face something will come, and the proof is—that I am scarcely sixteen and that I might already be a countess two and a half times over if I had wished. The *half* is on Pietro's account.

Wednesday, May 24.—To-night, on retiring, I kissed mamma.

"She kisses like Pietro," she said laughing.

"Has he kissed you?" I asked.

"He has kissed *you*" said Dina, laughingly, thinking she had said the most dreadful thing possible, and causing me to feel a sensation of lively remorse, almost of shame.

"Oh, Dina!" I cried, with such an expression that mamma and my aunt both turned on her a look of reproach and displeasure.

Marie kissed by a man! Marie, the proud, the severe, the haughty! Marie, who has made such fine speeches on that subject.

This made me inwardly ashamed. And indeed, why was I false to my principles? I cannot admit that it was through weakness, through passion. If I were to admit that, I should no longer respect myself! I cannot say that it was through love.

Friday, May 26.—My aunt remarked to-day that A——— was only a child.

"That is quite true," said mamma.

These words, of which I recognized the justice, made me feel that I have sullied myself for nothing; for, after all, I have committed this folly without the excuse of either interest or love. It is maddening!

After his departure for Rome I looked at myself in the glass, to see if my lips had not changed their color. A——— will have the right to say I loved him, and that the breaking of this engagement has made me very unhappy. A broken engagement is always a blot on the life of a young girl. Every one will say we loved each other, but no one will say the refusal came from me. We are neither sufficiently liked nor sufficiently great for that. Besides, appearances will justify those who may say so ; that enrages me! If it were not for those words of V , " Oh, child, how young you are still ! " I should never have gone so far. But I needed to hear his repeated offers of marriage to soothe my wounded vanity. You will observe that I have said nothing positive ; I let him talk, but, as I allowed him to take my hands in his and kiss them he failed to notice the tone of my voice, and in his happy and exalted mood suspected nothing. These thoughts console me, but they are not enough.

They say the blonde is the ideal woman ; as for me, I say the blonde is the material woman, *par excellence.* See those golden locks, those lips red as blood, those deep-gray eyes, that rose-tinted flesh, that Titian knows so well how to paint, and tell me what are the thoughts with which they inspire you ! Besides, we have Venus among the Pagans, and Magdalen among the Christians, both of them blondes. While the woman who is a brunette, who is really as much of an anomaly as a man who is fair,—the brunette, with her eyes of velvet and her skin of ivory, may remain pure and divine in our thoughts. There is a fine picture of Titian's in the Borghese Palace called " Pure Love and Impure Love." " Pure Love " is a beautiful woman with rosy cheeks and black hair, who is regarding with a tender look her infant child whom she is holding in the bath. " Impure Love " is a reddish blonde who is leaning against something,—just what, I do not remember,—with her arms crossed above her head. For the rest, the *normal* woman is fair, and the *normal* man dark.

The different types we see that are in seeming contradic

tion to this rule are sometimes admirable, but they are none
the less anomalies. I have never seen any one to be compared to the Duke of H——: he is tall and strong; he has
hair of a beautiful reddish gold hue, and a mustache of the
same color; his eyes are gray and small, but piercing; his
lips are modeled after those of the Apollo Belvidere. There
is in his whole person an air of grandeur and majesty, of
haughtiness even, and indifference to the opinions of others.
It may be that I see him with the eyes of love. Bah! I do
not think so! How is it possible to love a man who is dark,
ugly, extremely thin? who has beautiful eyes, it is true, but
who has all the awkwardness of a very young man, and
whose bearing is by no means distinguished, after having
loved a man like the Duke, even though it be three years
since I have seen him? And remember that three years in a
young girl's life are three centuries. Therefore I love no
one but the Duke! And the Duke will not be very proud of
my love, and will care very little about it. I often tell myself stories; I think of all the men I have ever known or
heard of—well, not even to an Emperor could I say, "I love
you," with the conviction that I was speaking the truth.
There are some to whom I could not say it at all.—Stay! I
have said it in reality! Yes, but I thought so little about
it at the time that it is not worth while to speak of that.

Sunday, May 28.—I am reading Horace and Tibullus.
The theme of the latter is always love, and that suits me.
And then I have the French and the Latin texts side by
side; that gives me practice. Provided only that this marriage affair that I have brought about by my own thought-
lessness does not injure me! I much fear it may. I ought
not to have given A—— any promise; I should have said
to him: "I thank you, monsieur, for the honor you have
done me, but I can give you no answer until I have consulted with my family. Let your people speak to mine

about it, and we shall see. As for me," I might have added, to soften this answer, " I shall have no objection to offer."

This accompanied by one of my amiable smiles, and my hand to kiss, would have been sufficient. I should not then have compromised myself ; they would not have gossiped about me at Rome, and all would have been well. I have sense enough, but it always comes to my assistance too late.

Wednesday, May 31.—Has not some one said that great minds think alike ? I have just been reading La Rochefoucauld, and I find he has said a great many things that I have written down here—I, who believed I had originated so many thoughts, and it turns out that they are all things that have been said long since.

I am troubled about my eyes. Several times, while painting, I was obliged to stop ; I could no longer see. I use them too much, for I spend all my time either reading, writing, or painting. I went over my compendium of the classics this evening, and that gave me occupation. And then, I have discovered a very interesting work on Confucius—a French translation from the Latin. There is nothing like keeping the mind occupied ; work is a cure for everything, especially mental work. I cannot understand women who spend their time knitting or embroidering—the hands busy and the mind idle. A multitude of frivolous or dangerous fancies must crowd upon the mind at such a time, and if there is any secret trouble in the heart, the thoughts will dwell upon that, and the result must be disastrous. . . .

Ask those who know me best what they think of my disposition, and they will tell you that I am the gayest, the most light-hearted, as well as the most self-reliant person they ever saw, for I experience a singular pleasure in appearing haughty and happy, invulnerable to a wound from any quarter, and I delight in taking part in discussions of all sorts, both serious and playful. Here you see me as I am. To the world I am altogether different. One would suppose, to see me, that I had never had a care in my life, and that I was accustomed to bend circumstances and people alike to my will.

Saturday, June 3.—Why does everything turn against me? Forgive me for shedding tears, O my God! There are persons more unhappy than I; there are those who want for bread, while I sleep under lace coverlets; there are those who bruise their feet against the stones of the street, while I tread on carpet; there are those who have only the sky for a canopy, while I have above my head a ceiling hung with blue satin. Perhaps it is for my tears that you punish me, my God; ordain, then, that I no longer weep. To what I have already suffered there is now added a feeling of personal shame—shame before myself. They will say: "Count A—— asked her in marriage, but there was some opposition, so he changed his mind and withdrew."

See how good impulses are recompensed!

Sunday, June 4.—When Jesus had healed the lunatic, his disciples demanded of him why they had not been able to do so, and he answered: "Because of your unbelief: for verily I say unto you, if ye have faith as a grain of mustard-seed, ye shall say unto this mountain, Remove hence to yonder place, and it shall remove; and nothing shall be impossible to you."

On reading these words my mind was, as it were, illumined, and for the first time in my life, perhaps, I believed in God. I rose to my feet, I was conscious of myself no longer. I clasped my hands together, and raised my eyes to heaven; I smiled; I was in a state of ecstasy. Never, never will I doubt again; not that I may receive a reward for my faith, but because I am convinced—because I believe. Up to the age of twelve I was spoiled ; my lightest wishes were obeyed, but my education was never thought of. At twelve years I asked for masters ; they were given to me, and I made out a programme for myself. I owe everything to myself. . . .

Thursday, June 8.—. . . . To think only *that we live but once*, and that this life is so short ! When I think of this my senses forsake me and my mind becomes a prey to despair ! *We live but once !* And I am losing this precious life, hidden in obscurity, seeing no one. *We live but once !* And my life is being ruined. *We live but once !* And I am made to waste my time miserably. And the days are passing, passing, never to return, and carrying a part of my life with them, as they pass.

We live but once ! Must this life, already so short, be still further shortened, ruined, stolen—yes, stolen—by miserable circumstances ?

Saturday, June 10.—" Do you know," I said to the doctor, " that I spit blood, and that it is necessary that my health should be attended to ? "

" Oh, mademoiselle," replied Walitsky, " if you continue to go to bed at three o'clock in the morning, you will have every ailment under the sun."

" And why do you suppose I go to bed late ? Because my mind is disturbed. Give me a tranquil mind and I will sleep tranquilly."

" You might have had that if you chose. You had the opportunity at Rome."

" Who would have given it to me ? "

" A   , if you had consented to marry him without asking him to change his religion."

" Oh, my friend Walitsky, how shocking ! A man like A·   ! Think of what you are saying ! A man who has neither an opinion nor a will of his own ; you have made a very foolish speech ! "

And I began to laugh softly.

" He neither comes to see us nor writes," I continued ; "he is a poor boy *whose importance we have exaggerated.* No, my dear friend, he is only a boy, and we were wrong to think otherwise."

I preserved the same calmness in uttering these words as I had shown during the rest of the dialogue—a calmness that resulted from the conviction I had of having said only what was just and true.

I went to my own room, and my spirit all at once became, as it were, illuminated. I comprehended at last that I had done wrong in allowing a kiss—a single one, indeed, but still a kiss— and in giving a rendezvous downstairs; that, if I had not gone out into the hall or elsewhere, to seek a tête-a-tête, the man would have had more respect for me, and I should now have no occasion for either anger or tears.

(How I love myself for having spoken thus ! What refinement of feeling !—Paris, 1877.)

Everything is at an end ! I knew well this state of things could not last. I long to lead a tranquil life. I will go to Russia—that will improve the situation—and bring papa back with me to Rome.

Monday, January 12 ; *Tuesday, January* 13.—I, who desired to live half a dozen lives at once, I do not live even a quarter of a life. I am held in chains. But God will have pity upon me ; my strength has left me,—I feel as if I were going to die. Yes, I must either acquire what God has given me the power to discern and to comprehend, in which case I shall be worthy of a future or die. For, if God cannot with justice grant me all I ask, he will not have the cruelty to make an unhappy creature live to whom He has given comprehension, and the ambition to acquire what she comprehends.

God has not made me such as I am without design. He cannot have given me the power to understand all things in order to torture me by denying me everything. Such a supposition is not in accordance with the nature of God, who is just and merciful. I must either attain the object of my ambition or die. Let it be as He wills. I love Him ; I believe in Him ; I bless Him ; and I beg Him to pardon me for all the wrong I may have done. He has endowed me with the comprehension of what is great, in order that I might attain it, and I will show myself to be worthy of the gift. If I am not worthy, then God will allow me to die.

Wednesday, June 14.—In addition to the triumph I have given this little Italian, which deeply vexes me, I foresee, besides, the scandal that will result from this affair.

I did not anticipate an adventure of this nature ; I foresaw nothing of the sort ; I had never imagined that such a thing could happen to me ; if I am as beautiful as I say, why then am I not loved? I am admired, I am made love to, but I am not loved—I, who have so much need of love ! It is the novels I have read that have turned my head ! No ; but I read novels because my head is turned. I read over and over again the novels I have already read, seeking out the love-scenes with lamentable eagerness. I devour them, because I think I am loved—because I think I am not loved !

I love, yes ; I will give no other name to what I feel.

But no ; this is not what I long for. I long to go into society ; I long to shine ; I long for high rank, for riches, pictures, palaces, jewels ; I long to be the center of a brilliant circle—political, literary, charitable, frivolous. I long for all this. May God grant it to me !

My God, do not chastise me for these wildly ambitious

thoughts. Are there not people who are born in the midst of all this, and who find it natural to possess it, and who thank God for it?

Am I culpable in desiring to be great? No, for I desire to employ my greatness in manifesting my gratitude to God, and in being happy. Is it forbidden to wish to be happy?

Those who find their happiness in a modest and comfortable home, are they less ambitious than I? No, for they have no comprehension of anything beyond. He who is content to live humbly, in the midst of his family, is he thus modest and moderate in his wishes through wisdom? No, no, no! He is so because he is happy thus; because to live obscurely is for him the height of happiness. And if he does not desire excitement, it is because excitement would render him unhappy. There are those, too, who have not the courage to be ambitious; those are not sages, but cowards; because they desire, in secret, what they do not possess, but make no effort to obtain it, not through Christian virtue, because of a timid and incapable nature. My God; if I reason badly, enlighten me, pardon me, pity me!

Thursday, June 22.—When I used to hear Italy praised I was incredulous; I could not understand why there was so much enthusiasm about this country, and why it was spoken of as if it were different from other countries. It is because it is different from other countries. It is because one breathes there another atmosphere. Life is not the same as elsewhere; it is free, fantastic, large, reckless and yet languid, fiery yet gentle, like its sun, its sky, its glowing plain. Therefore it is that I soar upward on my poet's wings (I am sometimes altogether a poet, and almost always one on some side of my nature), and am ready to exclaim with Mignon:

> Italia, reggio di ciel,
> Sol beato !

Saturday, June 24.—I was waiting to be called to breakfast when the doctor arrived, quite out of breath, to tell me he had received a letter from Pietro. I turned very red and without raising my eyes from my book asked:

"Well, what does he say?"

"They refuse to give him any money. But you will yourself be able to judge from the letter, better than I."

I took good care to show no eagerness to see it. I was ashamed to manifest so much interest in the matter as that would imply.

Contrary to custom I was the first at table. I ate my breakfast with impatience, but I said nothing.

"Is what the doctor has told me true?" I asked at last.

"Yes," responded my aunt. "A—— has written to him."

"Where is the letter, doctor?"

"In my room."

"Show it to me."

The letter bears date of June 10, but as A—— directed it simply "Nice," it has traveled all through Italy before arriving here.

"I have done nothing all this time," he writes, "but ask my family to allow me to go to Nice, but they absolutely refuse to hear of it"; so that it is impossible for him to come, and there is nothing left him but to hope in the future, which is always uncertain.

The letter was in Italian; they waited for me to translate it. I said not a word, but gathering up my train with affected deliberation, so that they might not attribute my departure to agitation, I left the room and crossed the garden, my countenance calm, but hell within my heart.

This letter is not in answer to a telegram from some Monaco acquaintance, that one should laugh at it. It is in answer to me; it is an announcement. And it is to me! To me who had soared so high in imagination; it is to me he says this. What remains for me to do?

To die? God does not will it. To become a singer? I have neither the health nor the patience for it.

What then? What then?

I threw myself on a sofa, and with my eyes fixed stupidly on vacancy tried to comprehend the meaning of the letter, to think of what course to pursue.

It is impossible to describe my suffering. Besides, there comes a time when complaints are useless. Crushed as I am of what should I complain?

I cannot describe the profound disgust and discouragement I feel. Love! Word henceforth without meaning to me! This, then, is the truth? This man has never loved me; and he looks upon marriage only as the means of acquiring his freedom. As for his protestations, I do not take them into account. I have spoken of them to no one. I do not place sufficient confidence in them to speak of them seriously. I do not say that he has always lied to me. A man almost always believes in his protestations the moment he is uttering them, but afterward?

And notwithstanding all these reflections, I am burning to be revenged. I will bide my time, but be sure I will be revenged. I went into my room, wrote a few lines, and then, suddenly losing heart, burst into tears. Oh, after all, I am nothing but a child. These sorrows are *too heavy* for me to bear *all alone.* I thought of awaking my aunt, but she would think I was crying from disappointed love, and I could not endure that. To say that love has no part in my tears would be to speak the truth. I am ashamed of that feeling now.

I might write all night without being able to express what I feel; and if I could succeed in expressing it, I should say nothing new, nothing that I have not already said.

Sunday, July 2.—Oh, what heat! Oh, what *ennui!* But I am wrong to say *ennui* (that one can never feel who has so many resources within one's-self as I have). I do not feel *ennui ;* for I read, I sing, I paint, I dream; but I am restless and sorrowful. Is my poor young life, then, doomed to be spent in eating and drinking, and domestic quarrels? Woman lives from sixteen to forty. I tremble at the thought of losing even a single month of my life. If this is to be, why have I studied, and sought to know more than other women, priding myself on being as learned as great men are said in their biographies to have been.

I have a general idea of many things, but I have devoted my attention chiefly to painting, literature, and physics, so that I might have time to read everything—everything interesting, that is to say. It is true that once I begin, I find everything interesting. And all this produces in me a genuine fever.

If this is to be so, why have I studied and reflected? Why were genius and beauty and the gift of song bestowed upon me? That I might wither in obscurity and die of sadness. If I had been ignorant and stupid I might then, perhaps, have been happy. Not a living soul with whom to exchange a word! One's family does not suffice for a creature of sixteen—above all, a creature such as I am. Grandpapa, it is true, is a man of intelligence, but he is old and blind; he irritates one with his eternal complaints about the dinner and about his servant Triphon.

Mamma has a good deal of intelligence, very little learning, no knowledge of the world, no tact whatever ; and her faculties have deteriorated through thinking of nothing but the servants, my health, and the dogs. My aunt is a little more polished ; she is imposing, even, to those who know her but slightly.

Have I ever mentioned their ages ? If it were not for ill-health, mamma would be still a superb woman. My aunt is a few years younger, but looks older ; she is not handsome, but she is tall and she has a good figure.

Monday, July 3.—I leave Nice to-morrow. I feel an indefinable sadness at leaving Nice. I have selected the music I shall take with me, and some books—the encyclopædia, a volume of Plato, Dante, Ariosto, Shakespeare, and several English novels, by Bulwer, Collins, and Dickens.

I went into my room, followed by all the dogs. I drew the white box over to the table. Ah, that is my chief regret—my journal! That is the half of myself. I was accustomed to glance over some one of its volumes every day, when I wished to recall Rome or Nice, or something still further back in the past.

And as if expressly for me—on this the eve of my departure—the moon shone brightly, lighting up the beauties of my city with her pale and silvery light. *My city?* Yes, *my city.* I am too insignificant a person for any one to care to dispute its ownership with me. Besides, does not the sun belong equally to every one ? I entered the drawing-room ; the moon's rays poured in through the large, open windows, and lighted up the white plaster wall, and the white covers of the chairs. One feels melancholy without knowing why, on a summer night like this.

To leave my journal behind, that is a real grief.

This poor journal, the confidant of all my struggles toward the light, all those outbursts, which would be regarded as the outbursts of imprisoned genius if they were to be finally crowned by success, but which will be regarded only as the idle ravings of a commonplace creature if I am destined to languish forever in obscurity. To marry and have children? Any washerwoman can do that.

What then do I desire? Ah, you know well what I desire—I desire glory !

It is not this journal that will give it to me, however. This journal will be published only after my death ; for I show myself too *nakedly* in it to wish it to be read during my

lifetime.   Besides, it would not in that case be the comple-
ment of an illustrious existence.

An illustrious existence!   Vain illusion! resulting from
an isolated life, much reading of history, and a too lively
imagination.

I know no language perfectly.   My own is familiar to me
only in connection with domestic affairs.   I left Russia at
the age of ten, and I speak English and Italian well.   I
think and write in French, yet I believe I still make mistakes in spelling.   And often, to my unutterable vexation,
I find some thought which I had vainly sought to put into
fitting words, expressed by some celebrated author with
fluency and grace.   Here is an instance : " To travel, whatever we may say to the contrary, is one of the saddest
pleasures in life ; when you begin to feel yourself at
home in some foreign land, it is because you have already
begun to make it your country."   It is the author of Corinne
who says this.   And how many times have I lost patience,
trying vainly, pen in hand, to express the same thought, and
burst out, at last, into some such words as these : "I hate
new cities !   It is a martyrdom for me to see new faces !"
We all think alike, then ; the only difference is in the way we
express our thoughts ; as men are all made out of the same
material, but how widely do they differ in feature, form,
complexion, and character !

One of these days I shall no doubt come across some such
thought as this, but expressed with spirit, eloquence, and
grace.

There, this volume is finished.   When I arrive in Paris I
will begin a new one that will no doubt suffice for Russia
also.

I shall take Pietro's last letter with me.

I have just read it again.   He is unhappy !   Why, then,
has he not more energy ?

It is easy for me—obeyed as I am by every one—to talk ;

but for him—And then those Romans—there are no
other people in the world like them.

Poor Pietro! The thought of my future glory forbids me
to allow my mind to dwell seriously upon him. I feel as if
it reproached me for the moments I dedicate to him.

Dear Divinity, reassure thyself. Pietro is nothing more
for me than an amusement—*a strain of music in which to
drown the lamentations of my soul.* If I reproach myself for
allowing my thoughts to dwell upon him, it is because he
can be of no service to me. He cannot even be the first
rung of the divine ladder that leads to fame.

GRAND HOTEL, PARIS, July 4.

Amor, ut lacryma, oculo oritur in pectus cadit.
—PUBLIUS SYRUS.

Wednesday, July 5.—I left Nice yesterday at two in the
afternoon, accompanied by my aunt and Amalie my maid.
Mamma cried for fully three hours at the thought of our
separation, so that I was amiable and affectionate with her.
At half-past two we reached Paris; it must be confessed
that if Paris is not the most beautiful, it is at least the most
charming, the most *spirituelle* of cities.

Thursday, July 13.—We went to see the Countess M——
this evening. She spoke to me on the subject of marrying.

"Oh, no," I said, "I have no wish to marry. I want to
be a great singer. See, dear Countess, we must do this ; I
will disguise myself as a poor girl, and you and my aunt will
take me to the most celebrated singing-master in Paris, as
a little Italian *protegée* of yours who gives promise of being a
singer."

"Oh! oh !" cried the Countess in remonstrance.

"That is the only way to learn the truth concerning my
voice," I resumed tranquilly. "And I have one of last

year's dresses that will just produce the desired effect!" I
added, pursing up my mouth and pushing out my lips.

"After all, it is an excellent idea!" she said at last.

Friday, July 14.—Since morning I have been taking the
greatest care of myself; I have not coughed once more
than was necessary. I have not moved. I am dying of
heat and thirst, but I have not taken even a drink of
water. . . .

We set out at last, with Madame de M   , and proceeded
to No. 37 Chaussee d'Antin, when M. Wartel, the most celebrated singing-master in Paris, lives.

Madame de M   had spoken to him of me as a young
girl from Italy who had been particularly recommended to
her, and whose family desired to know what hopes she gave
of becoming a great singer.

We reached the house at three . . . and were shown into
a little *salon* adjoining the one in which the master was giving a singing lesson. At last four o'clock struck. I felt my
limbs tremble and my strength fail me.

Wartel made me a sign that meant "come in." I did not
understand.

"Come in, mademoiselle, come in," he said.

I entered the *salon,* followed by my two protectresses,
whom I begged to return to the room we had left, lest their
presence should intimidate me, and in truth I felt very much
afraid.

Wartel is an old man, but his accompanist is quite
young.

"Do you read music?" asked the master.

"Yes," I replied.

"What pieces can you sing?"

"None; but I can sing a scale or an exercise."

"Take an exercise, then, Monsieur Chose. What is your
voice—soprano?"

"No, monsieur, contralto."

"We shall see."

Wartel, who did not rise from the arm-chair in which he was seated, made me a sign to begin, and I proceeded to sing the exercise with diffidence at first, then desperate, and at last satisfied.

"Well," said the master, "your voice is rather a mezzo-soprano than a contralto. It is a voice that will gain in range. Have you ever taken lessons?"

"Never, Monsieur; that is to say, ten lessons only."

"Well, you must work hard. Can you sing a romance?"

"The aria from Mignon!" cried my aunt from the other room.

"Very well; sing the aria from Mignon."

As I sang, the countenance of Wartel, which at first had expressed only attention, showed a slight surprise which gradually deepened into amazement; at last he went so far as to keep time to the music with his head, smiling agreeably as he did so, and finally to join in himself.

"Good, very good! now make her sing a—" I have forgotten the word he used.

The accompanist made me sing the—(it signifies little what its name was), he made me run through all my notes.

"As far as *si* natural," said the old man. "Yes, it is a mezzo-soprano; and that is better, much better, for the stage."

I continued standing.

"Sit down, mademoiselle," said the accompanist, examining me from head to foot with his eyes.

I sat down on the edge of the sofa.

"In fine," said the severe Wartel, "you must work hard; you will succeed."

"How long will it take to develop her voice?" said Madame de M .

"You can understand, madame, that that will depend

upon the pupil herself ; some do not need so long—those who have intelligence."

"This one has more than is necessary."

"Ah, so much the better ; in that case it will be easier."

"But, finally, how long will it take ? "

"To develop her voice, to perfect it, fully three years ; yes. fully three years' work, fully three years ! " he repeated.

I was silent, meditating vengeance against the perfidious accompanist, whose looks seemed to say, "This little girl has a good figure, she is pretty ; that will be amusing."

After a few words more we rose : Wartel remained seated, and extended his hand kindly to me. I bit my lips.

" Listen," I said at the door, "let us go back and tell them the truth."

My aunt took out her card, and we returned, laughing. I told the severe maestro of my stratagem.

What an expression the face of the accompanist wore ! I shall never forget it ; I was avenged.

Sunday, July 23.—Rome—Paris—the stage, singing, painting !

No, no ! Russia before everything ! That is the foundation of everything. Since I am posing as a sage, let me play my part consistently ; let me not be led astray by any will-o'-the-wisps of imagination.

. Russia first of all, if God will only help me.

I have written to mamma. Here I am, out of love, and up to my ears in business. Oh, if God will only help me, then all will go well.

May the Virgin Mary pray for me !

Thursday, July 27.—We arrived this morning in Berlin.
The city made a singularly agreeable impression on me ; the houses are extremely handsome.

Friday, July 28.—Berlin reminds me of Italy, of Florence. It reminds me of Florence because my aunt is with me here, as she was at Florence, and the life we lead is the same. Before going anywhere else we went to the Museum. Whether from ignorance or prejudice, I had not expected to see so fine a collection of works of art as we found here. As usual, it was the sculpture that most engaged my attention; it seems to me that I have one sense more than other people—a sense devoted especially to the comprehension of sculpture.

Here I am lodged like Faust,—before me an antique German bureau, at which I am seated with books, manuscripts and rolls of paper around me.

Where is the devil? Where is Margaret? Alas! the devil is always with me; my mad vanity—that is the devil. O ambition unjustified by results! O vain aspirations toward an unknown goal!

I hate moderation in anything. I want either a life of continual excitement or one of absolute repose. Why the thought should occur to me now I know not, but I do not love A——. Not only do I not love him, but I do not even think of him any longer, and *all that* appears to me a dream.

While I do not admire the plainness and the materialism of the Germans, I must concede to them many good qualities: they are very polite, and very obliging. What I like most in them is the respect they entertain for their history and for their rulers. This shows they are still far from being contaminated by the infection of what is called republicanism. No other form of government can be compared to the ideal republic; but a republic is like ermine—the slightest blemish upon it renders it worthless. And where will you find a republic without blemish?"

No, life here is impossible; this is a frightful country. Fine houses, broad streets—but nothing for the spirit or the imagination. The most insignificant town in Italy is the equal of Berlin in this respect.

Sunday, July 30.—Nothing can be gloomier than Berlin. The city bears the stamp of simplicity—a simplicity without beauty or grace. The innumerable monuments that encumber the bridges, the streets, and the gardens seem unmeaning and out of place. Berlin reminds one of the pictures on certain clocks, where, at stated intervals, the soldiers come out from the barracks, the boatmen row, and ladies in hoods, holding little children by the hand, pass by.

Now that the time has arrived when I shall cross the borders of Russia, and be left without either my aunt or mamma, my courage fails, and I begin to be afraid. The law-suit, the uncertainty—and then, and then—I don't know why, but I fear that I shall be able to alter nothing.

In two hours more we leave Berlin. To-morrow I shall be in Russia. Well, then, no ; I will not be afraid. I am strong. Only, if my journey should prove to be in vain ! But it will not do to think of that. One must not despair beforehand.

Oh, if any one could know what I feel !

The country here is flat, and thickly wooded, but the foliage, although fresh and luxuriant, has a certain look of sadness, after the rich and flourishing verdure of the South. We were conducted to an inn called the Russian Hotel, and installed in two small chambers with whitewashed ceilings and bare wooden floors, and furniture equally simple and unpretending.

Thursday, August 3 ; *Friday, August* 4 (*July* 23, Russian style).—Yesterday at three o'clock I went to meet the train, and fortunately found my uncle, who had already arrived, waiting for me. . . . At midnight I entered the carriage ; my aunt cried ; I held my eyes level and motionless, so that

the tears might not overflow.   The conductor gave the sig-
nal, and, for the first time in my life, I found myself alone !
I began to sob aloud ; but don't imagine I derived no profit
from it !   I studied from nature the art of crying.

"Enough ! my child," I said at last, sitting erect.   It
was time.   I was in Russia.   On descending from the carriage I was received in the arms of my uncle, who was accompanied by two gendarmes and two custom-house officers.
I was treated like a princess ; they did not even examine
my luggage.   The station is large, and the officials are well-
bred and extremely polite.   I fancied myself in some ideal
country, everything is so well-managed. . . .   My com-
patriots awaken no particular emotion in me, no species of
ecstasy such as I have experienced on revisiting other countries that I had seen before ; all I feel is a sort of sympathy
for them and a sensation of extreme ease.   It was still daylight at half-past nine.   We had already passed Gatchina,
the ancient residence of Paul I., who was so persecuted all
his lifetime by his haughty mother ; and soon arrived at
Tsarskoe Selo, within twenty-five minutes of St. Petersburg.

Sunday, August 6.—It is raining, and I have taken cold ;
I have written in my letter to mamma, " St. Petersburg is a
filthy place !   The streets are disgraceful for the capital of
a country ; one is mercilessly jolted over the rough paving-
stones ; the Winter-Palace is a barracks, and so is the
Grand Theater ; the cathedrals are richly decorated, but
outlandish and badly planned."

I tried to call up some emotion on looking at the portrait
of Pietro A——, but he is not handsome enough to make
one forget that he is a despicable man, a creature one cannot
but regard with contempt.   I am no longer angry with him ;
I despise him too much for that—not from personal feeling,
but because of his manner of life, of his weakness of character.   Stay, I am going to define for you the word weak-

ness.   The weakness which inclines us to the good, to tenderness, to the forgiveness of injuries, may be called by that
name, but the weakness which inclines us to evil-doing and
wickedness is called *cowardice.*

I thought I should feel the separation from my family
more than I do.   I am, however, *not happy;* but that is
rather owing to the presence of disagreeable and common
people (my poor uncle, for example, notwithstanding his
beauty), than to the absence of those I love.

Monday, August 7, 1876 (*July* 26).—I have just come
from the post-office, where I went to get my photographs
and a dispatch from my father.   He had telegraphed to
Berlin that my coming would be for him a "real happiness."

Thursday, August 10 (*July* 29), 1876.—This is a memor-
able evening.   I have finally ceased to regard the Duke of
A   as my cherished ideal.   I saw at Bergamasco's a
portrait of the Grand Duke Vladimir, from which I could
not tear myself away ; a more perfect and pleasing type of
beauty could not be imagined.   Giro grew enthusiastic
with me over it, and we ended by kissing the portrait on
the lips. . . .   I adored the Duke when I might have adored
a Prince Imperial of Russia !   It was stupid, but one cannot command these things ; and then, in the beginning I
regarded H—— as my equal, as a man whom I might
aspire to marry.   Well, that is past.   Who will be my idol
now ?   No one.   I shall live for fame, and in the hope of
finding—a *man.*

Behold me, then, free !   I have no longer an idol to
worship ; I am in search of some one to adore, and I must
find one soon, for life without love is like a bottle without
wine.   The wine must be good wine, however.

Abundance in not the only merit of the fare here.   It is
also of the most delicate quality.   When one eats well, one

is in a good humor, one regards good fortune with greater joy and evil fortune with greater equanimity, and one feels well-disposed toward one's neighbors. Gluttony is a monstrous thing in a woman, but to love good eating to some extent is as much a merit as it is to be intelligent or well-dressed ; without taking into account that simple and delicate food preserves the health, and, as a consequence, youth, the freshness of the complexion, and the roundness of the contours. Let my figure testify to this. Marie Sapogenikoff was right in saying that a figure like mine was worthy of a more beautiful face ; and observe that I am far from being ugly. At thirteen I was too large, and every one thought me sixteen. At present I am slender, but fully developed, remarkably rounded, perhaps too much so. I compare myself with all the statues I see, and I find none of them with contours as rounded, or with hips as large, as mine. Is this a defect? The shoulders, however, require a slightly fuller curve.

At the station Grousskoe we were met by two carriages, six peasant-servants, and my good-for-nothing brother. Paul is tall of stature, and rather stout ; but he is beautiful as a Roman statue.

We arrived at Chapatowka, after a drive of an hour and a half, during which I could detect the existence of much petty rivalry and spite on my father's side toward the Babanines. I held my head high and kept my brother in check, who, indeed, was enchanted to see me. I will not take part with either side. I need to be on good terms with my father.

The house is small, and consists of a single story. It has a large garden, not very well kept. The women of the peasantry are remarkably well-formed, pretty, and *piquante* in their costume, that follows every contour of the figure and allows the leg to be seen as far as the knee.

My Aunt Marie received us on the steps. After I had

taken a bath we went in to dinner. I had several skirmishes
with Paul. He tries to pique me, without meaning it, perhaps, and only in obedience to the impulse given him by
my father. I put him haughtily in his place, however, and
it is he who is humbled when he sought to humble me. I
can read what is in the depths of his heart : Incredulity
as to my success and petty resentment in regard to our
relative positions in the world. The only name they give
me here is " Queen." My father seeks to dethrone me, but
I will make him yield to my power. I know his nature,
for he and I are alike in many things.

Thursday, August 15 (*August* 3).—I was pacing slowly up
and down, leaning on my brother Paul's arm, and my
thoughts idly wandering, when, in passing under the trees
whose interlaced branches formd a green canopy above
that almost touched our heads, it occurred to me to think
what A—— would say if he were walking here with me and
I were leaning on his arm. He would say, bending slightly
toward me, in those soft and penetrating tones he kept for
me alone, " How happy I am, and how much I love you ! "
No words could give an idea of the tenderness of his
accents in speaking to me, in saying those things that were
meant for me—alone. Those tiger-cat manners, those
burning glances and those enchanting tones, veiled and
vibrating, that murmured endearing words as if they were a
complaint or a supplication—so humble, so passionate, so
gentle were they—were for me alone !
But it was a superficial tenderness, that meant nothing ;
and if he looked at me tenderly, it was because this was his
natural expression, as there are persons who appear always
eager, others who appear always astonished, and others
vexed, when they are none of these things in reality.
Oh, how I should like to know the truth in regard to *all
of this !* I should like to return to Rome married, other-

wise it would be a humiliation.   But I have no desire to
marry.   I want to remain free, and, above all, I want to
study.   I have discovered the right path at last.

And, frankly speaking, to marry in order to spite A——
would be a piece of stupidity.   .

That is not the question, however, but I wish to live as
other women live.

I am dissatisfied with myself to-night, without knowing
exactly why.

. . . . We had no sooner reached the open country than
my father suddenly asked me :

" Well, are we going to have a skirmish to-day, as we had
yesterday ? "

" Just as you choose ! " I answered.

He took me brusquely in his arms, wrapped his cloak
around me, and rested my head on his shoulder.

I closed my eyes ; that is my way of showing tenderness.

We remained thus for a few moments.

Then I begun to talk of foreign countries—of Rome, and
of the pleasures of society, taking good care to make him
understand that our position there is a good one ; I spoke
of Mgr. de Fallous, the Baron Visconti, and the Pope.   I
enlarged, then, on the society of Poltava.

" To spend one's life losing money at cards," I exclaimed ;
" to ruin one's-self in the heart of a province drinking champagne in taverns ; to lead a purely animal existence and let
one's faculties rust in inaction.   Whatever one does, one
should always keep good company."

" Come ! you seem to want to insinuate that I keep bad
company," he said, laughing.

" I ? No, indeed !   I speak only in general terms ;   I
allude to no one in particular."

I dwelt so long upon the subject, that at last he asked me
what a large apartment in Nice, in which one could give
entertainments, would cost.

" You know," he said, " if I should go settle down there for the winter, the position would be a different one."

" Whose position ? "

" That of · the birds of the air," he answered, laughing, as if piqued.

" My position ? " I said.   " Yes, that is true ; but Nice is a disagreeable city.   Why could you not come this winter to Rome ? "

" I ?   H'm ! well, h'm ! "

All the same, the first seed is sown, and it has fallen on good ground.   What I fear is the influence of others.   I must accustom this man to my society, render myself agree-able to him, necessary to him, so that my Aunt T—— may find a barrier raised between her brother and her evil influences.

Wednesday, August 23 (August 11).—I have written almost as much in detail to mamma as I have written in my journal. That will do her more good than all the medicines in the world.   I pretend to be enchanted. but I am not so, as yet. I have related everything exactly as it happened, but I am not sure of my success until the end of the story.   In fine, we shall see ; God is good.

Pacha is my real cousin—the son of my father's sister. This man puzzles me.   This morning, in speaking of my father, I remarked that children criticise their parents' actions, and when they marry and have children of their own, do the very things themselves they disapproved of in their parents.

" That is perfectly true," he said ; " but my children will not criticise me, for I shall never marry."

After a moment's silence I said : " Every young person says the same thing."

" Yes, but in my case it is different."

" And why so ? " .

" Because I am twenty-two years old, and I have never yet been in love ; I have never cast a second glance at any woman." ·

" That is quite natural. Before the age of ·twenty-two one has no right to fall in love.",

" What ! and the boys who fall in love at fourteen or fifteen ? "

" That sentiment has nothing at all to do with love."

" That may be so, but I am not like others. I am passionate ; I am haughty, that is—I mean to say that I respect myself ; and then—"

" But all those qualities you mention are good ones."

" Good ones ? "

" Yes, of course."

Afterwards he remarked, apropos of something I do not remember, that if his mother were to die he would lose his reason.   ·

" Yes, for a time ; and then—"

" Oh, no ; I should lose my reason ; I know it."

" For a time ; every feeling yields eventually to newer impressions."

" Then you deny the eternity of the feelings ? "

" Decidedly."

" It is strange, Moussia," he said to me, " how quickly one forms an attachment when one is free from other ties. The day before yesterday I called you Maria Constantinovna ; yesterday Mademoiselle Moussia, and to-day—"

" Moussia, simply, as I told you to do."

" It seems to me as if we had always lived together ; your manners are so simple and engaging."

" Are they not ? "

. . . . My father was waiting for us in the colonnade.

" Well, did I deceive you ? " I asked.   " Do I look badly in a riding-habit ? Ask Pacha how I ride. Do I look well ? "

"Yes, very well—h'm ; very well, indeed."

He examined me with satisfaction.

I am very far from regretting having brought thirty gowns with me ; my father is to be won over only through his vanity.

At this moment M—— arrived, with his luggage and a servant. When he saluted me I responded with the customary compliments, and then went to change my dress, saying I would return.

I returned attired in a gown of Oriental gauze, with a train two yards long, a silk bodice open in front, *a la Louis XV.*, and fastened with a large white bow. The petticoat was in one piece, and the train was a square one.

M—— spoke of dress, and admired mine.

They call him stupid, yet he can talk on every subject—music, art, science. It is true that it is I who do all the talking, and he does nothing but answer, "You are perfectly right ; it is quite true."

I was silent about my studies, fearing to frighten him, but I was provoked into speaking of them at table. I used a Latin quotation, and discussed classic literature and the modern imitations of it with the doctor.

They all cried out that I was wonderful ; that there was nothing about which I could not talk—no subject of conversation in which I did not find myself at home.

Papa made heroic efforts to conceal his pride. Finally a *poulet aux truffes* started a culinary discussion, during which I displayed a knowledge of gastronomy that made M—— open his mouth and eyes with still greater amazement.

And then putting into practice my powers of sophistry, I went on to give my views in regard to the advantages of good cooking, sustaining that it made men virtuous.

After dinner we went upstairs. The rooms are very large, especially the ball-room ; the piano was placed there only yesterday.

I played. Poor Kapitanenko made the most desperate gestures to prevent Paul from talking.

"*Mon Dieu*," cried the good man, "I forget while I listen that I have been vegetating here in a province for the last six years ; I begin to live again !"

When I had finished "Le Ruisseau " they all kissed my hand.

Papa sat on a sofa with half-closed eyes. The Princess worked on at her embroidery without speaking. She is a good sort of woman, though.

When the others were gone I said to my father: "This is the way we shall live after we leave Russia. You will come with me ?"

"I will think of it ; yes—perhaps."

Friday, August 25 (*August* 13).—My father proposed an excursion to Pavlovska, his other estate. He is very good to me, but to-day I was extremely nervous, and scarcely spoke ; the least attempt at speech threatened to make me burst into tears.

Thinking, however, of the effect this complete absence of pomp and festivity would have upon mamma, I told my father I should like to see something of society and amusements.

"Very well," he answered ; "if you wish it, it shall be done. Shall I take you to see the wife of the Prefect?"

"Yes."

"Very well ; it shall be done."

Reassured on this point, I was able to inspect the work on the farm with a tranquil spirit, and even to enter into all its details—something I found not at all amusing, but which I thought I might make use of in the future to astonish some one by my knowledge on the subject, mixing up a *mot de connoisseur* in such matters as the planting of barley and the good points of wheat with a quotation from Shakespeare or a discourse on the Platonic philosophy.

You see that I try to derive some profit from everything.

Pacha procured an easel for me, and near dinner-time I received two large canvases sent me from Poltava by M   .

"How do you like M   ?" asked papa.

I told him.

"Well," said Pacha, "I did not like him at all, at first, and now I like him very much indeed."

"And me—did you like me at first?" I asked him.

"You? Why?"

"Come, tell me."

"Very well, yes; I liked you; I expected to find you different; I thought you did not speak Russian; that you were affected, and—and, now, you see how it is!"

"It is very well."

Pacha grew enthusiastic, to the point of asking me to give him my likeness to wear in a locket all his life.

"For I love and honor you as I do no one else," he cried.

The Princess opened her eyes wide, and I laughed, and offered my cousin my hand to kiss.

At first he refused, coloring deeply, but ended by obeying me.

A strange and untamed nature! This afternoon I spoke of my contempt for humanity.

"Ah, that is how it is!" he cried. "I am, then, only a dastard—a wretch!"

And, flushed and trembling, he left the room hastily.

Saturday, August 26 (August 14).—The country is killing!

I with surprising rapidity sketched two portraits to-day— my father's and Paul's. The whole thing occupied thirty-five minutes.

My father, who thinks my talent for painting something to be truly proud of, examined them and was pleased. As for me, I was enchanted ; for to paint is to do something toward furthering one of my aims in life. Every hour not spent in that, or in coquetry, presses like a weight upon my head. To read ? No, to act !

This morning my father entered my apartment. After a few commonplace phrases, Paul having left the room, he suddenly grew silent, and as I felt he had something to say to me that I too wished to speak of, I remained purposely silent also, as much for the pleasure of seeing his embarrassment and hesitation as in order to avoid broaching the subject myself.

" H'm—well, then,—what do you say ? " he asked.

" I, papa ? Nothing."

" H'm !—you said—h'm !—that you wished me to go with you to Rome,—h'm ! And how, then ? "

" Very simply."

" But—"

He hesitated, moving my combs and brushes about from one place to another.

" But if I should go with you—h'm ! and your mamma— she might not come. And then—you see if she did not come—h'm ! what then ? "

" Mamma ? Mamma will come."

" Ah ! "

" Besides, mamma will do anything I want her to do. She exists no longer ; there is only I."

Then, visibly relieved, he put a number of questions to me, as to the manner in which mamma passed her time—in regard to an infinity of things, in fact.

The Cardinal is dying.

Despicable man ! (The nephew, I mean.)

Tuesday, August 29 (*August* 17).—I dreamed that Pierre was dead. I approached his bier and placed around his neck a rosary of topazes, to which was attached a cross of gold.   No sooner had I done this, however, than I saw that the dead man was not Pietro.

To dream of death is a sign of marriage, I believe.

A young man was in love with a girl who loved him in return.   After some time he married another, and when he was asked the reason of his fickleness, he answered :

" She kissed me,—consequently she has either kissed others, or she will kiss them."

" He was quite right," said my uncle Alexander.   And every man reasons in the same way.

A mode of reasoning which is in the highest degree un-just, but that does not prevent me being now shut up in my room, beside myself with rage.

I took it for granted that they meant me.   But think of the cause I had for the supposition.

Grant me, O Heaven, the power to forget !   O my God have I then committed a crime, that thou shouldst punish me in this way ?

That which neither education, nor books, nor advice could teach me, experience has taught me.

Friday, September 8 (*August* 27).—Despicable fear, I shall conquer thee at last.   Did I not take it into my head yester-day to be afraid of a gun ?   It is true that Paul had loaded it, and that I did not know how large a charge of powder he might have used, and that I was unacquainted with the gun. It might have gone off, and that would be a stupid death ; or, I might be disfigured for life.

So much the worse !   It is only the first step that is diffi-cult.   Yesterday I fired at fifty paces, and to-day I fired without any fear whatever.   May God forgive me, but I think I hit the mark every time.

We read Poushkine aloud to-day, and discussed the passion of love.

" Oh, I should like to be in love to know what it is like ! "

I said ; "Or perhaps I have already been in love ? In that case, love is a contemptible thing that one picks up—in order to cast it away again."

" You will never be in love," said my father.

" If that should prove to be the case, I would thank Heaven for it," I answered.

I wish, and I do not wish, to love.

Yet in my dreams I *love.* Yes, but an imaginary hero.

And A——? I to love him ? No; is it thus one loves? No. If he were not the nephew of the Cardinal, and if he were not surrounded by priests, and monks, and ruins, and— the Pope, I should not have loved him.

Besides, what need have I to explain? You know all better than I do. You know then that the music at the opera, with A—— in the barcaccia, produced together a charming effect, and you ought to know how great the power of music is. That was an amusement, but it was not love.

When, then, shall I really love? I shall still continue to pour out on all sides the superabundance of my affection, still grow enthusiastic, still shed tears—and for creatures who are less than nothing!

Saturday, September 9 (*August* 28).—The days are passing; I am losing precious time, and in the best years of my life.

What *ennui!* Never a witty saying! Never a polished phrase! Unhappily I am a pedant, and I love to hear an- cient literature and the sciences discussed. Find me any of this here if you can! Cards and nothing else! I would shut myself up and read, but since my object in coming here was to make myself loved, that would be a bad way to set about doing it. . . .

Thursday, September 2 (14.)—Here I am still in this de-

table city of Poltava! I am more familiar with Kharkoff.
I spent a year there before going to Vienna. I remember
a'l the streets and all the shops. This afternoon at the station I recognized a physician who had attended grandmamma, and I went over and spoke to him.

I long to return—there! "Knowest thou the land where
the orange-tree blooms?" Not Nice, but Italy.

GAVRONZI, *Sunday, September* 17.—While waiting for my
future fame I went to a hunt, arrayed in masculine attire,
and with a game-bag slung around my shoulder.

We set out, my father, Paul, the Prince, and I, at about
two o'clock in a *char-a-banc.*

Now I find myself without a word with which to describe
our excursion, not knowing the name of—in fine, of anything pertaining to the chase. The brambles, the reeds,
the shrubs, the trees, were all so thick that we could hardly
make our way through them. The branches brushed
against us on all sides, the air was deliciously pure, there
was no sun, but a fine rain fell such as is the delight of
hunters—when they feel warm.

We walked, walked, walked.

I made the tour of a small lake, armed with my gun, and
ready to fire, expecting at every instant to see a duck rise.

But—nothing! I was already asking myself whether I
should fire at the lizards that hopped about my feet, or at
Michel, who walked behind me, and whose admiring gaze
I could feel fixed upon me in my masculine attire.

I chose the happy medium and fired at a crow (killing
him instantly) that was perched upon the topmost branch
of an oak, suspecting nothing, the less so as his attention was
arrested by my father and Michel, who had thrown themselves on the ground in a clear space in the wood.

I pulled out its tail-feathers and made myself an aigrette.

The others did not shoot once; they did nothing but walk.

Paul killed a thrush, and that was the whole of the chase.

Friday, September 22.—O Rome! the Pincio, rising like an island from the plain traversed by aqueducts; the Porta del Popolo; the obelisk, the churches of Cardinal Gastolo, at either side of the entrance to the Corso; the Corso itself, the Palace of the Republic of Venice; and those dark and narrow streets, those palaces black with the dust of centuries, the ruins of a little temple to Minerva, and finally the Coliseum. I think I see them all before me now; I close my eyes and I walk through the streets of the city, I visit the ruins, I see—

It is not with me as it is with those who say "Out of sight, out of mind." A thing is no sooner out of my sight than it acquires for me a double value; I dwell upon its minutest details, I admire it, I love it.

I have traveled a great deal; I have seen many cities: but two of them only have raised me to the highest pitch of enthusiasm.

The first is Baden-Baden, where I spent two summers when I was a child; I can still remember those delicious gardens. The second is Rome—

I love Rome, only Rome.

And St. Peter's! St. Peter's, where a ray of light entering through the roof falls upon the floor and casts there shadows and tracks of light as regular as the architecture of its columns and altars—a ray of light that, by the aid of shadows only, creates in the midst of this marble temple a temple of light.

With closed eyes I transport myself in imagination to Rome, and it is night. And to-morrow the hippopotamus will come from Poltava, and I must make myself beautiful, and I shall be beautiful.

The country has done me a great deal of good; my

complexion was never fresher nor more transparent than now.

Rome!—and I will not go to Rome! Why? Because I will not go. And if you knew what it has cost me to come to this resolution, you would pity me. Indeed I am already in tears.

The first touch of cold weather has compelled me to make use of my fur coat. Kept from the air as it has been, it has preserved the odor of Rome, and this odor—this garment!—

Have you ever observed that it needs but a perfume, a strain of music, a color, to transport one in imagination to any particular place? To spend the winter in Paris— oh, no!

Thursday, September 28.—I cry with *ennui.* I wish to leave this place. I am unhappy here. I am losing my time, my life! My faculties are rusting in inaction. I am exasperated—yes, that is the word.

Friday, September 29.—I was in despair yesterday, for it seemed to me as if I were chained down here for life. The thought of this exasperated me, and I wept bitter tears.

Tuesday, October 17.— . . . "Pacha," I said, "what would you do to the person who had wounded me—cruelly wounded me?"

"I would kill him," he responded quite simply.

"You use very fine words, but you are laughing, Pacha."

"And you?"

"I have been called a devil, a hurricane, a demon, a tempest; I am all this since yesterday." . . .

When I grew a little calmer I began to give expression to the most contradictory opinions regarding love.

My cousin has thoughts ideally lofty, and Dante might have borrowed from him his divine love for Beatrice.

"I shall doubtless fall in love," he said, "but I will never marry."

"What is that you are saying, young man? Do you know that one deserves a beating for such words?"

"Because," he continued, "I desire my love to endure forever—at least in my imagination—in all its divine purity and strength. Marriage often kills love, just as it may give it being."

"Oh! oh!" I cried, indignantly.

"He is quite right," said his mother, while the bashful orator blushed and grew confused, ashamed of his own words.

All this time I was looking at myself in the glass, cutting the hair over my forehead, which had grown too long.

"There," I said to the "young man," throwing him a handful of reddish gold hair, "I will give you that as a remembrance."

Not only did he take it, but his voice trembled and he looked agitated as he did so; and when I would have taken it from him he gave me a pleading look, like a child who has got hold of a toy that appears to him a treasure, and that he fears to lose.

I gave my cousin "Corinne" to read, after which he went away.

Corinne and Lord Melvil were walking across the bridge of Saint Ange. "It was in crossing this bridge," said Lord Melvil, "returning from the Capitol, that my thoughts for the first time dwelt seriously on you." I do not know what there is in those words to affect me so powerfully, but when I read them yesterday they actually made me feel faint. And every time I come across them, on opening the book, I have the same feeling.

Has not some one said words like those to me?

There is a sort of magic in some simple word, perhaps on account of their very simplicity. Or is their power derived rather from association?

Monday, October 23.—Yesterday we got into a coupe drawn by six horses and set out for Poltava.

The journey was a gay one. The tears shed on leaving the paternal roof caused a general effusion of sentiment, and Pacha declared he was madly in love.

"I swear that it is true," he cried, "but I will not say with whom."

"If it is not with me," I said, "you shall receive my malediction."

I complained that my feet were cold; he took off his pelisse and wrapped it about them.

"Pacha, swear to me that you will tell me the truth."

"I swear."

"With whom are you in love?"

"Why do you ask?"

"It concerns me to know; we are relations. And then, I am curious; and then—and then—it amuses me."

"'You see, it amuses you!'"

"Without doubt, but you must not take the word in a bad sense; you are a very good fellow."

"You see you are laughing; you would ridicule me afterwards."

"Here you have my hand and word that I will not ridicule you." But there was a smile upon my face while I spoke.

"With whom are you in love?"

"With you."

"Truly?"

"On my word of honor. I am not given to many words, as they say in novels. Must I fall upon my knees and talk a lot of nonsense to prove it to you?"

"Oh, my dear fellow, you are following in the footsteps of some one I know."

"As you will, Moussia; but I am speaking the truth."

"But that is folly."

"Oh, not a doubt of it, that is what pleases me! I love without hope, which is what I needed. I needed to suffer, to torment myself, and then, when the object of my passion is gone away, I shall have something to dream about, something to regret. I shall endure tortures, that will be my happiness."

"Young man!"

"Young man? Young man?"

"But we are brother and sister."

"No, cousins."

"It is the same thing."

"Oh, no!"

Then I set myself to work to tease my lover—always the lover I do not want.

Tuesday, October 24.—I never had a childhood, but the house where I lived when I was a child, if not dear to me, possesses an attraction for me. I am familiar with everything and everybody there. The servants, grown old in our service, are surprised to see me so tall, and I should enjoy many sweet recollections if it were not for the anxieties that poison my mind. . . .

My ·Agrippine gown had a great success. I walked up and down while I sang to conquer the timidity that always seizes me when I sing.

Why write? What have I to recount?

I must bore people to death.—Patience!

Sixtus V. was only a swineherd, and Sixtus V. became Pope.

Sunday, October 29 (17).—It is not probable that I shall ever again see Tcherniakoff. I spent a long time wandering from room to room, and found a tender pleasure in doing so. People laugh at those who associate sentiment with pictures and articles of furniture, and who bid them farewell on going away; who find friends in those pieces of wood and stuff that through their association with us receive, as it were, something of our life, and seem to be a part of our existence.

Laugh then, if you will!   The finest feelings are the most easily ridiculed, and where mockery enters, delicacy of feeling disappears.

Wednesday, November 1.—When Paul had gone out I found myself alone with that excellent and admirable being called Pacha.

"Then you like me still?" I said.

"Ah, Moussia, how would you have me speak to you?"

"Quite naturally. Why this reserve? Why not be simple and frank? I will not laugh at you, and if I should laugh, it is only because I am nervous—nothing else. Then you no longer like me?"

"Why do you say that?"

"Oh, because—because—I don't remember now."

"One cannot account for those things."

"If you no longer like me, you may say so; you are frank enough for that, and I—indifferent enough. Come, is it my nose? Or my eyes?"

"One can see that you have never been in love."

"Why do you say that?"

"Because from the moment one begins to look critically at the features—to ask whether the nose is more perfect than the eyes, or the eyes more perfect than the mouth—it is evident that one has never been in love."

"That is quite true. Who told it to you?"

"No one."

"Ulysses?"

"No," he replied, "one can't tell what it is one likes—I will be frank with you—it is your air, your manner, above all your disposition."

"It is amiable, is it not?"

"Yes, unless you are acting a part, and it would be impossible to do that at all times."

"Another truth. And my face?"

"It has beauties—it is a classic face."

"Yes, I was aware of that. What more?"

"What more? There are women one sees passing by that one calls beautiful, but that one does not give a second thought to. But there are faces—that are beautiful and charming, that create a lasting impression, that produce a sensation that is delightful and agreeable."

"Precisely so. What else?"

"How you question!"

"I want to avail myself of this opportunity to learn a little of what people think of me. I shall not easily find another whom I can question in this way without compromising myself. And how did all that take possession of you? Did it come to you suddenly, or by degrees?"

" By degrees."

" H'm, h'm."

" That is the best way ; the impression is a more lasting one. What you conceive a sudden affection for you cease to care for as suddenly, while the affection that comes by degrees—"

" Endures forever."

" Yes, forever."

Our conversation lasted a long time, and I began to entertain considerable respect for this man whose affection for me is as reverent as a religion, and who has never profaned its purity by a word or a look.

" Do you like to talk of love ? " I asked him suddenly.

" No ; to speak of it with indifference is a profanation."

" It amuses one, though."

" Amuses ! " he cried.

"Ah, Pacha, life is a wretched affair. Have I ever been in love?

" Never," he answered.

" Why do you think so?"

" Because of your character. You could love only through a caprice—to-day a man, to-morrow a gown, the day after a cat."

" I am delighted when people think that of me. And you, my dear brother, have you ever been in love?"

" I have told you so ; you know it very well ; I have told you so."

" No, no, it is not that I am speaking of," I said quickly ; "but before."

" Never."

" That is strange. Sometimes I think that I am deceived in you, and that I take you for something better than you are."

We talked for a while on indifferent subjects, and then I went to my room. Here is a man—no, let me not think too well of him ; the disappointment would be too disagreeable. He told me a short time since that he was going to become a soldier.

" To fight for glory, I tell you frankly," he added.

Well, these words, uttered out of the depths of his heart, half-timidly, half-daringly, and true as truth itself, have given me extraordinary pleasure. It may be that I flatter myself, but I imagine that ambition was a feeling hitherto unknown to him. I think I see now the effect produced upon him by a few words I let fall in regard to ambition, one day, while I was combing my hair. The "young man"* suddenly rose to his feet and began to walk up and down the floor.

"I must do something ; I must do something," he cried.

Tuesday, November 7.—I have broken my looking-glass !

---

* *Homme vert,* in the original.

That portends some misfortune.   This superstitious thought freezes me with terror.   I look out of the window, and all I see is frozen too.   It is long since I beheld a scene like this.

Pacha, with the eagerness natural to the young to show new-comers novelties, ordered a little sleigh to be got ready, and took me out in triumph for a drive.   The sleigh is very impertinent to call itself by that name, for it is nothing more than a few miserable pieces of wood nailed together, stuffed with hay, and covered with carpet.   The horse, being quite close to us, threw the snow into our faces, as well as into my sleeves, my slippers, and my eyes.

" You asked me to go with you to Rome," said the young man, suddenly.

" Yes, and not through a caprice.   You would confer a favor upon me by coming—and you will not ! You do nothing for me ; for whom, then, would you do anything ? "

" Oh, you know very well why I cannot go."

" I do not."

" Because—I love you."

" But you would render me so great a service by coming ! "

" I render you a service ? "

" Yes ! "

" No, I cannot go.   I will think of you from afar.   And if you knew." he continued, in gentle and touching accents, " if you knew what I sometimes suffer,—one must possess as much moral courage as I do to appear always indifferent and always calm.   When I see you no longer—"

" You will forget me."

" Never."

" But—in that case ? "

My voice had lost all trace of raillery.   I was touched.

" I don't know," he answered.   " I only know that this state of things makes me too miserable."

" Poor fellow ! "

I quickly recovered myself.   This pity from me was an insult.

Why is it so delightful to listen to the confession of the sufferings of which one is the cause !   The more unhappy any one is for love of you the happier you are.

"Come with us," I said.   "My father does not wish to take Paul.   Come with us."

" I—"

"You cannot—I know it.   Enough !   I will ask you no more."

I assumed an inquisitorial air, like one who is preparing to be amused by the confession of a folly.

"Then I have the honor of being your first love," I said. "Admirable !—You are a deceiver."

"Because my voice does not change its tone, and because I do not shed tears ?   I have an iron will, that is all."

"And I wanted to give you—something."

"What ?"

"This."

And I showed him a little image of the Virgin suspended around my neck by a white ribbon.

"Give it to me."

"You do not deserve it.

"Ah, Moussia," he cried with a sigh, "I assure you that I do deserve it.   What I feel for you is like the attachment of a dog for its master, a devotion without limit."

"Come nearer, young man, and I will give you my bene-diction."

"Your benediction ?"

"Yes.   If I have made you talk in this way, it is because I desire to know what those who are in love feel, for suppose I should take it into my head to fall in love some day, I should want to recognize the symptoms."

"Give me that image," said the young man, without removing his eyes from it.

He knelt on the chair on the back of which I was lean-ing, and tried to take the image in his hand, but I stopped him.

" No, no, around your neck," I said.

And I put the ribbon around his neck, warm as it still was from contact with mine.

" Oh !" he cried, "thanks for that ! thank you ! thank you !"

And he kissed my hand *only*, for the first time.

Wednesday, November 8.—This evening I sat down at the piano to play the " Reading of the Letter of Venus," a charming *morceau* from " La Belle Helene."

But " La Belle Helene " is a ravishing opera. Offenbach had only just begun his career when he wrote it, and had not yet debased his genius by writing insignificant oper-ettas.

I played for a long time—I cannot now remember what—but something, I remember, that was slow and passionate, tender and charming, as only Mendelssohn's "Songs Without Words," well rendered, can be.

Afterwards I drank four cups of tea, while we talked about music.

" Music exercises a powerful influence over me," said the "young man." "I feel something altogether strange while I listen to it—it produces a—sentimental effect upon me, and I say then things that I should never dare to say otherwise."

" Music is a traitress, Pacha ; distrust her, she will cause you to do a great many things you would not do in your calmer moments. She seizes hold of you, twines herself around you, makes you lose your senses—and then it is terrible !"

Afterward I spoke of Rome. Pacha listened and sighed, in his corner ; and when he approached the light the expression on his countenance told me more plainly than all the words in the world could have done, what the poor fellow suffered.

(Observe this ferocious vanity, this eagerness to ascertain the extent of the ravages one has caused! I am a vulgar coquette, or—no, I am a woman, nothing more.)

" We are rather melancholy this evening," I said softly.

" Yes," he answered ; "your playing, and then—I don't know what the matter is, but I think I have a fever."

"Go to sleep, my friend," I said ; " I am going to my room ; but first help me to carry my books."

Thursday, November 9.—My sojourn here will at least have given me an opportunity of becoming acquainted with the splendid literature of my country. But what do her poets and writers speak of ? *The South.*

And first let me mention Gogol, our humoristic star. His description of Rome made me shed tears, and sigh ; one can form no idea of him without reading his works.

Some day they will be translated ; and those who have had the happiness to see Rome will then understand my emotion.

Oh, when shall I leave this country ?—gray, cold, arid, even in summer, even in the sunshine. The foliage is sickly, and the sky is less blue than—*down yonder.*

Friday.—I have been reading until just now. I am disgusted with my diary—troubled, disheartened.

Rome.—I can say nothing more. I remained fully five minutes with my pen in my hand, without knowing what to write, my heart was so full. But the time is approaching, and I shall see A—— again. The thought of seeing A—— again fills me with terror. And yet I believe that I do not love him, I am even certain of it. But that memory, my chagrin, my uncertainty regarding the future, the fear of being slighted! A—— ! How often this name returns to my thoughts and how hateful it is to me !

You think I wish to die? Fools that you are! I love life as it is, and the vexations, the tortures, the tears that God has sent me—I bless them and I am happy.

In fact, I have so accustomed myself to the idea of being unhappy, that when I think over my troubles alone in my room, and far away from the world, I say to myself that perhaps after all I am not so much to be pitied.

Why weep then?

Saturday, November 11.—This morning at eight o'clock I left Gavronzi, and not without some slight emotion caused—by regret at leaving the place? No, by the interruption of a habit.

The servants were all assembled in the courtyard, and I gave to each one of them some money, and to the housekeeper a gold bracelet.

Wednesday, November 15.—Last Sunday I set out on my homeward journey, accompanied by my father. During my last two days in Russia, I saw a good deal of Prince Michel and the others.

There was no one at the station to see me off but the members of my own family, but there were several strangers there who looked with curiosity at our "traps."

Alexander, Paul, and Pacha entered the compartment with us; the ringing of the third bell announced the departure of the train, and they all crowded around me.

"Paul! Paul!" cried the young man, "let me at least say good-by."

"Let him come here," I said.

He kissed my hand, and I kissed him on the cheek, near the eye. It is the custom in Russia, but I have never been able to approve of it.

We were only waiting for the bell to sound, and it did not delay long.

" Well ? " I said.

" There is still time enough," said the young man.

The train began to move slowly, and Pacha began to talk very fast, but without knowing a word of what he was saying.

" Good-by, good-by," I cried, "jump off."

" Yes, farewell, good-by."

And he jumped on to the platform after having once more kissed my hand—the kiss of a faithful and obedient dog.

" Come, come," cried my father from our compartment, for we were in the passageway of the coach.

I returned to him, but I was so troubled at the spectacle of grief of which I was the cause, that I lay down at once and closed my eyes to think and dream at my ease.

Poor Pacha ! Dear and noble boy ! If I regret anything I leave behind me in Russia, it is this heart of gold, this loyal character, this upright spirit.

Am I really troubled ? Yes.   As if it were possible to be so insensible as not to feel a just pride in possessing such a friend.

1877.

NICE, *Wednesday, January* 17.—When shall I know, then, what this passion called love is, of which people talk so much ?

I could have loved A——, but now I despise him.   The Duke of H—— I loved extravagantly when I was a child— a love due to the effect produced on an excitable imagination by the wealth, the name, and the eccentricities of the man.

Tuesday, January 23.—Last night I was seized by a fit of despair that found utterance in moans, and that finally

drove me to throw the dining-room clock into the sea.
Dina ran after me, suspecting some sinister design on my
part, but I threw nothing into the sea except the clock.   It
was a bronze one—a Paul, without the Virginia—in a very
becoming hat, and with a fishing-rod in his hand.   Dina
came back with me into my room, and seemed to be very
much amused about the clock.   I laughed, too.

Poor clock !

Thursday, February 1.—Mamma and I went out for an
airing.   On reaching home I sat down to read Livy.   The
heroes of antiquity, the classic folds of the toga, the Capitol,
the dome, the masked ball, the Pincio—Oh, Rome !

ROME, *Thursday, February* 8.—I fell asleep at Vintimille,
and only woke up, mind and body, when we arrived at
Rome.   Against my will I was obliged to remain there till
evening, as the train for Naples does not leave till 10 o'clock.
A whole day in Rome !

At twenty minutes past ten we left Rome.   I fell asleep,
and we are now at Naples.   My sleep was not so sound,
however, as to prevent my hearing an ill-tempered passenger complaining to the conductor of the presence of Prater
in the coach.   The gallant conductor took the part of
our dog.

But here is Naples.   Does it happen to you as it does to
me?   On nearing a great and beautiful city I grow restless,
my heart palpitates ; I feel as if I should like to clasp the
city in my embrace.

It took us more than an hour to reach the Hotel du
Louvre.   There was an obstruction in the way—what cries,
and what confusion !

The women here have enormous heads ; they look like
the women they exhibit along with the tigers, serpents, and
other animals, at the menageries.

In Rome I like only what is old ; at Naples there is nothing to admire but what is new.

NAPLES, *Monday, February* 26.—I continued my excursions to-day. We visited San Martino, an ancient convent. I have never seen anything more interesting. Museums, as a general thing, give one a chill. That of San Martino attracts and charms. The antique carriage of the Syndic, and the gallery of Charles III., enraptured me ; and those corridors, with their mosaic floors, those ceilings with their magnificent moldings ! The church and the chapels are something marvelous. As they are not large, every detail of the workmanship can be fully appreciated. Polished marbles, precious stones, mosaics on all sides, overhead and underfoot, on the ceiling as well as on the floor ! With the exception of those of Guido Reni and of Spagnoletto, the pictures are the most remarkable I have ever seen : the patiently wrought works of Fra Buenaventura, the ancient porcelains of Capo-di-Monte, the portraits on silk, and a painting on glass representing the story of Potiphar's wife. The court-yard of white marble, with its sixty columns, is of rare beauty.

Our guide told us that there are but five monks remaining in the convent—three brothers and two laymen, who dwell somewhere upstairs, in a neglected wing of the building.

We went up into a sort of tower, with two balconies suspended one above the other, and I felt as one might feel looking over the edge of a precipice ; the view is distractingly beautiful. One sees the mountains, the villas, and the plains of Naples through a sort of blue mist that is only an illusion of the senses, produced by distance.

"What is going on at Naples to-day ?" I asked the guide, as I listened to the noises that reached us from the city.

"Nothing ; it is only the Neapolitan people," he answered, smiling.

"Is it always so?"

"Always."

There rose up above this mass of roofs a clamor, a cease-less sound of cries, like a series of shouts, of which one can form no idea in the city itself. In truth, this noise that rises up above the city with the blue mist produces a species of terror in the mind, and, by making one strangely conscious of the height at which one stands, causes a sensation of vertigo.

The marble chapels charmed me. A country that pos-sesses treasures such as there are to be found in Italy, is the richest country in the world. To compare Italy with the rest of the world is like comparing a magnificent painting to a whitewashed wall.

How did I dare to judge Naples a year ago? I had not even seen it then.

Saturday, March 3, 1877.—I went to the chapel in our hotel this evening. There is an infinite charm in letting the thoughts dwell upon love when one is in a church. You see the priest, the images, the glow of the tapers shining through the obscurity—all this took me back to Rome! Divine ecstasy, celestial perfume, delightful transports—ah, how describe them here! Only in song could feelings such as pervaded me be expressed.

Rome! Its statues, its mosaics, its wonders of art, anti-quity, the middle ages, its great men, its monuments of the past, St. Peter's with its columns and its mysterious shad-ows—I thought of all these.

What is to be gained by weeping? Tears will do no good. Unhappiness is to be my destiny—that, and an artist's fame. And what if I should fail?

Make your minds easy; I was not born to spend my life in some obscure corner of the world, letting my faculties rust through neglect.

I will not now speak of love, for I once made use of that word lightly ; I will no longer invoke the help of God ; all I wish for is to die.

Lord God, Jesus Christ ; suffer me to die ! My life has been a short one, but the lesson taught me has been hard. Everything has been against me. I desire only to die. My thoughts are as incoherent and disordered as the lines I trace ; I hate myself, as I hate everything that is contemptible.

Let me die, my God ! Let me die ! I have lived long enough !

A peaceful death ! To die while singing some beautiful air of Verdi ; no rebellious feeling rises up within me at the thought, as formerly ; then I desired to live that others might not triumph and rejoice over me. Now all that is indifferent to me ; I suffer too much.

Sunday, April 1.—I am like the patient and untiring alchemist who spends whole days and nights beside his retorts that he may not miss the moment he has longed for and waited for. Every day it seems to me that *it* is going to happen. And I think of it and wait for it. And how do I know whether it has happened or not ? I examine myself curiously and with eager eyes in the glass, and I ask myself anxiously if this be not perhaps *it*. But I have formed such an opinion of *it*, that I have come to think it does not exist, or rather that it has already happened, and that there was nothing wonderful in it, after all.

But all my imaginings, then, and the novelists and the poets? Would they with one accord have made their theme a feeling that does not exist, solely for the purpose of dignifying by its name the grossness of human nature? No ; for in that case it would be impossible to account for our preferences.

Friday, May 11.—Have I mentioned that Gordigiani came to see us; that he gave me great encouragement, and predicted an artistic future for me ; that he found much to praise in my sketches, and wished very much to paint my portrait ?

FLORENCE, *Saturday, May* 12.—My heart is oppressed at the thought of leaving Florence.

To go to Nice ! I look forward to it as I would to going to live in a desert. I should like to shave my head that I might not have the trouble of arranging my hair.

We have packed our trunks, we are going ! The ink dries upon my pen while I try to write in vain, so oppressed am I by grief.

NICE, *Wednesday, May* 16.—I have been running about all the morning in search of a few trifles that I want for my antechamber, but in this wretched place one can find nothing. I went to the shop of a painter on glass, to a tin-smith's, and I don't know where else.

The thought that my diary may not prove interesting, the impossibility of making it interesting by preparing surprises for the reader, torment me. If I wrote only at intervals I might be able to do so, perhaps, but these notes written down each day will be read with interest only by some thinker, or some student of human nature. Whoever has not the patience to read it all, will be able to read none of it, and, above all, will be able to understand none of it.

I am happy in my comfortable and pretty nest in the midst of my garden full of flowers. Nice no longer exists for me ; I am in my country-house.

NICE, *Wednesday, May* 23.—Oh, when I think that we have only a single life to live, and that every moment that passes brings us nearer death, I am ready to go distracted !

I do not fear death, but life is so short that to waste it is infamous.

One pair of eyes is not enough if one desires to accomplish anything. Reading and drawing fatigue me greatly, and while I am writing these wretched lines at night I grow sleepy.

Ah, what a happy time youth is !

With what happiness shall I look back, in times to come, on these days devoted to science and art ! If I worked thus all the year round—but a day, or a week, as the chance may be ! Natures so richly endowed as mine consume themselves in idleness.

I try to tranquillize my mind by the thought that I shall certainly begin work in earnest this winter. But the thought of my seventeen years makes me blush to the roots of my hair. Almost seventeen, and what have I accomplished? Nothing ! This thought crushes me.

I think of all the famous men and women who acquired their celebrity late in life, in order to console myself ; but seventeen years for a man are nothing, while for a woman they are equal to twenty-three for a man.

To go live in Paris, in the North, after this cloudless sky, these clear, calm nights ! What can one desire, what can one hope for, after Italy ! Paris—the heart of the civilized world, of the world of intellect, of genius, of fashion—naturally people go there, and remain there, and are happy there ; it is even indispensable to go there, for a multitude of reasons, in order to return with renewed delight to the land beloved of God, the land of the blest, that enchanted, wondrous, divine land of the supreme beauty and magic charm of which all that one could say would never equal the truth !

When foreigners come to Italy they ridicule its mean little towns, and its lazzaroni, and they do this with some cleverness and not without a certain show of reason. But forget

for the moment that you are clever ; forget that it is a mark
of genius to turn everything into ridicule, and you will find,
as I do, that tears will mingle with your laughter, and that
you will wonder at all you see.

Tuesday, May 29.—The nearer I approach to the time
when my youth shall be over, the more indifferent do I
become to everything. Few things affect me now, while
formerly anything had power to move me, so that in reading
over this record of the past I see, from the impression they
made upon me, that I attached too much importance to
trifles.

Trust in others, and that sensitiveness of feeling that is
the bloom of the character, are soon lost.

I regret the loss of this freshness of feeling all the more,
as when it is once gone it is gone forever. Without it one
is more tranquil, but one no longer enjoys as much. Disappointment ought not to have come to me so early in life.
If it had not come, I feel that I might have achieved great
things.

I have just finished a book that has disgusted me with
love—the story of a charming princess who had fallen in
love with an artist. Fie ! I do not say this with the stupid
intention of seeking to belittle the profession of an artist,
but—without knowing why, I have always had aristocratic
tendencies, and I believe as much in race where men as
where animals are in question. It is true that often—always,
indeed, in earlier times the foundation of a noble race was
based on moral and physical training, the effects of which
were transmitted from father to son. And of what consequence is the origin of a thing ?

On glancing through those pages of my journal that record
the A—— episode I am filled with wonder and admiration
for myself to see how just and true were my reflections concerning it at the time it occurred. I had forgotten them,

and I was a little uneasy lest it might be thought that I had entertained an affection (a past affection) for Count A——. Fortunately, however, no one can think so now, thanks to this dear journal.   No, truly, I did not think I had made so many just reflections at the time, and, above all, that I had felt them.   That was a year ago, and I feared I had written a great deal of nonsense ; but no, I am quite satisfied with myself.   The only thing that I cannot understand is how I could have behaved so foolishly and reasoned so wisely.

I must repeat to myself again that no advice in the world— nothing but personal experience—could ever have kept me from doing anything I wished to do.

That is because the woman who writes these words and the woman she is writing about are two different persons. What do all these sufferings matter to *me?*   I write them down ; I analyze them ; I transcribe my daily life, but to *me*, to *me myself*, all that is completely indifferent.   It is my pride, my self-love, my interests, my complexion, my eyes, that suffer, that weep, that rejoice ; but *I*, I take part in it all only to observe, to narrate, to write about and reason coldly concerning all these trifles, like Gulliver among the **Liliputians.**

I have a great deal more to say in explanation of myself, but enough for the present.

Monday, June 11.—While they were playing cards last night I made a rough sketch of the players by the unsteady light of the two wax candles, and this morning I transferred the sketches to canvas.

I am delighted to have made a picture of persons sitting down in different attitudes ; to have copied the position of the hands and arms, the expression of the countenance, etc., I had never before done anything but heads, which I was satisfied to scatter over the canvas like flowers.

PARIS, *Saturday, July* 7.—I think I may truly say that I have been growing much more sensible for some time past ; that I begin to see things now in a more natural light, and that I have abandoned a great many illusions and a great many regrets.

True wisdom can be learned only from personal experience.

Sunday, July 15.—I am so weary of life that I should like to die. Nothing amuses me, nothing interests me. I desire nothing, I hope for nothing. Yes, there is one thing I wish for—not to be ashamed of being as I am. I desire to be able, in a word, to do nothing, to think of nothing, to live the life of a plant, without feeling remorse for it.

Reading, drawing, music—but *ennui ! ennui ! ennui !* In addition to one's occupations one requires some amusement, some interest in life, and this is why I am weary of it.

I am tired of life, not because I have not married—no, I am sure you think better of me than to imagine that—I am tired of life because everything has gone wrong with me, and because I am tired of it.

Paris kills me ! It is a cafe, a well-kept hotel, a bazar. I must only hope, however, that when winter comes, what with the opera, the Bois, and my studies, I shall be able to accustom myself to it.

Tuesday, July 17.—I have spent the day looking at veritable marvels of artistic and antique embroidery, gowns that are poems, all sorts of splendors that have given me a glimpse of a luxury I had scarcely an idea of before.

Ah, Italy !—If I devoted a month twice a year there to my wardrobe, I had no need to think of it again. Dress is so stupid when one makes it a matter of special study.

Wednesday, July 18.—The mere word " Italy "causes me

an emotion such as no other word, such as no one's presence, has ever done.

Oh, when shall I be there !

It would annoy me exceedingly if any one were to suppose I wrote these Ah's and Oh's through affectation.

I don't know why this should be the case, however ; and, besides, I affirm and declare that all I say, stupid and disagreeable though it may be, is the truth.

The thing is that I wish to write now in a different style, quite simply ; and I fear that on comparing this with my former exaggerated way of saying things, people will no longer be able to understand what I want to say.

I want to express myself quite naturally, and if I make use of a few figures of speech, do not think it is for ornament ; oh, no ! it is simply for the purpose of describing as nearly as possible the confusion of my thoughts.

It vexes me greatly to be able to write nothing that is pathetic. I long so much to make others feel what I feel ! I weep, and I say I *weep!* That is not what I want. I want to make you feel the whole thing—I want to touch your hearts !

That will come, and other things will come with it, but it must not be sought after.

Thursday, July 26.—I have spent almost the whole day drawing ; in order to rest my eyes I played for a while on the mandolin ; then again came drawing, then the piano. There is nothing in the world to be compared to Art ; and it is as much a source of happiness for the beginner as for the master. One forgets everything in one's work ; one regards those outlines, those shadings, with respect, with emotion—one is a creator, one feels one's-self almost great.

Through fear of injuring my eyes I have given up reading at night for some little time past. I begin to see things blurred, even at so short a distance as from the carriage to the sidewalk. This troubles me. What if, after losing my voice, I should be obliged to give up drawing and reading also ! In that case I should no longer complain, for that would mean that in all my other sufferings no one was to blame, and that they were the will of God.

Monday, July 30.—Fauvel has stopped my excursions to Enghein, and will perhaps send me to Germany, which would again turn everything upside down. Walitsky is a skillful doctor and understands a great deal about sickness ; I was in hopes he was mistaken in wishing me go to Soden, but it seems that Fauvel is of the same opinion.

Sunday, August 5.—When one is in want of bread, one does not ask for sweets ; therefore it is that I am ashamed to speak of my artistic hopes at present. I no longer dare to say that I would like such or such an arrangement made to enable me to work better, or that I want to go to Italy to study. To say such things now would cost me a great effort.

Even if I were to have everything I desire, I think it would no longer make me happy as it might have done before.

Confidence, once lost, can never be restored ; and to lose this—as is the case with every irrevocable loss—is an inconsolable sorrow.

I am disenchanted with life ; I take notice of nothing, and no one interests me ; I wear an anxious look, instead of my former confident expression, thus depriving my countenance of its principal charm ; I sit silent and apart while others are conversing around me ; my friends look at me with astonishment at first, and then leave me to myself. Then I try to be amusing, and I am only odd, extravagant, impertinent, and stupid.

Monday, August 6.—Do you suppose that the condition of Russia causes me no anxiety ? Who is there so unhappy or so contemptible that he forgets his country in her hour of danger ?

Do you think one hundred thousand slaughtered Russians would now be lying dead if my prayers could have availed to save them, or my anxious thoughts to protect them ?

Tuesday, August 7.—I have been stupefying myself at the Bon Marche, which pleases me, as everything else does that is well arranged. We had some friends to supper ; they laughed, still—I am sad, wretched. . . . So then, IT IS IMPOSSIBLE ! Horrible word ! Hideous, maddening word ! To die, my God, to die ! To die and leave nothing behind ! To die like a dog—to die as a hundred thousand other women have died whose names scarcely survive upon their tombstones ! To die !—

Mad creature, who will not see what it is that God desires ! God wishes me to renounce everything and to devote myself to art ! In five years to come I shall still be young, still beautiful perhaps. But what if I become only a mediocre artist such as there are already too many of ?

With other things to interest one, that might do, but to devote one's life to it and not to succeed !

What is life without society ? What can one who leads a solitary existence hope to accomplish ! This thought makes me hate the whole world, my family, myself ; it makes me blaspheme ! To live ! To live ! Holy Mary, Mother of God, Lord Jesus, help me !

But if, I wish to devote my life to art, I must go to Italy ! Yes, to Rome.

This is the wall of granite against which I dash my head at every instant !

I will remain here.

Sunday, August 12.—I have sketched the portrait of Antoinette, our chambermaid. She has a charming face, with large, bright blue eyes of an exquisitely sweet and innocent expression. The sketch is always a success with me, but to finish a portrait one must have studied.

Friday, August 17.—I am convinced that I cannot live outside of Rome. In fact my health is visibly deteriorating, but at least I have no wish in the matter. I would give two years of my life never to have been in Rome.

Unhappily, one learns how to act only when there is no longer need for action.

The thought of painting enrages me. Because there are the materials in me to accomplish wonders, and yet, so far as study is concerned, I am less fortunate than any poor boy whom some benevolent person sends to school because he has been discovered to possess talent. I hope, at least, that posterity, in revenge for the loss of the pictures I might have painted, will decapitate every member of my family.

Do you fancy I still wish TO GO INTO SOCIETY? No, no ; I am soured and disappointed, and if I wish to become an artist, it is for the same reason that malcontents become republicans.

I think, after all, I slander myself in saying this.

Saturday, August 18.—When I was reading Homer I compared my aunt, on one occasion, when she was angry, to Hecuba at the burning of Troy. No matter how much ashamed we may be to confess our admiration for the classics, no one, I think, can escape in secret from the charm exercised over the mind by the ancient writers. No modern drama, no romance, no sensational comedy of Dumas or of George Sand, has left so clear a recollection or so vivid and profound an impression upon me as the description of the fall of Troy.

I almost feel as if I had witnessed those horrors; as if I had heard those cries, and seen those flames, with Priam's family, unhappy ones, seeking refuge behind the altars of their gods, to be followed there by the flames and delivered by them at last from their sufferings.

I have thrown aside in disgust the "Journal d'un Diplomate en Italie." This French elegance of style, this politeness, these hackneyed phrases of admiration, are an insult to Rome. When a Frenchman is describing anything I always picture him to myself as dissecting it with a long instrument held delicately between his fingers, and eyeglasses on his nose.

Rome should be, as a city, what I imagined I should be as a woman; any expression of admiration uttered in the presence of others, where we are concerned, is a profanation.

Sunday, August 19.—I have just finished reading "Arcadia," by Ouida. This book has left a sad impression on me, yet 1 almost envy the lot of Gioja.

Gioja grew up to womanhood under the joint influence of Homer and Virgil; after her father's death she went on foot to Rome, and received there a terrible disappointment, for she had expected to see the Rome of Augustus.

For two years she studied in the studio of Marix, the most celebrated sculptor of the time, who secretly loved her. But she had no thought for anything except her art until the appearance of Hilarion, a poet whose poems drew tears from every one, and who himself turned everything into ridicule; a millionnaire—as beautiful as a god, and who was adored by all who knew him. While Marix worships her in silence, Hilarion causes Gioja to fall in love with him to gratify a whim.

The ending of the romance saddened me, yet I would accept without hesitation the lot of Gioja. First, she worshiped Rome, then she experienced the delight of an absorbing passion. And if she was deserted, it was by *him;* if she suffered, it was through *him;* and I cannot picture to myself how one can be unhappy because of anything that comes from the man one loves—as she loved, and as I shall love, if I ever love!

She never discovered that he had sought to make her love him for a whim.

"He has loved me," she says, "it is I who have been unable to retain his affections."

She won fame; her name, uttered in accents of admiration mingled with wonder, was on every one's lips.

She never ceased to love him; he never descended in her eyes to the rank of common men; she believed him always to be perfect, almost divine; she did not wish to die then, because he lived. "How can one kill one's self," she says, "while the man one loves still lives?"

And she died in his arms, hearing from his lips the words, "I love you."

But in order to love thus, one must find a Hilarion. The man one loves thus must belong to no obscure family; Hilarion was the son of a noble Austrian and a Greek princess. The man one loves thus should never know what it is to be in want of money; he should never falter in any of his undertakings, nor be afraid of anything or of any one.

This man, finally, must never find the door of a palace or of a club barred to him; he must never find himself obliged to hesitate regarding the purchase of a statue he desires to possess, or the propriety of any one of his actions, however foolish it may be. He must be superior to the slights, the annoyances, the difficulties of other men. He must be a coward only in love, but a coward like Hilarion who could break a woman's heart with a smile, and who would weep to see a woman want for anything.

Such a man should find, wherever he travels, a palace of his own in which he may repose, a yacht to transport him wherever his fancy may lead him, jewels, servants, horses, flute-players even, if he should desire them.

Thursday, August 23.—I am in Schlangenbad!

Fauvel has ordered me to rest, as he says. I do not think myself cured yet, however, and in the matter of disagreeable things I never deceive myself.

I shall soon be eighteen. Eighteen years are not a great many to one who is thirty-five, but they are a great many to me, who in the brief period of my existence as a young girl have had few pleasures and many griefs.

Art! If I had not that magic word before me in the distance I should have died already.

But for Art one has need of no one; we depend entirely upon ourselves, and if we fail, it is because there was nothing in us, and that we ought to live no longer. Art! I picture it to myself like a great light shining before me in the distance, and I forget everything else but this, and I shall press forward to the goal, my eyes fixed upon this light. And now—oh, no, no! now, my God, do not terrify me! Some horrible thought tells me that—Ah, no: I will not write it down, I will not bring bad luck upon myself! My God!—I will make the attempt, and if— Then there will be no more to be said, and—let God's will be done!

I was at Schlangenbad two years ago. What a difference between then and now!

Then I hoped all things; now I hope for nothing. . . .

Thanks to my habit of carrying a "heap of useless things" about with me I can make myself at home anywhere by the end of an hour—my dressing-case, my writing materials, my mandolin, a few good big books, my foot-warmer, and my photographs—that is all. But with those any room in an inn may be made comfortable. What I am most attached to are my four large red dictionaries, my Livy, bound in green, a small copy of Dante, a medium-sized

Lamartine, and my likeness, cabinet size, painted in oil and framed in dark blue velvet, encased in a Russia leather case. With this my bureau assumes at once an air of elegance, and when the light of the two wax candles falls on these warm and pleasing colors, I feel almost reconciled to Germany.

Dina is so good, so amiable! How I should like to see her happy!

And a word in regard to that; what a vile humbug the life of certain persons is!

Monday, August 27.—I have added a clause to my evening prayer—these five words: My God, protect our armies!

I, eighteen years old—it is absurd! My talents still undeveloped, my hopes, my passions, my caprices, will be ridiculous at eighteen. To begin to learn to paint at eighteen, when one has had the pretension of being able to do everything quicker and better than other people!

There are people who deceive others, but I have deceived myself.

Saturday, September 1.—I spend a great deal of my time alone, thinking and reading, without any one to direct me. Perhaps this is well, but perhaps also it is ill.

Who will assure me that my head has not been filled with erroneous notions, and my judgment distorted by false methods of reasoning? That is a question that will be decided when I am dead.

Forgive, forgiveness: here are a verb and a noun extensively used in the world. Christianity commands us to forgive.

What is forgiveness?

It is the renunciation of vengeance or of the desire to inflict punishment for an offense received. But when we have had neither the intention of taking vengeance nor of inflicting punishment, can we be said to forgive? Yes, and no. Yes, because we assure ourselves and others that we have forgiven; and we act as if the offense had never existed. No, because one is not master of one's memory, and so long as we *remember* we have not *forgiven.*

I have spent the whole of the day in the society of my family, and I mended with my own hands a Russia leather shoe belonging to Dina ; then I washed a large wooden table, as any chambermaid might do, and set to work to make on this table varenki (a paste made of flour, water, and fresh cheese). My people were amused to see me kneading the paste with sleeves turned up, and a black velvet cap upon my head, like Faust.

Sunday, September 2.—How can people who are free to do as they choose go to spend a day at Wiesbaden ?

We went there nevertheless, in order to see the most ridiculous people in the world celebrate the defeat of the most cultured.

Thursday, September 6.—I will stay in Paris. This is what I have definitively resolved to do, and my mother also. I spent the whole evening with her. Everything would have gone very well if she had not been ill, as she was, particularly toward night. She has not left her bed since.

I have resolved to remain in Paris, where I will pursue my studies, going to a watering-place in the summer for relaxation. All my caprices are exhausted. Russia was what I needed, and I am now completely reformed. And I feel that the moment has at last come to pause in my course. With my abilities, in two years I shall have made up for lost time.

So, then, in the name of the Father, of the Son, and of the Holy Ghost, and may the divine protection be with me. This is not a resolution made to be broken, like so many former ones, but a final one. •

PARIS, *Wednesday, September* 19.—I don't know why exactly, but I think I shall like to live in Paris. It seems to me that a year in the *atelier Julian* will lay a good foundation.

.

Tuesday, October 2.—To-day we removed our belongings to 71 Champs Elysees. Notwithstanding the confusion I found time to go to the *atelier* Julian, the only one of any note here for women. The hours of work are from eight in the morning till noon, and from one in the afternoon to five.

To-day not being the fourth, which is an unlucky day for me, I was eager to begin work on as many things as possible.

I sketched a three-quarter head in crayon in ten minutes at the studio, and Julian told me he had not expected anything so good from a beginner. I left the studio early, as all I wanted was to make a beginning to-day. We went to the Bois. I plucked five oak-leaves there and took them to Doucet, who in half an hour made me a charming little blue scapular. But what shall I wish for? to be a millionnaire? To get back my voice? To obtain the *Prix de Rome* under the guise of a man? To marry Napoleon IV? To go into the great world?

I wish more than anything to get back my voice.

The day passes quickly when one draws from eight in the morning till noon, and from one in the afternoon to five. Only to go to the studio and back takes almost an hour and a half. To-day I arrived a little late, so that I worked but six hours.

When I think of the entire years that I have lost it makes me angry enough to give up everything! But that would only make matters worse. Come, be miserable and hateful as you will, but be satisfied, at least, to have at last succeeded in making a beginning. And I might have begun at thirteen? Four entire years lost!

THE THREE LAUGHS

I might be painting historical pictures by this time if I had begun four years ago. All that I have done is worse than nothing ; it must be undone again.

At last I am working with artists—real artists, who have exhibited in the *Salon*, and whose pictures are bought—who even give lessons themselves.

Julian is satisfied with the beginning I have made. "By the end of the winter," he said to me, "You will be able to paint very good portraits."

He says some of the women pupils give as much promise as the men ; I would have worked with the latter but that they smoke, and then there is no difference in the work. Formerly the women pupils did not draw from the nude, but since they have been admitted to the Academy there is no difference made in that respect between them and the men.

The servant at the studio is just like one of those they describe in novels.

" I have always lived among artists," she says, "and I am not by any means one of the *bourgeoisie ;* I am an artist."

I am happy, happy !

Friday, October 5.—" Did you do that by yourself ? " M. Julian asked me on entering the studio to-day.

" Yes, Monsieur."

I grew as red as if I had told a falsehood.

" Well, I am satisfied with it, very well satisfied with it."

" Truly ? "

"Very well satisfied."

In the studio all distinctions disappear. One has neither name nor family ; one is no longer the daughter of one's mother, one is one's self,—an individual,—and one has before one art, and nothing else. One feels so happy, so free, so proud !

At last I am what I have so long wished to be. I have

wished for it so long that I scarcely believe it now to be true.

Apropos, whom do you think I saw in the Champs Elysees to-day?

None other than the Duke of H—— occupying a *fiacre* all by himself.

The handsome, vigorous young man with yellow locks and a delicate mustache now looks like a big Englishman ; his face is very red, and he has little red whiskers that grow from the tip of the ear to the middle of the cheek.

Four years, however, change a man greatly ; at the end of half an hour I had ceased to think of him.

Sic transit gloria Ducis.

The sense of shame disappears in the presence of perfect beauty, for supreme beauty leaves room in the mind for no other feeling than admiration.

And so with other things. The music that allows the defect of the stage-setting to be noticed is not perfect. An act of heroism that, after it has taken place, has left the judgment free, is not the heroic act you have dreamed of. . . .

To be supreme of its kind a thing must occupy the mind to the exclusion of every feeling that is not connected with it.

Thursday, October 11.—M. Julian told the servant at the studio that Schoeppi and I were the pupils who gave greatest promise of being artists. Schoeppi is a Swiss. M. Julian added that I may become a great artist.

The weather is so cold that I have taken cold, but I can forgive all that provided only I can learn to draw.

To draw ? And why ?

To compensate me for everything I have been deprived of since the day I was born ; to supply the place of everything I have ever longed for, and everything I still long for ;

to enable me to achieve success by my genius, by—by any-thing you choose, provided only that I achieve success !

Saturday, October 13.—It is on Saturday that M. Tony Robert-Fleury comes to the studio.   He is the artist who painted *Le Dernier Jour de Corinthe*, which was purchased by the State for the Luxembourg.   The most distinguished artists of Paris come to the studio from time to time to give *us* the benefit of their advice.

When he came to me and proceeded to *pronounce judgment* I interrupted him, saying :

"I beg your pardon, Monsieur, but I began only ten days ago."

"Where did you draw before?" he asked, examining my drawing.

"Nowhere."

"How, nowhere?"

"Yes, I took thirty-two lessons in painting for my own amusement."

"But that is not studying."

"No, Monsieur, for that reason—"

"You had never drawn from nature before coming here?"

"Never, Monsieur."

"That cannot be possible."

"But I assure you—"

And as he appeared still incredulous, I added :

"I will give you my word of honor that it is as I say, if you wish."

"Well, then," he said, "you have extraordinary talent for painting ; you are specially gifted, and I advise you to work hard."

Let me go on with and conclude the history of my suc-cess.

" How is this, Mademoiselle ? " said Julian this evening, standing in front of me with his arms folded.

I felt something like fear, and asked him, reddening, what the matter was.

" Why, this is splendid," he said ; " you work all day long on Saturdays, when every one else is taking a little relaxation ! "

" Why, yes, Monsieur, I have nothing else to do ; I must do something."

" This is fine.   Do you know that M. Robert-Fleury is not at all dissatisfied with you ? "

" Yes, he has told me so."

" This poor Robert-Fleury !   He is still somewhat in-disposed."

And the master, installing himself beside me, began to chat with me—a thing he very seldom does with any of his pupils, and which is very much appreciated.

Mme. D—— dined with us to-day ; I was quiet, reserved, silent, scarcely amiable, indeed.   I had no thought for any-thing but art.

As I am writing, I stop and think of all the labor that will be necessary—the time, the patience, the difficulties that will present themselves.

It is not as easy to become a great painter as it is to say the words ; even if one has the genius, there exists still the necessity for the indispensable mechanical labor.

And a voice within whispers to me : " You will feel neither the time nor the difficulties that may present themselves; you will achieve success before you are aware of it."

And I believe this voice !   It has never yet deceived me, and it has too often predicted misfortune for it to speak falsely this time ; I hear it, and I feel that I am justified in believing it.

I shall take the *Prix de Rome !*

Tuesday, October 16.—M. Robert-Fleury came to the studio this afternoon and honored me with his special attention.

I spent all the morning at the studio, as usual, from nine till half-past twelve. I have not yet succeeded in arriving there at eight precisely.

At noon I come home to breakfast and return to the studio at twenty minutes past one, to remain till five, and again in the evening at eight to remain till ten. That gives me nine hours a day.

This does not fatigue me in the least ; if it were physically possible for me to do more, I would do it. There are people who call this work ; I assure you that for me it is play, and I do not say this in order to boast of it. Nine hours are so little, and to think that I cannot work even so long as that every day, the distance is so great from the Champs Elysees to the Rue Vivienne, and very often there is no one to accompany me in the evening.

It will be dark at four o'clock in winter ; I will go to the studio in the evenings then at all costs.

We drive to the studio in a coupé in the morning, and in a landau in the latter part of the day.

You see the question is to accomplish in one year the work of three. And, as I am making rapid progress, these three years' work in one will be equal to six years of work for a person of ordinary ability.

I am talking now like the fools who say, "What it would take another two years to accomplish she will accomplish in six months." There can be no more mistaken way of reasoning than this.

The question is not one of time ; if that were the case, there would be nothing to do but work for so many years. Doubtless with patience any one might achieve a certain amount of success. But what I will accomplish in a year or two the Danish girl will never accomplish. Whenever I undertake to correct the mistakes of humanity I become confused and irritated, because I never have the patience to finish a sentence completely.

In brief, if I had begun three years ago, I might be satisfied with six hours' study daily; but as it is, I need nine, ten, twelve—as many hours as I can devote to it, in short. Of course, even if I had begun three years ago, I would still do well to work as many hours as possible, but—what is past, is past ! "

Thursday, October 18.—Julian, speaking of my drawing from the nude to-day, said that it was extraordinary, remarkable, for a beginner. And the fact is, if it is not remarkable, at least the composition is good, the torso is not bad either, and the drawing is very well for a beginner.

All the pupils got up and came over to look at my drawing, while I blushed to the roots of my hair.

Heavens, how happy I am !

Last night's drawing was so bad that M. Julian advised me to do it over. Wishing to make it too good, I spoiled it this evening. It was better before I retouched it.

Saturday, October 20.—Breslau received a great many compliments to-day from Robert-Fleury, and I not one. The drawing from the nude was good enough, but the head was bad. I ask myself with terror when I shall be able to draw well.

I have been working just two weeks, taking out the Sundays. Two weeks !

Breslau has been working at the studio two years, and she is twenty ; I am seventeen ; but Breslau had taken lessons for a long time before coming here.

And I, miserable creature that I am ?

I have been taking lessons only two weeks !

How well that Breslau draws !

Monday, October 22.—The model to-day was an ugly one, and every one refused to draw. I proposed that we should all go to see the *Prix de Rome*, on exhibition at the School of Fine Arts. Half the party went on foot, and Breslau, Madame Simonides, Zilhardt, and I in a carriage.

The exhibition had closed yesterday. We walked on the quays for a while ; we looked at the old books and engravings, we discussed art. Then we drove *in an open fiacre* to the Bois. Do you understand what that means? I did not want to say anything—it would have been to spoil their pleasure. They were so amiable and behaved with so much decorum, and we were just beginning to feel at ease with one another. In short—things were going on very well, when we chanced to meet the landau containing my family which followed our *fiacre.*

I made a sign to our driver not to take the lead ; they had seen me and they knew it, but I did not care to speak to them in the presence of my artist-friends. I wore my little cap, my hair was in disorder, and I looked confused.

My family, naturally, were furious, and, worse than that, ashamed.

I was terribly embarrassed.

Altogether a disagreeable event.

Wednesday, October 24.—M. Robert-Fleury came to the studio last night, and told me I had done wrong in absenting myself from the lesson, as I was one of the best of the pupils. M. Julian repeated this to me in a sufficiently flattering manner.

It was already flattering to have my absence noticed by a professor like Robert-Fleury.

And when I think that I might have begun to work four years ago at least—at least ! And I never cease to think of it.

Saturday, November 3.—M. Robert-Fleury had already

corrected all the drawings when I arrived at the studio to-day. I gave him mine and hid myself behind his seat, as usual. Well, I-was forced to come out from my place of concealment, he had so many pleasant things to say to me.

" There is still a crudeness in the outlines, indeed, but the freedom and truth of the drawing are admirable," he said. " The action of this is really very good. Of course it is true that you are wanting in experience, but you have that which is not to be learned. Do you understand? *That which is not to be learned.* What you do not yet possess is to be learned, and you will learn it."

"Yes," he repeated, "it is admirable, and if you will only study hard you will do very well—and remember it is I who say so."

" And I say so too," I answered.

Thursday, November 8.—There is only one thing that could have taken me away from the studio for the whole afternoon, and that is Versailles.

On the stairs I came face to face with Julian, who was surprised to see me leaving so early. I explained to him how it was, and said that nothing but Versailles could have taken me away from the studio. He said that was so much the more to be commended, as I had so many temptations in the way of amusements.

" I find pleasure nowhere but here, Monsieur," I said.

" And you are right ; you shall see how glad you will be that it is so two months hence."

" You know my desire is to be a great artist, and that I am not learning drawing as—an amusement."

" I should hope so ! That would be to put a bar of gold to the same use as a bar of copper, and that would be a crime ; I assure you that with your ability—I see evidence of that in the admirable things you have already done—

you do not need more than a year and a half to accomplish wonders."

"Oh!"

"I repeat it, wonders!"

"Take care, Monsieur, I shall go away enchanted."

"I speak the truth, you shall see for yourself ; by the end of this winter you will be able to draw very well. I give you six months in which to familiarize yourself with colors, without neglecting your drawing—to accomplish wonders, in a word."

Merciful Heaven! During the drive home I did nothing but laugh and cry for joy ; and I already began to indulge in dreams of receiving five thousand francs for a portrait.

So much happiness makes me afraid. A year and a half for portraits, but for a picture? Let us say two or three years more—we shall see.

Saturday, November 10.—M. Robert-Fleury was tired and indisposed to-day, and corrected scarcely half of our drawings. No one received a compliment from him, *not even I ;* I was a little surprised at this, as Julian had thought my work very good. Yes, but I was dissatisfied with it myself. I am disgusted.

Afterwards I made some sketches ; one of them, a sort of caricature, turned out a success. Julian made me put my name to it, and placed it in his album.

How much more easily we are affected by disagreeable things than by pleasant ones!

For a month past I have heard nothing but words of commendation, with the exception of one occasion, a fortnight ago. This morning I was scolded, and I have forgotten everything but the scolding. But it is so always. A thousand persons applaud ; a single one hisses, and his voice drowns the voices of all the others.

Wednesday, November 14.—To-day I went to look for some books and plaster casts in the neighborhood of the School of Medicine. I was delighted; the streets were full of students coming out of the various schools—those narrow streets with shops where musical instruments are sold. I was enchanted with everything. Ah! *sapristi!* I can understand now the magic charm, if one may say so, of the Latin Quarter.

Talk to me now of the Latin Quarter if you will—that is what reconciles me to Paris; one might fancy one's-self in another country—almost in Italy; it is another sort of life altogether, something that I cannot describe.

My mother was horrified to see me go to a shop where "one sees such things—oh, such things! naked peasants." Bourgeoise! Wait till I shall have painted a fine picture—When the flower is in bloom, the fruit ripe, no one thinks of the soil from which they have sprung.

I think only of the end in view, and I press on to that end without pausing or turning aside.

I love to go to workshops and to places where, thanks to my modest costume, I am taken for a Breslau, as it were; they look at me in a certain benevolent, encouraging fashion, altogether different from before.

I can never forgive myself for not knowing as much as Breslau. The thought that troubles me is this: I have learned a little of everything, but nothing thoroughly, and I am afraid the same thing may happen in this case. But no, by the way in which I am progressing, this is going to be serious. That one has not done a thing before is no reason why one should never do it. But each *first time* I am incredulous.

Friday, November 23.—That miserable Breslau has composed a picture—"Monday Morning, or the Choice of the Model." Every one belonging to the studio is in it—Julian standing between Amelie and me.

It is correctly done, the perspective is good, the like-nesses—everything.

When one can do a thing like that, one cannot fail to become a great artist.

You have guessed it, have you not ? I am jealous. That is well, for it will serve as a stimulus to me.

But it is six weeks since I began to draw. Breslau will be always in advance of me, because she began before me. No ; in two or three months more I shall be able to draw as well as she does—that is to say, very well. It pleases me, besides, to have found a rival worthy of me ; if there were only the others I should go to sleep.

Grandpapa is ill, and Dina is at her post, devoted and attentive. She has grown much prettier, and she is so good !

Monday, November 26.—I took my first lesson in anatomy at four o'clock to-day, just after my drawing lesson. It lasted till half-past four.

M. Cuyer is my teacher ; he was sent to me by Mathias Duval, who has promised to obtain permission for me to visit the School of Fine Arts. I began with the bones, of course, and one of my bureau drawers is full of vertebræ— natural ones.

This is frightful when one thinks that the other two contain perfumed paper, visiting cards, etc.

Sunday, December 9.—Dr. Charcot has just gone. I was present during the consultation and listened to what the doctors said afterward, for I am the only self-possessed person in the house, and they treat me as if I were a doctor like themselves. At all events they do not expect a fatal result at present.

Tuesday, December 11.—Grandpapa can no longer speak. It is horrible to see this man, who so short a time ago was

stili strong, energetic, young—to see him lying there almost
a corpse.

Wednesday, December 12.—At one o'clock the priest and
the deacon came and administered the last sacraments to
grandpapa. Mamma wept and prayed aloud ; after their
departure I went to breakfast. How much of the animal
there still, of necessity, remains in man.

Saturday, December 15.—As was to be expected, Breslau
has met with a great success ; that is because she draws
well. As to me, they found my head very good, and my
drawing from the nude not bad.

I am—I don't know what. Breslau has been drawing for
three years, and I for only two months ; no matter, it is
abominable ! Ah, if I had begun three years ago—only
three years ago, that is not so long—I should be famous
to-day.

Saturday, December 22.—Robert-Fleury said to me to-
day : "One must never be satisfied with one's-self." Julian
said the same thing, and as I have never been satisfied with
myself, these words have given me food for reflection. And
when Robert-Fleury said a great many agreeable things to
me afterward, I told him it was well he did so, for that
I was altogether dissatisfied with myself, disheartened,
despondent—which made him open his eyes wide with
astonishment.

And I was in truth disheartened. From the moment I
cease to be admired I grow discouraged ; that is unfortunate.

After all I have made unheard-of progress. He repeated
to me that I had extraordinary talent. I "catch the likeness." I "group well." I " draw correctly." " What more
would you have. Mademoiselle ? Be reasonable," he ended.

He remained a long time standing beside my easel.

"When one can draw like that," he said, pointing first to the head and then to the shoulders, "one has no right to draw shoulders like those."

The Swiss girls and I went, disguised, to Bonnat, to ask him to receive us in the men's studio.

Naturally, he explained to us that those fifty young men not being under any surveillance whatever, it would be impossible for him to do as we asked. Afterward we went to see Munkacsy—I don't know if I spell the name correctly—a Hungarian painter, who has a magnificent house, and who is a great genius.

Saturday, December 29.—M. Robert-Fleury was very well pleased with me to-day. He stood for at least half an hour before a pair of feet, life size, that I had drawn, and asked me again if I had never painted before; if I indeed wished to make a serious study of painting; and how long I intended to remain in Paris? He expressed a desire to see the first things I had done in colors, and asked me how I had come to do them. I told him I had done them for my own amusement. As he stayed talking so long they all came behind him to listen, and in the midst (I dare to say it) of the general amazement he declared that if I wished I might begin to paint at once.

To this I replied that I was not dying to paint, and that I should prefer to perfect myself first in drawing.

Sunday and Monday, December 30 *and* 31.—I feel very melancholy; we are not keeping the Christmas holidays this year, and that makes me sad. I went to see the Christmas-tree at the house of the Swiss girls; it was very gay and pretty, but I was sleepy, as I had worked till ten o'clock. We had our fortunes told. Breslau is to receive wreaths; I the *Prix de Rome,*

1878.

Friday, January 4.—How strange it is that my old nature should lie so completely dormant. Scarce a trace of it is to be seen. Occasionally some souvenir of the past reawakens the old bitterness, but I immediately turn my thoughts to—to what ? To art. This is amusing.

Is this, then, the final transformation ? I have so long and so eagerly pursued this aim, this means of contriving to live without passing the day cursing myself or the rest of the creation, that I can scarcely believe that I have found it.

Dressed in my black blouse, there is something in my appearance that reminds one of Marie Antoinette at the Temple.

I begin to become what I desired to be, confident in my own powers, outwardly tranquil. I avoid quarrels and intrigues ; I am scarcely ever without some useful occupation.

In short, I am gradually perfecting my character. Understand what I mean by perfection ; perfection, that is to say, for me.

Oh, time ! Time is required for everything.

Time is the most terrible, the most discouraging, the most unconquerable of all obstacles, and one that may exist when no other does.

Whatever may happen to me, I am better prepared for it now than I was formerly, when it enraged me to have to confess that I was not perfectly happy.

Sunday, January 6.—Well, then, I agree with you ; time is passing, and it would be infinitely more amusing to spend it as I formerly desired to do, but, since that is impossible, let us await the results of my genius; there will still be time enough for the other.

We have changed our place of residence; we are now living at 67 Avenue de l'Alma. From my windows I can see the carriages on the Champs Elysees. I have a *salon*-studio of my own.

Monday, January 7.—Am I, or am I not to believe in my future as an artist? Two years are not a lifetime, and when two years are passed I can return, if I wish, to a life of idleness, of amusement, of travel. What I want is to be famous!

I will be famous!

Saturday, January 12.—Walitsky died at two o'clock this morning.

When I went to see him last night he said to me, half-jestingly, half-sadly, "Addio, Signorina," in order to remind me of Italy.

Perhaps this is the first occasion during my life on which I have shed tears free from egotism or anger.

There is something peculiarly affecting in the death of a being altogether inoffensive, altogether good; it is like seeing a faithful dog die that has never done harm to any one.

As he felt slightly better toward one o'clock the women retired to their own rooms; only my aunt remained with him. Then his breath failed him so that it was necessary to dash water into his face.

When he had recovered himself a little he rose, for he desired at all hazards to bid adieu to grandpapa, but he had scarcely gone into the hall when his strength failed him; he had only time to cry out in Russian, "Adieu!" but in so strong a voice that it wakened mamma and Dina, who ran to his assistance, only to see him fall into the arms of my aunt and Triphon.

I have not yet been able to realize it; it is so terrible! It seems impossible!

Walitsky is dead! It is an irreparable loss; one would never suppose that such a character could exist in real life.

We read of people like that in books. Well, then, I desire that he may now be conscious of my thoughts; that God may concede him the power to know what I say and think of him. May he, then, hear me from whatsoever be his place of abode, and, if he has ever had reason to complain of me, he will pardon me now because of my profound esteem and sincere friendship for him, and because of the sorrow for his loss which I feel in the innermost recesses of my soul!

Monday, January 28.—To-morrow the prizes are to be awarded. I so much fear being badly placed!

Tuesday, January 29.—I had such a terror of the *concours* that poor Rosalie was obliged to make superhuman efforts to make me get up.

I expected either to receive the medal or to be classed among the very last.

Neither the one nor the other was the case. I am just in the same place that I was two months ago.

I went to see Breslau, who is still sick.

They sang "Traviata" at the Italiens to-night, with Albani, Capoul, and Pandolfini in the cast—great artists all of them; but I was not pleased. In the last act, however, I felt, not the desire to die, but the thought that I was destined to suffer thus and to die thus, just as all was going to turn out happily.

This is a prediction that I make concerning myself.

I wore a baby-waist, which is very becoming when one is slender and well made. The white bows on the shoulders and the bare neck and arms made me look like one of Velasquez's infantas.

To die? It would be absurd; and yet I think I am going to die. It is impossible that I should live long. I am not constituted like other people; I have a great deal too much of some things in my nature, a great deal too little of others, and a character not made to last. If I were a goddess, and the whole universe were employed in my service, I should still find the service badly rendered. There is no one more exacting, more capricious, more impatient, than I am. There is sometimes, perhaps even always, a certain basis of reason and justice in my words, only that I cannot explain clearly what I want to say. I say this, however, that my life cannot last long. My projects, my hopes, my little vanities, all fallen to pieces! I have deceived myself in everything!

Wednesday, February 13.—My drawing does not progress, and I feel as if some misfortune were about to happen to me; as if I had done something wrong and feared the consequences, or as if I anticipated receiving an insult.

Mamma makes herself very unhappy through her own fault; there is one thing I beg and implore her not to do, and that is to touch my things or put my room in order. Well, no matter what I may say, she continues to do so, with a pertinacity that resembles a disease. And if you only knew how exasperating this is, and how it increases my natural impatience and my inclination to say sharp things, which stood in no need of being increased!

I believe that she loves me tenderly. I love her tenderly, also, but we cannot remain two minutes together without exasperating each other, even to the extent of shedding tears. In a word, we are very uncomfortable together, and we should be very unhappy apart.

I will make every sacrifice that may be required of me

for the sake of my art. I must bear in mind that that is myself.

Therefore, I will create for myself an independent existence, and what must come, let it come.

Saturday, March 16.—" I have noticed for some time past," said Robert-Fleury to me this morning, " that there is a certain limit beyond which you cannot go ; that is not as it should be. With your really great ability you should not stop short at easy things, the more as you succeed in the more difficult ones."

I know it well! But next Monday you shall see that I will cross the limit of which Robert-Fleury speaks. The first thing is to convince one's-self that one must succeed, and that one will succeed.

Saturday, March 23.—I promised that I would cross the limit of which Robert-Fleury spoke.

I have kept my word. He was greatly pleased with me. He repeated that it was worth while to work hard with such ability as I possessed ; that I had made astonishing progress, and that in a month or two more—

Saturday, April 6.—Robert-Fleury really gives me too much encouragement ; he thought the second place was my due, he said, and it did not surprise him at all that I should receive it.

And to think that M   on leaving our house to-night probably went home to dream of me, and imagine, perhaps, that I am dreaming of him—

Whilst I, *en deshabille*, with my hair in disorder and my slippers thrown off, am asking myself if I have not succeeded sufficiently in bewitching him, and, not satisfied with asking myself, am asking Dina also.

And yet—O Youth !—I might once have thought that this

was love.   Now I am more sensible, and I understand that it
is merely an amusement to feel that you are causing some one
to fall in love with you, or rather to perceive that some one
is falling in love with you.   *The love one inspires and the love
one feels* are two distinct sentiments which I confounded
together before.

Good Heavens ! and I once thought I was in love with
A·   , with his long nose that makes me think of that of
M   .   How frightful !

How happy it makes me to be able to clear myself from
this suspicion—how happy !   No, no, I have never yet
loved, and if you could only picture to yourself how happy
I feel, how free, how proud, how worthy—of him who is
to come !

Friday, April 12.—Julian met Robert-Fleury at the cafe
yesterday, and the latter said I was a truly remarkable and
interesting pupil, and that he expected great things of me.
It is such words as these that I must constantly bear in
mind, especially when my spirit is invaded by a species of
inexplicable terror, and I feel myself sinking in an abyss of
doubt and of torturing thoughts of all kinds, for none of
which are there any real grounds.. ⁻

It has happened very often, for some time past, that they
have put three candles in my room together,—that signifies
a death.

Is it I who am to depart for the other world ?   I think
so.   And my future ?   And the fame that awaits me ?   Ah,
well, they would be of no value to me in that case.

If there were only a man on the scene, I should fancy
myself in love, so restless am I ; but, besides there being no
one, I am disgusted with the whole thing.

I begin to believe that I have a serious passion for my
art, and that reassures and consoles me.   If it were not for
this restlessness and this terror, I might be happy !

I remember that in my childhood I had a superstitious fear somewhat similar to the feeling I have at present. I thought I should never be able to learn any other language but French; that the other languages were not to be learned. Well, you see there was absolutely nothing in it; yet that was as much a superstitious fear as my present feeling is.

Saturday, April 20.—I glanced through a few pages in my journal before closing it last night, and came by chance across A——'s letter.

This made me think of the past, and I sat dreaming of it, and smiling and dreaming again. It was late when I went to bed, but the time spent thus was not lost ; such moments are precious, and cannot be had at will ; there are no moments lost when one wills it except when we are young ; we must make the most of them and be grateful for them, as for everything else that God has given us.

Owing to Robert-Fleury I was unable to go to confession before mass to-day, which has obliged me to defer taking communion until to-morrow.

My confession was a peculiar one ; it was as follows :

" You have committed some sins, no doubt," said the priest, after the customary prayer. " Are you prone to idleness?"

"Not at all."

"To pride?"

"Very much so."

"You do not fast?"

"Never."

"Have you injured any one?"

"I do not think so—perhaps; in trifles it may be, father, but not in anything of importance."

"Then may God grant you pardon, my daughter."

I have recovered my mental balance. I proved this to-night by conversing with the others without running into exaggerations of speech; my mind is tranquil, and I have absolutely no fear, either physical or moral. It has often happened to me to say: "I am terribly afraid" of going to such a place, or of doing such a thing. This is an exaggeration of language which is common to almost every one and which means nothing. What I am glad of is that I am accustoming myself to talk with every one. It is necessary to do that if one desires to have a pleasant *salon*. Formerly I would single out one person to converse with, and neglect the others entirely, or almost entirely.

Saturday, April 27; *Sunday, April* 28.—I foolishly took the notion into my head to invite some men to attend the midnight mass at our church. On our right were the Ambassador and the Duke de Leuchtenberg and Mme. Akenkieff, his wife. The Duke is the son of the Grand Duchess Marie, who died at Florence, and the nephew of the Emperor. This couple were at Rome when I was there, and Mme. Akenkieff was not then received at the Embassy. At present, however, she plays the part of Grand Duchess to perfection. She is still beautiful and has a majestic carriage, though she is almost too slender.

The husband is devoted in his attentions to the wife; it is admirable and altogether charming.

The Embassy gave an Easter supper, which took place at two in the morning, after the mass. It was given in the priest's house, which was chosen for the purpose on account of its proximity to the church. It was the Ambassador, however, who issued the invitations and received the guests, so that we had an opportunity to sit at the same table as the Grand Duke and his wife, the Ambassador, and all the best people of the Russian colony in Paris.

I was not very gay, though in reality not sad at heart; for this will send me back to my studies with renewed ardor.

Why does not Prince Orloff, who is a widower, fall in

love with me and marry me? I should then be Ambassadress in Paris, almost Empress. M. Anitchkoff, who was ambassador at Teheran, married a young girl for love when he was fifty-five.

I did not produce the effect I had intended. Laferriere disappointed me, and I was compelled to wear an unbecoming gown. I had to improvise a chemisette, as the gown was *decollette* and that would not do. My gown affected my temper, and my temper my appearance—everything.

Monday, April 29.—There is no better way of spending the time from six in the morning till eight in the evening, taking out an hour and a half for breakfast, than in some regular occupation.

Changing the subject: I will tell you that I think I shall never be seriously in love. I invariably discover something to laugh at in the man, and that is the end of it. If he is not ridiculous, he is stupid, or awkward. or tiresome; in fine, there is always something, if it were only the tip of his ear.

Yes, until I have found my master nothing else shall captivate me; thanks to my readiness in discovering the defects of people, not all the Adonises in the world could tempt me to fall in love.

Friday, May 3.—There are moments when one would give up all the intellectual pleasures in the world, glory and art itself, to live in Italy a life of sunshine, music, and love.

Thursday, May 9.—I might possess a beautiful hand if my fingers had not been vilely disfigured by playing on stringed instruments, and by biting my nails.

My form like that of a Greek goddess, my hips too much like those of a Spanish woman, perhaps; my bust small and perfect in shape; my feet, my hands, and my childlike countenance—of what use are they, since no one loves me?

Thursday, May 30.—As a general thing, the family and friends of great men do not believe in their genius: in my case it is too much the other way; that is to say, that it would not surprise my family if I were to paint a picture as large as Medusa's raft, and receive the cross of the Legion of Honor for it. Is this a bad sign? I hope not.

Friday, May 31.—The hardest thing to bear is to be continually disappointed in those nearest to us. To find a serpent where one had expected to find flowers, that is indeed horrible. But these constant shocks have produced in me at last a species of indifference to them. No matter what is passing around me I take no notice now. I put my head out of the door only to go to the studio.

You think, perhaps, that this is the resignation of despair; it is the result of despair, but it is a sweet and tranquil feeling, although a sad one.

Instead of being rose-colored my life is gray, that is all. I have accepted my fate and I am resigned to it.

My character has changed completely, and the change seems to be a permanent one; I no longer have need even of wealth; two black blouses a year, a change of linen that I could wash myself on Sundays, and the simplest food, provided it does not taste of onions and is fresh, and—the means to work; these are all I want.

No carriages; the omnibus or to go on foot: at the studio I wear shoes without heels.

But why live at all then? In the hope that better days will come, and that is a hope that never abandons us.

Everything is relative: thus, compared to my past tortures the present is ease; I enjoy it as an agreeable change. In January I will be nineteen: Moussia will be nineteen. It is absurd; it is impossible; it is frightful.

Sometimes I am seized with a fancy to dress myself, to go out for a walk, to go to the opera, to the Bois, to the *Salon,* to the Exhibition; but I say to myself, "What for?" and I sink back again into my former state of apathy.

For every word I write I think a million thoughts; I express my thoughts only by fragments.

What a misfortune for posterity!

It may not be a misfortune for posterity, but it prevents me from being able to make myself understood.

I am jealous of Breslau; she does not draw at all like a woman. Next week I will work so hard!—you shall see. The afternoons shall be devoted to the Exhibition, and the *Salon.* But the week after— I am resolved to be a great artist, and I will be one.

Monday, June 3.—In heart, soul, and thought I am a republican.

Let titles be preserved, but let there be equality of rights before the law; any other sort of equality than this is impossible.

Let ancient families continue to be respected, foreign potentates honored; let arts and all that contributes to the comfort and the elegance of life be protected. The republicans are reproached with having in their ranks a few miserable wretches. And where is the party that has not had such?

If France were to become altogether Legitimist or altogether Imperialist, would every one then be pure and virtuous?—Good-night—I write so fast that what I am saying is little better than the ravings of a lunatic.

Wednesday, June 12.—To-morrow I resume my work, which I have neglected since Saturday. My conscience reproaches me for it, and to-morrow everything will return to its accustomed order. . . . .

M. Rouher surprised me in many things. I was surprised at myself for employing so much tact and so much delicate flattery. Gavini and the Baron evidently approved of me unreservedly, and M. Rouher himself was pleased. They talked of votes, of laws, of pamphlets, of loyalists, of traitors, before me. Did I listen? You may well believe it. It was like the opening of a door into Paradise.

I am sorry I am a woman, and M. Rouher is sorry he is a man. "Women," he said, "are exempt from the annoyances and the cares that we have."

"Will you permit me to remark, Monsieur," I said, "that men and women alike have their cares and their annoyances ; the only difference is that the cares of men bring with them honors, fame, and popularity ; while the cares of women are attended by no advantage whatever."

"You believe, then, Mademoiselle, that our cares always bring us those compensations?"

"I think, Monsieur," I answered, "that that depends upon the man."

It must not be supposed that I entered all at once into the conversation like this ; I remained quietly in my corner for fully ten minutes, embarrassed enough, for the old fox did not seem to be charmed at the presentation.

Shall I tell you something?

I was enchanted.

Now I have a mind to repeat to you all the fine things I said, but I must not. I will only say that I did my best not to use hackneyed phrases, and to appear full of good sense ; in that way you will think my speeches finer than they really were.

Gavini remarked that the Bonapartists were happy in having the sympathies of all the pretty women with them, bowing to me as he said so.

"Monsieur," I answered, addressing myself to M. Rouher, "I do not give my sympathies to your party as a woman, I give them as an honest man might do."

Wednesday, July 3.—M   came to say good-by, and as it was raining, he proposed to accompany us to the Exhibition.

We accepted ; before we went, however, he and I being alone together for a moment, he entreated me not to be so cruel.

"You know how madly I love you," he said, "and how much you make me suffer. If you could but know how terrible a thing it is to see only mocking smiles, to hear only words of raillery when one truly loves ! "

" You only imagine all that."

"Oh, no, I swear it to you ; I am ready to give you the proofs of it—the most absolute devotion, the fidelity and the patience of a dog ! Say but a word ! say that you have some confidence in me—why do you treat me as a buffoon, as a being of an inferior race ? "

" I treat you as I treat everybody."

" And why ? since you know that my affection is not like that of everybody—that I am heart and soul devoted to you ? "

" I am accustomed to inspiring that sentiment."

" But not such a love as mine. Let me believe that your feelings toward me are not altogether those of hatred."

"Of hatred ? Oh, no ; I assure you they are not that."

" The most terrible feeling of all for me would be indifference."

" Ah, well !—"

" Promise me that you will not forget me in the few months I shall be away."

" It will not be in my power to do so."

" Let me remind you from time to time that I am still in existence. Perhaps I may amuse you, perhaps I may make you laugh. Let me hope that sometimes, occasionally, you will send me a word—a single word."

" What is it you are saying ? "

"Oh, without signing your name ; simply this: 'I am well ' ; only this, and that will make me so happy."

" Whatever I write I sign my name to, and I never deny my signature."

" You will grant me your permission to write ? "

" I am like *Figaro;* I receive letters from all quarters."

" God ! if you but knew how maddening it is never to be able to obtain a serious word—to be always scoffed at ! Let us talk seriously. You will not let it be said that you had no pity for me in the moment of my departure ! If I might only hope that my devotion, my regard for you, my love—impose any conditions you choose, put me to the test. If I might only hope that one day you will be kinder, that you will not always mock me ? "

" As far as tests are concerned," I replied very seriously, "there is only one test that can be relied upon."

" And that ? I am ready to do anything."

" That is time."

" Be it so, then. Put my affection to the test of time ; you shall see that it will stand it."

" That would cause me great pleasure."

" But tell me, have you confidence in me ? "

" How, confidence ? I have confidence enough in you to entrust you with a letter with the certainty that you will not open it." .

" No ! not that ! but an absolute confidence."

" What grand words ! "

" And is not my love for you something grand ? " he said softly.

" I ask nothing better than to believe it ; such things flatter a woman's vanity. And, stay, I should really like to have some confidence in you."

" Truly ? "

" Truly."

This is enough, is it not ? We went to the Exhibition,

and I was vexed to see that M   was in high spirits, and made love to me as if I had accepted him.

I experienced a feeling of genuine satisfaction this evening. I find that M   's love produces precisely the same emotions in me as did that of A——. You see, then, that I did not love Pietro! I was not even for a moment in love with him, though I came very near being so. But you know what a horrible disinchantment that was.

You understand that I have no intention of marrying M   .

" True love is always a sentiment to be respected," I said to him ; " you have no reason to be ashamed of yours ; only don't get foolish notions into your head."

" Give me your friendship."

" Vain word ! "

" Then your—"

" Your demands are exorbitant."

" But what am I to say, then ? You are not willing that I should try to gain your affection by degrees—that I should begin by friendship—"

" Friendship ! A chimera ! "

" Love, then ? "

" You are mad."

" And why ? "

" Because I hate you ! "

Friday, July 5. . . . After the concert my aunt took the arm of Etienne, Dina Philippini's, and I the other's. The night was so lovely that we walked home. M   , who was restored to good-humor, spoke to me of his affection for me. It is always thus ; I do not love him, but the fire of his love warms me ; this is the same feeling that I mistook for love two years ago !

I was touched by the words he spoke ; he even shed tears. As we approached the house I grew more serious ;

I was moved by the beauty of the night and by those melodious words of love. Ah, how delightful it is to be loved! There is nothing in the world so delightful as that. I know now that M—— loves me. One does not act a part like that. And if it were my money he wanted, my disdain would have caused him to abandon his pretensions before this; and there is Dina, whom every one believes to be as rich as I, and plenty of other girls he might marry if he chose. M—— is not a beggar; he is in every sense a gentleman. He could have found, and he *will* find, some one else to love.

M   is very amiable. Perhaps it was wrong of me to let him hold my hand in his as long as he did when we were about to part. He kissed it; but I owed him that much; and then he loves me and respects me so much, poor fellow! I questioned him as if he were a child. I wanted to know how it had happened, and when. He fell in love with me at first sight, it seems. " But it is a strange kind of love," he said; "other women are to me only women, but you are a being superior to the rest of humanity; it is a curious sentiment. I know that you treat me as if I was a hump-backed buffoon; that you have no feeling, no heart; and yet I love you. And I—at the same time that I adore you I know that our characters are not congenial."

I listened to all he had to say, for to tell the truth a lover's speeches are more amusing than all the plays in the world, unless when one goes to them to show herself. But that, too, is a sort of adoration; you are looked at, you are admired, and you feel your being expand like the flower under the rays of the sun.   ·

SODEN, *Sunday, July 7.*—We left Paris for this place at seven. . . . Imagine yourself transported from Paris to Soden. " The silence of death" feebly describes the calm that reigns at Soden. I am confused by it as one is confused by too much noise. . . .

Dr. Tilenius has just gone. He put the necessary questions to me regarding my illness, but did not say afterwards, like the French doctor :

"Very good ; this is nothing ; in a week we shall have you well, Mademoiselle."

To-morrow I am to begin a course of treatment.

The trees here are beautiful, the air is pure, the landscape sets off my face. At Paris I am only pretty, if I am that ; here there is in my appearance a certain poetic languor ; my eyes are larger, and my cheeks less rounded.

SODEN, *Tuesday, July* 9.—How tired I am of all these doctors ! I have had my throat examined—pharyngitis, laryngitis, and catarrh ! Nothing more !

I amuse myself reading Livy and taking notes of what I read in the evening. I must read Roman history.

Tuesday, July 16.—I am resolved on being famous, whether it be as an artist or in any other way. Do not think, however, that I am studying art only through vanity. Perhaps there are not many persons more completely artistic in their natures than I—a fact which you, who are the intelligent part of my readers, must have already perceived. As for the others, I regard them with contempt. They will find me only fantastic, because, without desiring to be so, I am peculiar in everything.

Wednesday, July 24.—Dr. Tomachewsky, who is physician to the opera-troupe at St. Petersburg, must know something ; besides his opinion is the same as that of Dr. Fauvel and the others ; and then I know myself that the waters at Soden, from their chemical composition, are hardly at all suited to my disease. If you are not very ignorant, you must know that they send only convalescents and consumptives to Soden.

At six o'clock this morning my aunt and I, accompanied by Dr. Tomachewsky, went to Ems, to consult the doctors there.

We have just returned.

The Empress Eugenie is at Ems.   Poor woman !

Friday.—For some days past I have been thinking of Nice.   I was fifteen when I was there, and how pretty I was !   My figure, my feet, and my hands were not perhaps as perfect as now, but my face was ravishing.   It has never been the same since.   On my return to Rome, Count Laurent almost made a scene about me.

" Your face has changed," he said ; " the features, the coloring are as before, but the expression is not the same. You will never again be like that portrait."

He alluded to the portrait in which I am represented resting my elbows on the table and my cheek on my clasped hands.*   " You look as if you had fallen naturally into that position, and with your eyes fixed upon the future, were asking yourself, half in terror, ' Is that what life is like ? "

At fifteen there was a childlike expression in my face that was not there before, and has not been there since, and this is the most captivating of all expressions.

Wednesday, August 7.—My God, ordain that I may go to Rome.   If you only knew, my God, how I long to go there ! My God, be merciful to your unworthy creature !   My God, ordain that I may go to Rome !   No doubt it will not be possible for me to go, for that would be to be too happy !

It is not Livy who has been putting these thoughts into my head, for I have neglected my old friend for several days past.

---

* See Frontispiece.

No ; but only to remember the Campagna, the Piazza del Popolo, and the Pincio, with the rays of the setting sun shining upon it !

And that divine, that adorable morning twilight, when the rays of the rising sun begin to give form and color to surrounding objects—what a blank everywhere else ! And what sacred emotions the remembrance of the wondrous, the enchanted city awakens ! Nor am I the only one whom Rome inspires with these feelings, which no words can be found to express—feelings due to the mysterious influence exercised over the mind by the blending of the traditions of the fabulous past with the sanctified associations of the present, or perhaps—But no, I cannot explain what I would say. If I were in love, it is in Rome, in the presence of the setting sun, as its last rays fall upon the divine dome, that I would make the avowal to him I loved.

If I were to receive some crushing blow, it is to Rome I would go to weep and pray with my eyes fixed upon that dome. If I were to become the happiest of human beings, it is there, too, that I would go.

Paris, *Saturday, August* 17.—This morning we were still at Soden.

I detest Paris. I do not deny that it may be possible to live there happier and more contented than elsewhere ; that one may lead there a completer, a more intellectual, a more renowned existence. But for the kind of life I lead one needs to love the city itself. I find cities, like individuals, sympathetic or antipathetic to me, and I cannot succeed in liking Paris.

I am afflicted with a terrible disease. *I am disgusted with myself.* It is not the first time I hate myself, but that does not make it the less terrible.

To hate another whom one may avoid is bad enough, but to hate one's-self—that is terrible,

Thursday, August 29.—I don't know by what providential chance I happened to be late this morning, but they came at nine, before I was yet dressed, to tell me that grandpapa was worse. Mamma, my aunt, and Dina were crying. . . . At ten the priest arrived and in a few minutes all was over.

Wednesday, September 4.—Kant has said that the material world exists only in the imagination. That is going too far, but I accept his system when the domain of feeling is in question. In effect, our feelings are caused by the impressions produced on us by things or persons; but, since objects are not objects—in other words, since they possess no objective value and exist only in our minds—But in order to follow up this train of argument, it would be necessary for me not to have to hurry to bed, and think at what hour in the morning I must begin my picture to have it finished by Saturday. . . .

I have a passion for all those learned, patiently conducted, *abracadabrante* follies—these arguments, these deductions, so logical, so learned. There is only one thing about them that grieves me, and that is that I feel them to be false, though I have neither the time nor the inclination to find out why.

I should like to have some one to discuss all these matters with. I lead a very lonely life. But I declare beforehand that I have no desire to impose my own opinions on other people, and that I would willingly acknowledge the justness of their arguments when I saw them to be in the right.

Without wishing to be thought ridiculous by the pretension, I long to listen to the discourse of learned men; I long, oh, so much, to penetrate into the precincts of the intellectual world; to see, to hear, to learn. But I neither know how to set about doing so myself, nor whom to ask advice of; and I remain here in my corner, dazed and wondering, not knowing what direction to take, and catching glimpses on all sides of treasures of art, of history, of languages, science—a whole world in short. I long to see everything, to know éverything, to learn everything!

Friday, September 13.—I am not in my right place in the world. . . . There are statues that are admirable, set on a pedestal in the middle of a grand square, but put them in a room and you will see how stupid they look, and how much they are in the way. You will knock your head or your elbow against them a dozen times a day, and you will end by finding detestable and unbearable that which, in its proper place, would have excited the admiration of every one.

If you find "statue" too flattering a word for me, change it for—whatever word you choose.

When I have finished Livy I shall read Michelet's history of France, and afterward the Greek authors, whom I know only from allusions to them or quotations from them in other books, and then—My books are all packed away, and we must take a more settled lodging than our present one before unpacking them.

I have read Aristophanes, Plutarch, Herodotus, a little of Xenophon, and that is all, I think. And then I am very familiar with Homer, and slightly so with Plato.

Thursday, October 3.—We spent almost four hours to-day at a dramatic and musical international entertainment. They gave scenes from Aristophanes in hideous costumes, and so abridged, arranged, and altered that it was frightful.

What was superb, however, was a dramatic recitation — Christopher Columbus—in Italian, by Rossi. What a voice! What intonation! What expression! What truth to nature! It was better than the music. I think one could feel the charm of it even without understanding a word of Italian.

I almost worshiped him as I listened.

Ah, what a power lies in spoken words, even when they are not our own words, but those of another! The handsome Mounet-Sully recited afterward, but I shall say nothing of him. Rossi is a great artist; he has the soul of an artist; I saw him talking with two men at the door of the theater, and he had a common air. He is an actor, it is true, but so great an actor as he is should have a certain greatness of character even in every-day life. I noticed his eyes; they are not those of a common man, though the charm exists only while he speaks. Then it is wonderful! What nihilists are those who despise the arts!

What a frightful existence mine is! If I possessed genius I might be able to change it, but my genius must be taken on trust; you have nothing but my word for it. Where have I given any proof, any evidence of genius?

Monday, October 7.—Stupid people may fancy that I want to be another Balzac. I have no such intention; but do you know why he is so great? It is because he describes with naturalness, without fear, and without affectation all that he has felt. Almost every intelligent person has had the same thoughts, but who has expressed them as he has?

No, it is not true that almost every one has had the same thoughts, but in reading Balzac one is so struck with his truth, with his naturalness, that one thinks one has. It has happened to me a hundred times in conversation, or in reflection, to be horribly tormented by thoughts that I had not the power to disentangle from the frightful chaos of my mind.

I have also another pretension; it is this: when I make any just or profound observation I fear people may not understand me.

Perhaps, indeed, they do not understand me as I wish to be understood.

Good-night, good people.

Sunday, October 20.—I ordered the carriage at nine o'clock this morning, and accompanied by my *demoiselle d'honneur*, Mlle. Elsnitz, went to visit Saint-Philippe's, the church of St. Thomas Aquinas and Notre Dame. I went up into the tower and examined the bells just as any English-woman might have done. Well, there is a Paris to be ad-mired—it is old Paris; and one might be happy there, but only on condition of keeping away from the boulevards and the Champs Elysees; in fine, from all the new and beautiful quarters of the city which I detest, and which irritate my nerves. In the Faubourg Saint-Germain, however, one feels altogether different.

We went afterward to the School of Fine Arts; it is enough to make one cry out with rage.

Why can I not study there? Why can I not have a course of instruction as complete as that? I went to see the exhibition of the *Prix de Rome*. The second prize was awarded to a pupil of Julian's. Julian is consequently very happy. If I am ever rich I will found a school of arts for women.

Saturday, October 26.—My painting was much better than the previous ones, and my drawing from the nude very good. M. T—— distributed the prizes at the *concours*— Breslau first, I second.

In short, I ought to be satisfied.

Sunday, November 3.—Mamma, Dina, Mme. X—— and I went to-day to take an airing together. They want to marry me, but I told them plainly, so as not to be made use of to enrich some monsieur, that I was quite willing to marry, but only on condition that the person should be either rich, of a good family and handsome, or else a man of genius, or of note. As for his character, if he were Satan himself, I will take charge of that.

Saturday, November 9.—It is a shameful thing! There was no medal at all! All the same, I am first; I think I should have been so even if Breslau had exhibited, in which case they would have made two firsts. This has nothing to do with the matter,—however, the fact is the same.

Wednesday, November 13.—Robert-Fleury came to the studio this evening. It would be useless to repeat the words of encouragement he spoke after giving me a long lesson; if what they all say be true, you will know by the time you read this what opinion to entertain of me.

It is a happiness, all the same, however, to find that people take you altogether in earnest. I am very silly; I entertain the greatest hopes with regard to myself, and when people tell me I have realized them I am transported with joy, as if I had never had any hopes at all. I am as much surprised at my good fortune, and as delighted with it, as a monster might be with whom the most beautiful woman in the world had fallen in love.

Robert-Fleury is an excellent teacher: he leads one onward by degrees, so that one is conscious at every step of the progress one is making. To-night he treated me somewhat like a pupil who has learned her scales and to whom for the first time a piece of music is given to play. He has lifted the corner of the veil and disclosed to me a vaster horizon. It is a night that will hold a place apart in my studies.

In the matter of drawing I am the equal of Breslau, but she has had more practice than I. Now, I must give myself a certain number of months to paint as she does, for, if I cannot do that, there is nothing extraordinary in my work. But she will not stand still during the eight or ten months I shall allow myself. I should therefore be obliged to progress so fast as to make up this time in the eight or ten months we shall continue working together, which does not seem to me probable. Well, by the grace of God, we shall see.

I looked all of a sudden so beautiful, after I had taken my bath this evening, that I spent fully twenty minutes admiring myself in the glass. I am sure no one could have seen me without admiration; my complexion was absolutely dazzling, but soft and delicate, with a faint rose tint in the cheeks; to indicate force of character there was nothing but the lips and the eyes and eyebrows.

Do not, I beg of you, think me blinded by vanity: when I do not look pretty I can see it very well; and this is the first time that I have looked pretty in a long while. Painting absorbs everything.

What is odious to think of is that all this must one day fade, shrivel up, and perish!

Thursday, November 21.—Breslau has painted a cheek so true to nature, so perfect, that I, a woman and a rival artist, felt like kissing it.

Friday, November 22.—I am terrified when I think of the future that awaits Breslau; it fills me with wonder and sadness.

In her compositions there is nothing womanish, commonplace, or disproportioned. She will attract attention at the *Salon*, for, in addition to her treatment of it, the subject itself will not be a common one. It is stupid, indeed, of me to be jealous of her. I am a child in art, and she is a woman. For the moment the light seems hidden, and everything is dark before me.

Friday, December 27.—This week has been lost to me for

study. For the past three days I have wanted to write
down some reflections—what about, I do not exactly know;
but, distracted from my purpose by the singing of the
young lady on the second story, I began to glance through
the account of my journey in Italy, and afterward some
one came to interrupt me, and I lost the thread of my
ideas, together with that feeling of gentle melancholy in
which it is so pleasant to indulge.

What surprises me now is to see what grandiloquent
words I employed to describe the simplest incidents.

But my mind was full of lofty sentiments, and it irritated
me to have no wonderful, startling, or romantic situations
to describe, and I *interpreted* my feelings. Artists will
know what I mean. This is very well; but what I cannot
understand is how a girl who pretends to be intelligent did
not better learn to estimate the value of men and things. I
say this because the thought has just suggested itself to me
that my family ought to have enlightened me on such subjects, and told me, for instance, that A—— was a person of
no worth, and one on whose account one should not give
one's-self the slightest trouble. It is true that they took a
mistaken view of the matter altogether, my mother having
even less experience of the world than I, but that is only
by the way, and, as I had so high an opinion of my own
intelligence, I should have made some use of it, and treated
him as I did others, instead of bestowing so much attention
on him, both in my journal and elsewhere.

But I was burning with the desire to have something
romantic to record, and, fool that I was! things could not
have turned out less romantic than they did. In a word, I
was young and inexperienced; notwithstanding all my folly
and all my boasting, this is the confession I must make at
last, no matter what it costs me to do so.

And now I think I hear some one say : " A strong-minded

woman such as you should never have occasion to retract her words."

Sunday, December 29.—I have lost my hold on art, and I cannot take up anything else in its place. My books are packed up, I am losing my knowledge of Latin and of classic literature, and I am growing altogether stupid. The sight of a temple, a column, or an Italian landscape fills me with loathing for this Paris, so cold, so learned, so wise, so polished. The men here are ugly. This city, which is a paradise for superior natures, has no charms for me. Ah, I have deceived myself : I am neither wise nor happy. I long to go to Italy, to travel, to see mountains, lakes, forests, seas. In the company of my family, with parcels, recriminations, annoyances, the petty disputes of every day ? Ah, no ; a hundred times no ? To enjoy the delights of travel one must wait for ——. And the time is passing. Well, so much the worse. I might marry an Italian prince at any time, if I wished to do so. Let me then, wait.

You see if I married an Italian prince I might still be an artist, since the money would be mine. But then I should have to give him some of it. Meantime I shall remain here and work on at my painting.

On Saturday they thought my drawing not at all bad.— You understand that it is only with an Italian I could live in France, where I wish to live, according to my own ideas ; and in Italy—ah ! what a delightful life ! I shall spend my time between Paris and Italy.

1879.

Thursday, January 2.—What I long for is to be able to go out alone ! To come and go ; to sit down on a bench in the Garden of the Tuileries, or, better still, of the Luxembourg ; to stand looking into the artistically arranged shop windows ; to visit the churches and the museums ; to stroll through the old streets of the city in the evening.

Friday, January 10.—Robert-Fleury came to the studio this evening. . . .

If my art does not soon bring me fame, I shall kill myself, and end the whole matter at once. This resolution I took some months ago. When I was in Russia I thought of killing myself, but the fear of a hereafter deterred me. I shall give myself till thirty, for up to that age one may still hope to acquire fortune, or happiness, or glory, or whatever it is one desires. So then that is settled, and if I am sensible, I shall torment myself no more either now or in the future.

Saturday, January 11.—They think at the studio that I go a great deal into society; this, together with the difference in station, separates me from the other pupils, and prevents my asking them any favors as they do among themselves ; as, for instance, to accompany me to the house of an artist or to a studio.

I worked faithfully all the week up to ten o'clock on Saturday night, then I came home and sat down to cry. Heretofore I have always asked the help of God in my troubles, but as He does not seem to listen to me at all, I scarcely believe in Him any longer.

Those who have experienced this feeling will understand all the horror of it.

Tuesday, January.—I did not awake this morning till half-past eleven. The prizes were awarded by the three Professors, Lefebvre, Robert-Fleury, and Boulanger. I did not go to the studio until one o'clock, to learn the result. The first words I heard on entering were :

" Well, Mlle. Marie, come and receive your medal."

Wednesday, January.—I have been dreaming all day of a blue sea, white sails, a luminous sky.—On entering the studio this morning I found P—— there. He goes to Rome in a week, he says, and while we were talking he mentioned Katorbinsky and others of our friends ; and I—I felt myself grow faint, before the vista opened up to me by his words, of sculptured stones, of ruins, of statues, of churches. And the Campagna,—that " desert,"—yes, but I adore that desert. And there are others, thank Heaven ! who adore it too.

Sunday, February 16.—Yesterday I received a scolding.

" I do not understand how it is that with your talent you find it so difficult to paint," said Julian.

Nor I either, but I seem paralyzed ; there is no use in keeping up the struggle any longer. There is nothing left me but to die. My God, my God ! Is there, then, nothing to be hoped for from any one ? What is detestable to think of is, that I have just filled up the fire-place with wood without any necessity for it, for I was not at all cold, while there are miserable creatures who are at this very moment, perhaps, crying with cold and hunger. It is reflections such as these that are most effectual in drying the tears I love to shed. And yet I sometimes think that I would as soon be at the lowest depths of misery as where I am ; for when one has touched bottom, there is nothing further to be feared.

Tuesday, February 18.—I threw myself on my knees beside my bed just now to implore God for justice, pity, or pardon ! If I have not merited the tortures I endure, let Him grant me justice ! If I have committed evil deeds, let Him grant me pardon ! If He exists, and is such as we are taught to believe Him to be, He should be just, He should pity, He should pardon. I have only Him left me ; it is natural therefore that I should seek Him and entreat Him not to abandon me to despair ; not to lead me into sin ; not to suffer me to doubt, to blaspheme, to die.

Doubtless my sufferings are no greater than my sins ; I am continually committing petty sins that amount to a frightful total in the end.

Just now I spoke to my aunt harshly, but I could not help it. She came into my room while I was crying, with my face buried in my hands, and calling on God to help me. Ah, misery of miseries !

No one must see me weep ; it might be thought my tears were caused by disappointed love, and that—would make me shed tears of rage.

Wednesday, February 19.—I must do something to amuse myself. I say this from the stupid habit we have of repeating what we read in books. Why should I amuse myself ; I still find pleasure in being miserable ; and then I am not like other people, and I detest doing the things other people do to preserve their moral or their physical health, for I have no faith in them.

NICE, *Friday, February* 21.—Well, I am at Nice !

I had a longing to luxuriate in pure air, to bask in the sunshine, and to listen to the sound of the waves. Do you love the sea ? I love it to distraction ; it is only in Rome that I forget it—almost.

I came here with Paul. We were taken for husband and wife, which annoyed me exceedingly. As our villa is rented. we put up at the Hotel du Parc—our old Villa d'Acqua-

Viva, that we occupied eight years ago. Eight years!—This is a pleasure trip. We are going to dine at London House. Antoine, the *maître-d'hôtel*, came to pay his respects to me, as did several of the shop women also; and all the drivers smiled and bowed, and the one we selected complimented me on my height—he recognized me; and then another offered his services, saying he had served Mme. Romanoff; and afterward I met my friends of the Rue de France. All this is very agreeable, and these good people have given me a great deal of pleasure.

The night was beautiful, and I stole out alone and did not return to the house until ten o'clock. I wanted to wander on the sea-shore, and sing to the accompaniment of the waves. There was not a living soul near, and the night was enchanting, especially after Paris. Paris!

Saturday, February 22.—What a difference between this place and Paris! Here I awake by myself; the windows remain open all night. The room I occupy is the one in which I used to take drawing-lessons from Binsa. I see the first rays of the sun gilding the tops of the trees beside the fountain in the middle of the garden, as I used to see them then every morning. My little study has the same paper on the walls as then—the paper I chose myself. Probably it is occupied by some barbarian of an Englishman. I was able to recognize it only by the paper, for they have made a new corridor that confuses me.

We will dine at London House while we remain at Nice. One sees every one there, especially during the Carnival.

Sunday, February 23.—Yesterday we went to Monaco. This nest of *cocottes* is more hateful to me than I can find words to express. I remained in the place only ten minutes, but that was enough, as I did not play.

Monday, February 24.—I am always happy when I can take a solitary walk. The sea was unspeakably beautiful to-night; before going to hear Patti I went to listen to the sound of the waves. It had been raining, and the air was delightfully fresh and pleasant. How soothing it is to the eyes to let them rest on the deep blue of the sky and of the sea at night!

PARIS, *Monday, March* 3.—We left Nice yesterday at noon. The weather was superb, and I could not help shedding tears of genuine regret at leaving this delightful and incomparable country. From my window I could see the garden, the Promenade des Anglais, and all the elegance of Paris. From the corridor I could see the Rue de France, with its old Italian ruins, and its lanes, with their picturesque lights and shadows. And all the people who knew me—"That is Mademoiselle Marie," they would say, when I passed by.

I should now like to leave Paris. My mind is distracted, and I have lost all hope. I no longer expect anything; I no longer hope for anything; I am resigned, with the resignation of despair. I grope my way darkly in search of light, but find none. I breathe a sigh that leaves my heart more oppressed than before.—Tell me, what would you do in my place?

Wednesday, March 5.—To-morrow I begin to work again! I will give myself another year—a whole year, during which I will work harder than ever. What good will it do to despair? Yes, we can say that when we are beginning to get out of our difficulties, but not while we are in the midst of them.

Saturday, June 21.—For almost thirty-six hours I have done nothing but cry, and last night I went to bed exhausted,

As I was about to leave the studio at noon yesterday, Julian called to the servant through the speaking-tube; she put her ear to the tube, and then said to us with some emotion:

"Ladies, M. Julian desires me to tell you that the Prince Imperial is dead."

I gave a cry and sat down on the coal-box. Then as every one began to talk at once, Rosalie said:

"A moment's silence if you please, ladies. The news is official; a telegram has just been received. He has been killed by the Zulus; this is what M. Julian says."

The news had already begun to spread; so that when they brought me the *Estafette*, with the words in capital letters, "Death of the Prince Imperial," I cannot express how much I was shocked.

And then, no matter to what party one may belong, whether one be a Frenchman or a foreigner, it is impossible to avoid sharing in the feeling of consternation with which the news has been everywhere received.

One thing I will say, however, which none of the papers has said, and that is that the English are cowards and assassins. There is something mysterious about this death; there must be both treachery and crime at the bottom of it. Was it natural that a prince on whom all the hopes of his party were fixed should be thus exposed to danger,—an only son? I think there is no one so devoid of feeling as not to be moved at the thought of this mother's anguish. The most dire misfortune, the cruelest of losses, may still leave some gleam of hope in the future, some possibility of consolation. This leaves none. One may say with truth that this is a grief like no other. It was because of her that he went; she gave him no peace; she tormented him.; she refused to allow him more than five hundred francs a month—a sum upon which he could hardly contrive to live. The mother and son parted on bad terms with each other!

Do you perceive the horror of the thing? Can you understand how this mother must feel?

England has treated the Bonapartes shamefully on every occasion when they were so blind as to ask the help of that ignoble country, and it fills me with hatred and rage to think of it.

Sunday, August 3.—My dog Coco II. has disappeared. You cannot conceive what a grief this is to me.

Monday, August 4.—I could not sleep last night thinking of my poor little dog. I even condescended to shed a few tears for him, after which I prayed to God that I might find him again. I have a special prayer that I repeat to myself whenever I want to ask for anything. I cannot remember ever to have said it without receiving some consolation.

This morning they wakened me to give me my dog, which had been found, and the ungrateful creature was so hungry that he showed scarcely any joy at seeing me.

Mamma exclaims that it is a miracle to have found him, as we have already lost four dogs and never found any of them before. She would not be so surprised, though, if I were to tell her of my prayer. I confide it only to my diary, however, and I am not quite satisfied with myself in doing even this. There are secret thoughts and prayers which to repeat aloud makes one seem foolish or ridiculous.

Saturday, August 9.—Shall I go or stay? The trunks are already packed. My physician does not appear to believe in the efficacy of the waters of Mont-Dore. No matter, I shall have rest there. And when I come back I shall lead a life of incredible activity. I will paint while there is daylight, and model in the evening.

Wednesday, August 13.—At one o'clock yesterday we arrived at Dieppe.

Are all seaport towns alike? I have been at Ostend, at Calais, at Dover, and now I am at Dieppe. They all smell of tar, of boats, of ropes, and of tarpaulin. It is windy; one is exposed to the weather on all sides, and one feels miserable. It is like being sea-sick. How different from the Mediterranean! There one can breathe freely and there is something to admire; one is comfortable, and there are none of the vile smells that are here. I would prefer a little green nest like Soden or Schlangenbad, or what I imagine Mont-Dore to be, to this place.

I have come here to breathe good air, ah,—well! doubtless outside the city and the port the air is better. None of these Northern sea-ports please me. From none of the hotels, below the third story, is a view of the sea to be had. O Nice! O San Remo! O Naples! O Sorrento! you are not unmeaning names; your beauties have not been exaggerated, nor profaned by guide-books! You are indeed beautiful and delightful cities!

Saturday, August 16.—We laugh a good deal, though I find this place very tiresome! but it is in my nature to laugh; it is something altogether independent of the humor I am in.

In former times, when I was at any watering-place I took pleasure in watching the passers-by; it amused me.

I have grown completely indifferent to all that now; it is all the same to me whether men or dogs be around me. Painting and music are still what I most enjoy. I expected to play a very different part in the world from the one I am playing; and since it is not what I thought it would be, what it is matters little.

Tuesday, August 19.—I took my first sea-bath to-day, and the whole thing disgusted me so much that I would have been glad of an excuse to cry. I would rather wear the dress of a fisher-girl than clothes that look common ; my disposition is, besides, an unfortunate one.   I crave an exquisite harmony in all the details of life ; very often things that are thought by others beautiful or elegant shock me by their lack of artistic grace.   I would like my mother to be elegant or *spirituelle,* or at least dignified and majestic. Life is a wretched affair, after all.   In truth, it is not right that people should be made to suffer thus.

These are trifles, you say ?   Everything is relative, and if a pin wounds you as sharply as a knife, what have the sages to say in the matter ?

Wednesday, August 20.—I think I can never experience any feeling into which ambition does not enter.   I despise insignificant people.

Friday, August 29.—Fatalism is the religion of the lazy and the desperate.   I am desperate, and I can assure you that I am entirely indifferent to life.   I would not make use of this hackneyed phrase, if this feeling were a transitory one ; but I am so always, even when I am most happy.   I have a contempt for death ; if there is nothing beyond—the thing is quite simple ; and if there is, I commend myself to God.   But I do not think that in any case I shall be in Paradise ; the unhappiness I suffer here will find a continuance there ; I am doomed to it.

Monday, September 1.—I hope you have noticed the great change that has been taking place in me for some time past. I have become serious and sensible ; and then, too, I can better appreciate certain ideas now than formerly.   Many things in regard to which I had no settled convictions I now begin to understand.   I can see, for instance, how one may cherish as profound a sentiment of devotion to an idea, and entertain for it a passion as strong, as for an individual.

Devotion to a prince, or to a dynasty, is a sentiment that might arouse my enthusiasm, that might move me to tears, and even impel me to action under the influence of some powerful emotion, but there is a secret feeling within me that makes me distrust these fluctuating emotions. Whenever I consider, in regard to great men, that they have been the slaves of other men, all my admiration for them vanishes. Perhaps it may be because of a foolish vanity on my part, but I look upon all these *servants* as little less than contemptible, and I am only truly a royalist when I put myself in the place of the king.

As far as I myself am concerned, I might be willing to bow the head before a king, but I could neither love nor esteem a man who would do so.

I might accept a constitutional monarchy like that of England or of Italy, but even in those there is much to object to. It disgusts me to see those salutes to the royal family ; they are a useless humiliation. Where the ruler is in sympathy with the people, as was the case with Victor Emmanuel, who was the exponent and advocate of a great idea, or with Queen Margaret, who is both amiable and good, this may be tolerated ; but it is much better to have a ruler who is chosen by the people, and who, as a consequence, will always be in sympathy with them.

The old order of things is the negation of progress and of intelligence.

PARIS, *Wednesday, September* 17.—To-day, Wednesday, which is a lucky day of the week for me, and the 17th, a lucky day of the month, I made my arrangements to begin modeling.

Wednesday, October 1.—The papers have come, and I have just finished reading the two hundred pages that make the first number of Mme. Adam's review. This disturbed me a little, and at four o'clock I left the studio to go for a walk in the Bois. I wore a new hat which attracted a good deal of attention. Now, however, I have become indifferent to such things. Mme. Adam has reason to be very happy, I think.

Thursday, October 30.—France is a delightful country and an amusing one ; the country of riots, of revolutions, of fashion, of wit, of grace, of elegance—of everything, in a word, that gives animation, charm, and variety to life. But we must look for neither a stable government, a virtuous man— virtuous, that is to say, in the antique sense of the word—a marriage based upon love, or true art. The French painters are very good, but, with the exception of Gericault, and at present of Bastien-Lepage, the divine spark is wanting. And never, never, never, will France produce works equal to those which England and Holland have produced, in a certain style.

France is a delightful country, where pleasure and gallantry are concerned, but how about other things? It is always this, however ; and other countries, with all their respectable and solid qualities, are very often dull. And then, if I complain of France, it is because I am unmarried. France for young girls is an infamous country—the word is not too strong a one. Trade, traffic, speculation, are honorable words in their proper place, but applied to marriage they are infamous ; yet they are the only words that can justly be applied to French marriages.

Monday, November 10.—I went to church yesterday. I go occasionally, so that I may not be thought a nihilist.

Friday, November 14.—If I have written nothing here for some days past, it is because I have had nothing interesting to say.

Thus far, I have always been charitably disposed toward my fellow-beings ; I have never spoken ill of others, nor repeated the evil I have heard spoken of them ; I have always defended any one who was slandered in my presence, no matter who it might be, in the selfish expectation that others would do as much for me in return ; I never seriously entertained the idea of injuring any one, and if I have de-sired fortune or power, it has not been from selfish motives, but rather with the purpose of performing such acts of gen-erosity, of goodness, of charity, as it now astonishes me to think of—although in regard to this last particular, I have not been very successful ; I shall always continue to give twenty sous to a beggar in the street, because such people bring tears to my eyes—but I really fear now that I am growing wicked.

And yet it would be a noble thing to remain good, em-bittered and unhappy as I am. It would be amusing, how-ever, to be wicked—to injure others, to speak evil of them—since it is all the same to God, and He takes cognizance of nothing. Beside, it is very evident that God is not what we imagine Him to be. God is, perhaps, nature ; and all the events of life are directed by chance, which sometimes brings about those strange coincidences and events that make us believe there is a Providence. As to our prayers to God, our communion with Him, our faith in Him, I have learned to my cost that there is nothing in them.

To feel within one's-self the power to move heaven and earth and to be nothing ! I do not proclaim this thought aloud, but the anguish of it may be read upon my counten-ance. People think such thoughts are of no consequence so long as one does not utter them aloud, but feelings like these always come to the surface.

Wednesday, November 19.—Robert-Fleury came to see me this evening, and, besides the profit I derived from the

good advice he gave me, we spent a pleasant evening together in my studio beside the samovar ; he explained very
clearly to me how it was necessary to arrange the light.
Fleury neither receives pay nor has he any selfish interest
in the matter ; besides, he is a person whose words are to
be relied upon, and he repeated to me this evening what he
told Mme. Breslau—that her daughter and myself are the
only pupils in the studio who have exceptional talent for
drawing. The others are worth nothing. He passed them
all in review, and I was amused to see how unceremoni-
ously he treated their pretensions.

In short, he has taken me absolutely under his wing. So
to compensate him in some way for this, I have given him
an order for a portrait of myself, small size, and this has
already begun to detract from my pleasure in his society,
on account of the expense.

Saturday, November 21.—As I expressed a great deal of
admiration to-day for a sketch he had made for the ceiling
of the Luxembourg, he (Tony) offered it to me in the most
amiable manner possible, saying it gave him pleasure to
present it to one who knew as much about art as I did, and
who could appreciate it so well.

"But there must be a great many," I said, "who appreciate your painting."

"No, no, it is not the same thing, it is not the same
thing," he replied.

I am already more at my ease with him, and am scarcely
at all afraid of him now. After seeing him for two whole
years at the studio, once or twice every week, it seems very
odd to chat with him and have him help me on with my
pelisse. A little more and we shall be good friends. If it
were not for the portrait, I should be well contented, for
my master is as amiable with me as possible.

Monday, November 23.—We went to-day to invite Julian to dine with us, but he made a thousand excuses, saying that, if he accepted the invitation, it would take away all his authority over me, and that then there would be no means of getting on, particularly as the least mark of complaisance toward me on his part was regarded as favoritism. They would say I could do as I liked at the studio because he dined with us, because I was rich, etc. The good man is right.

Tuesday, November 24.—The studio at No. 37 has been taken and is almost arranged.

I spent the whole day there ; it is a very large room, with gray walls. I sent there two rather shabby Gobelins which conceal the side of the wall furthest from the entrance, a Persian carpet, some Chinese matting, a large square Algerian seat, a table for modeling, a number of pieces of stuff, and some satinette draperies, of a warm, undecided color.

I also sent a number of casts—the Venus of Milo, the Venus of Medicis, and the Venus of Nîmes ; the Apollo, the Neapolitan Faun, an *écorché*, some bas-reliefs, a portmanteau, an urn, a looking-glass that cost me four francs twenty-five centimes, a clock that cost thirty-two francs, a chair, a stove, an oak chest of drawers, of which the upper part serves as a color box, a tray with everything necessary to make tea, an inkstand and some pens, a pail, a jug, and a number of canvases, caricatures, studies, and sketches.

To-morrow I shall unpack some drawings—but I fear that they will make my paintings appear still worse than they are—an arm and a leg, natural size, of an *écorche*, a lay-figure, and a box of carpenter's tools ; the Antinoüs is still to be sent.

Wednesday, December 30.—I think that I am going to be

ill. I am so weak that I cry without any cause. On leaving the studio to-day I went to the Magasin du Louvre. It would take a Zola to describe this excited, busy, disgusting crowd, running, pushing, with heads thrust forward, and eager eyes. I felt ready to faint from heat and weakness.

What a melancholy ending to the year! I think I shall go to bed at eleven and sleep while waiting for midnight— to have my fortune told.

1880.

Thursday, January 1.—I went to the studio this morning; so that by working on the first day of the year I may work the whole year through. We made some visits afterward, and then went to the Bois.

Saturday, January 3.—I cough continually! but for a wonder, far from making me look ugly, this gives me an air of languor that is very becoming.

Monday, January 5.—Well, things are going badly.

I have begun to work again, but as I did not take a complete rest, I feel a languor and a lack of strength such as I never felt before. And the *Salon* so near! I have talked it all over with Julian, and we are both agreed that I am not ready.

Let me see : I have been working for two years and four months, without deducting time lost, or spent in traveling— little enough, yet after all it is a good deal. I have not worked hard enough, I have lost time ; I have relaxed my efforts, I—in a word, I am not ready. "The constant pricking of a pin would drive one mad," Edmond has said, " but a blow from a club, provided it were not given in a vital part, might be courageously borne." It is true ; the same eternal comparison—Breslau. She began in June, 1875, which gives her four years and a half, with two years at Zurich or Munich ; total, six years and a half, without deducting either time spent in travel or time lost from study, as in my case. She had been painting a little more than two years when she exhibited. I have been painting a year and four months, and I cannot exhibit with as much credit as she can.

As far as I myself am concerned, this would not matter ; I could wait. I am courageous ; if I were told I had to wait a year, I could answer from my heart, " Very well." But the public, and my family—they would believe in me no longer. I might send a picture, but what Julian desires is that I should paint a portrait, and this I could do only indifferently well. See what it is to be of importance ; there are pupils in the studio who have exhibited, who cannot paint a fifth as well as I, and no one has said anything about it. But when it is I who am in question—" Why do it ? " they say. " You do not want to teach, nor to be paid fifty or a hundred francs for a picture ; what you want is fame. To exhibit such a thing as the others might very well do, would be unworthy of you."

This is my own opinion, too ; but the public and my family, and our friends and relations in Russia, what will they say?

Saturday, January 17.—The doctor would have me believe that my cough is a purely nervous one, and it may be so, for I have not taken cold ; neither my throat nor my chest hurts me. I simply experience a difficulty in breathing, and I feel a pain in the right side. Be that as it may, I came home at eleven, and, all the time wishing that I might fall suddenly ill so as not to have to go to the ball, dressed myself for it. I looked beautiful.

Tuesday, January 20.—When I came home from the studio to-day I found that Mme. G—— had been here, expecting to find me in my room, and that she was furious because I do not take care of myself just as if I were an old woman.   And then, the tickets we were promised for to-morrow have been given to Mme. de Rothschild.

Oh, not to have to ask for tickets !   To be independent !

Saturday, January 31.—I went to-night to a concert and ball, given for the benefit of the suffers by the inundations in Murcia, at the Continental Hotel, under the patronage of Queen Isabella, who, after listening to the concert, descended to the ball-room, where she remained an hour.

I am not very fond of dancing, and to whirl around in the arms of a man does not seem to me to be very amusing. On the whole, though, it is a matter of indifference to me, for I could never understand the feeling of the Italians with respect to the waltz.

When I dance I think of nothing but the persons who are observing me.

I should like to do every day as I have done to-day : to work from eight until noon ; and from two until five ; at five to have the lamp brought in and draw till half-past seven.

At half-past seven to dress ; to dine at eight, read until eleven, and then go to bed.

To work from two till half-past seven, however, without stopping, is a little fatiguing.

For this year's *Salon* I have thought of this : A woman seated at a table reading, her elbow resting on the table, and her chin in the palm of her hand, while the light falls on her beautiful blonde hair.   Title—The Divorce Question, by Dumas.   This book has just appeared, and the subject is one that is agitating the whole world.   The other picture is simply Dina in a white crepe-de-chine, seated in a large antique easy-chair, her hands in her lap, and her fingers loosely interlaced. The attitude is so easy and graceful that I hastened to make a sketch of her one evening she had seated herself thus by chance, while I was trying to pose her. It is somewhat in the style of Mme. Recamier, and in order that the waist may not look too immodest I shall add a colored sash.

To-day, I float in air, I feel myself a superior being,— great, happy, capable of all things. I have faith in my future.

Monday, February 16.—We went to the Theatre Français to-night to see the first representation of "Daniel Rochat," by Sardou. It was a really important event. We had an excellent box containing six seats. There was a splendid house ; every one of any importance, socially or politically, being there.

As to the play itself I must see it again. I thought it in some parts diffuse and tiresome ; but the audience shouted, applauded, and hissed so much, some approving, others condemning, that I could scarcely hear half of the piece. The hero is a great orator,—a sort of atheistic Gambetta. The heroine is a young girl,—an Anglo-American Protestant, extremely liberal in her views, and a republican, but a believer.

You can imagine what might be made out of such materials at the present time.

Wednesday, March 3.—I must give up going out in the evening for the present, so that I may be able to rise refreshed in the morning and begin my work at eight o'clock.

I have only sixteen days left in which to complete my picture.

Friday, March 12.—If mamma goes away to-morrow,

Dina will accompany her ; there are only seven days left now, and I shall never be able to find a model ; even if I succeed in finding one to-morrow, there will be only six days, then, and it would be impossible to finish my picture in that time. I must therefore give up the hope of exhibiting this year, and I will not conceal from you the fact that I have shed tears of rage, not only on account of that, but also at the thought that nothing succeeds with me. I conceive an idea for a picture—a sensational subject that would produce an effect, whatever shortcomings there might be in the execution, and give me in a day the reputation I could scarcely hope to acquire otherwise in a year— and now there is an end to everything. The labor of so many days is lost, and lost without hope of a return. This is what may be called a misfortune. Think of me as you will, but while Paul's romantic sorrows left me unmoved, this sorrow of my own exasperates me and plunges me into despair. Yet there is something more in this feeling than selfishness, though what it is I cannot explain. And even if there were nothing in it but selfishness, I am unhappy enough, and forlorn enough, to excuse my being selfish.

Friday, March 19.—At a quarter-past twelve Tony arrived. Why had I not begun sooner? he asked; the picture was charming, enchanting, he declared: what a pity it was that it was not finished! On the whole, he consoled me, but he said that I must ask for more time.

"You might send it as it is," he added, "but it would not be worthy of you; this is my sincere opinion; ask for more time, and you will produce something really good."

Then he turned up his sleeves, took the palette and brush, and dashed in a stroke here and there to show where more light was wanted. But I will retouch it all—if they grant me the time. He stayed more than two hours. He is a charming fellow; he entertained me greatly, and I was in such good-humor that it mattered little to me what became of the picture.   Those dashes of the brush were in fact an excellent lesson.

I had already recovered my spirits even before I knew the result of mamma's efforts with Gavini, who had written to Turquet.   Well, I am to receive my six days' grace. I do not know precisely whom to thank for this, but we went to the opera with the Gavinis to-night, and I thanked the elder Gavini.   It is to him, I think, that I owe it.   I was radiant, triumphant, happy.

Monday, March 22.—Tony is surprised to see how much I have accomplished in so short a time.   All the same, with the exception of the background, the hair, and the flesh, the painting has a muddy look.   There is no freshness about it.   I might have done better. ́   This is Tony's opinion also; he is satisfied with it, however, and says that, if there were any possibility of its being refused at the *Salon*, he would be the first to tell me not to send it.   He says he is surprised to see how much I have accomplished.   "It is well conceived, well composed, and well executed; it is full of harmony, of charm, of grace."

Ah, yes, but I am dissatisfied with the flesh.   And to think they will say this is my manner!   It is like parchment!   I shall be obliged to have recourse to glaze!   I who adore freshness and simplicity in painting, who have always made it my aim to secure the effect at the first stroke!   I can tell you that it costs me not a little to exhibit a thing the execution of which falls so far short of what I should like it to be—a thing so different from my ordinary work. It is true that I have never done anything that has altogether pleased me, but this is muddy, it is a daub.   Tony says that Breslau shows the influence of Bastien-Lepage in her painting this year.   She shows his influence as I show hers.

Tony is as good as he can be.   And to say that I might

have done better! Miserable self-depreciation; miserable want of self-confidence! If I had not begun to hesitate and to say to myself, "To be, or not to be!"—But let me not commit the folly of grieving for a thing that is past.

I cannot tell why my mind should dwell on Italy to-night. This is a subject that awakens torturing thoughts within me, and one that I seek to avoid thinking of as far as possible. I have given up reading Roman history; it excited my imagination too much, and I have fallen back on the French Revolution and the history of Greece. But when I think of the Italian sunshine, the Italian air,—when I think of Rome, I grow wild!

Even Naples—Ah, Naples by moonlight! And what is curious is that there is no man in the case. When I think that I might go there if I chose, I am almost mad.

Thursday, March 25.—I have given the final touches to my picture: there is nothing now to be done to it, unless to do it all over again. It is finished, as far as so wretched a thing can be finished.

This is my *début;* my first independent public act. At last it is accomplished; my number is 9091, "Mademoiselle Marie-Constantin Russ." I hope it will be accepted; I will send the number to Tony.

Wednesday, April 7.—I must not forget to say that Julian announced to me this morning that my picture has been accepted. Curiously enough, I experienced no feeling of satisfaction at the news. Mamma's delight irritates me; this kind of a success is unworthy of me.

We spent the evening at Mme. P——'s,—amiable people, but surrounded by a curious set; the dresses were of another century; no one of any note was there: I was sleepy and cross. And poor mamma left her seat to present to me the Mexican, or the Chilian, "who laughs." He makes fright-

ful grimaces which give him a habitually sneering expression. It is a nervous affection, and along with it he has a
round, smooth face! He has twenty-seven millions, and
mamma has taken it into her head that I might marry this
man—it would be almost as if I were to marry a man without a nose! Horrible! I might marry an old man, an
ugly man—they are all alike to me—but a monster, never!
Of what use would his millions be to me with this laughing-
stock attached to them. There were several people there
we knew, but it was enough to put one to sleep—amateurs
who made faces and showed their teeth while they sang, a
violinist who could not be heard, and a handsome man who,
after sweeping his audience with a triumphant glance, gave
us Schubert's "Serenade," with his hand resting on the piano.
But for that matter I cannot understand how a gentleman
can thus make an exhibition of himself in public.

The women, their heads dressed with that white powder
that gives the hair so dirty an appearance, looked as if they
had just been stuffing mattresses or threshing straw. How
foolish, how disgusting a practice it is!

Thursday, April 29.—We dine with the Simonides this
evening. Everything about their menage is curious (I
made the acquaintance of the wife at Julian's); the husband
is young and handsome, the wife is past her thirty-fifth year,
though still beautiful; they are very much attached to each
other. They live in retirement, seeing no one with the exception of a few artists, and produce the most extraordinary
drawings and paintings, something after the style of the
Renaissance, and on subjects surprising by their naivete!
"The Death of Beatrice," "The Death of Laura" (the woman
who concealed her lover's head in a flower-pot, from which
flowers sprouted afterward), and all in the manner of centuries ago. Madame wears costumes of the time of Boccaccio;
to night she wore a soft Japanese crepe, with long, narrow

sleeves, such as the Virgin is represented wearing, fastened behind, and a plain skirt hanging in straight folds; a girdle of antique galloon, which made her look rather short-waisted; a bouquet of lilies of the valley in the corsage, pearls around her neck, and earrings and bracelets of gold of antique workmanship. With her pale complexion, her black wavy hair, and her gazelle-like eyes, she looked like a fantastic apparition. If she only had the sense to dress her hair simply, instead of tumbling it up and making her head look like a fright, she would be very striking.

Friday, April 30.—My little American friend, whose name is Alice Brisbane, came at ten, and we left the house together. I had set my mind on going alone or with but a single companion to see how my picture was hung. I went to the *Salon*, then, very nervous, and imagining the worst that could possibly happen, so that I might not be disappointed. None of my forebodings were realized, however, for my picture was not yet hung.

As for Bastien-Lepage, his picture produces on the beholder, at the first glance, the effect of space—of the open air. Jeanne d'Arc—the real Jeanne d'Arc, the peasant girl—leans against an apple-tree, of which she holds a branch in her left hand, which, as well as the arm, is of extreme perfection; the right arm hangs loosely by her side; it is admirable—the head thrown back, the strained attitude of the neck, and the eyes that look into the future— clear, wonderful eyes; the countenance produces a striking effect; it is that of the peasant, the daughter of the soil, startled and pained by her vision. The orchard surrounding the house in the background is nature's self; but there is a something—in a word, the perspective of it is not good; it seems to crowd forward on the view, and spoils the effect of the figure.

The figure itself is sublime, and it produced on me so

strong an impression that I can scarcely restrain my tears as I write.

This was what most interested me in the *Salon*. Now for myself : We were all going to visit the *Salon* together, after breakfast, or at least so I thought. . . . But no ; my aunt went to church, instead, and mamma wanted to go too, and it was only when they saw that I was astonished and offended, that they decided to accompany me, and then with a very bad grace. I do not know if it was the modest place I occupied that displeased them, and made them unwilling to go, but it is really very hard to have such a family ! Finally, ashamed of her indifference, or whatever else it may have been, mamma went with me, and Dina also, and we met at the *Salon*, first, the whole studio, then some acquaintances, and finally Julian.

Saturday, May 1.—One of the most stupid, unlooked for, and annoying things imaginable has just happened to me ! To-morrow is Easter Sunday, and we were to go to-night to high mass, at which the whole Russian colony, beginning with the embassy, was to be assembled—all the beauty and elegance and vanity of the colony in the front seats. The Russian women and their gowns were of course to be passed in review and commented upon by everybody.

Well, at the last moment they brought me my gown, and it looked like nothing but a heap of old gauze. I went, however, but no one shall ever know the secret rage I felt. My waist was hidden by a badly made corsage, all askew ; my arms were cramped by ill-fitting sleeves, much too long ; altogether I presented a ridiculous appearance, and, in addition to all this, the gauze, that I had seen only by daylight, looked positively dirty at night.

Friday, May 7.—Mme. Gavini came again to-day to tell mamma that I am wearing myself out ; that is true, but it is not with painting ; to avoid wearing myself out it would be only necessary for me to go to bed every night at ten or eleven o'clock, while, as it is, I stay up till one, and waken in the morning at seven.

Last night it was that idiot S—— who was the cause of this. I was writing and he came over to speak to me ; then he went to play cards with my aunt ; then I waited up in order to hear a few silly words of love from him. And twenty times he bade me good-night, and twenty times I told him to go, and twenty times he asked permission to kiss my hand ; and I laughed and said at last, " Very well, it is all the same to me." Then he kissed my hand, and I am sorry to have to confess that this kiss gave me pleasure, not because of the person who bestowed it, but—for many reasons. And after all, one is only a woman.

I could still feel this kiss upon my hand this morning, for it was not a kiss bestowed simply through politeness.

Ah, what creatures young girls are !

Do you suppose I am in love with this young man with the long nose? No, you do not? Well, the A—— affair was nothing more than this. I had been doing my best to fall in love, and the Cardinals and the Pope lent their assistance ; my imagination was excited ; but as for love— oh, no ! Only as I am not now fifteen, and, besides, am not as silly as I was then, I exaggerate nothing, and relate the occurrence just as it took place.

The kiss upon my hand troubled me especially because I saw that it had given me pleasure. Consequently, I have resolved to treat S—— with coldness in the future ; but he is such a good fellow, and so simple-minded, that it would be stupid of me to act a part ; it would not be worth while ; it is better to treat him as I did Alexis B——, which is what I do. Dina, he, and I remained together to-night till eleven o'clock, S—— and I reading verses and making translations from the Latin, and Dina listening. I was

surprised to see that this young fellow knows a great deal,—
at least a great deal more than I. I have forgotten a good
deal of what I knew, and he is just fresh from his studies
for his degree of bachelor of arts. Well, I should like to
make a friend of him—but, no, he does not please me well
enough for that, but—a friendly acquaintance.

Saturday, May 8.—When I am spoken to, even in a loud
tone of voice, I cannot hear! Tony asked me to-day if I
had seen anything of Perugino, and I answered "No,"
without understanding what he said.

Thursday, May 13.—I have such a buzzing in my ears
that I have to make the greatest efforts to prevent the distress it causes me from being perceived.

Oh, it is horrible! With S—— it is not so much matter,
because he sits near me, and whenever I wish I can tell
him that he bores me. But the G   s raise their voices
when they speak to me ; and at the studio they laugh at
me, and tell me I am growing deaf. I pretend that it is
only absent-mindedness, and make a jest of it, but it is
horrible !

Sunday, May 16.—I went to the *Salon* alone early this
morning; only those who had cards of admission were
there. I looked for a long time at the Jeanne d'Arc, and
still longer at the " Good Samaritan " of Morot. I seated
myself in front of the Morot, with a lorgnette in my hand, so
as to study it carefully. It is the picture that, of all I have
seen, has given me the greatest pleasure. There is nothing
cramped in it ; all is simple, true, natural ; every object in
it is copied from nature, and there is nothing that recalls
the hideous conventional beauty of the school. It is charming to look at ; even the head of the ass is perfect ; the
landscape, the mantle, the very toe-nails, Everything is

harmonious, everything is correct, everything is as it should be.

The head of the Jeanne d'Arc is sublime. These two paintings are in two adjoining rooms. I went back and forth from the one to the other. I was looking through my lorgnette at the Morot and thinking of that poor fellow —, when he passed in front of me, without seeing me, however, and when I was going away I again saw him from the garden pointing out my picture to another person who looked like a journalist.

Friday, June 18.—I have worked all day to-day at my painting. In the evening S—— came. I attributed his evident depression to his being in love, but there was something more than this the matter. He goes to Bucharest or to Lille as director of his brother's bank. But, besides this, and above all, he desires to get married ; ah, his heart is set upon it ! As for me, I smiled and told him he was bold and presumptuous, and explained to him that I had no dowry, as all my dowry would be no more than enough for pin-money, and that he would have to lodge me and feed me, and provide me with amusement at his own cost.

Poor fellow, I felt sorry for him all the same.

He kissed my hands a hundred times, entreating me to think of him sometimes. " You will think of me sometimes ? Speak, I entreat you ; tell me you will sometimes think of me," he said.

" Whenever I find time."

But he begged so hard that I was obliged at last to give him a hasty yes. Ah, our adieus were tragic—at least on his side. We were standing near the door of the drawing-room, and I gave him my hand to kiss, so that he might carry away with him a romantic recollection of our parting, and then we gravely shook hands.

I remained pensive for a full minute after he had gone. I shall miss this boy. He is to write to me.

Sunday, June 20.—I spent the morning at the *Salon,* which closes this evening. The " Good Samaritan " has received the medal of honor.

The landscape of Bastien-Lepage is not perfect, it spoils the figure ; but what an admirable figure ! The head is a piece of art that stands absolutely unrivaled. I found Morot's picture almost tiresome to-day, while Bastien-Lepage I admired more than ever. I went from the one to the other, and then to a " Sleeping Head," of Henner, and a little nymph by him also. Henner is grace itself. It is not altogether nature, but—but no, it must be nature ; it is adorable. His " Nymphs by Twilight " is incomparable and inimitable. He nevers varies, but is always charming. His nude figures at the Luxembourg are not so good as his later work. His last year's picture is the best of his work that I have seen. I longed passionately to buy it. I look at it every day. Ah, if I were only rich ! The effect the Morot produces on me is a singular one. I find him tiresome beside Bastien-Lepage and Henner. Henner !—his charm is inexpressible !   .

MONT-DORE, *Tuesday, July* 20.—I went to Julian's yesterday with Villevielle, to get my keys, which I had forgotten. This man encourages me greatly, and I leave Paris in good spirits.   One consolation is that I am no longer afraid of Breslau. " The thing with her " (meaning me), Julian says, " is that it is not painting, but the object itself ; and even when she does not quite reach it, you can see that the effort has been in that direction."

We are badly lodged, the house is full, and the cooking atrocious.

Wednesday, July 21.—I have begun a course of treatment. They come for me with an air-tight sedan-chair, and a costume of white flannel trousers reaching to the feet, and a cloak with a hood.

Then follow a bath, a douche, drinking the waters, and inhalations. I agree to everything. This is the last time I shall submit to all these things, and I should not do so now, if it were not for the fear of growing deaf. My deafness is much better ; almost well, in fact.

Friday, July 23.—Who will restore me my youth—my squandered, stolen, vanished youth ! I am not yet twenty, and the other day I pulled out three gray hairs. I am proud of them ; they are the terrible proof that I have exaggerated nothing. If it were not for my childish figure I should look like an old woman. Is this natural at my age ?

I had a wonderful voice ; it was a gift from God, and I have lost it. Song for a woman is what eloquence is for a man—a power without limit.

In the park which my window overlooks I saw Mme. Rothschild to-day, with her horses, her grooms, etc. The sight of this fortunate woman gave me pain ; but I must be brave. Besides, when suffering becomes too severe there comes deliverance from it. When it reaches a certain point then we know it must begin to diminish ; it is while awaiting this crisis of the heart and soul that we suffer ; when it has once come, then our sufferings begin to admit of consolation—then one can call Epictetus to one's aid, or one can pray ; but there is this about prayer : it stirs the emotions.

Tuesday, July 27.—I tried to paint a landscape to-day, but it ended in my flinging away the canvas ; there was a little girl of about four years old standing beside me watching me while I painted, and instead of looking at my landscape I looked at the child, who is to sit for me to-morrow. How can any other subject be preferred to the human form?

I have such a pain running from the right ear down the neck that it almost drives me crazy. I have said nothing about it—it would only trouble my aunt; and then I know it is caused by my sore throat.

Here I have been for the last twenty-four hours suffering tortures. I find it impossible to sleep, or to do anything else whatever. Even my reading I have to leave off at every moment. I think it is this pain that makes everything look black around me. Misery of miseries!

Saturday, July 31.—Before I left Paris I read "Indiana," by Georges Sand, and I can assure you I did not find it amusing. As I have only read "La Petite Fadette," "Indiana," and two or three other novels of hers, perhaps I ought not to express an opinion on the subject; but so far I do not enjoy this author at all.

I thought of taking a ride to-day, but I have no mind for anything, and when I spend the day without working I suffer the most frightful remorse, and there are days when I can do nothing; on such occasions I say to myself that I could work if I tried, and then follow self-reproaches, and it ends by my exclaiming, "Better give it all up! Life is not worth the trouble!" And then I sit down and smoke cigarettes and read novels.

Tuesday, August 17.—I have never had the perseverance to finish any piece of writing. Something, of interest takes place; it occurs to me to write an article about it; I sketch this out, and on the following day I see in one of the papers an article resembling mine, or at least one that renders mine useless. My studies in art have taught me that in order to succeed in anything persistent effort in the beginning is indispensable. "The first step is the most difficult one." This proverb never struck me so forcibly as now.

And then there is the question also, and above all, of *environment.* Mine may be characterized, notwithstanding the best will in the world, as stultifying. The members of my family are, for the most part, ignorant and commonplace. Then there is Mme. G   , who is a worldly woman, *par excellence ;* and you know who our *habitues* are. M   and some insignificant young people. So that I can assure you if it were not for my own companionship, and my reading, I should be even less intelligent than I am.

Wednesday, August 18.—We took a long ride to-day,— five hours on horseback, and with this debilitating treatment, and I am literally tired to death.   ·

I fear the result of the treatment will prove this stupid doctor here, who pretended that I was weak, to be in the right. It is true that he assured me, when I had got through with it, that in order to have borne twenty-one baths as well as I did, I must have been very strong. Medicine is a sorry science.

We ascended to the summit of Sancy ; the mountains that frame in the horrible Mont-Dore, seen from this height, appear flat. The spectacle from the top of Sancy is truly sublime ; I should love to see the sun rise from there. The far horizon has a bluish tint that reminded me of the Mediterranean, and that is all there is that is beautiful about the place. The ascent on foot is very fatiguing, but when one has reached the top one seems to dominate the world.

Thursday, August 19.—I am good for nothing this morning ; my eyes are tired, my head aches. And to think I shall not leave here till Saturday ! To-day it is too late, to-morrow is Friday, and if I were to travel on Friday, I should think all the stupid things that invariably happen to me on such occasions happened on that account.

PARIS, *Sunday, August* 29, *eight o'clock.*—How comfortable and pretty my studio looks !

I have been reading the illustrated weekly papers, and some pamphlets. Everything goes on in the same routine as before, just as if I had not been away.

Two o'clock.—I console myself by thinking that my troubles are only the equivalent of the troubles of other kinds that other artists have to suffer, as I have neither poverty nor the tyranny of parents to bear—for it is those, is it not, that artists have chiefly to complain of ?

I make some good resolution, and then on a sudden I commit some folly, as if I were acting in a dream ! I despise and detest myself, as I despise and detest every one else, including the members of my own family. Oh, one's family ! My aunt employed a dozen little stratagems on the journey to make me sit on the side of the car on which the window did not open. Tired of resisting I at last consented, on condition that the window on the other side should be opened ; and no sooner had I fallen asleep than they closed it again. I woke up exclaiming that I would break open the window with my heels, but we had already arrived. And then at breakfast, afterward, such frowns, such looks of anguish, because I did not eat. Evidently these people love me, but it seems to me that when people love one they should be able to understand one better.

Just indignation renders one eloquent.

And then—mamma is always talking about God : " If God wills it "; " With the help of God." When one invokes the name of God so often it is only as an excuse for leaving a number of petty duties undone.

This is not faith, nor even religion ; it is a mania, a vice, the cowardliness of laziness, of incapacity, of indolence. What can be more unworthy than to seek to cover all one's shortcomings by the word " God." It is not only unworthy, it is criminal, if one believes in God. " If it is written that such a thing is to happen, it will happen," she says, so as to avoid the trouble of exerting herself, and—remorse.

If everything were ordered beforehand, God would be nothing more than a constitutional president, and free will, vice, and virtue idle words.

Tuesday, September 7.—It is raining ; all the most disagreeable events of my life pass in review before me, and there are some of them, far back in the past, that to think of makes me start in my chair and clinch my hands as if a physical pain had suddenly seized me.

In order that I should grow better, it would be necessary for me to change all my surroundings ; I know beforehand all that mamma or my aunt will say or do in such or such circumstances, what they will wear receiving visitors, when they go out to take an airing, when they are in the country—and all this irritates me frightfully ; it produces the same effect upon me as it would to listen to the cutting of glass.

It would be necessary for me to change my surroundings completely, and then, when my spirit was more tranquil, I should no doubt love them as they deserve to be loved. Meantime, however, they worry me to death. When I refuse any dish at table they wear the most frightful looks ; they employ every device to avoid the use of ice at table, as they fancy it might hurt. me. When I open a window they steal to it like thieves to close it again ; and do a thousand other silly things of the kind that irritate my nerves. But I am possessed with a hatred for everything belonging to this house. What gives me most uneasiness is that my faculties are rusting in this solitude ; all these somber colors tinge my thoughts with gloom and throw my mind back upon itself. I fear that these dark surroundings may leave a lasting impression upon my character, and render it sour, morose, and embittered. I have no wish that this should be so, but I fear that it will be the case, owing to the efforts that I am compelled to make to prevent the rage with which they are continually inspiring me, from appearing on the surface.

Friday, September 10.—A profound emotion for my aunt to-day ! Dr. Fauvel, who examined my lungs a week ago and found nothing the matter with them then, examined them again to-day and discovered that the bronchial tubes are affected. He seemed serious, moved, and somewhat confused at not having foreseen the gravity of the disease ; then followed prescriptions for the remedies used by consumptives—cod-liver oil, painting the chest with iodine, hot milk, flannel underwear, etc., and finally he advised me to consult Dr. See or Dr. Potain, or to call them in in consultation with him. You may imagine the expression in my aunt's countenance ! For my part all this amuses me; I have suspected something of the kind for a long time past ; I have been coughing all the winter, and I cough still, and experience difficulty in breathing besides. The wonder would be if nothing were the matter with me ; I should be well pleased if something were the matter, so as to be done with it. My aunt is terrified ; I, delighted. The thought of death does not frighten me. I should not dare to kill myself, but I should like to be done with life. If you but knew—I shall wear no flannel and I will not stain my chest with iodine. I have no desire to get well. I shall have life enough and health enough without that for all I want to do.

Friday, September 17.—I went again yesterday to see the

doctor who was treating me for my deafness. He confessed to me that he had not thought the trouble so serious,
and told me that I shall never again be able to hear as well
as formerly. I was completely overwhelmed by his words.
It is horrible! I am not deaf, it is true, but my ear per-
ceives sound only through a mist, as it were. For instance,
I can no longer hear, and perhaps shall never be able to
hear again, the tick-tick of my alarm clock, unless by putting my ear close to it. This, indeed, may be called a misfortune. In conversation many things escape me. Well,
let me thank Heaven, that I have not also became blind or
dumb.

Tuesday, *September* 28.—Since last night I have been
happy. I dreamed of *him*. He was ill, and he looked
ugly, but that did not matter; I know now that love is not
dependent for its existence on the possession of beauty by
the beloved object. We talked together like two friends as
we used to do, as we would do now if we were to meet
again. All I asked for was that our friendship might not
transgress the limits beyond which it would become subject
to change.

This was the dream I cherished in my waking hours, also.
In a word, I have never been so happy as I was last night.

Wednesday, *September* 29.—Since yesterday my complexion has been wonderfully fresh and clear and beautiful, and
my eyes brilliant and animated. Even the contour of my
face is more delicate and more perfect than before. Only
it is a pity that this is at a time when there is no one to see
me. It is a silly thing to say, but I remained standing for
half-an-hour before the glass for the pleasure of looking
at myself; it is a long time since this has happened.

Friday, *October* 1 —Oh, Frenchmen who complain that

you are neither free nor happy! The same state of things exists now in Russia as existed in France during the Reign of Terror—by a word, a gesture, one may bring ruin on one's-self. Ah, how much there still remains to be done that men might be even approximately happy!

Sunday, October 3.—I am very sad to-day.

No, there is no help for me. For four years I have been treated by the most celebrated doctors for laryngitis, and my health has been going from bad to worse during all that time.

For the last four days I was able to hear well; now, however, the deafness is beginning again.

Well, I will make a prediction:

I am going to die, but not just yet—that would be too much good fortune—that would be to end my sufferings at once. I shall go on dragging out a miserable existence for a few years longer with my cough, my colds, fevers, and other ailments.

Monday, October 4.—I wrote to my music-teacher at Naples, a short time since, for some music for the mandolin. I have just received his answer. I confess, notwithstanding my *realistic* tendencies (a word very little understood) and my republican sentiments, I am very sensible to the charm of the flowery style of these Italians.

And why should not the two things go together?

But this style must be left to the Italians; in others it appears ridiculous. Ah, when shall I be able to go to Italy?

How tame every other place is after Italy! Never has any other country, never has any one's presence produced in me so strong an emotion as the mere recollection of Italy now awakens within me.

Why should I not return there? And my painting? Do

I know enough to go on in the right direction without further instruction? I cannot say.

No, I will remain in Paris this winter. I will go to spend the Carnival in Italy. The winter of 1881–1882 I will spend at St. Petersburg. If I do not marry a rich man then, I shall return to Paris or to Italy in 1882 or 1883. And then I will marry a nobleman with fifteen or twenty thousand francs a year, who will be very glad to accept my income and myself. Am I not wise to allow myself three years of liberty before capitulating?

Tuesday, October 5.—There is nothing left me to do but to resign myself to the inevitable ; or rather to summon all my courage, and, standing face to face with myself, ask myself if *this* be not, after all, a matter of indifference. To have lived in one manner or in another, what does it matter? I must learn to conquer my sensations, and to say with Epictetus that it is in one's own power to accept evil as a good, or rather to accept with indifference whatever happens. One must have suffered horribly to be reconciled to this species of death as a way out of life, and it is only after one has endured indescribable sufferings, after one has sunk into a state of complete despair, that one begins to comprehend how it is possible to lead this living death. And yet, if one were to make the effort one might learn to accept one's fate with calmness at least. This is not a vain delusion ; it is something possible.

When one has reached a certain point in physical suffering one loses consciousness, or else falls into a state of ecstasy. The same thing takes place in the case of mental suffering. When it has reached a certain point the soul soars superior to it, one regards as insignificant one's former sufferings, and goes forward to one's fate with head erect, as the martyrs did of old.

For the fifty years or so I may still have to live, of what

consequence would it be whether they were passed in a prison or in a palace, among people or in solitude? The end would be the same. What I am troubled about, then, is the sensations experienced during this period, and which, when they have passed, leave no trace behind? But what does a thing matter which is of short duration, and which, when it is past, leaves no trace of its existence? What it concerns me to do, since I have the power, is to utilize my life in the pursuit of art—this may give evidence of my existence after I am dead.

Saturday, October 9.—I have done nothing this week, and inaction has made me stupid. I glanced through the account of my journey to Russia, and it interested me very much.

Georges Sand is a writer with whom I have no sympathy; and she does not even possess, in the same degree as Gautier, the vigor, the audacity, that inspire one with admiration, if not with liking, for him. Georges Sand—well, she is well enough. Among contemporary writers I like Daudet best. His works, it is true, are only novels, but they are full of just observations, of truth to nature, of genuine feeling; his characters live.

As for Zola, I am not on very good terms with him. He has thought fit to attack, in *Figaro*, Ranc, and others of the Republican party, with a virulence that is both in bad taste and unbecoming alike to his great genius and his high literary position.

But what do people see in the writings of Georges Sand? Novels beautifully written, yes; but what more? As for me, I find her novels tiresome, which is never the case with Balzac, the two Dumas, Zola, Daudet, or Musset. Victor Hugo, in his most wildly romantic prose-writing, is never tiresome; one feels the spell of his genius. But Georges Sand! How can any one have the patience to read three hundred pages filled with the sayings and doings of Valentine and Benedict, the uncle, a gardener and so on. Her theme is always the same : the equalizing of classes by means of love—which is an ignoble one.

Let social distinctions be abolished—well and good ; but let it be done by a more dignified means than this.

To present the picture of a countess in love with her valet, and to write long dissertations on the subject—in this does the genius of Georges Sand consist. She has written some good novels, it is true, containing some very pretty descriptions of country life ; but I require in a writer something more than this.

I am reading " Valentine " at present, and the book irritates me, because, while it is interesting enough to make me wish to finish it, every time I lay it down I find that it has left nothing in my mind but a vaguely disagreeable impression. I feel as if I lowered myself by this species of reading ; I dislike the book, and yet I go on reading it and shall go on with it to the end, unless it should prove as tiresome as the " Dernier Amour," of the same author. " Valentine," however, is the best of Georges Sand's novels that I have read ; the " Marquis de Villemer," too, is good. I believe there is no groom in love with a countess in it.

Sunday, October 10.—I spent the morning at the Louvre, and was dazzled by what I saw there. I see now that I never had a clear understanding of art before ; I looked, and admired in set phrases like the great majority of people. Ah, when one can feel and comprehend art as I do now, one has no ordinary soul. To feel that a thing is beautiful, and understand why it is beautiful—this is a great happiness.

Monday, October 11.—I set to work on my picture to-day, full of yesterday's excitement. It is impossible not to

achieve success when one has had revelations such as I had
yesterday.

Tuesday, October 19.—Alas ! All this will end, after dragging out a few more years of miserable existence, in death.
I have always felt that it must end in this way. One
could not live long with a brain like mine. I am like those
too precocious children who are doomed to an early death.

I required too many things for my happiness, and circumstances were such that I was deprived of everything, even
physical well-being.

Two or three years ago—even six months ago—each time
I went to a new doctor in the hope of recovering my voice,
he would ask me if I did not feel such and such a symptom,
and when I answered no, he would say: "No, there is
nothing in the bronchial tubes or the lungs ; it is the larynx
only that is affected." Now I begin to feel all the symptoms the doctors imagined I had then. Therefore the
bronchial tubes and the lungs must now be affected. True
it is nothing as yet, or almost nothing. Fauvel ordered
iodine and a blister ; naturally I cried out in horror ; I
would rather break an arm than suffer myself to be blistered.
Three years ago a doctor at one of the watering-piaces in
Germany found some trouble—I don't know just what—in
the right lung, under the shoulder-blade. This made me
laugh heartily. And again at Nice, five years ago, I felt
something like a pain in the same spot. The only thing I
feared, however, was that I was going to become hump-
backed, as two of my aunts, sisters of my father, were ;
and now again, a few months since, the doctors asked me if
I felt anything there. I answered, no, without thinking.
When I cough now, or even when I draw a full breath, I
feel the pain there, in the right lung, at the back. All these
things together make me believe that there may be really
something there. I take a sort of pride in showing that I

am ill, yet I am scarcely pleased at it.   It is an ugly death—
a very slow one, four, five, ten years perhaps, and one grows
so thin, and loses all one's good looks.

I have not as yet grown much thinner ; I am just as one
ought to be ; the only thing is that I look tired.   I cough
a great deal, and I find difficulty in breathing.   And yet for
the past four years I have been under the care of the most
celebrated doctors ;   I have taken the waters they have
ordered, yet not only have I not recovered my beautiful
voice—so beautiful that it almost makes me cry to think of
it—but I grow worse and worse every day, and, let me write
the horrible word, a little deaf.

Provided death come quickly, however, I shall not complain.

Friday, October 22—It is raining, and the weather is
cold,—bitterly, frightfully cold.   So I am in sympathy with
the weather, and I cough without ceasing.   Ah, what misery, and what a horrible existence is mine !   At half-past
three there is no longer light enough to paint, and if I read by
artificial light my eyes are too fatigued to paint on the
following day.   The few people I might see I shun through
the fear of not being able to hear what they say.   There are
some days when I can hear very well, and others when I can
scarcely hear at all, and then I suffer nameless tortures.   It
cannot be that God will allow this state of things to continue.   I am ready to suffer every kind of misery, however,
provided only I am not asked to see any one.   Every time
the bell rings I shudder.   This new and horrible misfortune
makes me dread everything that I had before desired.
Think what it must be for me who am by nature gay and
fond of jesting !   I laugh as much as Mlle. Samary of the
Theatre Français ; but this is rather from habit than
any wish to conceal my feelings.   I shall always laugh.
All is over with me ; not only do I believe that all is over,

but I desire that it should be so.   There are no words with
which to express my dejection.

Monday, October 25.—I am reading "Les Chatiments ";
Yes, Victor Hugo is a genius.   Perhaps I do wrong even
to suspect that I have found certain of his lyrical transports
extravagant, not to say tiresome.   No, it is not the case;
he is beautiful, he is sublime, and, notwithstanding the
exaggerated expressions he at times makes use of, he is
human, he is natural, he is charming.   But I like his passages
of touching simplicity best—the last act of Hernani, for
instance, where Dona Sol pleads with the old man for pity ;
and the words of the old grandmother whose grandchild had
received two bullets in the brain.

Monday, November 1.—Our studio now enjoys the same
advantages as the studio of the men, that is to say, we draw
from the nude every day from the same model in the same pose
as they do ; consequently we can now paint compositions
of more importance than before.   This would have been useless to me for the last few months, but I have now reached
the point at which I am able to profit by it.   We are only
eight in the studio now ; the other pupils, to the number
of twenty-two, have gone to Julian's new studio, 51 Rue
Vivienne, which is on the same basis as this was formerly.

Tuesday, November 2.—For a week past I have had my
breakfast brought from the house to the studio.   This is
much more sensible than to run back and forth between
the Rue Vivienne and the Champs Elysées, and thus lose
the best hours of the day.   In this way I am able to work
from eight o'clock till noon, and from one till four.

Wednesday, November 10. —It is horrible to have worked
without ceasing for three years, only to find out at the end
of them that one knows nothing.

Tuesday, November 16.—I fear that I spoke of the church with some exaggeration the other day. I afterward felt some compunction in the matter, and it depended on the merest chance whether I should get up out of bed or not, to make the *amende honorable.* For it cannot be denied that the church has been the means of diffusing a truer knowledge of God, it has greatly ameliorated the condition of human society, and it has carried the name of God and civilization among savage nations. Without meaning any offense to religion, I think the work of civilization might have been carried on without the aid of Catholicism, but—on the whole, the church has been a useful institution, as the feudal system was, and, like it too, it has served, or almost served, its turn. There are too many things in Catholicism that shock the understanding, without being therefore odious, however— sacred things mixed up with childish legends. The world is too enlightened now for these holy falsehoods to be any longer respected. But we are passing through a transition period, and unhappily the masses are not yet sufficiently enlightened to be able to dispense with these idle superstitions, that bring contempt upon religion and conduce to atheism.

True, there are men who are sincerely religious, but are there not also men who are sincere monarchists?—for there are people who believe that monarchical institutions are necessary to the prosperity of certain countries. Stay, I did not think of this the other day, when I said one needed to have the soul of a lackey to advocate a monarchical form of government.

Sunday, December 5.—Dr. Potain came this morning, and he wishes me to spend the winter in the south, at least until March ; otherwise I shall not be able to breathe at all soon, or even to leave my bed. Truly I am getting on finely! For the last four years I have done everything the best physicians have ordered me to do, and I am going from bad to worse. I have even laid violent hands on my beauty in accordance with their orders. I have painted the right side of my chest with iodine, and the pain is still there. Can it be possible that the continual annoyances I suffer have undermined my health? And yet the larynx and the bronchial tubes are not generally affected by mental conditions. I don't know what to think. I do everything they tell me to do ; I avoid imprudences, I wash myself with warm water only, and yet I grow no better.

Villevieile told me yesterday that Tony, when he came to the studio on Saturday to correct the drawings, asked to see our pictures for the *concours*, and said of mine that the eyes were drawn in a peculiar manner, but that there were some good things about them, and that the coloring was charming. He was not satisfied with the paintings for the *concours*, in general. If I do not receive the medal, I shall at least have made a good study.

Tuesday, December 21.—I have no longer a buzzing in the ears, and I can hear very well.

Wednesday, December 22.—A picture by a pupil of the Rue Vivienne was awarded the medal ; she is a new pupil— a young American. I received first mention.

Sunday, December 26.—Potain wishes me to go away at once. I refused point-blank, and then, half-laughingly, half-seriously, I began to complain to him of my family. I asked him if the throat could be affected by continual fits of anger, and he said decidedly it could. I will not go away. It is delightful to travel, but not in the company of my family, with their tiresome little attentions. I know that I should rule them all, but they irritate me, and then,—no, no, no !

Besides, I scarcely cough at all, now. Only, *all this* makes me unhappy. I fancy I can no longer extricate myself from it—from what? I haven't the least idea ; but I cannot restrain my tears. Do not suppose they are tears of disappointment at not being yet married—no, those are not like other tears. After all, perhaps it is that ; but I don't think so.

And then, everything is so gloomy around me and I have no outlet for my feelings ; my poor aunt leads so isolated a life, we scarcely ever see each other ; I spend the evenings reading or playing.

I can no longer either speak or write of myself without bursting into tears. I must indeed be ill. Ah, how foolish it is to complain ! Does not death end everything ?

Why, then, notwithstanding all our fine phrases, notwithstanding our certainty that death ends everything, do we still persist in complaining of the ills of life ?

I know that my life, like that of every other human being, will end in death—in annihilation ; I consider all the circumstances of existence, which, however flattering they may seem, are mean and wretched enough in my eyes, and yet I cannot resign myself to die ! Life, then, is a force, it is *something ;* it is not merely a transient state of being, a period of time that it matters little whether it be spent in a palace or in a prison ? There is, then, something beyond, some higher truth than we are able to give expression to in the foolish phrases in which we strive to give utterance to our thoughts on those subjects ? This, then, is life,—not a transient state, a thing of no value,—but life, the dearest treasure we possess, all that we possess, in fact !

People say it is nothing, because it is not eternal. Ah, fools !

Life is ourselves ; it belongs to us, it is all that we possess ; how then is it possible to say it is nothing ! If life be nothing, tell me, then, what *something* is.

Thursday, December 30.—I went to see Tony to-day, and came home feeling somewhat comforted. We talked a great deal about myself in a general way ; he said no one ever expected great results after only three years' study ; that I want to go too fast, that he is convinced I shall succeed, and much more to the same effect. In short, I requested him so earnestly to be frank with me that I think he spoke as he felt. Besides, he has no interest in trying to deceive me ; and then, what he said was not much after all. I have recovered my spirits, however, in some degree, and I am ready to begin work on my picture.

What a good, kind fellow Tony is ! He says the greatest painters have begun to be something only after a dozen years or so of study ; that Bonnat, after seven years of study, was still unknown ; that he himself exhibited nothing until after eight years. Of course I know all this, but, as I had counted on winning a name before my twentieth year, you can imagine what my feelings are.

1881.

Saturday, January 8.—I have a genuine passion for my books: I arrange them on the shelves, I count them, I gaze at them ; only to look at these shelves filled with old books rejoices my heart. I stand back from them to look at them admiringly, as I would at a picture. I have only seven hundred volumes, but as they are almost all large ones, they are equivalent to a much greater number of the ordinary size.

Sunday, January 9.—Potain refuses to attend me any longer, as I do not obey his orders. Ah, it would please me very well to go away—to go to Italy, to Palermo. Oh for the cloudless sky, the blue sea, the beautiful, tranquil

nights of Italy!   Only to think of seeing Italy again makes
me wild!   It is as if there were some great good in store for
me which I am not yet ready to enjoy.   No, that is not
what I want to say.   It is as if some great happiness awaited
me which I want to enjoy free from every care, from every
anxiety.   When I say to myself, "I will go to Italy," I
think immediately afterward, "No, not yet."   I must
first strive, first work, and then—how soon I cannot tell—
complete repose.   Italy!   I know not wherein the charm
consists, but the effect this name has upon me is magical,
marvelous, indescribable.

Oh, yes, it is necessary for me to go away!   I must be
very ill indeed, for Charcot, Potain, and the others to order
me away!   I feel that the air of the South would have made
me well at once, but the fault is theirs.

And why does not mamma return?   They say it is unrea-
sonable on my part to want her to do so, but the fact that
she does not come remains the same.   Well, at last it is all
over!   I have another year, perhaps—1882 is the important
year I had looked forward to in all my childish dreams.   I
had fixed on 1882 as the year that was to decide my destiny—but in what sense I could not tell.   By my death,
perhaps.   At the studio to-night they dressed up the skeleton to represent Louise Michel, with a red scarf, a cigar-
ette in its mouth, and a palette-knife for a poignard.   In
me, too, is concealed a skeleton; to that must we all come
at last.   Annihilation!   Horrible thought!

Thursday, January 13 (The Russian New-Year's Day).—
I still cough a little, and my breathing is painful; otherwise I
am not noticeably changed; I am neither thin nor pale.
Potain has left off coming; my malady, he thinks, needs
only sunshine and fresh air to cure it.   He is honest, Potain
is; and he does not wish to fill me with useless drugs.   But
I take ass's-milk and water-wort.   I am sure that a winter

spent in a warm climate in the open air would cure me, but—I know better than any one what it is that is the matter with me; I have always had a delicate throat, and constant agitation of mind has contributed to make it worse. After all there is nothing the matter with me but the cough and my deafness, and that is of very little consequence, as you may see.

Saturday, January 15.—To day M. Cot, who is to take turns with Tony at the studio, entered upon his duties. I showed him nothing I had done, though Julian had pointed me out to him as the person he had spoken to him about. "It is Mademoiselle," he said, "who is going to do this," showing him the large canvas they had so much trouble to bring into the studio yesterday.

Tony is a man who understands his business—an artist of reputation, an academician, a man of recognized authority in his art, and the lessons of such a man are always an advantage. It is in painting as it is in literature: first learn the grammar of the art, and your own nature will tell you whether you are to write dramas or songs. So that if Tony were to be assassinated I would take in his place Lefebvre, Bonnat, or even Cabanel—which would not be pleasant. Painters by temperament, like Carolus, Bastien-Lepage, and Henner, compel you to imitate them against your will; and they say one learns only the faults of those one copies. And then I would not choose for my master a painter of single figures only. I want to see an artist surrounded by historical pictures; the figures in his picture, the *persons*, lend him the support of their names, and would compel me to listen to his counsels; though there are pictures of a single figure which I would prefer to half a dozen pictures with half a dozen figures in each of them.

The least interesting face in the world may become interesting under certain conditions. I have seen, in the case of models, the most commonplace heads rendered superb by a hat, a cap, or a piece of drapery. All this is in order to tell you with becoming modesty that every evening, after coming home from the studio, I wash my hands and face, put on a white gown, and drape a white muslin handkerchief around my head, after the manner of the old women of Chardin, or the young girls of Greuze. This gives my head a surprisingly charming effect. To-night the handkerchief, which was rather large, was draped *à l'Egyptienne*, and I don't know how it was, but my face looked *regal*. As a general thing this word would not be applicable to my countenance, but the drapery wrought the miracle. This has put me in good spirits.

I have fallen into this habit of late. To remain with my head uncovered in the evening makes me uncomfortable, and my "sorrowful thoughts" like to be under shelter. I fancy myself more at home, thus—more at my ease, as it were.

I have not learned to understand how one can sacrifice one's life for the beloved object—for a mortal like one's self—and for love of him.

But I can understand how one might suffer tortures and death itself for a principle—for liberty, for anything that could serve to ameliorate the condition of humanity.

For my part I would be as ready to defend all these fine things in France as in Russia; one's country comes after humanity; after all, there are between different nations but shades of differences; and I am for simplicity and broadness of view in treating every question.

I am not easily carried away by my feelings on this point; I am neither a Louise Michel nor a nihilist,—not at all; but if I thought liberty were seriously menaced, I should be the first to take up arms in her defense.

Wednesday, January 26.—After coming home from the

studio on Tuesday I grew feverish; and I sat in the dark in my arm-chair, shivering and half-asleep until seven o'clock. I kept my picture constantly before my eyes, as has been the case every night during the last week.

As I had taken no nourishment during the day except a little milk, the night was still worse. I could not sleep, for I had set my alarm-clock, and it wakened me; but the picture was still before me, and I working on it in imagination. I did the opposite of everything I ought to have done, however, impelled by an irresistible desire to efface all that was well done. It was impossible for me to remain quiet: I tried to convince myself it was but a dream. In vain. "Is this, then, the delirium of fever?" I asked myself. I think there was something of that in it. I know now what it meant, and I should not regret it, if it were not for the fatigued feeling I have—more especially in my limbs.

But the strangest part of it was that, in my delirium, I fancied I was waiting for Julian to give me his advice concerning one of the figures I had changed.

He came yesterday and found that everything I had done was wrong; before my dream I had effaced all that was good in the picture.

And last night, by a curious coincidence, I could hear perfectly well.

I feel bruised all over.

Thursday, February 3.—I have now before my eyes the portrait of my father and mother, taken just before they were married. I have hung them up as "documentary evidence." According to Zola and other philosophers of greater fame, it is necessary to know the cause if we would understand the effects. My mother at the time of my birth was young and full of health, and exceedingly beautiful, with brown hair, brown eyes, and a dazzling complexion; my father was fair, pale, delicate in health, and was himself the son of a robust father and a sickly mother, who died young, leaving four daughters, all more or less deformed from their birth. Grandpapa and grandmamma were endowed with vigorous constitutions, and they had nine children, all of them healthy and robust, and some of them, mamma and Etienne for instance, handsome.

The sickly father of our illustrious subject has become strong and healthy, and the mother, blooming with health in her youth, has become feeble and nervous, thanks to the horrible existence she has been compelled to lead.

I finished " L'Assommoir" the day before yesterday. I was so forcibly impressed with the truth of the book that it almost made me sick. I felt as if I had lived among those people and talked with them.

Monday, February 7.—My picture, set aside for a time on account of a figure I could not get to my liking, goes forward again. I feel as light as a feather.

My favorite Bastien-Lepage has exhibited a portrait of the Prince of Wales, in the costume of Henry IV., with the Thames and the English fleet in the background. The background has the same tone as the " Joconde." The face is that of a sot ; it has altogether the air of a Holbein,—it might be taken for one. I don't like that. Why imitate the style of another?

Ah, if I could only paint like Carolus Duran ! This is the first time I have seen anything I thought worth coveting—anything I should like to own, myself, in the way of painting. After that everything else seemed to me mean, dry, and daubed.

Saturday, February 12.—At noon to-day the servant came running into the studio, her face flushed with excitement. M. Julian has received the Cross of the Legion of Honor.

Every one was rejoiced, and A. Neuvégliss and I ran to order a splendid basket of flowers, with a large red bow, at Vaillant-Roseau's.   Vaillant-Roseau is not an ordinary florist, he is an artist—150 francs was not too dear.

Villevielle returned at three for the express purpose of felicitating the master.   Julian wore his ribbon, and, for the first time in my life, I had the pleasure of seeing a perfectly happy man.   He declared he was this.   "There may be people who have still something to wish for," he said ; "as for me I have everything I desire."

Then Villevielle and I went downstairs to the studio of the director to see the basket ; there were rejoicings, felicitations, and even a little emotion.   He spoke to us of his old mother, for whom he feared the news might be too much ; and then of an old uncle who would cry like a child, he said, when he heard it.

"Only think—a little village down yonder!   I imagine what an effect it will have—a poor little peasant-boy who came to Paris without a sou—Chevalier of the Legion of Honor ! "

Sunday, February 13.—I have just received a very affectionate letter from mamma ; here it is :

"GRAND HOTEL, KARKOFF, *January* 27.
My adored angel, my cherished child Moussia, if you but knew how unhappy I am without you, especially as I am uneasy on account of your health, and how I long to go to you at the earliest possible moment !

"My pride, my glory, my happiness, my joy !   If you could imagine the sufferings I endure without you !   Your letter to Mme. Anitskoff is before me ; I read it over and over again like a lover, and I water it with my tears.   I kiss your little hands and your little feet, and I pray the good God that I may soon be able to do so in reality.

"I tenderly embrace our dear aunt.
                                        "M. B."

Monday, February 14.—The head in Alice Brisbane's portrait was finished in two hours, and Julian told me not to retouch it. And at other times one spends a week in making a daub. A part of the bodice and of the skirt is also painted in.

Thursday, March 3.—I am very ill. I have a violent cough, I breathe with difficulty, and there is an ominous sound in my throat. I believe this is what they call laryngeal phthisis.

I opened the New Testament lately, a thing I had not done for some time past ; and on two different occasions, within a few days of each other, I was struck by the appositeness to my thought of the passage at which I chanced to open. I have begun again to pray to Jesus ; I have returned to the Virgin, and to a belief in miracles, after having been a deist, and, for a short time, even an atheist. But the religion of Christ, as He taught it, bears little resemblance either to your Catholicism or to our orthodoxy, the rules of which I do not observe, limiting myself to following the precepts of Christ, and not concerning myself about allegories which have been taken in a literal sense, nor with the superstitions and other absurdities introduced into religion later on, by men, from political or other motives.

Friday.—I have finished my picture, with the exception of a few final touches.

Saturday, March 19.—Julian cries out that he is furious with himself for having given me the subject he did for my first picture. " Ah, if it were only your second," he says. " Ah, well," I answered, " let us leave it then for next year."

Thereupon he looked at me with eyes shining with hope

at finding me capable of renouncing the vain satisfaction of exhibiting an unfinished and mediocre picture. He would be delighted if I renounced it ; and so should I ; but the others ?—my friends ? They would say my work had been thought too ill of by the professors ; that I was not able to execute a picture ; in short, that my picture was rejected at the *Salon.*

I have spoken seriously to Julian, and explained my feelings to him. He comprehends the state of things very well, and so do I. He says I shall be honorably received, and achieve even a certain measure of success ; but this is not what we have dreamed of. The men below will not come and stand before my picture, and say, " What ! is it a woman who has painted that ? " Finally, to save my pride, I proposed to make it appear as if an accident had happened to the picture ; but he would not consent. He had expected a success ; he confesses that he is not altogether satisfied, but that it may do. And under these conditions I exhibit !

Well, it is done with, and I am rid of my picture, but how anxious I shall be until the first of May is over ! If I only have a good number !

Thursday.—I have just found a little jar of tar under my bed. It was placed there by Rosalie to benefit my health. And by the advice of a fortune-teller ! My family thought this mark of devotion on the part of a servant very touching ; mamma was very much affected ; but I poured a jug of water over the carpet under the bed, broke a pane of glass, and went to sleep in my study through rage.

Tuesday, March 29.—I learned at the studio that Breslau's picture was accepted, and I have heard nothing of mine. I painted until noon, and then went for a drive, that appeared to me interminably long.

Wednesday, March 30.—I pretended to be asleep until

ten o'clock, so as not to go to the studio, and I am very unhappy.

Friday, April 1.—April-fooling apart, I am to be queen. Julian came himself at midnight last night to tell me so, after leaving Lefebvre's. Bojidar went to find out from Tidiere, one of the young men downstairs, without my asking him, and declares that I am No. 2. This seems to me too much to expect..

Sunday, April 3.—Never have I heard Patti sing with greater spirit than last night. Her voice had such power, such freshness, such brilliancy! Heavens! what a beautiful voice I had! It was powerful, dramatic, entrancing! It made a chill run down one's back to hear it. And now, not even the memory of it left!

Shall I never recover it, then? I am young; it may be possible.

Patti does not touch the heart, but she can bring tears of enthusiasm to the eyes. To listen to her voice reminds one of an exhibition of fireworks. In one passage, last night, her notes were so pure, so brilliant, so bird-like, that I was completely carried away.

Tuesday, April 5.—A great surprise! My father is here! They came to the studio for me, and when I went home I found him in the dining-room with mamma, who paid him a thousand little attentions. Dina and Saint-Amand, who were there also, were charmed with the spectacle of this conjugal happiness.

Wednesday, April 6.—I was delayed until nine by my father, who insisted upon it that I should not work to-day; but I am too much interested in my torso for that, and I shall not see the august family again until dinner-time, after which they go to the theater and I remain at home alone.

My father *cannot conceive how one can be an artist*, or how being one can redound to one's credit. I sometimes think he only pretends to have such ideas.

Sunday, May 1.—Alexis came early; he had a ticket admitting two persons, so that, as I have one also, we can all four go—Monsieur, Madame, Alexis, and I. I am not too well pleased with my dress—a costume of dark-gray wool, and a handsome, but rather commonplace, black hat. We found my picture at once; it is in the first *salon*—to the left of the *salon d'honneur*, in the second row. I am delighted with the place, and very much surprised to see the picture look so well. Not that it looks well, but I expected to see it look frightful, and it is not bad.

Through an error, however, they have omitted my name in the catalogue. (I have called their attention to it, and it will be rectified.) One cannot see the pictures very well on the first day. One wants to see everything at once. Alexis and I left the others from time to time, to look around a little; then we lost sight of them entirely, and I took his arm, for I do as I choose; I come and go without fear of any one. We met a crowd of acquaintances, and I received a great many fine compliments that did not seem as if they were dragged in by the hair. This is but natural; these people, who understand nothing about the matter, see a large picture with a good many figures in it, and they think it is everything it should be.

A week ago I gave a thousand francs to be distributed among the poor. No one knows of this. I went to the principal office, and quickly slipped away when I had finished the business that brought me, without waiting for thanks. The director must have thought I stole the money, in order to give it away. Heaven grant me a return for my money!

Abbema, who was walking through the rooms with Bojidar, sent me word that he was pleased with my picture ; he says that it is strong, full of spirit, etc. A few moments afterward we met and made the acquaintance of the celebrated friend of Sarah Bernhardt. She is a very good girl and I value her praises.

We breakfasted in the building ; altogether we spent six hours with Art. I shall say nothing of the pictures. I will only say that I think highly of Breslau's picture ; it has great beauties, but the drawing is bad, and the colors too thickly laid on in places. And then, such fingers, like the claws of a bird ! Such noses, with slits for nostrils ! Such nails ! And such stiffness and heaviness in the execution ! In short, the picture is of the impressionist school and Bastien-Lepage is the master she copies.

Where does one see such colors and such perspective in nature ?

Notwithstanding all this, however, it possesses beauties ; and those three heads, placed between the portrait of Wolff and the " Mendicant " of Bastien-Lepage, attract a good deal of attention.

Friday, May 6.—I went this morning to the *Salon,* where I met Julian, who made me acquainted with Lefebvre. The latter said to me that my picture possessed great merit. At home here they are always talking of the changes that are to take place. They all irritate me. My father's ideas are absurd at times. He does not himself think so, but he persists in speaking as if it were of the greatest importance that I should consent to spend the summer in Russia. " People will see then," he says, " that you do not live apart from your family."

Have I ever lived apart from them ? Well, I shall wait for whatever chance may bring ; but, at all events, I will not travel. I shall remain tranquilly (!) here, and I can then be miserable at my ease in my arm-chair, where, at least, I am physically comfortable.

Oh, this dreadful lassitude ! Is it natural to feel thus at my age ?

And this it is that drives me to despair. If I should ever meet with any good fortune would I have the capacity to enjoy it ? Could I avail myself of any opportunity that might present itself ? I think at times I can no longer see as well as other people—though still well enough.

In the evenings when I am tired out and half asleep, divine harmonies float through my brain ; they rise and fall, like the strains of an orchestra, but independent of my volition.

Saturday, May 7.—My father wishes to leave Paris to-morrow, and mamma is to accompany him. This will un-settle everything.

And I, am I to accompany them ? I could sketch there in the open air and return in time for Biarritz.

On the other hand, they say Ems would benefit me. Ah, everything is indifferent to me. There is nothing left me to hope for.

Sunday, May 8.—I am almost glad to see that my health is giving way, since Heaven has denied me happiness.

But when it is completely ruined, everything will perhaps change, and then it will be too late.

Every one for himself—that is true ; but my family pre-tend to love me so much, and they do nothing for me. I am nothing now ; there seems to be a veil between me and the rest of the world. If one only knew what there is beyond—but we do not ; and then, it is precisely this feel-ing of curiosity I have about it that makes the thought of death less terrible to me.

I cry out a dozen times a day that I want to die ; but

that is only a form of despair. One says to one's-self, " I desire to die," but it is not true ; it is only another way of saying that life is unendurable ; one always, and in every case, desires to live, especially at my age. Besides, there is no need to grieve about me. I have life enough still to last for some time longer. No one is to be blamed in the matter ; it is God who wills it so.

Sunday, May 15.—Nothwithstanding everything—in a word, I am to go to Russia with them, if they will wait a week for me. I should find it unendurable to be present at the distribution of prizes. This is a very great chagrin that no one knows anything about except Julian ; and I shall leave Paris on account of it. I went incognito to consult a famous doctor, C   . I shall never recover my hearing, he says. The pleura of the right lung is diseased, and has been so for some time ; and the throat is in a very bad state. I asked him about all this in such a way that, after making a careful examination, he was obliged to tell me the truth.

It will be necessary for me to go to Allevard, and under- go a course of treatment. Well, I will do so on my return from Russia ; and from there I will go to Biarritz. I will go on with my painting in the country ; I will sketch in the open air, and that will benefit my health. I write all this filled with rage.

But here in the house the situation is enough to make one weep. Mamma in despair, on the one side, at having to go, and I unwilling to go with her, and equally unwilling that my aunt should be obliged, in accordance with the non- sensical notions of the family, to stay here to take care of me.

My strength is exhausted. I remain the whole day with- out opening my lips, so that I may not have to burst into tears. I feel suffocating ; there is a constant buzzing in my ears, and I have a curious sensation, as if my bones were breaking through the flesh, and this were melting away. And my poor aunt, who wants me to be happy, and to talk to her and to stay here with her ! I repeat it, my strength is exhausted, I have no faith in anything good happening, and I think everything evil is possible. I desire neither to go nor to stay, but I think that if I were to go they would not remain there so long. Besides—I cannot say ; it is the thought of Breslau's receiving the medal that makes me wish to go. Ah, I am unlucky in everything ! I must then die miserably—I who had so much faith in the future ; who prayed so fervently. Well, after the most moving arguments on all sides, our departure has been fixed for Saturday.

Friday, May 20.—In two words, I have again begun to hesitate about going to Russia. Potain came to see me to-day, and I count on his aid to be able to remain without causing my father too much vexation. Well, there is a possibility of my not going.

But it is Bojidar who has given me the fatal blow. The committee made its examination of the pictures in the *Salon* to-day, and admired Breslau's picture greatly! My tears, which had been already flowing, fell in torrents at this news. My father and mother think it is what Potain has said that is troubling me, and I cannot tell them the truth; but I shed tears enough for both causes.

After all Potain has said very little that is new, and he has made it possible for me to remain here if I wish to do so. But Breslau's picture is the thing! I have asked Potain to represent my condition to my family as worse than it is, and to say to them that my right lung is affected, so that my father may not be vexed at my remaining here. .

Monday, May 23.—Finally everything was packed up

and we went to the station. Then, at the moment of departure, my hesitation communicated itself to the others; I
began to cry, and mamma with me, and then Dina and my
aunt; and my father asked what was to be done. I responded by tears; the bell rang; we ran to the cars, in
which no seat had been secured for me, and they entered
an ordinary compartment (which I objected to doing). I
was going to follow them, but the door was already closed,
as the compartment was full, and they went away without
our even saying good-by. It is all very well for people of
the same family to abuse one another, and say they detest
one another, but when it comes to parting they think of
those things no longer. I cried at the thought of going
with them, I cry now because I am left behind. I scarcely
think at all of Breslau. But, after all, I shall be able to
take better care of my health here, and then I shall not
lose time.

Tuesday, May 24.—I am in despair at not having gone
with the others. . . . I shall telegraph to them to Berlin to
wait for me there.

BERLIN, *Wednesday, May* 25.—Accordingly I left Paris
yesterday. Before leaving I went to see Tony, who is very
ill, and for whom I left a letter of thanks, and to Julian's;
he was not at home, which was as well perhaps, as he might
have made me change my mind and remain, and it was necessary for me to go. For the last week no one of the family dared look at the others for fear of bursting into tears!
And when I was left alone I wept constantly, thinking, at
the same time, how cruel this was for my aunt. She must
have seen, however, that I also wept when the question was
one of leaving her. She thinks I do not care for her at all,
and when I consider what a self-sacrificing life this heroic
creature has led, I am melted to tears. She has not even

of being loved as a good aunt! But then
I love better. In fine, I am at Berlin; my

What is the culmination of horror is my deafness; this is
could have received. I now dread

world would be at my command if I could only hear as
before. And in my disease this happens only once in a
the physicians I
," they would say: "

And it has happened precisely to me. You cannot imagine what a state of tension
I am in continually infirmity.
I succeed in doing so with those who have always known
with those whom I seldom see; but at the studio, for
they know it there.
how it affects the intelligence! How is it possible

(near Knauf), *Thursday, May 26.*—I needed to
take this long journey, nothing is to be seen on any side
but immense plains. The view is grand: I am delighted
a sense of infinity; where there are villages or forests to be
seen it destroys the effect. What charms me especially here
the lowest of them. The people of the custom-house chat
with you as if they were acquainted with you. But I have

are still thirty before me. These distances make one dizzy to think of.

GAVRONZY, *Sunday, May* 29.—Last night we reached Poltava.

Paul has grown frightfully stout.

This morning Kapranenko, Wolkovisky, and some others came to see us. My father is very happy, but a little troubled at seeing the melancholy effect this country produces on me after five years of absence. I do not seek to conceal this feeling, and now that I am more familiar with my father I no longer try to humor him.

At dinner a dish dressed with onions was served. I got up and left the dining-room; the Princess and Paul's wife were surprised. Paul's wife is quite pretty; she has superb black hair, a fine complexion, and not a bad figure; she is

. . . . *June* 4—Julian writes that Tony R. F. took cold while driving home from his mother's in an open carriage, and that he has been between life and death ever since. He mourns for him as if he were already dead.

Sunday, June 5.—I telegraphed to Julian yesterday for news about Tony. I am extremely anxious on his

Monday, June 6 (*May* 25).—Tony is out of danger! am delighted. Rosalie burst into tears at the news; she said that if he had died, it would certainly have made me ill. She exaggerates a little, but—she is a good girl. A letter from Julian, containing the good news, arrived at the same . . . .

. . . . peasant-girl, life-size; she stands leaning against a hedge of interwoven branches.

Monday, June 27 (15).—I have sketched out one of my pictures for the Salon. I am delighted with the subject; it is all planned out, and I am burning with impatience to begin.

Wednesday, July 6 (*June* 24).—I have finished my picture: it is better than anything I had done so far; the head, which I have done over three times, is especially good.

Monday.—Nini, her sister, and Dina came for me, where I was working out of doors, to take me back with them to the house. Some one chanced to allude to the superstition that the breaking of a mirror portends misfortune. This reminded me that on one or two occasions I have found three candles together in my room. Does this portend that I am going to die? There are times when the thought of death turns me cold. But I have less fear when I let my mind dwell upon God, though this does not reconcile me to the thought of death. Or perhaps it means that I shall become blind; but that would be the same thing as to die, for I should then kill myself. What shall we find on the other side, though? But what does it matter? At least we escape from our present sorrows. Or perhaps I shall lose my hearing completely; perhaps I shall grow deaf. The very thought of this word, that it scorches my pen to write, enrages me. My God—but I cannot now even pray as formerly. What if it should portend the death of a near relation—of my father, for instance? Or of mamma? I should never be able to console myself, in that case, for the many unkind words I have spoken to her.

Doubtless what most displeases God with me is that I take note of all the inward movements of my soul, thinking, involuntarily, that such a thought will be set down to my credit, such another to my discredit. For, from the moment in which we recognize a thought to be good, all the merit

of it is lost.   If I have some generous, or noble, or pious
impulse, I am immediately conscious of it ; as a consequence
I involuntarily experience a feeling of satisfaction on
account of the benefit that must accrue to my soul from
this.   And because of these thoughts the merit of the
action resulting from this impulse is lost.   Thus, a moment
since it occurred to me to go downstairs and throw myself
into mamma's arms, and ask her to forgive me for all my
past unkindness to her, and naturally the thought that followed this impulse was favorable to myself, and all the
merit of it was at an end.   I felt afterward that to have
carried out my intention would not have benefited me much,
for that, in spite of myself, I should have done it a little
cavalierly, or awkwardly ; for a genuine, serious expansion
of feeling between us would not be possible ; she has
always seen me turn everything into ridicule ; to do anything else would not seem natural in me ; she would think
I was acting a part.

Monday, July 11.—To-day is the feast of St. Paul.   I
have on a ravishing gown ; Dina, too, looks charming.   I
laughed and chatted awhile with Lihopay and Micha, as
amiably as if it amused me.   The others listened to our
witty sayings.   Then we danced, papa and mamma together,
having Paul and his wife for their *vis-a-vis.*   Dina, in the
wildest spirits, danced alone, one fantastic dance after
another, and really with a great deal of grace.   I, too, notwithstanding this dreadful affliction (my deafness) which is
turning me gray, danced for a few minutes, but without
gayety or even the pretense of it.

Friday, July 15.—We are at Karkoff ; I cough a great
deal and breathe with difficulty.   I have just been looking
at myself in the glass, expecting to see traces of my malady;
but no, there is nothing as yet.   I am slender but far from

being thin, and then my bare shoulders have a smooth and rosy appearance that does not agree with my cough, nor with the sounds to be heard in my throat. I cannot hear as well as formerly, however. I have taken cold, and that is probably the reason why my cough is worse. Ah, well!

Mamma and I went into one of the convents here, to-day, and mamma knelt down and prayed with fervor before an image of the Virgin. How can any one pray to a picture? I had, indeed, intended doing so, but I could not. It is different when the desire comes to me of itself, when I am in my own room—then I feel the better for having prayed. And I believe that God can cure me, but God only. Before doing so, however, He would have to forgive me first for so many little sins!

Saturday, July 16.—This morning Pacha, my old admirer, arrived here. He has grown stouter, but he is still the same rude and uncultivated, but harmless being, as before.

Thursday, July 21.—Here we are at Kieff, the "holy city," the "mother of Russian cities," according to St. Wladimir, who, having received baptism himself, afterward baptized all his people, with their own consent or without it, as the case might be, driving them into the waters of the Dnieper. Some of them must have been drowned, I fancy. What troubled the imbeciles most, however, was the fate of their idols, which were cast into the river at the same time that the people were baptized in its waters. The rest of the world is so ignorant with regard to everything that concerns Russia that I shall perhaps tell you something you did not know before, when I say that the Dnieper is one of the most beautiful rivers in the world, and that its banks are extremely picturesque. The houses in Kieff have an appearance of being thrown together in confusion, *pêle mêle*, no matter how, as it were. There is an upper city and a lower city, and the streets are very steep. This is not very agreeable, for the distances are enormous, but it is picturesque. Nothing remains of the ancient city. The Russian civilization of that time contented itself with constructing mean temples, without art or solidity, to which fact it is due that we possess few or no monuments of the past. If I were given to exaggeration, I should say that there are as many churches in the city as there are dwelling-houses. There are also a great many cathedrals and convents ; in fact, three or four of these buildings may at times be seen standing together in a row, all adorned with numerous gilded cupolas ; the walls and columns are whitewashed and the roofs and cornices are green. Often the entire façade of the structure is covered with pictures of the saints, and scenes from their lives, but all executed with extreme crudeness.

We first visited La Lavra, a convent which thousands of pilgrims from all parts of Russia come to visit every day.

The *iconostase*, or partition that separates the altar from the body of the church, is covered with images of the saints, either painted or inlaid with silver. The shrines, and the doors, which are completely covered with silver, must have cost an immense amount of money ; the coffins of the saints too, which are inlaid with wrought silver, and the candelabra and candlesticks, all of the same metal, must be of great value. They say these monks have in their possession sacks full of precious stones.

Mamma prayed with unexampled fervor. I am quite sure that Dina and papa prayed for me also.

The miracle did not take place, however. You laugh? Well, as for me I almost counted upon it. I attach no importance whatever to churches, relics, or masses ; no, but I relied on their prayers, on my prayers. And I rely upon them still. God has not yet heard my prayer, but perhaps one day He will. I believe only in God ; but is the God I

believe in a God who listens to us, and who concerns Himself in our affairs ?

God may not restore me to health, all of a sudden, in a
church. I have not deserved this ; but He will have compassion on me and inspire some doctor who will cure me—
or perhaps He will suffer time to do so. But I shall not
cease to pray.

As for mamma, she believes in images and relics—her
religion, in a word, is paganism—as is the case with the
greater number of people who are devout and—not very
intelligent.

Perhaps the miracle would have taken place if I had
believed in the power of images and relics. But at the
same time that I knelt and prayed I could not succeed in
doing this. I can more easily understand how one should
kneel down anywhere else, and pray to God quite simply.
God is everywhere. But how believe in these things ? It
appears to me that this species of fetichism is an insult to
God and a wrong done Him. In the case of the majority
of persons,—of the pilgrims, for instance,—God is lost
sight of ; they see nothing but a piece of dry flesh that has
the power to work a miracle, or a wooden image to which
they may pray, and which will hear their prayers. Am I
wrong ? Are they right ?

PARIS, *Tuesday, July* 26.—I am at last here ! This is
to live ! Among other places, I went to the studio ; they
received me there with kisses and cries of welcome.

Wednesday, July 27.—I mentioned to Julian a subject I
had thought of for a painting, but he was not very enthusiastic about it. And then for two hours he did nothing but
talk to me of my health, and that without any disguise.
He thinks my condition serious. He may well think so,
since two months' treatment have made no change in it for

the better.   I know myself that it is serious; that I grow
worse every day; that I am gradually fading away; and at
the same time I refuse to believe such horrible things.
Breslau has received her honorable mention.   She has already had some orders.   Madame M   , who has taken a
great interest in her, and at whose house she has met the
most celebrated artists in Paris, has given her an order for
her portrait, for the coming *Salon*.   She has already sold
three or four pictures; in short, she is on the road to fortune.   And I?—And I am a consumptive!   Julian tries
to frighten me so as to induce me to take care of myself.
I would take care of myself if I had any confidence in the
result.   It is a melancholy fate to befall one at my age.
Julian is in truth right.   In a year from now I shall see how
changed I shall be; that is to say that there will be then
nothing left of me.   I went to day to visit Colignon.   She
will die soon; there is one who is indeed changed!   Rosalie had prepared me for it, but I was shocked to see her;
she looks like death itself.

Can you not fancy you already see me feeble, emaciated,·
pale, dying, dead?

Is it not atrocious that this should be so?   But, dying
young, I shall at least inspire every one with pity.   I am
myself touched with compassion when I think of my fate.
No, it does not seem possible!   Nice, Rome, my girlish
dreams, the mad delights of Naples, art, ambition, illimit-
able hopes—all to end in a coffin, without ever having possessed anything—even love!

I was right; it is not possible to live, constituted as I
am, when one's life is such as mine has been from childhood.   To live to be old would have been too much to expect in such circumstances.

And yet we see people who are more fortunate than I
ever hoped to be, even in my wildest dreams.

For every other sorrow there may be found some consolation; but for the pangs of wounded vanity there is none; they are worse than death itself. And what of disappointed affection, of absence from those we love? These, at least, are not death. I can scarcely keep back my tears; I believe that my health is irretrievably ruined, and that I am going to die. But it is not that I complain of, it is my deafness! And then, just now, Breslau; but Breslau is a blow that was not needed. Everywhere beaten, everywhere repulsed.

Well, then, let death come.

Tuesday, August 9.—I went to the doctor's this morning; this is the third time in two weeks; he makes me go to him so that he may receive a louis for every visit, for the treatment is always the same.

Truly it is enough to drive one mad. They say that in a thousand cases of the disease I suffer from, in not more than one case does deafness occur, and that happens to be precisely my case. We see people who suffer from the throat, people who have consumption, every day, but they do not become deaf. Ah, it is such an unlooked-for misfortune! It was not enough that I should lose my voice, that I should lose my health, but this unspeakable torture must be added to my other trials. This must be a judgment upon me for complaining about trifles. Is it God who thus chastises me? The God of pardon, of goodness, of mercy? But the most cruel of men could not be more pitiless than this!

I am in a state of constant torture. To have to blush before my family; to be made to feel their complaisance in raising their voices when they speak to me! To be obliged to tremble every time I enter a shop lest I should betray my deafness! Then it is not so bad, however, but when I am with my friends—all the stratagems I am compelled to make use of to conceal my infirmity! No, no, no, it is too cruel, it is too frightful, it is too terrible! And the models—when I am painting! I am not always able to hear what they say to me, and I tremble every time I think they are going to address me. Do you think my work does not show the effects of this? When Rosalie is present she helps me, but when I am alone I grow dizzy, my tongue refuses to say, "Speak a little louder, I cannot hear very well!" My God! have pity upon me! And to cease to believe in God would be to die of despair! First, the sore throat, then the affection of the lungs, and now deafness. Now I must undergo treatment for that! But—I have always been under treatment. Dr. Krishaber is to blame for all this; it is in consequence of his treatment that I—

My God, must I then be so cruelly cut off from communication with the rest of the world? And it is I, I, I! who have to bear this. There are many people to whom it would not be so terrible a misfortune, but to me—

Oh, what a terrible thing!

Thursday, August 11.—I go to Passy every day, but I have no sooner begun work on a picture than I conceive a horror of what I have done. And I injure my eyes, and waste my time reading in order to quiet my nerves.

And there is no one whom I can consult in regard to my doubts. Tony is in Switzerland, Julian is in Marseilles.

It may be true that I have no greater cause for complaint than others have. This may be so; but it is equally true that I am no longer good for anything! Social life, politics, intellectual enjoyments—in none of these can I take a part, except through the medium of a fog, as it were, through which everything reaches my senses dulled and confused.

And should I venture to seek these pleasures, I would only run the risk of covering myself with ridicule or of being taken for a fool. All the eccentricities, the fits of

absent-mindedness, the brusqueness I must affect, only to
conceal from Saint-Amand the fact that I cannot hear well!
It is enough to discourage the stoutest heart. How is it
possible to confess that one is deaf, when one is young and
elegant, and pretends to be able to do everything? How
is it possible to solicit indulgence or pity in such circumstances? Besides, of what use would it all be? My head
feels splitting, and I no longer know where I am. Oh, no!
there is no God such as I have imagined God to be. There
is a Supreme Being, there is Nature, there is, there is—
but the God I have prayed to every day, this God does not
exist. That God should deny me everything—well and
good; but to torture me to death in this manner! To
render me more wretched, more dependent than any beggar
in the street! And what crime have I committed? I am
not a saint, it is true. I do not spend my life in churches;
I do not fast. But you know what my life has been—with
the exception of treating my family disrespectfully, who do
not deserve it from me, I have nothing to reproach myself
with. Of what use would it be to ask pardon every night
in my prayers for being compelled by circumstances to say
disagreeable things to my family? For if it be true that I
am to blame with regard to mamma, you know well it was in
order to spur her to action that I have spoken harshly to her.

Friday, August 12.—You think perhaps that I have
decided upon a subject for my picture? I can do nothing.
I am possessed by the horrible certainty of my incapacity.
Here is a month or more gone already, counting the time
lost in traveling, during which I have done nothing. I am
disappointed beforehand with my work; I see it in imagination, without a trace of animation, beauty, or genius. It is
odious! I can do nothing!

Saturday, August 13.—You are not ignorant of the fact

that my right lung is affected ; well, you will no doubt be glad to learn now that the left lung is affected also, though it is true that none of those idiots of doctors have told me so as yet. I felt the first symptoms of this in the catacombs of the relics at Kieff, but I thought it was only a temporary pain caused by the dampness. Since then I have felt it constantly ; to-night it is so severe that I can scarcely draw my breath. I feel it very distinctly between the shoulder-blade and the chest, in the spot where the doctors strike their little blows.

And my picture?

Sunday, August 14.—Last night I could scarcely sleep, and this morning I still feel the pain in my chest.

I have given up the idea of painting my picture—that is decided upon. But how much time I have lost with it!— more than a month.

As for Breslau, encouraged as she must be by her honor-able mention, things are no doubt prospering with her ; for me, my hands are tied ; I have no longer any confidence in myself.

Thursday, August 18.—. . . . I have been looking through my portfolios, where I can follow my progress step by step. I have often said to myself that Breslau knew how to paint before I had begun to draw. "But is this girl the whole world to you, then?" you will say. However this may be, I know it is no petty feeling that makes me fear this rival. I knew from the beginning that she had talent, whatever the professors or our fellow-pupils might say to the contrary. And you see that I was right. Only to think of this girl vexes me. I have felt a stroke of her pencil on one of my drawings like a blow on my heart. This is because I am conscious of a power in her before which I must at last succumb. She always made comparisons between herself and me; the dunces at the studio said she would never know how to paint; that she had no idea of colors; that she only knew how to draw—exactly what they say of me now. That ought to be a consolation to me; indeed it is the only one left me now.

In 1876 (in February) she received the medal for drawing She began to draw in June, 1875, after having studied for two years in Switzerland. As I myself saw, it was not until after she had struggled for two years against the most discouraging failures that she began to succeed in painting. In 1879 she exhibited in accordance with Tony's advice. At this time I had been painting for six months. In a month it will be three years since I first began to paint.

The question now is whether I am capable of doing anything equal to the pictures she exhibited in 1879. Julian says that her picture of 1879 was better than that of 1881, only, as they were not good friends, he made no effort to push her forward, although he refrained from doing anything to keep her back. Her picture of last year was placed, as mine was, in the *morgue*, that is to say, in the outer gallery.

This year she made her peace with Julian, and finding favor with the new school also, she was placed on the line. The medal follows, as a matter of course.

Saturday, August 20.—I have been to see Falguiere, the sculptor. I told him I was an American, and showed him some of my drawings, telling him of my desire to study sculpture; a few of these he thought excellent, and the others good. He directed me to a studio where he gives lessons, saying that should I not succeed in making arrangements there, his instructions were at my service either at my own house or at his. This was very kind on his part, but for a teacher I have Saint Marceaux, whom I adore, and I shall content myself with the studio,

BIARRITZ, *Friday, September* 16.—Having bade ourfriends adieu, we left Paris Thursday morning. We passed the night at Bordeaux, where Sarah Bernhardt was acting. We secured two stalls in the balcony for fifty francs. The play was "Camille." Unfortunately I happened to be very tired ; this actress has been so raved about that I can scarcely tell what I think of her myself. I expected to see her do every-thing in a different way from any one else, and I was a little surprised at the natural manner in which she talked, and walked, and sat down. I have seen her only four times ; once, when I was a child, in " The Sphynx," and again in " The Sphynx" not long ago, and in " L'Etrangere." I paid the greatest attention to her every movement. I think, perhaps, after all, that she is charming.

What there is no doubt about is that Biarritz is beautiful, beautiful !

The sea has been of an enchanting color all day. Such exquisite gray tints !

Saturday, September 17.—So far I have seen none of those extraordinary natural beauties that I expected to see at Biarritz. As for the beach, from an artistic point of view, it is ugly and disagreeable.

Oh, Nice ! Oh, bay of Naples !

Sunday, September 18.—My costume here is a simple gown of batiste or of white flannel. without trimming, but charm-ingly made, boots bought here, and a youthful-looking white hat, a hat such as a happy woman might wear. This forms an *ensemble* that attracts a great deal of attention.

Tuesday, September 27.—We spent the day *en famille,* yesterday at Bayonne ; to-day we spent at Fontarabia, also *en famille.* I seldom go out ; I would like to take a ride, but my riding-habit does not fit me, and then it would bore me to ride in the company of a Russian whom I scarcely know, and whom I find tiresome.

There is a roulette table here at which I tried my luck; when I had lost forty francs I stopped, and occupied myself in sketching instead. I sat in an obscure corner, and I hope no one observed me.

We left Biarritz on Thursday morning, and reached Burgos last night. I was struck by the majestic beauty of the Pyrenees. I made a rough sketch of the Cathedral; but how describe these painted sculptures, these gewgaws, this conglomeration of gilding and ornamentation that go to make up a magnificent whole? The chapels, however, with their immense gratings and shadowy recesses, are wonderful. In the Cathedral is the Magdalen of Leonardo da Vinci. Shall I confess that I found it ugly, and that it caused me no emotion whatever, which, for that matter, was the case with the Madonnas of Raphael also.

Since yesterday morning we have been in Madrid. We went this morning to the Museum. Compared with this collection the Louvre, Rubens, Philippe de Champagne, even Vandyke and the Italian painters, sink into insignificance. There is nothing in the world to equal Velasquez; but I am still too dazzled to be able to judge clearly. And Ribera! He is wonderful! These, these indeed are the true exponents of naturalism! Can there be anything more admirably, more divinely true to nature than these? Ah, how it moves me, and how unhappy it makes me to see such things! Ah, how it makes me long for genius! And they dare to compare the pallid pictures of Raphael, and the uusubstantial paintings of the French school, with these! And the coloring! It is impossible that one who feels color as I do should be unable to produce it.

At nine o'clock this morning I was already at the Museum, among the paintings of Velasquez, beside which those of every other artist look hard and cold, not excepting even those of Ribera, who, indeed, cannot be considered his equal.   In the " Portrait of an unknown Sculptor " there is a hand which is the clue to the secret of Carolus Duran's admirable execution : the latter, as is well known, purposes editing the works of Velasquez.

We•bought a Spanish guitar and a Spanish mandolin. The rest of the world has no idea of what Spain is like. And they say Madrid is less distinctively Spanish than the cities we have yet to see—Toledo, Granada, Seville.   Such as it is, I am enchanted to be here.   I am feverishly eager to get my hand in by copying something at the Museum, and afterward painting a picture, even if I should have to stay here two months to do it.

Thursday.—I have copied the hand of the Velasquez.   I went to the Museum, dressed quietly in black, with a mantilla, such as all the women here wear ; yet a great many persons came to stand behind my chair and look on while I worked—one man in particular.

It seems that in the matter of gallantry the men in Madrid are even worse than those in Italy ; they walk up and down under their mistresses' windows, playing the guitar ; they follow you and talk to you in the street, and they are persistent in their attentions.   Love-letters are exchanged in church, and every young girl has five or six of these admirers ; they are extraordinarily gallant with ladies, without, however, transgressing the bounds of delicacy ; they accost you in the street and tell you that you are beautiful and that they adore you ; they ask in all honor and good faith, knowing that you are a lady, to be allowed to accompany you.

Here you may see men spread their cloaks on the ground that you may pass over them.   For my part I find all this delightful.   Whenever I walk in the streets, tastefully and simply dressed, as is my custom, the men stop to look at me. This makes me feel a new life ; it is a romantic and novel existence, colored with the chivalry of the middle ages.

Sunday, October 9.—As I was painting at the Museum, two men, neither of whom was young or handsome, came up and asked me if I were not Mlle. Bashkirtseff. I answered that I was ; they appeared delighted. M. Soldatenkoff is a millionnaire from Moscow, who has traveled a great deal, and who adores art and artists. Pollack told me afterwards that Madrazo, the son of the director of the Museum, and himself an artist, admired my copy very much, and asked to be presented to me. Soldatenkoff asked me if I wished to part with the picture, and I was so foolish as to say no.

As for painting, I am on the way to learn a great deal about it here. I can see things now that I never saw before. I keep my eyes wide open ; I walk around on tiptoe ; I scarcely dare to breathe, so to speak, lest the spell should be broken, for it is a veritable spell ; I hope at last to realize my dreams. I think I know now how to set to work ; all my energies are directed toward the one absorbing aim—to produce something that shall be good, that shall be real flesh—something lifelike—and when I can do that I can do greater things; for everything— everything is in the execution. What is the "Vulcan's Forge" of Velasquez, or his "Spinners"? Take away from these paintings their wonderful execution, and nothing but commonplace figures remain. I know that many people will cry out in disapproval of this, beginning with the fools who pretend to adore feeling ; and feeling, indeed, is much ; it is the poetry of style, the chief charm of art. This is more true than we are apt to think. Do you admire the primitive style of art ? its crude and meagre forms, its smooth execution ? It is curious and interesting, but it is impossible to admire it.   Do you admire the Virgins in the cartoons of Raphael?   I shall be considered wanting in taste, but I confess that they do not touch me; there is in them a feeling and a nobility of style that command my respect, but I cannot admire them.   There are some other compositions of Raphael, however, as the "School of Athens" for instance, that are admirable, incomparable; especially engraved or photographed.   There is feeling in them, thought, true genius.   Observe that I dislike equally the gross flesh of Rubens, and the magnificent, but soulless, flesh of Titian.   Soul is as necessary in a painting as body.   The true artist should conceive as a man of genius, and execute as a poet.

Monday, October 10.—I dreamed last night that they were explaining to me what was the matter with my right lung ; into certain portions of it the air cannot penetrate, and this causes an accumulation—but it is too disgusting to describe ; let it suffice that the lung is affected.   And I am convinced that it is so, for I have felt a species of *malaise* for some time past—a debility, for which I cannot account.   In short, I have a strange sort of feeling as if I were different from other people ; as if I were surrounded by an enervating atmosphere, so to speak ; I feel a peculiar sensation in my chest, I have—But why describe all these symptoms ?—the disease will soon make itself sufficiently evident.

Wednesday, October 12.—I am finishing my copy of the "Vulcan" of Velasquez, and if I am to judge by what the public think of it, it must be good.   The poor devils of artists, who make copies on a reduced scale of celebrated pictures for sale, come often during the day to watch me while I work, and the young fellows from the School of Fine Arts, as well as many of the visitors, French, English,

and Spanish, discuss my work among themselves, and say
the most flattering things of me.

Friday, October 14.—At seven o'clock yesterday we set
out for Toledo. I had heard so much of this city that I
expected to see something wonderful. In defiance of
reason and common-sense I had pictured it to myself as
something in the style of the Renaissance and the Middle
Ages—with marvelous buildings, sculptured doors blackened with time, balconies exquisitely carved, etc. I knew
very well it must be quite different from all this, but such
was the image of it fixed upon my mind ; and the contrast
it formed with the thin walls and broken-down gates of
the city, as they presented themselves to my view, spoiled
Toledo for me. Toledo is situated on a height like a
citadel ; it is a labyrinth of little streets, narrow and
crooked, into which the sun never penetrates, and where
the inhabitants seem to be camping out, so little do their
houses resemble ordinary dwellings. It is a Pompeii preserved entire, but looking as if it might crumble into dust
at any moment, through age ; the soil is parched, and the
high walls burned by the sun ; there are wonderfully
picturesque courtyards, mosques converted into churches,
and daubed with whitewash, beneath which may be seen,
however, where this peels off, paintings and arabesques of
which the colors are still vivid, with ceilings of carved
wood divided into compartments, that have grown black
with time, and beams crossing each other curiously overhead. The cathedral is as fine as that of Burgos, and is
profusely ornamented ; its doors are marvels of beauty,
and the cloister, with its courtyard filled with oleanders
and rose-bushes, that have made their way into the galleries and twined themselves around the pillars and the
somber statues—there is an indescribable charm about all
this, when a ray of sunlight falls upon it.

No one, who has not seen them, can form an idea of the Spanish churches—the guides in rags, the sacristan in velvet, strangers walking around, or kneeling down praying, dogs barking—all this has a wonderful charm. One almost expects, on coming out of one of these chapels, to meet suddenly, behind some pillar, the idol of one's soul.

It is incredible that a country so near the center of European corruption should be still so primitive, so uncontaminated, so rude.

And what colonnades, what pilasters, what antique doors, studded with large Spanish or Moorish nails! Everything is a picture. One has not even the trouble of choosing ; all that is to be seen is odd and interesting.

Sunday, October 16.— One of the most curious things to be seen is the Rastro,—a street lined with booths, resembling the shops in Russian villages, where all sorts of things are to be found. And what life, what animation, under this burning sun ! It is wonderful ! Here marvelous articles of bric-a-brac are stored away in dirty houses. In little back-shops and up romantic staircases are to be found such stuffs as might make one wild with rapture.

And their wretched owners seem to be absolutely indifferent to the value of these things ; they pierce the most beautiful stuffs, with which the walls are covered, with nails on which to hang up old pictures ; they walk over embroideries spread out upon the floor, over pieces of antique furniture, pictures, sculptures, reliquaries, silver-ware, and old rusty nails all heaped together. I bought an embroidered curtain of a reddish salmon color, for which they asked me seven hundred francs and gave me for a hundred and fifty, and a cloth skirt embroidered with flowers of a pale pretty tint, for a hundred sous, after they had asked me twenty francs for it.

Escobar came to-day to take us to see the bull-fight.

Eight bulls had been announced to appear, and it was, 1 believe, the last Sunday of the season. The spectacle was a brilliant one ; the King, the Queen, and the Infanta were all in their places. There were music and sunshine, wild cries, stampings of the feet, and hisses ; handkerchiefs were waved, hats thrown in the air. The spectacle is a unique one of overpowering grandeur. I began after a time to enter into the spirit of the thing, and to take an interest in what was going on, though I had gone there against my inclinations, and with a shudder of disgust. In full view of this butchery, carried on with the utmost refinement of cruelty, I was able to maintain a tranquil air, sustained by my pride. I did not once turn my eyes away. One leaves the scene slightly intoxicated with blood, so to say, and feeling a desire to thrust a lance into the neck of every chance person one meets.

I stuck my knife into the melon I was cutting at table, as if it were a *banderilla* I were planting in the hide of a bull, and the pulp seemed like the palpitating flesh of the wounded animal. The sight is one that makes the knees tremble and the head throb. It is a lesson in murder. Yet these men are elegant and graceful, and notwithstanding their extreme agility their movements are dignified and noble.

Some people regard this duel between man and brute, in which the latter seems to have so much the advantage, both in size and strength, over the former, as a noble spectacle ; but can it with truth be called a duel, when one knows from the first which of the combatants it is that must succumb? I will confess that there is something to captivate the imagination in the sight of the *matador*, with his brilliant costume, that displays the graceful contours of his figure, as he places himself, after thrice saluting the spectators, just in front of the animal, and stands calm and self-possessed, his cloak on his arm, his sword in his hand.

And this is the best part of the performance, for so far there is scarcely any blood shed. As for the sufferings of the horses, the Spaniards themselves do not like that part of it. Have I become reconciled, then, to this barbarous amusement? I do not say that, but it has its grand, almost its heroic, side. In this amphitheater with its fourteen or fifteen thousand spectators, we seem to catch a glimpse of antiquity—that antiquity I so much admire. But on the other hand it has also its sanguinary, its horrible, its ignoble side. If the men who engage in it were less skillful; if they were more often to receive a serious wound or two, I should say nothing. But what revolts me in it is this exhibition of human cowardice. Yet it is said the profession of a *matador* requires the courage of a lion. I do not think so. These men know very well how to avoid the attacks of the brute, terrible it is true, but attacks which they themselves have provoked, and which they are prepared for. The real danger is in the case of the *banderillero*, where the man invites the attack of the animal, and just as the latter is about to transfix him with his horns, anticipates him by planting his *banderillas* between the shoulders of the brute. For this, exceptional courage and skill are required.

Wednesday, October 19.—I cough so violently that I fear it must end by causing some injury to the lungs. And along with this I am growing thin, or rather—yes, I am growing thin; look at my arm, for instance; when I stretch it out it has a delicate look, instead of its former insolently robust one. It is pretty, still, however. I do not complain as yet. This is the interesting period, when one is slender without being thin, and there is a certain air of languor in my appearance that is very becoming; but if I continue thus, in a year more I shall be a skeleton.

Thursday, October 20.—I spent two hours in Cordova this morning—just the time necessary to take a glance at the city, which is charming—in its way. And I adore cities like Cordova ; there are some Roman ruins that absolutely enchanted me, and the mosque is a veritable wonder.

Saturday, October 22.—Well, here we are in Seville, this much-vaunted city. Indeed I lose a great deal of time here. I have seen the Museum—a single hall full of Murillos ; I would have liked better to see something else, especially here ; there are only Virgins and other sacred pictures. I, rude and ignorant barbarian as I am, with whom the opinions of others have but little weight, have never yet seen a Virgin such as I imagine her to have been. The Virgins of Raphael are beautiful in photographs ; I confess that the Virgins of Murillo, with their round faces and rosy cheeks, appeal but little either to my imagination or my heart. I will make an exception in favor of that in the Louvre, however, which has been so extensively copied ; that is the one which is painted with most feeling ; indeed, it might almost be characterized as divine.

And the manufactory of cigars and cigarettes ! What an odor prevails there ! If it was only that of the tobacco, well and good ! But the building is crowded with women in bare necks and arms, little girls, and children, most of whom are very pretty. Our visit here was an interesting one. The Spanish women are endowed with a grace not to be found among any other people. Cigarette-rollers, women who sing in cafes, walk with the air of a queen. And the way in which the head is set upon the shoulders ! And such arms, round and beautifully molded, and rich in coloring. They are indeed captivating and wonderful creatures.

Tuesday, October 25.—We have seen the Cathedral,

which is, in my opinion, one of the most beautiful, as well as one of the largest, cathedrals in the world ; the Alcazar, with its delightful gardens, and the Bath of the Sultans ; afterward we took a stroll through the streets. I do not exaggerate when I say that we were the only women who wore hats, so that it is to our hats I attribute the attention we attracted.

If I had even been more elegantly dressed, but I wore a gray woolen dress, a black coat, and a black traveling hat. But strangers here are regarded somewhat as learned monkeys might be ; people stop to look at them, and either hoot at them or pay them compliments.

The children hoot at me, but the grown-up people tell me I am beautiful and *salada ;* to be salada is, as you know, to be very *chic*.

Seville is white—all white ; the streets are narrow ; through a few of them only can a carriage pass ; and yet it is not so picturesque as one would expect to find it. Ah, Toledo ! I perceive now what a barbarian I am !

These half-savage women and children in their rags are wonderful in coloring. The view is ravishing, notwithstanding the bare look of the white houses. But it rains all the time ; and then, I am *en famille.*

I expected to meet with no end of amusing adventures in Seville, and I am so bored that I remain in my room in the hotel almost all the time, and then, it rains without ceasing.

There is no romance here, no poetry, no youth even. There is nothing—I repeat it, there is nothing to interest me in Seville ; I feel as if I were buried alive—as I felt this summer in Russia. Why all this traveling ? And my painting ? It is now five months since I was at the studio. Of these five months I have lost three in travel—I, who have so much need to work. The mention of Breslau has awakened a world of thoughts within me, or rather it has brought nearer to me, it has rendered possible, and given a character of reality to that dream of the medal of the *Salon* which was so far in the distance, which I dreamed of in the romances I wove before going to sleep at night, as I dreamed of receiving the cross of the Legion of Honor, or of being Queen of Spain. When Villevielle came to announce to me the probability of Breslau's mention, she looked as if she thought it made me—in short, others, by admitting that I might dare to dream of a prize, have given me the daring to dream of it ; or rather, to say to myself that since others think I might hope to receive it, there must be a possibility of my doing so. In brief, for the past five months I have cherished this dream.

It appears as if I were digressing, but all the events of life are linked one with another. Lorenzo's studio would be a good subject for a picture.

Thursday, October 27.—Oh, happiness ! I have quitted that frightful Seville !

I say frightful, the more especially because since last night we have been in Grenada, because we have been sight-seeing since morning, and because I have already seen the inevitable Cathedral, the Generalife, and something of the caves of the Gypsies. I am in a state of rapture. At Biarritz and Seville I felt as if my hands were tied, as if everything were at an end—dead. From the little I saw of Cordova it impressed me as being an artistic city ; that is to say, I felt that I could have worked there with enthusiasm. As for Grenada there is only one thing I regret, and that is that I cannot remain here for six months or a year. I don't know on what side to turn, there are so many things to be seen. Such streets ! such views ! such outlines !

To-morrow I am to visit the Alhambra, and to sketch the head of a convict which I am going to paint.

Friday, October 28.—I spend yesterday, accordingly, in the prison of Grenada. The prisoners enjoy a delightful degree of liberty ; the courtyard looks like a market-place, the doors do not even appear to close well ; in brief this prison bears no resemblance whatever to the descriptions we read of the French prisons.

The prisoner condemned to death walks up and down the courtyard with the same freedom as the one condemned to imprisonment for a year or two for some trifling offense.

Saturday, October 29.—At last I have seen the Alhambra. I refrained purposely from devoting much attention to its beauties ; in the first place, so that I might not become too much attached to Grenada, and in the second place, because our guide interfered by his presence with my artistic enjoy-ment. I promise myself to revisit it, however.

Grenada, seen from the tower, is wonderfully beautiful— the mountains covered with snow, the gigantic trees, the shrubs, the exquisite flowers, the cloudless sky, and then the city itself, with its white h uses bathed in sunshine, sur-rounded by all these natural beauties ; the Moorish walls, the tower of the Generalife, and the Alhambra ! And, far as the eye can reach. a sea of space ; indeed, nothing but the sea itself is wanting to make this the most delightful country in the world. There is nothing that can be com-pared to the majestic grace of these superb draperies. My mind is filled with thoughts of Boabdil and his Moorish companions whom I can fancy I see walking through the halls of this palace, unique of its kind.

Sunday, October 30.—Grenada is as picturesque and artistic as Seville is commonplace, notwithstanding her famous school. The streets of Grenada are almost all wonderfully picturesque.

One is dazzled and distracted in every sense. One might

copy the first chance view one sees, and it would be a picture.

I shall return here next August to remain until the middle of October. ·

Monday, October 31.—I am glad that the cold drives me away, for otherwise I could not make up my mind to leave this country, and it is necessary for me to return to Paris. It is five months since I have seen Tony, and it is time for me to think of hiring a studio so as to be able to paint my picture for the *Salon* at my leisure, and with my utmost skill. The first year did not count ; the year after you know how short was the time I had in which to prepare my picture, besides the other drawbacks ; but this year I hope to send something really interesting.

I should like to paint the bric-a-brac shop of Lorenzo—a brilliant light falling on the staircase at the further end, with a woman in the background arranging some draperies on this species of *estrade.* In the foreground another woman bending down, engaged in cleaning some brass ornaments, and a man who stands looking at her with his hands in his pockets, smoking a cigar.

The women would be dressed in their ordinary chintz gowns, which I could buy in Madrid. I have almost all the other accessories ; all that would remain to be done is the arrangement of the *estrade*, which would cost a hundred francs or so. But it would be necessary to find a studio large enough. Well, we shall see. We are to set out to-night, and I can scarcely contain myself for joy.

My travels in Spain will have the good effect of curing me of eating simply for the sake of eating ; which is a waste of time and dulls the intelligence. I have become as abstemious as an Arab, and eat only what is strictly neces-sary—just enough to sustain life.

Wednesday, November 2.—Here we are again in Madrid, where I came a week ago, to remain three days in the hope of retouching a sketch of the shop of Lorenzo.

Although she had heard me speak of nothing but this for some days past, and knew how impatient I was to reach Madrid, it was quite natural, was it not, that my aunt should come, ready dressed to go out, and say to me ; " Well, shall we spend the day doing our shopping ? " And when I answered that I was going to paint, she looked at me in astonishment and told me I was crazy.

An idea strikes me : I think I have found a subject for a picture ; I collect all my energies : the vision takes form in my mind, I sketch it out, I am completely absorbed in my work ; I rack my brain to find a harmonious arrangement,—and just as I think I have found it, and am trying to fix it upon my mind before it vanishes, comes some one of that dear family who are so uneasy every time I cough, to interrupt me. And yet I am not exceptionally sensitive, either ! Compared with other artists, indeed, I regard myself as exceedingly practical, though not sufficiently so, as you see. Ah, thoughtless and careless family ! they will never understand that any one less strong, less energetic, less buoyant in spirit than I am would be already dead !

Saturday, November 5.—I am back in Paris ! What happiness ! I counted the hours, as I sat shivering in the railway coach, until we arrived. The recollection of the scorching sun and the burning air of Spain makes the cool, subdued tints of this beautiful city seem refreshing to my senses, and I think with delight of the ceramics of the Louvre—I who was bored to death by the very thought of them before.

Julian thought I should not return until much later—and then, ill ; that perhaps, indeed, I should not return at all.

Ah, how sweet is sympathy !—and above all, how sweet
is art !

Tuesday, November 15.—I have shown Julian a sketch
of a picture, which he approves of. But he no longer
inspires me with confidence ; he looks confused when he
speaks to me ; in short, I can imagine what he is thinking
about.

Tony is still left me, but I have not cultivated his friendship as I have Julian's, and then—well, we shall see.

Thursday, November 17.—Yesterday I could scarcely
drag myself about ; my throat pained me, my chest pained
me, my back pained me, I coughed, I had a cold in the
head, I could swallow nothing, and I was hot and cold by
turns a dozen times in the course of the day.

I am a little better to-day, but that is not saying much,
considering that I am now, and have been for a long time
past, under the care of the greatest physicians in the world !
For ever since the time when I first lost my voice they
have been treating me. Yes, that is the ring of Polycrates
that I have thrown into the sea,—very much against my
will, it is true.

Monday, November 21.—They sent for Potain on Wednesday ; he came to-day ; in the mean time I might have died.

I knew very well that he would again order me South ; I
set my teeth hard, and my voice trembled, and it was only
by an effort that I could keep back my tears.

To go South ! That is to acknowledge myself conquered. And the persecutions of my family make it a
point of honor with me to keep on my feet, in any case.
To go away would be to give all the *vermin* of the studio
cause for triumph—to make them say, " She is very ill ;
they have taken her South."

Tuesday, November 22.—I cannot describe the feeling of despair which this banishment to the South would cause me. I should feel as if everything were ended—I who came back intoxicated with the idea of leading a quiet life—a life devoted to study—hard study, study without relaxation; of keeping up with the times. And now to see all this at an end!

And while the others are steadily progressing here in Paris, the home of art, I shall be down there doing nothing, or making futile attempts to paint a picture in the open air, which is something frightfully difficult to do.

There is Breslau—it is not her picture of a peasant woman that has won her a reputation—my heart is ready to break at the thought of it all!

This evening I saw Charcot, who says the disease is no worse than it was last year; as for the trouble I have had for the past six days, it is a simple cold that I shall soon be well of. In regard to my going South, he thinks as Potain does—I must either go there or shut myself up in the house like a prisoner. Otherwise I run the risk of being seriously ill, seeing that the right lung is affected, although it appears there is still some hope of my getting well; it is a curable disease, confined to one spot, and it grows no worse, notwithstanding my pretended imprudences. They said the same thing last year, about going South, and I would not even listen to them. Now I hesitate, and I have done nothing since four o'clock but cry at the thought of leaving Paris, and again interrupting my studies.

It is true that if I am to be often as ill as I have been for these last few days I should profit little by remaining in Paris.

To yield, to acknowledge myself beaten, to say " Yes, the doctors are right,—yes, I am ill "—this is the thought that renders me desperate.

Saturday, November 26.—I was to have gone to see Tony, as you may remember, to show him my sketch, and decide upon some subject for a picture, that I was to paint under his guidance; but I have not left the house. I am weak, and I can eat nothing; I am probably still feverish. It is horribly sad to be kept in this state of inaction by—by—I don't know what, by want of strength; in short, Charcot has resumed his visits.

Mamma and Dina arrived yesterday, recalled by the foolish dispatches of my aunt. This morning Dina received a letter from her sister asking how I was.

I have taken cold, I know, but that might happen to any one.

But no; everything is ended; my hearing is in a deplorable state with this cold and this fever. What can I aspire to? What can I attain to? There is no longer anything to hope for. It is as if a veil had been torn from before my eyes, that day nearly a week ago. Everything is at an end—everything, everything.

Tuesday, November 29.—Well, this has lasted now for fourteen days, and will probably last fourteen days longer. Madame Nachet brought me a bunch of violets to-day, which I accepted as any one might have done, for notwithstanding the fever, which has not left me for two weeks, and a congestion of the right lung, otherwise pleurisy, and two blisters, I have not yet given in; I get up every day and act in every way like an ordinary person, only the quinine makes me deaf. The other night I thought I should die of terror, because I could no longer hear the ticking of my watch; and it seems I must go on taking it.

Otherwise I feel almost strong, and if it were not that I have been able to swallow nothing for the last fortnight, I should scarcely be aware that I am ill.

But my work, my picture, my poor picture! It is now

the 29th of November, and I shall never be able to com-
mence it before the end of December; I shall not be able
to finish it in two months and a half. What a piece of ill-
luck! And how useless it is when one has been born to
misfortune to struggle against Fate! You see painting
was a sort of refuge for me, and now at times I can hardly
hear; the consequences of this are the greatest embarrassment with the models, continual anguish of spirit, and the
impossibility of painting a portrait unless I make up my
mind to acknowledge my infirmity—a thing I have not yet
the courage to do. Then this illness, the impossibility of
going on with my work, and the necessity of shutting myself
up in the house for a month. It is too much!

Dina never leaves me; she is so good!

Paul and his wife arrived yesterday. The Gavinis and
Gery, Bojidar and Alexis also came. And I try to keep up
my courage and extricate myself from the embarrassing
situations that are continually presenting themselves, by
dint of joking and bravado.

The doctors are the subjects of our pleasantries just now.
As Potain cannot come himself every day, he has sent me a
doctor who will come in his stead.

And this serves to amuse me, because I pretend to be
crazy, and avail myself of this pretended madness to give
utterance to the wildest nonsense.

Wednesday, November 30.—Julian was here last evening;
I could see by his affected cheerfulness that he thinks me
very ill; as for me, I am in the deepest affliction; I can do
nothing, and my picture is at a standstill. But worst of all
is to be able to do nothing! Can you conceive the anguish
of that? To stay with your arms hanging idly by your
sides while others are studying, progressing in their work,
preparing their pictures!

I thought that God had left me painting as a refuge from

my troubles, and I gave myself up entirely to it, and behold! it has failed me, and now there is nothing left for me to do but weep.

Thursday, December 1; *Fri ay, December* 2.—The second of December already! I ought to be at my work; I ought to be looking for the draperies for my picture, and the large vase which figures in the background. But why these details? They only serve to make me shed tears. Yet I feel much stronger; I eat, I sleep, I am almost as well as usual.

But there is congestion of the left lung. That on the right side—the chronic trouble—is better, it seems; but that is of no consequence; it is the acute attack, which might be cured, that will keep me shut up in the house *for a few weeks longer*. It is enough to make one go drown one's-self.

Ah, how cruel it is of God to afflict me in this way! I had my annoyances—family troubles—but they did not touch my inmost heart. I had extraordinary hopes of being a great singer—and I lose my voice; this was the first blow; finally I become accustomed to the loss, I resign myself to it, I get over it, I console myself for it.

"Very well, then," Fate steps in and says, "since you have accommodated yourself to this, you shall be deprived of the power of working."

I can neither study, nor work on my picture, nor do anything else. Here is a delay of a whole winter.—I, who had put all my life into my work. Only those who have been situated as I am, can understand me.

Wednesday, December 7.—What exasperates me most is my illness; yesterday the horrible sub-Potain, who comes to see me once a day, as the great man can only put himself out twice a week to do so—the sub-Potain asked me, as it were casually, if I were preparing for my journey.

Their South !   The bare idea of it puts me in a rage !
At dinner I could not eat for thinking of it, and if Julian
had not come I should have cried all the evening with rage.

Well, then, so much the worse !   But I will not go to
their South.

Friday, December 9.—There is a drawing of Breslau's in
the *Vie Moderne.*   If I had not cried so much I might have
been able to make use of my time while I am ill in making
rough draughts and sketches ; but my hands are still
trembling.

The lung is now free from the congestion, but the temperature is still 38 degrees.   I am playing but a sorry part,
however, in giving you all these details.

I feel that there is no hope for me, and I dare not ask a
question lest I should hear of Breslau's next success.

Ah, my God, hear me, grant me strength, have pity upon
me !

Thursday, December 15.—Here are four weeks and two
days that I have been ill.   When the sub-Potain came I
made a scene by beginning to cry.   He did not know what
course to pursue in order to quiet me ; for abandoning the
subterfuges, nonsensical excuses, and other delightful things
with which I am in the habit of regaling him, I began to utter
complaints and to shed genuine tears, my hair falling loose
about my shoulders the while.   I stammered my infantile
complaints to him in the language of a child.   And to think
that I did it all in cold blood, and that I did not mean a
word of what I said !   And so it is with me when I take
part in a real play—I grow pale in earnest, and I shed genuine tears ; in short, I think I should make a magnificent
actress ; but for the present all I can do is to cough, and I
have scarcely even breath enough left me for that.

Monsieur my father arrived this morning.   Everything

goes on very well, with the exception of Paul's poor wife, who is quite disillusionized, seeing an indifference toward her on his part that is little short of hostility. As for me I am all that is right in regard to her; I gave her a very beautiful emerald given me by mamma, and for which I have no use.

I was a little sorry for it afterward: I might have given it to Dina, who adores jewels; but there is no help for it now.

I do not say that papa is irritating; on the contrary, he resembles me a little, physically as well as mentally (this is a compliment to him), but he will never be able to understand me.

Imagine that he has conceived the project of taking us to our country to spend Easter.

No, it is too much; it is too great a want of consideration, in the present state of my health to speak of taking me to Russia in February or March! I leave it to your own judgment. But let that pass—not to speak of all the rest! Ah, no, I who refused to go South! No, no, no! Let us speak no more of it, decidedly not.

Sunday, December 18.—I have been telling my trouble to Julian; and after doing his best to console me, he advised me to sketch every day whatever I saw that chanced to strike me. What is there to strike me? What do you suppose I should find to strike me in the surroundings amidst which I live? Breslau is poor, but she lives in an eminently artistic sphere; Marie's best friend is a musician; Schoeppi, although of the people, is original; and there is Sara Purser, artiste and philosopher, with whom one may hold discussions on the philosophy of Kant, on life, on the *ego*, and on death, that stimulate thought, and that impress upon the mind what one has heard or read—everything is artistic, even to the neighborhood in which she lives, *Les Ternes*. And the neighborhood in which I live, so clean, so regular, where not a sign of poverty is to be seen, not a tree that is not trimmed, not a street that is not straight. Do I, then, complain of my fate? No, but I wish to say that easy circumstances tend to prevent the development of artistic talent, and that the environment in which one lives is half the individual.

Wednesday, December 21.—To-day I went out for a drive! But wrapped in furs, the carriage-windows closed, and a bear-skin around my feet. Potain said this morning that I might go out if the wind ceased, and if I took precautions. The weather is splendid—and as for precautions!

But that is not the question; it is Breslau "that will not let go her prey." My picture for the *Salon* is accepted. What shall I have to show beside her picture this summer?

This girl is a power in my life; there are others, it is true; but she and I are of the same cage, not to say of the same nest, and I divined her genius from the beginning, and announced it to you, little as I then knew of art. I despise myself; I refuse to believe that I have any talent; I cannot understand why Julian and Tony should speak of me as they do; I am nothing; I have nothing in me. Compared with Breslau I seem to myself like a thin and fragile pasteboard box compared to a massive and richly carved oaken casket. I despair of myself, and so convinced am I of my worthlessness that if I were to say what I think to the masters I should convert them to my opinion.

But I will go forward blindly, all the same, my hands stretched out before me, groping for the light, ready to be engulfed if it must be so.

Thursday, December 29.—It is a week since I have written anything in my diary; this will show you that my glorious existence has been divided between work and society. There is nothing new; and yet there is, for I am well and I go out as usual. I went on Saturday to have some new gowns fitted, to the Bois, and to Julian's, with mamma and Dina. And on Sunday I went to church, so that they may not say I am at the point of death, as the charming Bertha tells every one.

On the contrary I have gained new life; my arms, that were so thin ten days ago, are now rounded; that is to say, that I am much better than I was before my illness.

A week more of this and I shall have to stop growing fat; I shall be just right then; for I do not wish to have again the large hips I had three years ago. Julian, who came to see me last night, thinks my figure much better as it is now. We laughed all the evening. I am painting the portrait of Paul's wife. Yesterday I had so far recovered my energy that I wanted to paint, all at once, the portraits of Dina, Nini, and Irma.

Friday, December 30.—They have spent the whole day here quarreling. In order to recover my tranquillity I went to see Tony, taking with me the sketch of the portrait of Paul's wife, to show him. He thought it very original in treatment and well begun. The sympathetic Tony seemed delighted at seeing me in good health again. After chatting gaily together on different matters we touched on the serious subject of art, speaking of Breslau in connection with it, among other things. "Her picture is certainly very good," he said; "she is richly endowed."

Ah, it would be impossible to transcribe my feelings here—to describe the fever, the fire, that consumes me. Oh, I must work day and night, without ceasing, to produce something that shall have merit! True, he told me that the day I wished I might produce a picture equal to any of hers; true, he thinks I have as much talent as she has, but I am ready to weep, to die, to hide myself anywhere—where I might be able—But would I be able? Ah,

Tony has confidence in me, but I have no confidence in myself. I am consumed by the desire to accomplish something, and I know my own powerlessness—But here I must stop. As my readers no doubt take me literally, they might believe what I say to be true—whereas I only say these things in the hope of being contradicted.

Ah, heavens! I spend my time writing down all this, and selecting words in which to describe the annoyances I suffer, while Breslau, wiser than I, spends hers drawing and painting.

———

1882.

The thing I take most delight in is my painting; I do not feel myself worthy of saying, "my art." In order to speak of art we must first have won a name; otherwise one has the air of an amateur, who deserves only to be laughed at.

.

Wednesday, January 4.—Julian spent the evening rallying me on my liking for Tony, and on his for me. At midnight we took chocolate. Dina was very amiable.

I always dress with particular care, and in an entirely different fashion from other times, when I go among artists—in long gowns, and flowing draperies; in society my waist would not be found sufficiently slender nor my gown sufficiently fashionable; so that all my pretty fancies—too extravagant for the world of society—will serve me in my ministry of the Fine Arts; I still cherish the dream of having a *salon* that shall be frequented by every one of note.

Friday, January 6.—Art, even in the case of the humblest of its votaries, elevates the soul, and makes one superior in some degree to those who are not of the sacred fraternity.

Wednesday, January 11.—To-morrow, our New Year's Eve, we give a soiree ; they have been making preparations for it for the last week ; more than two hundred and fifty invitations have been sent out, for a great many of our friends have made requests for them.   As no one is receiving yet, this will be an event, and I think we shall have some very *chic* people.   In short, it will be a pleasant affair. Etincelle makes allusion to it in her notes in *Figaro*, adding a eulogy of Mlle. Marie, who is beautiful and an artist, etc., etc.   But even if she had said nothing of all this, I should still regard her as the most charming of ugly people ; there are fifty women I know who are not so attractive as she is, and then she bears the undefinable Parisian stamp, as well as the stamp of a person of note.   Observe well what I say. for it is profoundly true—all people of note, whether they be men, women, or children, young or old, have a certain tone in the voice, a certain air, which is the same among them all, and which I will call the family likeness of persons of celebrity.

We are to have the two Coquelins.   The elder Coquelin came yesterday to inspect the rooms, and to consult with us respecting the pieces.   G—— was present, and he disgusted me with the airs he gave himself of being a connoisseur—a little more and he would have taken it upon himself to advise Coquelin, who is very agreeable, by the way, a very good fellow, who does not make you feel, the moment you speak to him, that sort of embarrassment which so many people experience in the presence of any one of note.

Friday, January 13.—The two Coquelins were superb ; and the rooms presented a charming appearance ; there were a number of pretty women present—the enchanting trio, the Marquise de Reverseaux, the daughter of Janvier de la Motte, Mme. Thouvenel and Mme. de Joly, the

Countess de Kessler,—in short, almost all the women were pretty, and, in the words of Tony (who did not come, however, nor did Julian), "very desirable guests." Mme. G—— was enchanted, and finished the evening by dancing with Count Plater.

The reception was preceded by a dinner.

As for artists, the brother of Bastien-Lepage is still absent ; so he was not with us (on Thursday we are to visit the real Bastien-Lepage) ; there was George Bertrand, who exhibited last year an admirable and touching picture called *Le Drapeau.* I alluded to it in a notice, and he wrote me a few amiable words in return. I sent him an invitation signed "Pauline Orell." It was Pollack who presented him to me. It was very amusing—he paid me a great many fine compliments, for, although I wished to hide them, Dina showed some of my studies to such of our guests as she thought had a right to see them. Carrier-Belleuse succumbed to the power of my eyes, and toward the end of the evening grew quite tender and sentimental.

Here is a man who is capable of falling very much in love ; perhaps he has done so already ; but—

We had supper at three o'clock ; Gabriel sat on my right ; about sixty persons had remained. Nini was charming, and looked very pretty : her shoulders were dazzling, and she wore an exquisite gown, as did Dina, mamma, and my aunt. I wore a gown made by Doucet and myself in partnership, an almost faithful reproduction of Greuze's *Cruche Cassée.* I wore my hair loose in front and fastened in a knot on the back of the head, high above the neck. A long chain of Bengal roses with loose leaves lost itself among the folds of the short skirt, which was of silk mull, pleated ; the bodice was of satin, laced in front, and very long, with a handkerchief crossed over the breast. There was a second skirt of mull, turned up with satin, open in front, and gathered up behind, forming panniers, of which one was

covered with roses. I looked charming. The odious sub-
Potain followed me like a shadow so as to catch me if I
should attempt to dance.

Sunday, January 15.—There was a long article of
Etincelle's about our soiree, but, as we had expected this
article, mamma and my aunt were not satisfied with it. She
compares me to the *Cruche Cassée*, and they are afraid that
this may be taken in Poltava as an insult. They are too
stupid ! The article is very good, only that, as she had
said two days ago that I was one of the prettiest women of
the Russian Empire, and she contents herself this time with
describing my gown, I am rather disappointed.

I am wrapped up in my art. I think I caught the sacred
fire in Spain at the same time that I caught the pleurisy.
From being a student I now begin to be an artist. This
sudden influx of power puts me beside myself with joy. I
sketch future pictures ; I dream of painting an Ophelia.
Potain has promised to take me to Saint-Anne to study the
faces of the mad women there, and then I am full of the
idea of painting an old man, an Arab, sitting down singing
to the accompaniment of a kind of guitar ; and I am
thinking also of a large affair for the coming *Salon*—a view
of the Carnival ; but for this it would be necessary that I
should go to Nice—to Naples first for the Carnival, and
then to Nice, where I have my villa, to paint it in the open
air. I say all this, and yet I wish to remain here.

Saturday, January 21.—Madame C—— came to take
me to see Bastien-Lepage. We found there two or three
American women, and the little Bastien-Lepage himself ;
he is very small, very fair, wears his hair *a la Bretonne* * has
a *retroussé* nose and the beard of a youth. I was altogether
taken aback. I adore his painting, but it is impossible to

---

* Cut square across the forehead,

regard him with the respect due to a master. You want to treat him as a comrade, and his paintings are there to fill you with admiration, astonishment, and envy. There are four or five of them, all life-size, and painted from nature. They are admirable ; one of them represents a little girl of eight or ten guarding some cows in a field ; the tree stripped of its foliage, and the cow resting under its branches, are touchingly poetic ; the eyes of the little girl have a look of childlike dreaminess in them—the dreaminess of one who lives in companionship with nature—that it would be impossible to describe. He has the air of a good little man who is very well satisfied with himself—this Bastien.

I returned home in time to help mamma to receive a number of visitors. This is what it is to give soirees in Paris, you see, as one of our friends says.

Saturday, January 22.—For the time being I am full of the idea of the Carnival ; I am making sketches for it in charcoal. If I only had the genius, it would be delightful to paint it.

Monday, January 30.—It is decided that we are to go to the Villa Gery at Nice. I spent a delightful day on Saturday. Bastien, whom I had seen the evening before at the ball given at the Continental Hotel for the benefit of the Breton life-savers, and presided over by the Queen, came to see me and remained more than an hour. I showed him some things of mine, and he gave me his opinion respecting them with a flattering severity. And then he said I was *marvelously* gifted. And it did not seem as if this was a compliment merely. For the moment I was so overcome with joy that I was on the point of taking the good man's face between my hands, and kissing him.

I am very well pleased, however, to have heard his opinion. He gives me the same advice as Tony and Julian, and says the very same things.   And then is he not a pupil of Cabanel?   Every artist has his own peculiar temperament, but as far as the grammar of the art is concerned, it is necessary to learn it from a master.   Neither Bastien nor any one else can communicate his gifts to another.   Nothing can be learned but what may be taught ; the rest depends upon one's-self.

Mme. de Peronny (Etincelle) came to-day, and I spent a delightful quarter of an hour in the company of this superior woman and great artist, first seated around the fire, and afterward under the palm.   I shall say nothing of our other visitors, whom I left in the official drawing-room with mamma.

NICE.—We left Paris at eight in the evening, Paul, Dina, I, Nini, Rosalie, Basili and Coco.   The Villa Gery is all that we could desire, and is situated in the open country only ten minute's distance from the Promenade des Anglais ; it has gardens and a terrace, and is a large and comfortable house.

We found everything ready to receive us ; and M. Picoux, the agent, had bouquets for each of us.

I took a trip on the tramway this evening that delighted me ; there was, in what I saw, a blending of the Italian and the French gayety, but without any of the vulgarity that is to be met with among the populace of Paris.   As I wrote to Julian, life here is as comfortable as it is in Paris, and as picturesque as it is in Grenada.   Within five yards of the Promenade des Anglais are to be found so many different costumes, so many different types of humanity, and all so picturesque !   Why go to Spain ?   Oh, the South ! Oh, Nice !   Oh, the Mediterranean !   Oh, my beloved country, through which I have suffered so much !   Oh, my earliest joys, and my profoundest griefs !   Oh, my childhood, my ambitious dreams !

Try how I will, those days will always form an epoch in my existence, and side by side with the recollection of the sufferings that darkened my early youth will remain the recollection of its joys—joys that will remain forever the sweetest flowers of memory.

I am boiling over with rage. Wolff has devoted a dozen lines—as flattering as they could possibly be—to Breslau.

But after all I am not to blame ; one does what one can. She has nothing to occupy her attention but her art ; while I invent new fashions for my gowns, I devise new ways of arranging draperies, I think of how to be revenged on the society of Nice. I do not say that I should have her talent even if I were to do as she does ; she obeys the instincts of her nature, I those of mine. But my hands are tied. The trouble is that I am so convinced of my powerlessness as to be tempted at times to give it all up. Julian says I might to do as well as she does if I wished. If I wished—but in order to have the wish it is necessary to have the power. Those who have succeeded because they *willed* to succeed were sustained by a secret strength which is wanting in me. And only to think that at times I have not only faith in my future power to succeed, but that I feel burn within me the sacred fire of genius ! Oh, misery !

But here, at least, no one is to blame, and that is less maddening. There is nothing more horrible than to have to say to one's-self, " If it were not for this or for that, I should have succeeded, perhaps." I know that I do all I can, and yet I have accomplished nothing.

O my God, grant that I may deceive myself, and that the feeling I now have of my mediocrity may be a mistaken one.

Friday, February 10.—I have received so rude a blow that it has caused me to spend three very unhappy days.

I shall not now paint my large picture. I will paint sim-

pler things—things more within the compass of my powers—studies.   I have taken a solemn resolution not to waste
another moment, and not to paint another stroke without
some purpose.   I shall concentrate my powers.   Bastien
has advised me to do this, and so have Julian and the fortunate Breslau.   Yes, fortunate, indeed ; to be as fortunate
as she is I would give, without a moment's hesitation, all
that people call my *happiness* and my *wealth*—a hundred
thousand francs to have independence and to have talent :
when one has these, one has everything.

But how fortunate she is, this girl! It makes me so
unhappy every time I think of that article of Wolff's.   Yet
it is not what is called *envy* that makes me feel this.   I have
not the heart to analyze this feeling and to select words in
which to describe it.

Monday, February 13.—I am making sketches in aquarelle
for the first time !   Every moment of the day is occupied,
and I have decided on a subject for my picture, for, in addition to the smaller things, I must take back a large study
to Julian.   It is three little boys standing near a gateway :
that seems to me an interesting subject, and one that ad-
mits of realistic treatment.   The blow I received in Wolff's
article has done me good.   I was for the moment crushed,
annihilated, and the reaction from this feeling has given me
the power to understand things in art that previously to
that had tormented me, for while I suspected their existence,
I could not discover them.   This has compelled me to make
salutary exertions.   I begin too, to understand now what I
used to read respecting the trials and struggles of artists.   I
used to laugh at all this as romantic stories that had no
foundation.   That famous *will* of Breslau—I have called it
to my aid, and I see that it is necessary to make great efforts
in order to obtain the success that one fancies has dropped
down from the skies.   The thing is that I have made no

real effort up to the present. The extreme facility with which I worked has spoiled me. Breslau obtains good results, but only after working hard for them ; as for me, when success does not come at once, and without effort, I can do nothing. I must conquer this feeling. Thus, in sketching a picture, in making charcoal sketches, for instance, I found it necessary to make great efforts, in order to attain to the desired purity of outline, and I have succeeded in accomplishing things of which I had before thought myself incapable, and which I thought others had accomplished by means of tricks, of sorcery almost, so difficult is it to concede to others the possession of those qualities in which we ourselves are lacking.

Wednesday, February 15.—It is only by degrees that we learn to see things as they really are. Formerly all that I could see in a picture was the subject and the composition, and now—ah ! if I could only copy what I see, I should produce something great. I *see* the landscape, I see, and I love the landscape, the water, the air, the coloring—the coloring !

Monday, February 27.—After a thousand hesitations and doubts I have destroyed my canvas ; the boys would not pose ; attributing my want of success in making them do so to my own incapacity, I tried again and again, and at last— it was happily settled. The frightful little monsters moved about, and laughed and cried and fought with each other— I shall simply make a study of them ; to make a picture wonld be too much torture.

PARIS, *Thursday, April* 20.—Well, it is not now as it was when I came back from Spain. I am not enchanted to see Paris again, I am only pleased. Besides, I am so preoccupied about my painting that I scarcely know what my feelings are. I tremble to think what will be said of it, and I am completely crushed by the thought of Breslau, who is treated by the public as if she were already a successful artist. I went to see Julian yesterday (we have been in Paris since yesterday morning), and he treats me no longer as if I were making a serious pursuit of painting. " Brilliant, yes," he says, " but no depth, no power of will." He had hoped for, he had expected, something better. All this, told me in the course of our conversation, wounded me deeply. I shall wait until he sees what I painted at Nice, but I no longer expect anything good

Saturday, April 22.—No, what was necessary to me in order that I should continue to live, was genius. I can never be happy in the same way as other people are. To be loved and to be famous, as Balzac says, this is to be happy ! And to be loved is only the natural consequence of being famous. Breslau, who is thin, cross eyed, and haggard, although her face is an interesting one, can never exercise any feminine attraction except through her genius, while, if I had her talent, I should be superior to any woman in Paris. But that must come. In the wild desire that it should come, I seem to see a hope that it will.

These journeys, these interruptions to my work, the lack of advice and encouragement—they are ruinous. One looks as if one had come back from China, one knows nothing of what is going on.

Ah ! after all, I think there is nothing I love like painting ; that must, as I believe, procure me every other happiness ! Mistaken vocation, mistaken talent, mistaken hopes ! And yet I slander myself. I went to the Louvre this morning. When one sees as clearly as I do, one ought to be able to interpret what one sees. Formerly I had the self-confidence of ignorance, but for some time past I have been able to see things in art that I had never seen before.

This morning it was Paul Veronese, who appeared to me in all his splendor, in all his glory. What incomparable richness of coloring ! How explain the fact that these glorious paintings have seemed to me until now only large, uninteresting pictures, dull in coloring and flat in execution ! The beauties to which my eyes were before sealed I can now appreciate. The celebrated paintings that I admired before only out of regard for the opinion of others, now delight me and hold me spellbound. I feel all the delicate gradations in the coloring ; I appreciate color, in short.

A landscape by Ruysdael compelled me to return to look at it a second time. A few months ago I could see in it nothing of what I saw there this morning—atmosphere, space ! In short, it is not painting, it is nature itself. Well, it is because my eyes have been practiced that I now perceive these beauties that I could not see before. And is it not possible for the same thing to happen with the hand ?

Sunday, April 23.—I have just been looking over the studies I made at Nice. The sole thought that *they* might find something to admire in them makes a shiver run down my back. For Tony, Julian, and Bastien appear to me themselves so insignificant compared to the immense effect their words are capable of producing on me !

I have as yet formed no plans for the future. On Monday I shall go to the studio to get into the habit of regular work again.

The sky is gray and stormy ; it rains, and a piercing win is blowing ; the state of the elements is in harmony with the condition of my mind ; what I feel then is due to a physical impression merely.

But there was something else I wanted to write about— a few reflections concerning love suggested by something I read this morning.

Love—this is the inexhaustible subject. To allow yourself to be loved by a man to whom you should be so superior
that he would regard you as a goddess descended from the
skies—this would have a certain charm. To know that
your glance would diffuse happiness around—there is a
benevolent side to this that is flattering to the generous part
of one's nature.

Tuesday, April 25.—My own anxiety was sufficient, without seeing around me the anxious countenances of my
family, who were all looking at me to see if I betrayed emotion. Well, to sum up, this is what Tony has said : The
costume of Dina very good, very good ; the man standing
on the sea-shore very good also ; the head of Thérèse not
altogether bad. The tones of the landscape, however, do
not harmonize with the costumes ; the smaller landscape is
very good ; the old man correct in drawing, but not suf-
ficently simple, and not sufficiently something else—in fine,
there is something good in it. "Well," you will say, " you
ought to be satisfied." Ah ! in addition to all this he said
I ought to follow a conscientious course of study, and that
he would pay particular attention to my progress ; he also
said that he was at my disposal whenever I chose to send
for him.

I ought to be satisfied—but no, I am almost crushed,
This was not enough ; he should have said to me ; " Good,
this time you have succeeded ; this is good ; your execution
is as good as Breslau's, and your other qualities are superior
to hers."

Nothing less than these words would have satisfied me;
or even sufficed to take me out of the despair in which I
have been plunged, on account of my painting, for more
than a year past. Why should I not be satisfied with all
these " goods " ?—when I still keep in my memory the " very

good " he bestowed on Breslau for a little picture she made in Brittany two years ago.

Yet when he said the same words to me regarding the little picture I did at Nice, it seemed to me as if they no longer possessed the same value. And why? Before my departure for Nice he said to me that Breslau's " Fisher Girl " was " very good," and now that this same " Fisher Girl " has been accepted, receiving a number 3, he says it is " not bad," only. In short, I am not satisfied. And why? In the first place, because my family based such extravagant hopes on these few studies of mine that only the most extravagant praises could satisfy them; and then—nerves, the effects of the spring weather. Whenever I am over-excited, as I am now, I feel a burning sensation in my arms, just above the elbow; it is very curious; explain to me, ye learned doctors, what this means.

Saturday, April 29.—I am not a painter; I learned drawing, as I learn everything, with facility—that is all. Yet when I was a child of three I used to draw profiles with chalk on the whist-tables in the country, and afterward, and always. One would swear it was a true vocation—and yet you see! But there is nothing more to be said, only so much time to be lived through; my arms fall down powerless by my sides. And after all, what is it that has happened? Nothing. Breslau has been studying much longer than I—almost twice as long. Admitting, then, that I am as gifted as she, things have followed their natural course; I have been painting for three years, while she has been painting for five.

Sunday, April 30.—Since morning I have been watching the varnishing of the pictures, with Villevielle, Alice, and Webb. I was in black and looked very well. I was amused to see how many people I know in Paris. Carolus Duran came to speak to me—this man is fascinating. Breslau's picture is hung very high, and produces a deplorable effect. I was so uneasy on account of her possible success that this was a great consolation. I do not deny it. Her friends came to me in distress, to learn my opinion, and I said that I did not think the picture a very good one, but that they should have given her a better place.

The conclusion to this brilliant day was a conversation with Julian, during which he reproached me with wasting my energies, with not justifying the magnificent promise I had given, etc. In short, he thinks I have gone beyond my depth ; so do I, and we are going to see if I cannot be brought into safe waters again. I told him I was aware of this deplorable condition of things, that it made me desperate, and that I thought all was over with me ; he reminds me of the clever things I have done, and says that a sketch of mine, which he has in his possession, makes every one stop to look at it, and so on. Ah, my God, take me out of this state of misery ! God has been good to me in not suffering me to be killed outright by Breslau—at least to-day. In short, I know not how to express my thought that it may not seem a base one. If her picture had been what I expected it would be, that would have been my death—in the pitiable condition in which my work is at present. I have not for a single instant wished that it might be bad— that would be ignoble, but I trembled lest she should meet with a decided success. I felt so strong an emotion on opening the newspapers that perhaps God took pity on me.

Tuesday, May 9.—Tony and Julian dined with us this evening. I wore a fantastic costume, and we sat chatting till half-past eleven. Julian was very amusing, after the champagne, and Tony very amiable, very abstemious, very tranquil, with his fine head and his languid air. One would like to stir to its inmost depths this tender and melancholy

soul where all is calm and still.   I cannot imagine this professor as indulging in any strong emotion.   He is dispas-
sionate and logical, and, where matters of the heart are in
question, he will quietly demonstrate their causes, and their
progress, as if he were explaining the qualities of a painting.
In a word, and to *sum up*, as he says, he is charming.

The portrait of a young girl, by Sargent, haunts me ; it
is ravishing.   It is an exquisite piece of work, worthy of a
place beside the paintings of Vandyke and Velasquez.

Saturday, May 20.—Ah, how discouraged I am !   What
have I accomplished since I came to Paris ?   I am no longer
even eccentric.   And in Italy, what did I accomplish ?
Once I allowed myself to be secretly kissed by that stupid
A   .   Well, and afterward ?   Ah, it disgusts me to think
of it !   Yet not a few young girls have done the same thing,
and do it every day, and no one speaks ill of them for it.   I
declare that when I hear, as I have heard just now, of the
remarks people make about us, and especially about me, so
strong is the emotion I feel that it overwhelms me.

We went yesterday to the *Salon* with E   , the brother
of Bastien, and Beaumetz.   Bastien-Lepage is going to
paint a picture representing a little peasant-boy looking at
a rainbow.   It will be sublime—you may take my word for
it.   What genius, what genius !

Monday, May 22.—I am convinced that I shall never
love any one—except one ; and he, it is probable, will never
love me.   Julian is right—the best way to revenge myself
would be by conquering a brilliant position in the world—
by marrying some man of note who is rich as well as
famous.   That would be magnificent !   Or to develop a
genius like that of Bastien-Lepage, that would make all
Paris turn round to look at me when I pass by.   Truly this
is charming !   I talk as if this might happen to me, who

have never had anything but misfortune all my life. Oh,
my God, my God! grant me my revenge! I will be so
compassionate to those who suffer!

Thursday, May 25.—We went this morning to see Carolus Duran. What a charming and admirable being he is!
People are disposed to laugh at him because he can do a
little of everything. He shoots well, he rides, he dances, he
plays the piano, the organ, and the guitar, and he sings.
They say he dances badly, but as for the other things, he
does them with inimitable grace. He fancies himself a
Spaniard, and a Velasquez. His appearance is very attractive,
his conversation interesting, and there is in his whole air
something so amiable, so frank, and so self-satisfied, he has
so evident an enjoyment in the admiration of his own proper
person, that one cannot bear him ill-will for it—on the contrary; and if one smiles at him occasionally, one is none
the less charmed by him, especially when one thinks of
those one has to put up with, who do not possess a quarter
of his merits.

He takes himself altogether *au serieux;* and which of us,
in his place, would not have his head a little turned?

Sunday, May 28.—The Duchess of Fitz-James came to-
day to say that she would present us this evening to her
daughter-in-law. There was to be a ball. Mamma declares
that no one could be more amiable than this lady. They
see each other quite often, but just how often I cannot say.
We agreed to call for her and go together.

Everything was perfect; the society was of the best; the
young girls looked fresh and charming; the gowns were
beautiful. The old Duchess has any number of nephews
and nieces and grand-children. The persons whose names
I heard mentioned are among the best known and the most
aristocratic in Paris, and those I met there all distin-

guished.   For my part, delighted as I was to find myself in this *salon*, I could not get the thought of a pastel I had finished this morning out of my head, so troubled was I by the remembrance of its defects.

And then one cannot go into society in this way—I should need a couple of months, at least, to accustom myself to it. But do you think that in my heart I find it entertaining?   I find it stupid, hollow, dull!   And to think that there are people who live only for this!   As for me, I should like to go out occasionally, just enougl to keep up an interest in what is going on in the world of fashion; but for relaxation only, as distinguished men go; so as not to seem like a Hottentot, or an inhabitant of the moon.

Monday, May 29.—Yesterday we went to the Bois with Adeline, who congratulated us on being launched into the most aristocratic society of Paris, and to-day we visit the Queen, the two Duchesses of Fitz-James, the Countess of Turenne, Mme. de Briey, and, finally, the American.

The question that chiefly occupies my attention now is the subject of my picture for next year's *Salon*.   The subject I should prefer, I feel profoundly; my heart and mind are alike captivated by it, and it is one that I have thought of for nearly two years past.   It is when Joseph of Arimathea has placed the body of Jesus in the tomb, and the stone has been rolled before it; the people have departed, the night is falling, and Mary Magdalen and the other Mary remain alone, seated before the mouth of the sepulchre.

Tuesday, June 20.—Well, there is nothing new to record; a few visits exchanged, and my painting—and Spain.   Ah, Spain!   It is a work of Theophile Gautier that has been the cause of this.   Can it be possible that I have been in Toledo, Burgos, Cordova, Seville, Grenada?   Grenada!   What!

Have I indeed been in all those cities, only to pronounce the names of which is to feel one's-self ennobled? Well, I have caught the infection: I must return there! I must see those wonders once more! I must return there alone, or with congenial companions. I have suffered enough already through the company of my family there. O Poetry! O Art! Ah, how short is life! And how unfortunate we are that it should be so short!

Wednesday, June 21.—I have effaced everything in my picture, and even disposed of the canvas, so as not to have it before my eyes! This is killing me! O Art! I shall never attain to a mastery of it. But, as soon as one destroys what one is dissatisfied with, one feels consoled, free, and ready to begin again. The studio in which I am painting was lent to Mlle. Loshooths by an American named Chadwick, who returned to-day, and we have restored his temple to him.

Friday, June 23.—At five o'clock L——, Dina, and I went to see Emile Bastien, who is to sit for me.

I shall paint with the palette of the true Bastien, with his colors, his brushes, in his studio, and with his brother for a model.

Well, it is a dream, a piece of childishness, a silly fancy! The little Swedish girl took his palette in her hands, and I took away some of the paint he had used as a souvenir; my hand trembled as I did so, and we both laughed.

Saturday, June 24.—It is decided that we are to take the the house in the Rue Ampere. It consists of a basement with a kitchen and billiard-room. The ground-floor, to which one ascends by a flight of ten steps, has a vestibule; then there is a pretty glass door opening on an antechamber, from which the staircase to the other stories ascends;

to the right is a room which they have converted into a par-
lor by making an entrance from it into a little chamber
which opens on the garden; a dining-room, and a courtyard which carriages can enter, and into which one descends
by steps from the drawing-room, and dining-room.

On the first story there are five bed-rooms, with dressing-
rooms adjoining, and a hall, with baths.   As for the second
story it belongs to me, and consists of an antechamber,
two bedrooms, a library, a studio, and a store-room.   The
studio and the library open into each other, forming a large
apartment, nearly thirty-six feet long, and twenty-one feet
wide.

The light is superb, entering on three sides, as well as
from above.   In short, for a hired house there could be
nothing that would suit me better.   It is No. 30 Rue Ampere, on the corner of the Rue Bremontier, and may be
seen from the Avenue de Villiers.

Wednesday, July 12.—I am making preparations to begin
my famous picture, which will be an extremely difficult
piece of work.   I must select a landscape like the one I
have pictured to myself.   And the tomb hewn out of the
rock—I should like to paint it near Paris—at Capri, for
instance, which is altogether Eastern; but it would be necessary to copy a real tomb, such as there must be many of
in Algeria, and still more in Jerusalem—any Jewish sepulchre hewn out of the rock.   And the models?   Oh, there
must be magnificent ones to be found there—and with the
original costumes.   Julian says this is a piece of folly.   He
can understand, he says, how a great artist—one who is
master of his art—should go to paint his picture on the
scene; he seeks the only thing in which he is lacking, a
knowledge of the real object he is to copy; but I who am
deficient in so many things!   Well, it seems to me it is just
for that reason that I should paint my picture on the scene,

ground is not yet finished, but the figure!—Ah,

What idiots are they who say he excels only in execution! He is an original, a powerful artist; he is a poet; he is a philosopher; other artists are mere workmen compared to him; he is grand, as nature is, as life is. The other day Tony Robert-Fleury was obliged to agree with me that, to copy Nature, one must be a great artist, and that none but a great artist can comprehend Nature so as to copy her faithfully. The ideal quality of the painter is manifested in his choice of a subject; as for the execution, it should be the perfection of what the ignorant call realism. Choose as your subject Enguerrand de Marigny or Agnes Sorel, if you will, but let their han s, their hair, their eyes be natural, ... subject itself matters little. Doubt- . . . . I view modern subjects are the most . . . . . . the only, the true realism is in the execution. No doubt it is more easy to . . . . the . . . . . Bastien-Lepage were to paint Mlle. de la Vallière or Mary Stuart, dead and turned to dust as they are, they .

. . . .

There was also a little portrait of the elder could find no words to express my admiration, e . . . . the act of making with his hand, his eyes wink

Wednesday, August 23.—Instead of working on any of my studies I have been going out. Yes Mademoiselle has been . . . . observations in the . . . . of . .

Wednesday, August 23.—I have read for the second book by Ouida, a woman who is not endowed with a . deal of realism; it is called ".

Tuesday, August 29.—This book has disturbed me; Ouida is neither Georges Sand, nor Balzac, nor Dumas, but she has produced a book which, for professional reasons, has thrown me into a fever. Her ideas and opinions concerning art, acquired among the studios in Italy, where she has lived, are extremely just.

She says, among other things, that with the true artist—not the artisan—the conception is immeasurably superior to the power of execution. Again, the great sculptor Marix, when he had seen the first attempts at modeling of the young heroine, the future woman of genius, says: "Let her come; she will accomplish all that she *desires* to accomplish." So Tony Robert-Fleury said, after he had carefully examined my drawings at the studio: "Work hard, Mademoiselle, you *will accomplish whatever you desire*" were his words.

But my work has, no doubt, been one-sided. Saint-Marceaux said that my drawings were the drawings of a sculptor, and I have always loved form beyond everything else.

I love color, also, but now, since I have read this book—and even before—painting appears a miserable thing compared to sculpture. And, then, I ought to hate it, as I hate every imitation, every imposture.

Nothing irritates me more than to see artificial objects imitated in painting on a surface necessarily smooth and flat, whether it be a work of art that is concerned, or a common wall-paper. The sight of such things enrages me as the sight of red enrages a bull. What can be more odious, for instance, than imitations of pictures on walls, as we sometimes see—even in the Louvre—or the friezes on the walls of furnished apartments imitating carved wood or lace.

What is it, then, that prevents me from being a sculptor? Nothing. I am free; I am so situated that all my artistic needs are supplied. I have an entire floor to myself—an antechamber, a bed-room, a library, a splendidly lighted studio, and finally, a little garden, in which I can work when I choose. I have had a speaking-tube put up, so that I may not be disturbed by any one coming upstairs and that I may not have to go downstairs too often.

And what am I painting, with all this? A little girl who has turned up her black petticoat over her shoulders, and who holds an open umbrella in her hand. I work in the open air, and almost every day it rains. And then—what does all this signify? What is it compared to a thought expressed in marble? And what use have I made of the sketch I did three years ago, in October, 1879? They gave us the subject—Ariadne—at the studio, and I was enthusiastic about it, as I was about the Holy Women at the Sepulchre. Julian and Tony thought the subject a good one. Here it is now three years since I first determined to learn modeling for the purpose of doing it in marble. I feel myself powerless where commonplace subjects are concerned. And the terrible words, "To what end?" keep my hands tied.

Yes, the prejudice in favor of linear perspective is a mistaken one, the preference for colors a false sentiment—coloring is a purely mechanical art which gradually absorbs all one's powers, and leaves no room for original conception.

The execution of the painter who is a thinker or a poet is generally of an inferior degree of excellence. How could I have deceived myself as I have done in regard to this truth, and clung to this art with such mad persistency?

August 30.—I am engaged in drawing my Magdalen, for which I have an excellent model. I saw three years ago the face I wanted for it, and this woman has the very same features, and the same terribly intense expression of despair.

No painting has ever affected me like the Jeanne d'Arc of Bastien Lepage ; there is something mysterious, supernatural, in her expression, born of the intensity of feeling produced by her vision—a feeling understood by the artist who has painted it as at once grand, human, inspired, and divine; *all that it was*, in fact, but which no one before him had comprehended.

Friday, September 1.—I have received a letter from mamma in which she tells me that our young neighbors are visiting at our house, with some friends of theirs, and that they are getting up a grand hunt. She is ready to return, but, as I had asked her to let me know if—she has done so. Well, this plunges me in a sea of uncertainty, doubt, and anxiety. If I go to Russia, there is an end to my picture for the Exhibition. If I had even been working all the summer, I might have the pretext of needing rest, but this is not the case. It would be splendid, of course, but nothing is less probable. And to travel for four days and nights in a railway-coach, and sacrifice the labor of a year to go and try to make a conquest of some one I have never seen—there is neither sense nor reason in it. If I begin to think of committing this piece of folly, I shall, perhaps, be guilty of it, for I no longer know what I am doing. I shall go to see Mother Jacob the fortune-teller about it; the same who foretold that I should have a serious illness.

For the sum of twenty francs I have just purchased good fortune enough to last me for at least two days. Mother Jacob has predicted, from the cards, the most delightful things for me—a little mixed up, it is true. But what turns up with most persistence is that I am going to achieve a brilliant success, of which all the newspapers will talk ; that I shall be a great genius, and that a change for the better is going to take place ; that I am to make a splendid marriage, to have great wealth, and to travel a great deal.

The delight all this gives me is insensate, if you will, but all it costs me is twenty francs ; I shall not go to Russia, but to Algeria, for if all these things are going to happen to me, they will happen to me there as well as in Russia.

Good-night ; this has done me good ; I shall work well to-morrow.

Wednesday, September 6.—I am not an artist. I desired to be one, and, as I am intelligent, I learned certain details of the art.—How then explain what Robert-Fleury said to me when I began : " You have already what is not to be learned." He deceived himself, that is all.

I paint, as I do anything else, with intelligence and skill— nothing more. Why then did I draw heads with chalk on the card-tables in our country-house when I was only four years old ?

All children draw. But whence the constant desire to draw—to copy engravings, both before we left Russia, and afterword, at Nice, when I was only eleven ? They thought then I had an extraordinary talent for drawing, and I studied, under various masters, for a couple of years.

Well, upon reflection, I find that I always had the desire to learn drawing, the impulse toward art ; that I made efforts, but without any one to direct them. And then came the journey to Italy—Rome. They say in novels that it is possible to appreciate the beauties of art without any previous instruction, but I confess that I have only learned gradually to appreciate the beauties, that is to say, the merits of paintings. In short, I have lost confidence, I have lost courage. I am deficient in some sense. I appre- ciate beauty of coloring, but—I cannot say precisely that I have not been able to attain it, for I have done two or three things which are good, both in coloring and execution. If I have done some good things, that means that I can do others—this is what encourages me. And I was going to abandon my *rôle* of artist and painter—especially of painter.

In short I paint not so badly, but I think I should do better as a sculptor—I have certain conceptions—of forms, gestures, attitudes—that cannot be expressed in color.

Sunday, September 24.—The days follow one another in unbroken monotony; from eight in the morning till five, painting; an hour for the bath before dinner; then dinner, eaten in silence, for I read the newspapers while I eat, interchanging an occasional word with my aunt. She must be bored to death, poor woman! Truly I am not very amiable; she has never enjoyed any happiness in life; formerly she sacrificed herself for mamma, who was the beauty of the family, and now she lives only for us, for me; yet I cannot succeed in being amiable and pleasant during the rare moments in which we are together; and then, I enjoy a silence during which my thoughts do not dwell upon my infirmities.

In RUSSIA, *Saturday, October* 14.—My aunt left me at the frontier, and I made the rest of the journey with Paul. We have to wait five hours here for the train. The place is called Znamenka. It is cold, and the sky is overcast; if it were not quite so cold, it would be delightful to be in the open air. I have been observing the peasants, with their garments discolored by exposure to the inclemency of the weather, and I see how true to nature are the paintings of Bastien-Lepage. "The tones are gray, the atmosphere is flat, it has no body," say those who are unaccustomed to observe nature out-of-doors, who know her only in the exaggerated effects of the studio. But this is precisely what nature is; his rendering could not be truer or more faithful. Ah, Bastien ought to be a happy man! And I who left Paris filled with chagrin at the thought of my ruined Fisherman!

But I will try to finish it in March, in time for the *Salon.*

It is Robert-Fleury who has advised me to retouch it; I am to leave the background and the dress as they are; there is nothing to be done but to retouch the head.

GAVRONZI, *Sunday, October* 15.—We went to bed at seven o'clock this morning, as we came direct to Gavronzi. Mamma, papa, Dina, and Kapitan were at the station to meet us. Paul's wife has a little boy two weeks old. The little girl is a year old, and is a charming child, with long, black lashes. The young P——s are to arrive to-morrow. Michka has gone to see them, instead of waiting here for me with the others.

Thursday, October 19.—Here we have them with us at last. They arrived in time for breakfast with Michka. Victor, the elder, is slender and dark, and has a large aquiline nose; he is rather stout, has full lips, is distinguished in appearance, and has agreeable manners. The younger, Basili, is about the same height, but much stouter; he is very fair, with a florid complexion, and cunning eyes; he seems quarrelsome, turbulent, brutal, and yes—vulgar. I wore the same gown as yesterday—a white wool, short and extremely simple, with kid shoes of antique red; my hair was twisted in a knot at the back of the head. This was not one of my brilliant days, but neither, on the other hand, did I look my worst.

I do not think I shall make a conquest of either of the brothers. There is nothing in me that could please them; I am of medium stature, well proportioned, and neither dark nor fair; my eyes are gray, and I have neither a large bust nor a wasp waist; and, as for my mental qualities, I think, without flattering myself, that I am sufficiently their superior not to be appreciated by them. And as a woman of the world I am no more charming than many other women of their own set.

On reaching the railway at St. Petersburg Sarah Bern-hardt was hissed by the populace because they were disap-pointed at not seeing her tall and dark, with enormous eyes, and a mass of tangled black hair.   Aside from this piece of stupidity I think the judgment formed here of the actress and the woman a just one, and I am altogether of the opin-ion of the Russian journals, which place Mlle. Delaporte above her.   For my part, with the exception of the music of her voice when she declaims, I find little in her to admire.

PARIS, *Wednesday, November* 15.—I am in Paris! We left Russia on Thursday evening.   Uncle Nicholas and Michka accompanied us as far as the first station, and Paul and his wife as far as Karkoff.   We remained twenty-four hours at Kieff, where Uncle Alexandre's daughter is at the Academy.   She is fourteen years old, and is a sweet girl.

Thursday, November 16.—I have been to see a great doctor, a surgeon who visits the hospitals.   I went incog-nito, and quietly dressed so that he might not deceive me.

Indeed, he is not a very amiable person.   He simply told me that I SHOULD NEVER RECOVER MY HEARING.   It may grow better, however, so that my deafness will be endur-able.   It is so already, in fact.   But if I do not follow strictly the treatment he prescribes for me, my deafness will increase. He has given me the address of a little doctor who will attend me for a couple of months, as he himself has only the time to see me twice a week, which is all that will be necessary.

For the first time I had the courage to say : " Doctor, I am growing deaf."   Up to the present I have used such expressions as, " I cannot hear very well," " My ears seem stopped," etc.   This time I have had the courage to say the hateful word, and the doctor has answered me with the brutality of his profession.

I only hope that the misfortunes foreshadowed in my dreams may be nothing more than *this*. But let me not trouble myself beforehand about what blows Providence may still have in store for me. For the time being I am only partially deaf.

And then he says that my hearing will certainly improve. So long as I am surrounded by my family, to watch over me and come to my assistance when I need them, it can be borne ; but how would it be if I were alone, and in the midst of strangers !

And what if it should fall to my lot to have a bad husband, or one who would be wanting in delicacy of feeling ! If *this* were even the price I had to pay for some great good fortune which had befallen me without my deserving it. But—Why do they say that God is good, that God is just ?

I shall never recover my hearing, then. It will be endurable, but there will always be a veil between me and the rest of the world. The wind among the trees, the murmur of the brook, the rain striking against the window-panes, whispered words—I shall hear none of these. With the K——'s I have not found myself once embarrassed, nor do I find myself embarrassed at table. So long as the conversation is animated I have nothing to complain of. But at the theater I miss a great deal of what is said, as I do also with my models,—the silence is so profound that they are afraid to raise their voices. Well, I had in a certain measure foreseen this for a year past ; I ought to be accustomed to the thought by this time. I am accustomed to it, but it is none the less horrible.

I have been stricken in that which was most dear to me, most necessary to my happiness.

Provided only that it stop here !

Friday, November 17.—So then I shall be henceforth less than the least of human beings—incomplete, infirm.

I shall stand in constant need of the complaisance and the co-operation of my family, and of the consideration of strangers.   Independence, freedom, all that is at an end.

I, who have been so haughty, shall have to blush and hesitate at every moment.

I write all this so as to accustom myself to the thought— not because I believe it yet ; it is too horrible.   I have not yet realized it ; it is too cruel, too hard to be believed.

The sight of my fresh and rosy countenance in the look-ing-glass fills me with pity.

Yes, every one knows it, or soon will know it,—those who have already taken such delight in disparaging me— " She is deaf."   O my God ! why this unexpected, this terrible blow ?

Tuesday, November 21.—I have been painting at the studio since yesterday.   I have returned to the simplest studies, taking note neither of the beauty of the model, nor of anything else.   " With six months of this *régime* " Julian says, " you will accomplish whatever you wish."   He is convinced that I have made no progress during the last three years, and I shall end by believing him.   In fact, since I began painting I have made but little progress.   Is this because I have not worked as hard as before ?   No, I have, on the contrary, worked harder than before, but I have undertaken subjects that are too difficult for me.

But Julian will have it that it is because I do not work hard enough, that I have made no progress.

I am tired of them all ; I am tired of myself !   I shall never recover my hearing.   Can you understand how hor-rible, how unjust, how maddening this is ?

I can bear this thought with calmness, for I was prepared for it ; but no—that is not the reason ; it is because I can-not believe it will be forever.

Do you understand what that means?—all my life long—until I die.

But I repeat, I cannot yet believe it to be true. It is impossible but that something can be done, impossible that it is to be forever, that I am to die with this veil between the universe and me, that I shall never, never, never hear again!

Is it not true that it is impossible to believe that this sentence is a final, an irrevocable one? That there is not the shadow of a hope?

This thought makes me so nervous when I am working, that I am in constant dread lest the model, or some one else in the studio, may have spoken without my having heard; or that they are ridiculing my infirmity; or that they are raising their voices so as to make me hear.

But when the model comes to me here, can I not say plainly that—what? That I cannot hear well? Let me try it, then. To make confession of my infirmity, like that! And so humiliating, so stupid, so pitiable an infirmity—an infirmity, in short!

I have not the courage to confess it, and I still cherish the hope that it may not be perceived.

Thursday, November 23.—All I have done this week is so bad that I myself cannot understand it. Julian called me to him, and spoke such useless, such cruel words to me,—I cannot understand it! Last year he said almost the same thing to me: and now, looking over last year's studies, he says: "That was good work; you would not be able to do so well now." To believe him, then, I have made no progress during the last three years; that is to say, he had begun his lamentations and his reproaches and his sarcastic speeches three years ago, ever since I began to paint, in fact.

Perhaps he thinks he will force me to work, in this way; on the contrary, it paralyzes me; I was unable to do anything for more than three hours—my hands trembled, my arms burned.

Last summer I painted a portrait of Irma, laughing, and every one thought it good. This summer, on my return from Spain, I made a pastel, after my illness, which every-one thought extremely good; and a picture which they thought good. What have I done since? I have spoiled my Fisherman; and then, I have been in Russia—six weeks of vacation; on my return I chanced upon a model I did not like, I chose a bad position; notwithstanding all this I forced myself to work against my will; I produced a wretched thing, which I destroyed. Then, I attempt to paint an arm; Julian comes to see it just as I have sketched it, and finds it very bad, and tells me so privately. That I am not a Breslau I know very well; that I need to study I know too; but between that and telling me that my case is hopeless, that I can no longer paint—upon my word, one would imagine that I knew nothing at all about art!

If I do not make as rapid progress in painting as I did in drawing, that is no reason why he should say such horrible things to me.

Monday, November 27.—Now that I have returned to the studio and he can no longer say I do not work, Julian tells me that I am pretending. This continual fault-finding becomes monotonous. The day before yesterday he said it was only during the last two years that I had made no progress. During those two years I was ill for five months, and convalescing for six months more. In the remaining time I have painted my picture for the *Salon*—a woman, life-size, painted from life in Russia, the Old Man of Nice, Therese, Irma, and Dina. So much for large paintings; I do not count several studies. That they are not good I know very well—but it is not as if my shoemaker had painted them for his own amusement.

I suppose he thinks his words will spur me on; that he is witty, perhaps. How exasperating this is! Of course I am not situated like Breslau, who moves in an artistic circle, where every word spoken, every step taken, bears some relation to art. But all that I can do, in the environment in which I am placed, I do.

No doubt I lose a great deal of time from study; in the evenings, for instance, which Breslau employs in drawing, and in sketching compositions, my attention is distracted and dissipated by the persons who surround me.

Environment—half one's progress depends upon that, during the time one is a student. Letting my thoughts dwell continually on this idea gives to my countenance an expression of concentrated rage, or rather of alienation from those who surround me. If I were not afraid of drawing down upon my head other misfortunes, I would say that God is unjust. Yet why should I say so? I have a horror of myself; I have grown stout; my shoulders, that were large enough already, are broader, my arms are rounder, and my chest fuller than before.

Tuesday, December 5.—I have just read "Honorine" at a sitting. What would I not give to be mistress of this fascinating style, that I might be able to interest my readers in my dull existence.

It would be curious if this record of my failures and of my obscure life should be the means of procuring for me the fame I long for, and shall always long for. But I should not be conscious of it then; and, besides, in order that any one should wade through these interminable pages, would it not be necessary that I should first win a name?

Two or three days ago we went to the Hotel Drouot, where there was an exhibition of precious stones. Mamma, my aunt, and Dina were lost in admiration of some of the ornaments; I, however, made little of anything, with the exception of some enormous diamonds which, for a single instant, I desired to possess; it would be delightful, I thought, to possess a pair of them; but such a thing was not to be thought of. I contented myself with thinking, therefore. that if I should one day marry a millionnaire, I might own a pair of earrings with diamonds of this size, or a brooch, for stones of such a size would be almost too heavy for earrings. This was the first time I had ever fully appreciated the beauty of precious stones. Well, last night those two stones were brought to me; my mother and my aunt had bought them for me, yet I had only said, without the slightest expectation of ever having them, " Those are the only diamonds I have ever cared to possess." They are worth twenty-five thousand francs; they are yellow, otherwise they would have cost three times that sum.

I amused myself with them during the whole evening; I kept them in my pocket while I was modeling. Dusautoy played, and Bojidar and the others chatted. I did not part with the stones all the evening, and I placed them beside my bed when I went to sleep.

Ah, if certain other things that seem as impossible might only be so easily obtained—even if they should prove to be yellow, and should cost only four thousand instead of twenty-five thousand francs !

Thursday, December 7.—I spent a few moments chatting with Julian, but we never have the long and friendly conversations together now that we used to have. We have no longer anything to talk about, everything has been said; we are waiting until I shall accomplish something. I reproached him with his injustice toward me, however, or rather with the means he took to spur me on.

My pastel is to be sent to a club, and then to the *Salon.*

"It could not be better," said Julian, and I felt like throwing my arms around his neck.

Well, then, I must paint a picture that artists will stop to look at. But I shall not be able to do that just yet. Ah, if I only thought that by working, no matter how hard, I might at last succeed! That would give me courage, but at present I feel as if it were impossible.

Thursday, December 14.—We went this morning to see the paintings which the real Bastien has brought back with him from the country. We found him engaged in making some alterations in his pictures. Our meeting was like that of good friends ; he is so amiable, so unpretending !

Perhaps he is not quite that ; but then he has so much genius ! But yes, he is charming.

As for the poor architect, he is completely cast in the shade by his brother's splendor. Jules brought with him several studies of " The Soir au Village ": a peasant returning from his labor in the fields, has stopped to talk with a woman who is going toward a house in the distance, the windows of which are lighted up by the rays of the rising moon. The effect of the twilight is marvelously rendered ; one can feel the calm of the hour pervading everything. It is full of poetry and charm, and the coloring is wonderful.

There is also a scene representing a Forge, at which an old man is at work. It is very small, and is as fine as those wonderful little dark pictures that are to be seen at the Louvre. Besides these there are landscapes and marine views—Venice and London—and two large pictures, an English flower-girl, and a little peasant-girl in a field.

At the first glance one is dazzled by the versatility and the force of this genius that disdains to confine itself to a single style, and that treats every style in a masterly manner.

This English boy is far superior to the two pictures I

have just mentioned. As for the boy of last year, entitled " Pas-meche," it is simply a masterpiece.

Sunday, December 17.—The real, the only, the great Bastien-Lepage came to see me to-day. I received him with embarrassment, for I was vexed and humiliated at having nothing worth while to show him.

He stayed looking at my pictures for more than two hours, although I did my best to prevent his seeing them. This great artist is extremely amiable ; he tried to put me at my ease, and we spoke of Julian, who is the cause of my present discouragement. Bastien does not treat me like a society girl. His opinion is the same as that of Tony Robert-Fleury and of Julian, only he does not make use of the horrible jests of the latter, who says all is over ; that I shall never be able to accomplish anything ; that there is no hope for me. This is what afflicts me.

Bastien is adorable ; that is to say, I adore his talent ; and I think my embarrassment in his presence was the most delicate and flattering compliment I could have paid him. He made a sketch in the album of Miss Richards, in which she had asked me to draw something, and, as the paint passed through, and stained the following page, he wished to lay a piece of paper between.

" Leave it so," I said ; " she will then have two sketches, instead of one." I don't know why I should do a favor to Miss Richards, but at times it amuses me to give pleasure to a person who does not expect it from me, or one who is a stranger to me.

Wednesday, December 20.—I have made no choice of a subject yet for the *Salon,* and nothing suggests itself.—This is torture !

Saturday, December 23.—The great, the real, the incomparable Bastien-Lepage and his brother dined with us this evening. We had invited no other guests, which made me feel a little embarrassed. As it was the first time they had dined with us, it might seem as if we were treating them with too much familiarity ; and then I was afraid, besides, of not being able to entertain them.

As to the brother, he is received here with almost the same familiarity as Bojidar, but our concern was for the real, the great, the only, etc. And the good little man, whose genius is worth more than his weight in gold, is flattered and pleased, I think, at being regarded in this way ; no one has yet called him a "genius." I do not call him so, either. I only treat him as such, and, by means of artifices, make him swallow the most extravagant compliments. Bojidar came for a few moments in the evening ; was in an amiable humor, and agreed with everything I said. We treat him like one of the family, and he is pleased to meet here celebrities such as Bastien.

But in order that Bastien may not think I carry my admiration for him to excess, I couple Saint-Marceaux with him whenever I speak of them. "You two," I say. He stayed until midnight. He thought a bottle I had painted very good. "That is the way you must work," he added, "with patience and concentration ; use your best efforts to copy nature faithfully."

Tuesday, December 26.—Well, it seems that I am really ill ; the doctor who is attending me is unacquainted with me ; he has no interest in deceiving me, and he says the right lung is affected ; that it will never be completely cured, but that, if I take care of my health, it will grow no worse, and I may live as long as any one else. Yes, but it is necessary to arrest the progress of the disease by heroic measures—by burning, and by a blister—everything that is delightful, in short ! A blister ! that means a yellow stain for a year or more.   I might, indeed, conceal the mark by wearing, in the evening, a bunch of flowers over the right shoulder.

I shall wait for a week longer ; if I am no better by that time, I shall consent to this atrocity.

Thursday, December 28.—So this, then, is what the matter is—I have consumption ; he told me so to-day. " Take care of yourself," he said ; " try to get well, or you will regret it."

He is a young man, and has an intelligent look, this doctor ; to my objections regarding the blister, and other wretched things of the kind, he answered that I would regret it if I did not follow his advice, and that he has never in his life seen so extraordinary a patient as I am ; and also that from my appearance no one would suppose that my lungs were affected.   And, indeed, although both my lungs are affected, the left much less seriously than the right however, I look the picture of health.

The first time I felt anything in the left lung was on leaving the sacred catacombs of Kieff, where we had gone to pray to God and to the saints for my recovery, reinforcing our prayers by paying to have a great many masses said.   A week ago scarcely anything was noticeable in the left lung.   He asked me if any of my family had had consumption.

" Yes," I replied, " my grandfather, and two of his sisters, the Countess of Toulouse-Lautrec, and the Baroness Stralborne, a great-great-grandfather, and two grand-aunts." At any rate, I have consumption.

My knees trembled slightly as I went downstairs, after my interview with this good man, who is interested in so eccentric a patient.   The disease might be checked if I would follow his orders ; that is to say, apply blisters to the chest, and go to the South—disfigure myself for a year and go into banishment. And what is a year compared to one's whole life? And my life is so beautiful!

I am quite calm, but I have a sense of strangeness at being the only one in the secret of my misfortune. And how about the fortune-teller who predicted for me so much happiness? Mother Jacob, however, told me that I should have a serious illness, and here it is. In order that her predictions may be altogether fulfilled there are still to come : A great success; wealth, marriage, and the love of a married man. This news about the left lung troubles me, though. Potain would never acknowledge that the lungs were affected ; he made use of the phrases usual in such cases—the bronchial tubes, bronchitis, etc. It is better to know exactly what the matter is; that will decide me to do all I can—except to go away this year.

Next winter I shall have my painting of the Holy Women as an excuse for this journey. To go this winter would be to begin over again the follies of last year. I will do everything that it is possible for me to do, then, except go South—and trust in the grace of God!

What has made this doctor speak so seriously is, that since he has been attending me my lungs have become much worse. He was treating me for my deafness, and I mentioned my chest to him by chance, and laughingly ; he examined my lungs and prescribed some remedies for them a month ago, and laid particular stress on blistering ; on this latter, however, I could not resolve, hoping that the trouble would not progress so rapidly as it has done.

I have consumption, then, but my lungs have been affected only for the past two or three years. And after all the trouble is not so serious as to cause my death, though it is very distressing!

But how, then, explain my blooming appearance, and the fact that the waists of my dresses, made before my illness, and when no one had any idea that there was anything the matter with me, are all too small for me? I suppose I shall grow thin all of a sudden.

Well, if I am granted ten years of life, and during those ten years love and fame, I shall be content to die at thirty. If there were any one with whom it would be possible to make this agreement, I would do so—to die—having lived up to that time—at thirty.

But I should like to get well; that is to say, that the progress of the malady might be arrested, for the disease is never cured, though one may live with it a long time—as long as any one else, in fact. I will apply as many blisters as they like to my chest, but I must go on with my painting.

Ah, I was right in predicting that it was my fate to die early. After being overwhelmed with misfortunes death now comes to end all. I knew well that I must die early; my life, as it was, could not last. This desire to possess all things, these colossal aspirations, could not continue, I knew it well; years ago at Nice I foresaw dimly all that would be necessary to make life possible for me. But others possess even more than I desired, and they do not die.

I shall speak to no one of my condition, with the exception of Julian, who knows it already. He dined with us this evening, and, finding myself alone with him for a moment, I nodded to him significantly, pointing to my throat and chest as I did so. He cannot believe it, I appear so strong. He tried to reassure me by telling me of friends of his in regard to whom the doctors had said the same thing, and had proved to be mistaken.

Then he asked me what my ideas respecting Heaven were. I told him Heaven had used me very ill. "As to my ideas respecting it," I added, "I have thought but little about it." He says he thinks, however, that I believe there is something after this life. "Yes," I said, "it is possible." I read him Musset's "Espoir en Dieu," and he responded by reciting Franck's invocation, "I must live!"

I, too, wish to live. Well, this position of one condemned to death almost amuses me. It is an opportunity
to pose; it is a new sensation; I hold a secret within me.
I have been touched by the hand of Death; there is a certain fascination in all this—it is a novelty, in the first
place.

And then to be able to talk *in earnest* of my death—that
amuses me, that is interesting. Only it is a pity that I cannot conveniently have any other audience than my con-
fessor Julian.

Saturday, December 30.—The disease progresses. There,
now I begin to exaggerate; yet, no, it is true that it progresses, and that I shall never be well again, and that the
good God, who is neither just nor good, will probably
inflict still further punishment upon me for daring to say
so! He inspires me with such dread that I shall submit
myself to His will—a submission which He will probably
not take into account, since it is the result of fear.

Provided only—the worst of it is that I cough a great
deal, and that ominous sounds are to be heard in my chest.
Well, let us leave everything till the fourteenth. If I can
only keep in any kind of health until then! If I only
remain free from fever; if I am not obliged to take to bed.
That is not likely, however. Yet perhaps the disease is
already beyond control, it is one that progresses so rapidly.
And both lungs! Ah, woe is me!

Sunday, December 31.—As it was too dark to paint, we
went to church; after that we went to the Exhibition, in the
Rue de Seze, of the paintings of Bastien, Saint-Marceaux,
and Cazin. This is the first time that I have seen any of
Cazin's paintings, and they have completely captivated me.
They are poetry itself; but Bastien's "Soir au Village" is in
no way inferior to any of the pictures of this poet-painter,

Cazin, and observe that Bastien has often been unjustly said to excel in execution only.

I spent a delightful hour there. How many things there were to be enjoyed! Never was there a sculptor like Saint-Marceaux. The words, so often used as to become hackneyed, "It is lifelike!" are in his case absolute truth. And, in addition to this important quality, which alone would be sufficient to make the success of an artist, there is in his work a depth of thought, an intensity of feeling, an indescribable something which shows Saint Marceaux to be an artist, not alone of great talent, but almost of genius.

It is only because he is young, and is still living, that I seem to exaggerate his merits.

For the moment I am disposed to place him above Bastien.

I have at present a fixed idea—it is to possess a picture by the one, and a statue by the other.

1883.

Monday, January 1.—Gambetta, who had been lying ill and wounded for many days past, has just died. Died, notwithstanding all his seven physicians could do to save him, notwithstanding all the interests of which he was the center, all the prayers offered up for his recovery! Why should I torment myself? Why should I hope to recover; Why should I grieve?—The idea of dying terrifies me, now, as if I had already come face to face with death.

Yes, I think it must come—soon, now. Ah, how I feel my littleness! And yet why? There must be something beyond the grave; this transitory existence cannot be all; it does not satisfy either our reason or our aspirations;

there must be something beyond; if there were not, this life would have no meaning, and God would be an absurdity.

The life to come—there are moments when one catches mysterious glimpses of it that terrify one.

Tuesday, January 16.—Emile Bastien took us to Gambetta's house at Ville d'Avray, where his brother is working.

Bastien-Lepage was seated at the foot of the bed, painting. Everything in the room remains as it was—the sheets, the eiderdown coverlet, that still retains the impress of the body, the flowers on the bed. The picture is truth itself. The head, thrown back, and taken in a three-quarter view, wears the look of nothingness that succeeds to intense suffering—a serenity that is lifelike, but that has in it also something of eternal peace. You fancy you see before you the man himself. The body, stretched motionless on the bed, and from which life has just departed, is strikingly impressive.

What a happy man Bastien-Lepage must be! I feel when in his presence a certain awkwardness. Although he has the physique of a young man of twenty-five, he has that air of unaffected and amiable serenity which is characteristic of great men—of Victor Hugo, for instance. I shall end by thinking him handsome; at all events he possesses the infinite charm conferred by the consciousness of power—in which, however, there is nothing of either arrogance or conceit.

On the wall is to be seen the mark left by the bullet which caused Gambetta's death. He called our attention to it, and the silence of this chamber, the faded flowers, the sunlight entering through the window,—all this brought the tears to my eyes. He was absorbed in his painting, however, and his back was turned to me; so, in order not to lose the benefit of this display of sensibility, I extended my hand to him abruptly, and hastily left the room, the tears running down my face. I hope that he observed them. It is hateful, yes, hateful, to have to confess that one is always thinking of the effect.   .

Monday, January 22.—For the past two months I have been going twice a week to see the doctor recommended to me by M. Duplay, who had not the time to attend me himself. The treatment that was to have produced such good results has not done so. I am no better, but they *hope* the disease will not progress. " And if it should not progress," he says, "you may consider yourself very fortunate." This is hard.

Thursday, February 22.—I have been playing airs from Chopin on the piano, and from Rossini on the harp, all alone in my studio. The moon shone brightly ; through the large window of the studio I could see the beautiful cloudless blue sky. I thought of my picture of the Holy Women, and was so carried away by the impression it made upon me, as it presented itself to my imagination, that I was seized with an irrational fear lest some one else should do it before me. This thought troubled the profound peace of the night.

I have been very happy this evening : I have been reading Hamlet in English, and I have been reveling in the music of Ambroise Thomas.

There are dramas that never lose their power to move the soul, characters that are immortal—" Ophelia," for instance, pale and fair ! we give her a place in our hearts. Ophelia ! She makes us long to experience an unhappy love. Ophelia with her flowers, Ophelia dead !—How beautiful is all this !

Ah, if God would only grant me power to finish my picture—my large picture, my real picture. My picture for this year will be only a sort of study—inspired by Bastien ?

Yes, of course ; his painting so closely resembles nature that whoever copies nature faithfully must resemble him.

His faces are living faces; they are not merely fine painting like the faces of Carolus, they are art ; in short they are the real flesh, they breathe, they live. The question here is not one of skill, nor of a fine touch. This is nature itself ; it is sublime !

Saturday, February 24.—My thoughts, as you know, are constantly occupied with Bastien-Lepage ; I repeat his name to myself continually, but I avoid speaking it aloud, as if to do so were something to be ashamed of. When I do mention it, it is with a tender familiarity which would seem to be only natural, considering his genius, but which might be misunderstood.

Good heavens ! what a pity it is that he cannot come to see me, as his brother does !

And what should I do if he were to come ? Make him my friend, of course ! What! Do you not believe there is such a feeling as friendship ? As for me I could worship those of my friends who are famous, and this not through vanity alone, but also because of the delight I take in their talents—in their intelligence, their ability, their genius. Those who are endowed with genius are a race apart ; when we have escaped from the region of mediocrity we revel in a purer atmosphere, where we may join hands with the elect, and dance a round in honor of— What was I about to say ? But the truth is, that Bastien-Lepage has a charming head.

I fear, indeed, that my painting may be found to resemble his. I copy nature faithfully, I know, but while I am doing so I am thinking of his pictures. And then, an artist of any genius who loves nature, and who desires to copy her faithfully, will always resemble Bastien.

Tuesday, February 27.—This has been a series of happy days. I sing, I chat, I laugh, and the name of Bastien-Lepage recurs constantly in my thoughts, like a refrain. Not himself, not the corporeal man, scarcely his genius— nothing but his name. Yet I am filled with a certain dread. What if my picture were to resemble his? He has lately painted a number of boys and girls—among others the celebrated " Pas-meche "; what could be finer than this?

Well, my picture represents two little boys who are walking along the pavement holding each other by the hand ; the elder, a boy of seven, holds a leaf between his teeth, and looks straight before him into space ; the other, a couple of years younger, has one hand thrust into the pocket of his little trousers, and is regarding the passers-by.

This evening I enjoyed an hour of intense happiness. Why? you ask. Did Saint-Marceaux or Bastien come? No, but I made a sketch for my *statue.*

You have read the word correctly. When the fifteenth of March is past, it is my intention to begin a statue. In my lifetime I have modeled two groups, and two or three busts, all of which I threw aside before they were finished ; for, working as I did, alone and without instruction, I could work only at something in which I was interested, into which I could throw my life, my soul, as it were— something real, in short, not a mere exercise for the studio.

To conceive a figure, to throw myself heart and soul into the work, this is what I wish to do.

It will be bad ? no matter ; I was born a sculptor. I carry my love of form to the point of adoration. Color can never exercise the same power over the soul as form does, though I adore color also. But form ! A noble gesture, a beautiful attitude, fixed in marble, look at it from what

JEAN AND JACQUES.

side you will, the outlines may change, but the figure still preserves the same significance.

Oh, happiness ! Oh, joy !

The figure is that of a woman who stands weeping, her face buried in her hands ; you know what the attitude of the shoulders is when one weeps.

I felt an impulse to kneel down before it ; I addressed a thousand foolish speeches to it. The clay model is thirty centimetres in height, but the statue itself will be life-size. But that will be an outrage on common-sense. And why ?

Finally I tore up a fine batiste chemise in which to wrap this fragile statuette. I love this clay more dearly than my own flesh.

And then, as my sight is not very good, when I can no longer see to paint I shall devote myself to sculpture.

How beautiful this moist white linen is as it follows every curve of this little figure. I wrapped it up with a sentiment of respect—so fine, so delicate, so beautiful is it.

Wednesday, February 28.—My picture will be finished to-morrow. I shall have spent nineteen days on it. If I had not had to do over one of the boys, it would have been finished in a couple of weeks. But he looked too old.

Saturday, March 3.—Tony came to see the picture. ·He is very much pleased with it. One of the heads is very good, he says.

Thursday, March 15.—My picture is at last finished ! I was still working at it at three o'clock, but a great many visitors came, and I was obliged to leave it,—Madame and Mademoiselle Canrobert, Alice, Bojidar, Alexis, the Princess, Abbema, Mme. Kanchine, and Tony Robert-Fleury came in the morning. They are all going to Bastien's to see his picture, " L'Amour au Village." It is a young girl standing with her back to the spectator, leaning against a hedge in an orchard ; her eyes are bent upon the ground, and she holds a flower in her hand ; a young man stands beside the hedge, facing the spectator ; his eyes also are cast down, and he is looking at his fingers which he is twisting together. The picture is exquisite in sentiment and full of poetry.

As for the execution—this is not art, it is nature's self. There is also a little portrait of Madame Drouot, the guardian-angel of Victor Hugo, which is wonderful in point of truth, sentiment, and resemblance. None of these pictures look like each other, even at a distance ; they are living beings who pass before your eyes. He is not a painter only, he is a poet, a psychologist, a metaphysician, a creator.

His own portrait, which stands in a corner of the room, is a masterpiece. And he has not done his best work yet—that is to say, we hope to see a large picture from him, in which he will give such proof of his genius that no one will dare to deny it any longer.

The young girl, with her hair in short braids, standing with her back to the spectator, is a poem.

No one has ever penetrated more deeply into the realities of life than Bastien. Nothing can be at the same time more elevated and more human than his painting. That the figures are life-size contributes to render the truth of his pictures more striking. Who can be said to surpass him? The Italian painters—painters of religious and, as a consequence, of conventional subjects? There are sublime painters among them, but they are necessarily conventional, and then—their paintings do not touch the heart, the soul, the intelligence. The Spanish painters? Brilliant and charming. The French are brilliant, dramatic, or academic.

Millet and Breton are poets, no doubt, but Bastien unites everything. He is the king of painters, not alone because of his wonderful execution, but on account of the sentiment expressed. The art of observing could not be carried further, and Balzac has said that almost the whole of human genius consists in observing well.

Thursday, March 22.—I sent for two workmen yesterday, who constructed the framework, life-size, for the statue I had modeled in clay. And to-day I worked on it, giving it the pose I desired. My mind is full of my picture, the Holy Women, which I will try to paint this summer ; and in sculpture, my first thought is Ariadne. Meantime I have done this figure, which is, in fact, the other Mary of the picture. In sculpture and without drapery, taking a younger model, it would make a charming Nausicaa. She has buried her face in her hands and is weeping ; there is in her attitude so genuine an abandonment, a despair so complete, so naïve, so sincere, and so touching, that I am captivated by it.

Sunday, March 25.—Since two o'clock yesterday I have been on the rack, as you may imagine when I tell you what has happened.

Villevielle came to see me and asked me if I had heard any news from the *Salon.* " No," I answered. " What ! you have heard nothing ? " she said. " Nothing." " You have passed." " I knew nothing of it." " There can be no doubt about it, since they have reached the letter C.' And this is all. I can scarcely hold the pen ; my hands tremble, I feel utterly powerless.

Then Alice came and said to me, " Your picture has been accepted."

" Accepted—but how ? Without a number ? " I asked.

" It is not yet known."

I had no doubt about its being accepted.

And all this has thrown mamma, my aunt, and everybody else into a state of agitation that it irritates me in the highest degree to see. I have had to make the greatest efforts in order to appear unconcerned, and to bring myself to see visitors.

I sent about forty telegraphic despatches. Later on I received a few lines from Julian, which I copy here word for word : " O naivete ! O sublime ignorance ! I am going to enlighten you at last.

" Your picture has been accepted, and with a number 3 at the least, for there is some one I know who wished to give you a number 2. You have conquered at last. Greeting and congratulations."

This is not happiness, but it is at least tranquillity.

I do not think that even a number 1 would have given me pleasure after these twenty-four hours' humiliating uncertainty. They say joy is more deeply felt after anxiety. Such is not the case with me. Difficulties, doubts, and suffering spoil everything for me.

Friday, March 30.—I worked until six o'clock ; as it was still daylight I opened the door leading out into the balcony, in order to hear the church clock striking, and to breathe the spring air while I played upon the harp.

I am very tranquil ; I worked faithfully all day, after which I took a bath, dressed myself in white, and sat down and played upon the harp ; now I am writing ; I am calm, contented, and happy in this apartment arranged by myself, where I have everything I want at hand ; it would be so pleasant to go on leading this life,—while waiting for fame. And even if fame were to come, I could sacrifice two months in the year to it, and live shut up in my room working the other ten months. And indeed it is only by so doing that those two months would be possible. What troubles me is to think that I must one day marry, but this is the only way in which to escape the wounds my self-love is constantly receiving.

" Why does she not marry ?" people ask. They say I

am twenty-five, and that enrages me ; while if I were once
married—but whom shall I marry ? If I were only well,
as before. But now if I marry, it must be some one who
has a good heart and delicacy of feeling. And he must
love me, for I am not rich enough to marry a man who
would leave me entirely to myself.

In all this it is not my heart that speaks. One cannot
foresee everything ; and then it would depend—And besides it may never happen. I have just received the following letter :

> " PALACE OF THE CHAMPS-ELYSÉES.
> ASSOCIATION OF FRENCH ARTISTS FOR THE AN-
> NUAL EXHIBITION OF THE FINE ARTS.

" MADEMOISELLE :

" I write to you here in the committee room to inform you
that the Head in Pastel has had a genuine success with the
committee. Receive my heartiest congratulations. I need
not tell you that your paintings have been very well received.

" You have met with a genuine success this year, which
makes me very happy.

> " With friendly regards,
> " TONY ROBERT-FLEURY."

Well, and what then ? The letter itself I shall pin down
here, but I must first show it to a few friends. Do you
imagine I am wild with joy ? Not at all ; I am quite calm.
Doubtless I am not worthy of experiencing a great joy,
since such a piece of news as this causes me no more emotion than if it were the most natural thing in the world.
And the fact of the letter being addressed to me makes it
lose much of its significance. If I knew that Breslau had
received a letter like it I should be greatly troubled. This
is not because I value only that which I do not possess, but
because of my excessive modesty. I lack confidence in
myself. If I were to take this letter literally, I should be

too happy. When good fortune comes to me I am slow to believe in it. I fear to rejoice too soon. And after all the cause for rejoicing is not so great.

Saturday, March 31.—Nevertheless I went to Julian's this morning, in order to hear a repetition of these flattering things. It seems Bouguereau said to him : " You have a Russian who has sent something that is not bad— not at all bad." "And you know," added Julian, "that this from Bouguereau, where one of his own pupils is not concerned, means a great deal." In short, it seems I shall receive some sort of mention.

Sunday, April 1 . . . . I cough a great deal, and although I have not grown visibly thinner, I fear I am seriously ill. Only I don't want to think about it. But if I am seriously ill, why do I present so healthy an appearance in every way ?

I try to discover some cause for my sadness, and I can find none, unless it be that I have done nothing for the last fortnight. The statue is falling to pieces ; all this has made me lose a great deal of time.

What vexes me is that the pastel should be thought so good, and the painting simply good. Well, then ! I feel that I am capable now of producing something equally good in painting—and you shall see !

I am not sad ; but I am feverish, and I find difficulty in breathing. It is the right lung that grows worse, that is all.

Tuesday, April 3.—The weather is delightful ; I feel new strength. I feel that I possess the power to produce something really good ; I feel it, I am sure of it.

So, then, to-morrow.

I feel within me the capacity to render with truth to

nature whatever strikes my imagination. I feel a new
force, a confidence in my own powers that will give me
thrice the ability to work that I had before. I shall begin
a picture to-morrow, the subject of which charms me. I
have another very interesting one for later on in the autumn
when the bad weather commences. I feel that now every
stroke will tell, and I am intoxicated with the thought of
my work.

Red-letter day, Wednesday, April 4.—Six little boys in a
group, their heads close together, half-length only. The
eldest is about twelve, the youngest six. The eldest of the
boys, who stands partly with his back to the spectator, holds
a bird's nest in his hands, at which the others stand looking.
The attitudes are varied and natural.

The youngest boy, whose back only is to be seen, stands
with folded arms and head erect.

This seems commonplace, according to the description,
but in reality all these heads grouped together will make an
exceedingly interesting picture.

Sunday, April 15.—My disease has reduced me to a state
of prostration that renders me indifferent to everything.
Julian writes to say that my picture is not yet hung ; that
Tony Robert-Fleury cannot PROMISE (sic) to have it hung on
the line ; but that, as it is not yet hung, all that can be done
in the matter will be done. That Tony Robert-Fleury
strongly (sic) hopes to receive some slight recompense in
the shape of a painting (sic) or a pastel ! Two months ago
I had not expected anything of the kind, yet I am as indifferent to it all now as if I were not concerned in it.
This mention, which I once thought it would make me
faint with emotion to receive, now that they tell me it is
probable, almost certain indeed, will, I feel, cause me no
emotion whatever.

There is a logic in the events of life by which each event prepares us for that which is to follow ; and this it is that diminishes my pleasure. I should have wished this news to come like a thunder-clap—I should have wished the medal to fall down from the skies, as it were, without giving time to cry out " Take care ! " and plunge me in a sea of happiness.   .

Wednesday, April 18.—If I receive a mention this year, I shall have progressed more rapidly than Breslau, who had already studied hard, before commencing with Julian. In short—

I have just been playing the piano. I began by playing the two divine marches of Chopin and Beethoven, and then went on playing whatever chanced to come into my head,— melodies so exquisite that I fancy I can hear them still. Is it not curious ! I could not play a single note of any one of them now, if I were to try, nor if I wished to improvise could I do so. The hour, the mood, a certain something is necessary, yet the most heavenly harmonies are running through my head. If I had the voice I could sing the most ravishing, the most dramatic, the most original airs. To what end ? Life is too short ; it does not give one time to accomplish anything. I should like to take up sculpture, without giving up painting. Not that I wish to be a sculptor, but because I have visions of the Beautiful which I feel an imperious necessity of giving form to.

Sunday, April 22.—Two pastels only have received a number 1—Breslau's and mine. Breslau's picture is not hung on the line, but her portrait of the daughter of the editor of *Figaro* is on the line. My picture is not on the line, either, but Tony Robert-Fleury assures me that it looks well, and that the picture under it is not a large one. The head of Irma is on the line, and in an angle—

in a place of honor, consequently. In short, he says my pictures are well hung.

We have people to dine with us almost every evening, and I often say to myself as I listen to their conversation, " Here are people who spend their lives doing nothing but making silly or artificial remarks. Are they happier than I ? " Their cares are of a different nature, but they suffer as much. And they do not take as much enjoyment in everything as I do. Many things escape their notice— shades of language or of coloring, for instance, which to me are sources of interest or of pleasure, such as are unknown to vulgar souls. But perhaps I am more prone than most people to observe the beauties of nature, as well as the countless details of city life, and if it be true that I am in one sense inferior to the rest of the world, since I am occasionally unable to hear as well as others, perhaps I am not without some compensation for it.

Ah, no ; every one knows it, and it is the first thing they say to each other when they mention my name. " She is a little deaf, did you know it ? " I do not understand how I am able to write the word. Is it possible to accustom one's-self to so terrible an affliction ? It is conceivable that this should happen to an old man or to an old woman, or to some miserable creature, but not to a young girl like me, full of ardor, full of energy, eager for life !

Friday, April 27.—I think that in art a certain glow of enthusiasm may supply in some sort the want of genius. Here is a proof of this : it is six or seven years since I have played on the piano ; that is to say, I have remained for whole months without touching it, and then played five or six hours at a time once or twice a year. Under such circumstances the fingers lose their flexibility, so that I now never play before people ; the merest school-girl would put me in the shade.

But let me only hear a masterpiece played, like the march of Chopin, or that of Beethoven, for instance, let me be seized by the desire to play it myself, and in two or three days, practicing not more than an hour a day, I shall be able to play it perfectly, as well as any one, as Dusautoy, for instance, who took the first prize at the Conservatory, and who practices constantly.

Monday, April 30.—I have had the happiness of talking with Bastien-Lepage.

He has explained his Ophelia to me !

This man is not an ordinary artist. He does not regard his subject from the standpoint of an artist, merely, but from that of a student of human nature, also. His observations revealed an intimate knowledge of the most secret recesses of the soul ; he does not see in Ophelia a mad girl only, she is a lovelorn creature as well. In her madness there is disenchantment, bitterness, despair, hopelessness ; she has been disappointed in love, and her disappointment has partly turned her brain. There can be nothing sadder, more touching, more heart-rending than this picture.

I am wild about it. Ah, how glorious a thing is genius ! This ugly little man appears to me more beautiful and more attractive than an angel. One would like to spend one's life listening to him and watching him in his sublime labors. And then he speaks so simply. In answer to a remark of some one he said, " I find so much poetry in nature," with an accent of such perfect sincerity that I was inexpressibly charmed.

I exaggerate, I feel that I exaggerate. But something of this there is.

Tuesday, May 1.—And the *Salon ?* Well, it is worse than usual. Dagnan does not exhibit. Sargent is mediocre ; Gervex commonplace ; Henner is charming ; his picture is a nude figure of a woman reading. The light is artificial, and everything is bathed in a sort of luminous mist, of so exquisite a tone that one feels as though enveloped in it. Jules Bastien admires it greatly. A painting of Cazin's, that I like less than his landscapes, is Judith departing from the city to meet Holofernes. I did not look at it long enough to come under its spell, but what struck me most forcibly in it was that the attractions of Judith are not sufficient excuse for Holofernes's infatuation.

I am not very enthusiastic about Bastien-Lepage's picture. The two figures are faultless. The figure of the girl standing with her back to the spectator, the head, of which nothing is to be seen but one cheek, the hand playing with a flower—there is in all these a feeling, a poetical charm, and a truth to nature which cannot be surpassed.

The back is a poem; the hand, of which we can just catch a glimpse, is a masterpiece; we feel all that he has desired to express. The girl bends down her head, and is at a loss as to what she shall do with her feet, which have assumed an attitude of charming embarrassment. The young man is very good also. But the girl is the embodiment of grace, of youth, of poetry. The figure is true to nature, and full of feeling, delicacy, and grace.

The landscape, however, is altogether disagreeable. Not only is it of too pronounced a green, but it obtrudes itself on the eye as well. There is a want of space. Why is this? Some say that the colors in the background are too thickly laid on. At all events it is heavy.

And Breslau? Breslau's picture is good, but I am not quite pleased with it. It is well executed, but the picture expresses nothing; the coloring is graceful, but commonplace. It represents a group—a brunette and a blonde, and a young man—drinking tea at the fireside, in a bourgeois interior, without character. They all wear a solemn expression; the air of sociability we look for in such a scene is wanting. She who talks so much about sentiment does not appear to be very richly endowed in that respect. Her portrait is good, that is all.

And I ?

Well, the head of Irma is pleasing, and the execution sufficiently bold. But the picture is unpretentious.

The painting has a somber look, and, although executed in the open air, it does not look natural. The wall is not like a wall—it is the sky, a piece of painted canvas, anything you choose. The heads are good; but the background is poor. They might have given it a better place, however, especially as things so inferior to it are on the line. Every one agrees that the heads—that of the elder boy, particularly—are very good. Probably I should have succeeded better with the rest of the picture, since the treatment is comparatively easy, if I had had more time.

Looking at my picture hanging there before me I learned more than I could have learned in six months at the studio. The *Salon* is a great school; I never understood this as well as now.

Wednesday, May 2.—I ought to go to the opera, but what for? That is to say, I thought for a moment of doing so in order to show myself to the best advantage; that Bastien might hear my beauty spoken of. And why do this? I do not know. Well, it was a stupid thought! Is it not silly to try to make people like me whom I care nothing about, and that through pique?—I shall think of it, however, the rather as it would be in reality for the King of Prussia that I should go, for after all I have no serious cause of complaint against this great artist. Would I marry him? No. Well, then, what do I want?

And why seek to analyze every sentiment so minutely. I have a wild desire to please this great man, and that is all. And Saint-Marceaux as well. Which of them most? No matter which: either would do. It would be an interest in life. This feeling has given a new expression to my face. I look prettier; my complexion is smooth, fresh, and blooming; my eyes are animated and brilliant. At all events it is curious. What would not real love accomplish, if a silly fancy can produce an effect like this?

After all, that is not the question. Jules Bastien dined with us this evening. I posed neither as a mad creature nor a child. I was neither silly nor mischievous. He was simple, gay, charming; we rallied each other incessantly; there was not an instant's embarrassment. He is very intelligent; and then I do not believe in specialties for men of genius; a man of genius can be and ought to be everything he wishes.

And he is gay too; I feared to see him insensible to that delicate humor that is half-way between wit and humbug. In short, like Roland's mare, he has every quality; the only thing is that he is dead—or almost so, as far as I am concerned. Is it not stupid?

Sunday, May 6.—There has been a great deal of talk about young Rochegrosse's picture. It represents Astyanax being torn from the arms of his mother Andromache, to be cast over the ramparts.

It is a *modern* and original treatment of an antique subject. He imitates no one and seeks inspiration from no one. The coloring and the execution are of unexampled vigor—there is no other artist of the present day who is capable of them In addition, he is the son-in-law of M. Th. de Banville,— so much for the press.

Notwithstanding this latter fact, however, he has wonderful gifts. He is only twenty-four, and this is the second time he exhibits.

This is the way one would like to paint—composition, color, drawing, all are indescribably spirited.

And this is the quality expressed by his name—Rochegrosse. It is like the rumbling of thunder. After the idyllic Bastien-Lepage. Georges Rochegrosse comes on you like a torrent. It is possible that later on his talent may become more concentrated, and that he will aim at being a poet and psychologist in painting, like Bastien-Lepage.

And I? What does my name express—Marie Bashkirtseff—I would willingly change it; it has a harsh, bizarre sound; though it has a certain ring of triumph in it too; there is even a certain charm in it, something expressive of arrogance, of renown; but it also has a quarrelsome, jerking sound. Tony Robert-Fleury—is it not cold as an epitaph? And Bonnat?—correct and vigorous but short and commonplace. Manet sounds like something incomplete—a pupil who will be known at fifty. Breslau is sonorous, calm, powerful. Saint-Marceaux is like Bashkirtseff, nervous, but not so harsh. Henner is tranquil and mysterious, with an indescribable something in it of antique grace.

Carolus Duran is a mask. Dagnan is subtle, veiled, delicate, sweet, and strong, with little beyond this. Sargent makes one think of his painting, of the false Velasquez, of the false Carolus, not so great as Velasquez, yet good, nevertheless.

Monday, May 7.—I have begun the little *gamins* over again from the beginning. I have drawn them full-length, and on a larger canvas; this will make a more interesting picture.

Tuesday, May 8.—I live only for my art; I go downstairs only to dine, and talk with no one.

I feel that I am passing through a new phase.

Everything seems petty and uninteresting, everything except my work. Life, taken thus, may be beautiful.

Wednesday, May 9.—We had some visitors this evening,

who were entirely different from our usual set and who would shock these very much, but whom I found very entertaining.

Jules Bastien, who lays such stress on concentrating all one's forces on one particular point, does not, for his own part, expend his energy uselessly. For myself, so superabundant are my energies that it is a necessity with me to have some outlet for them. Of course, if conversation or laughter fatigues one, it is better to abstain from them, but—he must be right, however.

We went up to my studio, and I almost quarreled with Bastien to prevent him looking at my large picture, the face of which was turned against the wall.

I praised Saint-Marceaux extravagantly, and Jules Bastien declared he was jealous of him, and that he would never rest until he had ousted him from the place he holds in my regard.

He has said this several times already; and although it may be only a jest, it delights me to hear him say it.

I must make him think that I admire Saint-Marceaux more than I admire him—in an artistic sense, of course.

"You like him, do you not?" I said to him.

"Yes, very much."

"Do you like him as much as I do?"

"Oh, no; I am not a woman; I like him, but—"

"But it is not as a woman that I like him."

"Oh, yes, there is a little of that in your admiration for him."

"No, indeed, I assure you."

"Oh, yes, unconsciously there is."

"Ah, can you suppose—?"

"Yes, and I am jealous of him; I am not dark and handsome, as he is."

"He resembles Shakspeare."

"You see!"

The real Bastien is going to hate me! And why should he hate me? I do not know, but I fear that he will. There is always a certain feeling of hostility between us— little things one cannot explain, but that one feels. We are not *in sympathy* with each other; yet I have gone out of my way to say things before him that might perhaps— make him like me a little.

In regard to art we think alike, but I dare not speak of art in his presence. Is this because I feel that he does not like me?

In short, there is a *something—*

Friday, May 18.—To set my heart upon possessing the friendship of Bastien-Lepage would be to give too much importance to this feeling, to distort it, so to say, and to place myself, in my own eyes, in a false position. His friendship would have been a great pleasure to me, as Cazin's or Saint-Marceaux's would be; but I am vexed to think I should have let my thoughts dwell upon him personally— he is not sufficiently great for that. He is not a demigod in art, like Wagner, and it is only in such a case that it would be admissible to entertain a profound admiration for him.

What I long for is to gather around me an interesting circle, but every time this hope seems about to be realized something happens to interfere; here is mamma gone to Russia, papa dying, perhaps.

I had planned to give a dinner followed by a reception, every Thursday, for instance, for society people, and on Saturday another dinner for artists; at the receptions on Thursdays I would have the most distinguished of the artists, who had dined with me on the previous Saturday.

And now there is an end to all this; but I will try again next year to carry out my plan, as tranquilly as if I were conscious of the power to succeed, as patiently as if I were to live forever, and as perseveringly as if I had been already successful.

I am going to begin a panel—Spring: A woman leaning against a tree, her eyes closed, and smiling as if she were in a beautiful dream. Around is a delicate landscape—tender greens, faint rose-tints, apple and peach trees in blossom, budding leaves—all that gives to Spring its magic coloring.

Bastien-Lepage is going to paint a picture representing the burial of a young girl, and his views in art are so just that he will be sure to make the landscape like this that I have been dreaming of. I *hope* it will not prove so, however, and that he will give us a landscape of a vile green, instead—yet it would vex me if he did not make a sublime picture of this subject.

Sunday, May 20.—Mamma arrived in Russia early on Friday morning; we received a dispatch from her on Saturday in which she says that papa's health is in a deplorable state.

To-day his valet writes that his condition is desperate. He says, too, that he suffers greatly; I am glad mamma arrived in time.

To-morrow the distribution of prizes takes place, and the *Salon* is to be closed for three days. On Thursday it will be re-opened.

I dreamed that I saw a coffin placed upon my bed, and that I was told a young girl was lying in it. And through the surrounding darkness glowed a phosphorescent light.

Tuesday, May 22.—I worked till half-past seven; but at every noise I hear, every time the bell rings, every time Coco barks, my heart sinks into my boots. How expressive this saying is; we have it also in Russia.—It is nine o'clock and no news yet—how many emotions! If I receive nothing, it will be very exasperating! They were all so sure of it at the studio—Julian, Lefebvre, and Tony have spoken so much of it among themselves, that it cannot be but that I shall receive something. In that case they might have telegraphed it to me; one can never hear good news too soon.

Ah, if I had received anything I should have heard of it already.

I have a slight headache.

Not that it is of so much consequence, however; but every one was so sure of it—and then uncertainty about anything is odious.

And my heart is beating, beating. Miserable existence! This, and everything else, and all for what? To end in death!

No one escapes—this is the fate of all. .

To end, to end, to exist no longer—this is what is horrible. To be gifted with genius enough to last for an eternity—and to write stupid things with a trembling hand because the news of having received a•miserable mention delays in coming.

They have just brought me a letter; my heart stood still for a moment—it was from Doucet about the waist of a dress.

I am going to take some syrup of opium to calm my nerves. To see my agitation one would suppose I had been thinking about my Holy Women; the picture is all sketched in, and when I work on it or think of it, I am in the same state of agitation as at present.

It is impossible for me to fix my thoughts upon anything.

A quarter-past nine. It could not be that the discreet Julian should have committed himself as he has done, and that I should not receive it! But, then, this silence!

My cheeks are burning; I feel as if I were enveloped in flame: I have sometimes had bad dreams in which I have felt like this.

It is only twenty-five minutes past nine.

Julian ought to have come before this; he must have known at six o'clock; he would have come to dine with us—I have received nothing then.

I thought that my picture would be refused when there was no possibility of that being the case. But that I should receive nothing now is very possible.

I have just been watching the carriages as they passed. Ah, it is now too late!

There is no medal of honor for painting, and Dalou will have received the medal for sculpture.

What does this matter to me?

Would I have given Bastien the medal of honor? No. He can do better than this "Amour au Village," consequently he does not deserve it. They might have given it to him for his sublime "Jeanne d'Arc," the landscape in which displeased me three years ago.

I should like to look at it again.

Thursday, May 24.—I have received it ! And I am once more reassured and tranquil, not to say happy. I might say satisfied.

I learned it from the papers. Those gentlemen have not taken the trouble to write me a word about it.

Nothing is ever so good or so bad in reality as it is in the anticipation.

Monday, June 11.—My father is dead.

We received the dispatch announcing his death at ten o'clock ; that is to say, a few minutes since. My aunt and Dina thought mamma ought to return here at once without waiting for the interment. I went to my room very much agitated, but I shed no tears. When Rosalie came to show me my new gown, however, I said to her, "It is not worth while, Monsieur is dead," and I burst into an uncontrollable fit of weeping.

Have I anything to reproach myself with concerning him? I do not think so. I have always tried to do my duty toward him. But in moments like these one always thinks one's-self in some way to blame. I ought to have gone with mamma.

He was only fifty years old. And he had suffered so much! And he had never injured any one. He was beloved by all around him; he was strictly honorable in all his dealings, upright, and an enemy to all intrigue.

Friday, June 15.—The Canroberts have written me a charming letter; indeed every one has shown me the greatest sympathy.

This morning, not expecting to meet any one I knew, I ventured to go to the Petit hall—an exhibition of a hundred masterpieces for a benefit of some kind,—of Decamps, Delacroix, Fortuny, Rembrandt, Rousseau, Millet, Meissonier (the only living artist represented) and others. And in the first place I must apologize to Meissonier, of whom I had little previous knowledge, and who had only very inferior compositions at the last exhibition of portraits. Yes, these are literally marvels of art.

But what had chiefly induced me to leave my seclusion was the desire to see the paintings of Millet, of whom I had heretofore seen nothing, and whose praises were continually dinned into my ears. "Bastien is only a weak imitator of his," they said. Finally I was tempted to go. I looked at all his pictures, and I shall go back again to look at them. Bastien is an imitator of his, if you will, because both are great artists and both depict peasant life, and because all genuine masterpieces bear a family resemblance to each other.

Cazin's landscapes resemble Millet's much more closely than do those of Bastien. What is most admirable in Millet, judging from the six paintings I saw at the Exhibition, is the general effect, the harmonious arrangement, the atmosphere, the transparency. The figures are unimportant and are simply treated, but broadly and correctly. And this it is in which Bastien has no equal to-day—the execution, at once careful, spirited and vigorous, of his human figures—his perfect imitation of nature. His "Soir au Village," which is only a sketch of small dimensions, is certainly equal to anything of the kind of Millet's ; there are in it only two small figures dimly seen in the twilight. I cannot think of his "Amour au Village," however, with patience. How faulty is the background ! How is it that he cannot see this ? Yes, in the larger paintings of Bastien there is wanting the tone, the general effect, that make the small pictures of Millet so remarkable. Whatever may be said to the contrary, everything else in a picture should be subordinate to the figure.

"Le Pere Jacques" in its general effect is superior to "L'Amour au Village"; this is the case with "Les Foins," also. "Le Pere Jacques " is full of poetry ; the girl gathering flowers is charming, and the old man is well executed. I know that it is extremely difficult to give a large picture that character, at once soft and vigorous, which is distinctive of Millet, but this is what must be aimed at ; in a smaller picture many details may be slighted. I speak of those pictures in which the execution is everything (not of those of the overscrupulous Meissonier), like those of Cazin, for example, who is the disciple of Millet. In a small picture that indescribable quality called charm, which is a result of the general effect rather than of any particular detail, may be given with a few happy strokes of the brush, while in a large picture this is not the case—there feeling must rest on a basis of science.

Saturday, June 16.—So then, I withdraw from Bastien's paintings the title of masterpieces. And why? Is it be-

cause his " Amour au Village " shocks me, or because I have
not the courage of my opinions ? We can only deify those
who are no longer living; if Millet were not dead, what
would be said of him ? And then there are only six paintings of Millet's here. Could we not find six equally excellent paintings among those of Bastien? " Pas-meche,"
" Jeanne d'Arc," the portrait of his brother, the "Soir au
Village," " Les Foins." I have not seen all his paintings,
and he is not dead. Bastien is less the disciple of Millet
than is Cazin, who resembles him greatly—with the difference that he is younger. Bastien is original ; he is
himself. One always imitates some one at first, but one's
own personality gradually asserts itself. And then poetry,
vigor, and grace are always the same, and it would be
disheartening, indeed, if the attempt to attain them were
to be called imitation. A picture of Millet fills you with
admiration, one of Bastien's produces the same effect upon
you ; what does that prove?

People of shallow minds say this is the result of imitation ; they are wrong ; two different actors may move you
in the same manner, because genuine and intense emotion
is always the same.

Etincelle devotes a dozen flattering lines to me. I am a
remarkable artist. I am a young girl, and a pupil of Bastien-
Lepage. Mark that !

I saw a bust of Renan by Saint-Marceaux, and yesterday
I saw Renan himself pass by in a fiacre. At least the likeness is good.

Monday, June 18.—Here is a little incident : I had
granted an interview for eleven o'clock this morning to the
correspondent of the *New Times* (of St. Petersburg), who
had written to me requesting one. It is a very important
periodical; and this M. B.—— has contributed to it, among
other things, some studies on our painters in Paris, and—

" as you occupy a conspicuous place among them, I hope you will permit me," etc.

Before going downstairs I left him alone with my aunt for a few minutes, that she might prepare the way by telling him how young I was, and other things of the kind, for the sake of effect. He looked at all my pictures, and took notes of them. "When did I begin to paint," he asked, " at what age, and under what circumstances?" and so on. I am an artist on whom the correspondent of a great newspaper is going to write an article.

This is a beginning; it is the mention that has procured me this. Provided only that the article be a favorable one. I do not know if the notes were correct, because I did not hear all that was said, and then the situation was embarrassing.

It was my aunt and Dina who told him—what? I shall await this article with anxiety—and it will not appear for a fortnight.

They laid particular stress upon my *youth.*

Thursday, June 21.—To-morrow the distribution of prizes takes place; they have sent me a list of the prizes to be given, with my name on it (section of painting); this is pleasant; but I have some hesitation about being present— it is hardly worth while, and then if—

What am I afraid of? I cannot tell.

Friday, June 22.—I thought for an instant, as I looked at the people present, that it would be terrible to rise and go forward to that table.

My aunt and Dina were seated behind me, for only those who were to receive prizes had the right to chairs.

Well, the day is at last over, and it was altogether different from what I had thought it would be.

Oh, to receive a medal next year, and to realize my

dreams at last ! To be applauded, to achieve a triumph ! And when I have received a second-class medal, no doubt I shall want a first-class one ? Of course.

And after that the cross ? Why not ? And afterward ? And afterward to enjoy the fruit of my labors, of my struggles, to go on working, to make as much progress as possible, to try to be happy, to love and to be loved.

Yes, afterward we shall see ; there is no hurry. I shall be neither uglier nor older, so to say, in five years to come than I am to-day. And if I were to marry hastily now, I might repent it. But, after all, it is indispensable for me to marry ; I am twenty-two years old, and people take me to be older ; not that I look to be so, but when I was thirteen, when we lived in Nice, I was taken to be seventeen, and I looked it.

In short, to marry some one who *truly loved me ;* otherwise I should be the most unhappy of women. But it would be necessary that this *some one* should be at least a suitable *parti.*

To be famous ! illustrious !—that would settle everything. No, I must not expect to meet an ideal being who would respect me and love me, and who would, besides, be a *good parti.*

Ordinary people are afraid of famous women, and geniuses are rare. .

June 24.—I have been thinking lately of the nonsensical things I used to write about Pietro. As, for instance, when I said that I always thought of him in the evenings, and that if he were to come to Nice unexpectedly I would throw myself into his arms. And people thought I was in love with him—my readers may think so.

And this has never, never, never, been the case.

Yet often of a summer evening, when vague longings fill the soul, one feels that one would like to throw one's-self into the arms of a lover.   This has happened to me a hundred times.   But then this lover had a name, he was a real being whom I could call by his name—Pietro.   But enough of Pietro !

I had a fancy for being the grandniece of the Cardinal, who might one day become Pope—but—nothing more.

No, I have never been in love ; and now I never shall be in love.   A man must be very superior to other men to please me now that I have grown so exacting ; he must be.   And to fall in love with some young fellow, simply because he is charming—no, that can never be.

Tuesday, July 3.—The picture does not go forward.   I am in despair.   And there is nothing to console me for it.

At last the article in the *New Times* has appeared.   It is very good, but it causes me some embarrassment, as it states that I am only nineteen, while I am older, and am taken to be even older than I am.

But it will produce a great effect in Russia.

And love—what of that ?

What is love ?   I have never experienced the emotion, for passing fancies founded on vanity cannot be called by that name.   I have preferred certain persons because the imagination needs something with which to occupy itself. I have preferred them because to do so was a necessity to my *great soul*, not because of their own merits.   There was this difference, and it is an enormous one.

To turn to another subject—that of art ; I scarcely know how I am progressing in painting.   I copy Bastien-Lepage, and that is deplorable.   An imitator can never be the equal of the master he copies.   One can never be great until one has discovered a new channel through which to express one's nature, a medium for the interpretation of one's own individual impressions.

My art has ceased to exist.

I can discern a trace of it in the " Holy Women "; but in what else ? In sculpture it is different, but as for painting !

In the " Holy Women " I imitate no one. And I think the picture will produce a great effect, not only because I shall try to execute the material part of the work with the utmost truth to nature, but also because of the enthusiasm with which the subject inspires me.

The picture of the little boys reminds one of Bastien-Lepage, though the subject is taken from the street, and is a very commonplace, every-day one. But this artist always causes me an indescribable feeling of uneasiness.

Saturday, July 14.—Have you read " L'Amour " of Stendhal ? I am reading it.

Either I have never been in love in my life, or I have never ceased to be in love with an imaginary being. Which is it ?

Read this book ; it is even more delicate than anything of Balzac ; it is more profoundly true, more harmonious, and more poetical. And it expresses divinely what every one has felt, what I myself have felt. But then I have always been too much given to analyzing my emotions.

I was never really in love, except at Nice, when I was a child and ignorant of the world.

And afterward when I had a sickly fancy for that horrible Pietro.

I can remember moments alone in my balcony at Nice, listening to some delightful serenade, when I felt transported with ecstatic joy, without any other cause for it than was to be found in the hour, the scene, and the music.

I have never experienced these feelings either in Paris or anywhere else, except in Italy.

Friday, August 3.—Bastien-Lepage is enough to drive one to despair. When one studies nature closely, when one seeks to imitate her faithfully, it is impossible not to think constantly of the works of this great artist.

He possesses the secret of rendering flesh with perfection ; they talk of realism, but the realists do not know what reality is ; they are coarse, and think they are natural. Realism does not consist in copying a vulgar thing, but in making the copy of whatever be represented an exact one.

Sunday, August 5.—People say that I had a romantic fancy for C   , and that that is the reason I do not marry, for they cannot understand why, having a handsome dowry, I am yet neither a marquise nor a countess.

Fools !   Happily you, the few superior people who read me, you, my beloved confidants, know what to believe. But when you read these words, all those of whom I speak will probably be dead, and C—— will carry to the tomb the sweet conviction of having been loved by "a young and beautiful foreigner, who, enamoured of this cavalier," etc. Fool !   Others also will believe it—fools !   But you know very well that this is not the case.   It would, perhaps, be romantic to refuse marquises for the sake of love ; but it is reason, alas ! that causes me to refuse them.

Sunday, August 12.—The bare idea that Bastien-Lepage is coming here has made me so nervous that I have not been able to do anything.   It is truly ridiculous to be so impressionable.

Our Pope dined with us.   Bastien-Lepage is very intelligent, but less brilliant than Saint-Marceaux.

I showed him nothing of my work ; I scarcely spoke ; that is to say, I did not shine ; and when Bastien-Lepage introduced an interesting subject I could not answer him, nor even follow his remarks, which were as terse and full of meaning as his paintings are.   If it had been Julian, I should have taken the lead, for this is the style of conversation I like best. He is very well-informed, and has a keen intellect, while I had feared to find him in some measure ignorant.

In short, when he said things to which I should have responded in such a way as to reveal the fine qualities of my head and heart, I let him go on speaking and remained silent.

I can scarcely even write, so completely has the day upset me.

I desire to be alone, completely alone, so as to commune with myself regarding the impression he made upon me, which was profound and interesting; ten minutes after his arrival I had mentally capitulated and acknowledged his mastery.

I did not say a single word that I ought to have said; he is indeed a god, and he is conscious of his power; and I have contributed to strengthen him in this belief. He is small, he is ugly, in the eyes of the vulgar crowd, but for me and for people like me he has a charming countenance. What is his opinion of me? I was embarrassed; I laughed too frequently; he says he is jealous of Saint-Marceaux. What a triumph!

Tuesday, August 21.—No, I shall not die until I am about forty, like Mlle. Colignon. At thirty-five I shall grow very ill, and at thirty-six or thirty-seven, a winter in bed, and all will be over.   :

And my will? All I shall ask in it will be a statue and a picture, the one by Saint-Marceaux, the other by Jules Bastien-Lepage, placed in a conspicuous position in a chapel in Paris, and surrounded by flowers; and on each anniversary of my death that a mass of Verdi or of Pergolesi, and other music, may be sung by the most celebrated singers in remembrance of me.

Besides this, I shall found a prize for artists of both sexes,

I should, indeed, prefer to live, but as I am not gifted with genius, it is better that I should die.

Wednesday, August 29.—Notwithstanding the heat, I cough continually, and, and, as I was reclining half asleep on the divan this afternoon, while my model was resting, I had a vision in which I saw myself lying on a couch, with a large wax taper standing lighted beside me.

That will be the denouement of all these miseries.

To die? I very much fear so.

And I do not wish to die; it would be horrible. I don't know how the case may be as regards happy people, but as for me, I am greatly to be pitied, since I have ceased to expect anything from God. When this supreme refuge fails us there is nothing left us but to die. Without God there can be neither poetry, nor affection, nor genius, nor love, nor ambition.

Thursday, September 13.—Stendhal says that our sorrows seem less bitter when we idealize them. This observation is a very just one. But how shall I idealize mine? It would be impossible! They are so bitter, so prosaic, so frightful, that I cannot speak of them, even here, without suffering horribly. How say that at times I cannot hear well? Well, the will of God be done! This phrase recurs to my mind involuntarily, and I have almost come to feel it. For I shall die, quite naturally and peacefully, notwithstanding all the care I can bestow upon myself. And this would be as well, for I am troubled about my eyes; for a fortnight past I have been able neither to paint nor to read, and I am growing no better. I feel a throbbing sensation in them, and little dark specks seem to float before me in the air.

Perhaps this is because I have been suffering for the last fortnight from a bronchial cold, which would have made

any one else take to bed, but notwithstanding which I go
about as usual, as if nothing were the matter.

I have worked on Dina's portrait in so tragical a mood
that I shall have more gray hairs when I am done with it.

Saturday, September 15.—This morning I went to the
Salon to see Bastien's pictures. What shall I say of them?
Nothing could be more beautiful. There are three portraits which, according to Julian, who dines with us this
evening, are the despair of artists. Yes, the despair.
Never has there been anything done to equal them. They
are life-like; they are endowed with soul. The execution
is so admirable that there is nothing to be compared to it;
it is nature itself. One must be mad to go on painting
after seeing these.

There is also a little picture called "Les bles Murs." A
man with his back to the spectator is reaping. The picture
is good.

There are two pictures life-size. " Les Foins " and " Les
Ramasseuses de pommes de terre."

What coloring! What composition! What execution!
There is a richness of tone in them that is to be found only
in nature itself. And the figures live!

The tones blend into one another with a simplicity which
is the perfection of art, and the eye follows each with genuine delight. .

When I entered the room I was not aware that the picture was there, but the moment I saw " Les Foins " I stopped
short before it, as one stops before a window that is suddenly opened, and discloses a beautiful landscape to the
view.

They do not do him justice; he is immeasurably superior
to every one else. There is no one to be compared to him.

I am very, very ill; and I have applied an immense
blister to my chest. After that, doubt my courage and my

desire to live, if you can. No one knows of it, however, except Rosalie ; I walk up and down my studio, I read, I chat, I sing, and my voice is almost beautiful. As I often spend Sunday without working, this surprises no one.

Tuesday, September 18.—It seems that the notice taken of me by the Russian press has drawn the attention of many people to me—that of the Grand Duchess Catherine among others. Mamma is intimately acquainted with her grand chamberlain and his family, and the question of appointing me to the post of maid of honor has been seriously discussed.

I must first be presented to the Grand Duchess, however. Everything has been done that could be done in the matter, but mamma was wrong to let things take their course, and return here.

And then—my *belle-âme* demands a sister-soul. I shall never have a friend. Claire says I can never have a girl friend because I have none of the little secrets and love-affairs that other girls have.

" You are too proper," she says ; "you have nothing to conceal."

Monday, October 1.—We were present at the ceremonies which took place to-day on the removal to Russia of the remains of Tourgenieff, our great writer, who died a fortnight ago. Afterward we went to the *Salon.* I could not refrain from a burst of enthusiasm (inward enthusiasm, however, for I feared they might think me in love with him), as I looked at the paintings of Bastien-Lepage.

Meissonier ? Meissonier is nothing but a prestidigitator ! He paints pictures with figures so minute that one would need to look at them through a microscope, and that cause one so much surprise that the feeling might almost be taken for admiration. But as soon as he departs from this minute style, when his heads are more than a centimetre long, his manner becomes hard and commonplace. But no one dares to say this, and every one admires him, although all his pictures for the *Salon* are merely good and correct.

But is this art,—to paint people in costume who play on the harpsichord or ride on horseback? For after all many *genre* painters can do as much as this.

Those of his paintings that I have seen that are really admirable are, in the first place, the "Joueurs de boules sur la route d'Antibes"; it is a scene copied from the life, although the costumes are antique ; and is luminous and transparent ; next his father and himself, on horseback ; then the "Graveur a 'l'eau-forte"; the movement and expression have been seized and depicted with truth. This man, absorbed in his own thoughts, carried away by them seemingly, touches and interests us, and the details are wonderful. There is also a cavalier of the time of Louis XIII., looking out of a window, of the same size ; the movement here is also just ; the action is human, natural, simple—it is a bit of real life, in fact.

Those of his pictures in which the heads are as much as two centimetres long are merely cartoons, and the larger his figures are the worse they are.

I pay my tribute to his genius and pass on ; he does not touch my feelings. But look at the portraits of Bastien-Lepage ! Most people would make an outcry if I were to say that they are much better than those of Meissonier. And yet such is the fact. There is nothing that can be compared to the portraits of Bastien-Lepage. Object to his other paintings if you will—you do not understand them, perhaps—but his portraits ! Nothing better of the kind has ever been done.

Saturday, October 6.—I have just read, at one sitting, a novel in French by our illustrious Tourgenieff, so as to be able to form an idea of the impression his books make upon foreigners. He is a great writer, a man of subtle intellect, an acute reasoner, a poet, a Bastien-Lepage. His descriptive passages are beautiful, and he interprets the most delicate shades of feeling in words as Bastien-Lepage interprets them in color.

And Millet—what a sublime artist! Well, he is as poetic as Millet. I use this foolish phrase for the benefit of those imbeciles who would otherwise be unable to understand me.

Whatever is grand, poetical, beautiful, subtle, or true in music, in literature, or in art reminds me of this wonderful artist and poet. He chooses subjects that are considered vulgar by fashionable people, and he extracts from them the most exquisite poetry.

What can be more commonplace than a little girl guarding a cow or a woman working in the fields? "But these have been already treated," you will say. Yes, but no other artist has ever treated them as he has done. He did well to choose them ; in a single picture he has given us a romance of three hundred pages. But there are perhaps, not more than fifteen of us who understand him.

Tourgenieff, also, has depicted peasant-life—the life of the poor Russian peasant ; and with what truth, what simplicity, what sincerity ! And how moving is the picture he has drawn, how poetic, how grand !

Unfortunately this can be appreciated only in Russia, and it is chiefly in these social studies that he excels.

Monday, October 22.—I should be well pleased if my malady proved to be an imaginary one.

It seems that at one time it was fashionable to have consumption, and that people tried to make it appear, and even to persuade themselves, that they had it. Ah, if it might turn out that this disease of mine were an imaginary one ! I desire to live in any case, and despite of everythin". I have neither love-sorrows, nor sentimental reasons, nor any other cause, to make me wish to die. I desire to achieve fame, and to enjoy whatever happiness is to be enjoyed on this earth.

Monday, November 5.—The leaves have all fallen, and I do not know how I shall be able to finish my picture. I have no luck. Luck ! How formidable a thing is luck ! What a mysterious and terrible power !

Ah, yes, it must be finished, but finished quickly, quickly !—in a fortnight. And then to astonish Robert-Fleury and Julian by showing it to them.

If I could do this, it would give me new life. I suffer because I have done nothing of any consequence this summer ; I experience the most frightful remorse. I should like to define my condition with more exactness—I am altogether without strength, as it were, and at the same time I am profoundly calm. I fancy that one who has just lost a great deal of blood might feel as I do now.

I have taken my resolution—I shall wait until May. And why should this state of things change in May ? After all, who knows ?

This has made me think of whatever virtues or talents I may possess, and I find a source of secret consolation in these thoughts. It has make me take part in the conversation, at dinner, with my family, like any other person— amiably, and with a calm and dignified air such as I had on the day I first wore my hair turned up.

In short, I experience a feeling of profound tranquillity. I shall pursue my work with calmness ; it seems to me that henceforth all my actions must be tranquil, and that I shall regard the universe with gentle condescension.

I am calm as if I were, or perhaps because I am, strong ; and patient, as if I were certain of the future.—And who knows ? I feel myself in truth, invested with a new dignity ;

I have confidence in myself ; I am a power. Then—what ?
May not this be love ? No ; but outside that feeling I see
nothing that could interest me. This is what was needed,
mademoiselle, devote yourself entirely to your art.

When I see myself famous in imagination it is as if I
were dazzled by a flash of lightning, as if I had come in
contact with an electric battery ; I start from my seat, and
begin to walk up and down the room.

It may be said that if I had been married at seventeen I
should be like every one else. This is a mistake. *In order
that I should marry like any one else* it would be necessary
for me to be *some one else.*

Do you suppose that I have ever loved ! I do not think
so. These passing fancies look like love ; but they could
not have been love.

I still continue to feel this excessive weakness ; I might
compare myself to an instrument of which the cords are
relaxed. What is the cause of this ? Julian says that I remind him of an autumn landscape, a desolate and deserted
walk enveloped in the fogs of winter. Just what I am, my
dear monsieur.

Monday, November 12.—Dumont, of *La Liberté*, is coming to see us. He detests the style of painting I have
chosen, but he paid me a great many compliments at the
same time that he asked me in astonishment how it was
that I, living as I do, in the midst of elegant and refined
surroundings, should love the ugly. He thinks my little
boys ugly.

"Why did you not choose pretty ones ?" he said ; "they
would have answered the same purpose."

I chose *expressive* faces, if I may dare to say so. And
then one does not see such miracles of beauty among the
little boys who run about the streets ; for those it would be
necessary to go to the Champs Elysees, and paint some of

the poor little be-ribboned babies who are to be seen there, guarded by their nurses.

Where, then, is action to be found? Where the savage liberty of primitive times? Where *true* expression? For even the *children* of the better classes study effect.

And then—in short, I am right.

Thursday, November 22.—The *Illustration Universelle* (of Russia) has given an engraving of my painting ("Jean et Jacques") on its first page.

This is the most important of the illustrated papers of Russia, and I am, so to speak, at home in it.

And I am not overjoyed at this? Why should I be? It pleases me, but I am not overjoyed on account of it.

And why not? Because this is not enough to satisfy my ambition. If I had received a mention two years ago, I should have fainted from emotion ; if they had given me a medal last year, I should have shed tears of joy upon the breast of Julian. But now—Alas! all the events of life follow each other in logical order ; they are all linked together, and each prepares us for the one which is to follow. If I receive a third-class medal next year, it will seem nothing more than natural ; if they give me nothing, I shall be indignant.

One never rejoices greatly at any event except when it comes unexpectedly—when it is in some sort a surprise.

Saturday, December 1.—After all, may I not have been deceiving myself all this time? Who will give me back the most beautiful years of my life—wasted, perhaps, in vain !

But there is a sufficient answer to these vulgar doubts of mine in the fact that I had nothing better to do ; besides, anywhere and everywhere, leading the same life as others I should have had too much to suffer. And then I should not have attained that moral development which confers upon me a superiority so embarrassing—to myself.   Stendhal had come in contact with at least one or two persons capable of understanding him, while I, unfortunately for myself, find every one insipid ; and even those whom I expected to find intelligent, I find stupid.   Is this because I am what is termed a *misunderstood being ?*   No ; but I feel that I have reason to be surprised and dissatisfied when people think me capable of things which reflect upon my dignity, my delicacy, my *elegance*, even.

You see I want some one who should understand me completely, to whom I could confide everything, and in whose word I should see my own thoughts reflected.—Well, my child, this would be love.

That may be, but without going so far—people who would be able to form an intelligent opinion concerning one, and whom one might talk to—even that would be pleasant ; and I know no such person.   The only one I knew was Julian, and he is growing every day more disagreeable ; he is even exasperating when he begins with his tiresome, teasing insinuations, especially in matters relating to art. He does not understand that I am not blind, and that I mean to succeed ; he thinks me infatuated with myself.

After all, though, he is still at times my confidant.   As far as an absolute parity of sentiments is concerned, that does not exist, except between lovers!   It is love, then, that works the miracle.   But may it not be rather this absolute parity of sentiments that gives birth to love?—The sister-soul.—As for me I find this image, which has been so much abused, a very just one.   But who is this sister-soul ? Some one, not even the tip of whose ear can one catch sight of.

It would be necessary that not a word, not a look, of his should be at variance with the idea I have formed of him. Not that I demand in him an impossible perfection, or that he should be a being superior to humanity; but I require that his caprices should be interesting caprices that would not lower him in my eyes; that he should be in conformity with my ideal—not the hackneyed ideal of an impossible demigod, but that everything in him should please me, and that I should not unexpectedly discover in him some stupid, dull, weak, foolish, mean, false, or mercenary trait; one such blemish only, no matter how small it might be, would be sufficient to ruin him in my eyes.

Sunday, December 2.—In short, my heart is absolutely empty, empty, empty. But I must indulge in these dreams in order to amuse myself. I have experienced almost all those feelings which Stendhal mentions, however, apropos of true love, which he calls passionate love—those innumerable caprices of the imagination; those childish follies of which he speaks. Thus I have often seen the most hateful people with pleasure, because they had chanced to be near the beloved object on that particular day.

Besides, I think that no one, whether man or woman, who is always busy, or who is constantly preoccupied by the thought of fame, can love like one who has nothing but love to think of.

Monday, December 3.—I am intelligent, I give myself credit for wit, for penetration, for every intellectual quality in fact, and I am unprejudiced. Well, having these conditions, why should I not be able to form a clear judgment of myself?

Have I really any talent for, or shall I really ever be anything in art? *What is my unbiassed opinion concerning myself?*

These are terrible questions—because I think little of myself compared with the ideal to which I strive to attain— compared with others, however—

But one cannot form a correct judgment concerning one's-self, and then—as long as I am not a genius—and I have never produced anything that could enable any one—even myself—to form a definite judgment concerning me.

Monday, December 10.—Hundreds of people whose names are never heard of accomplish as much as I have done, and never complain that they have no outlet for their genius. If you find yourself embarrassed by your genius, it is because you have none; any one who has genius will have the strength to support it.

The word *genius* is like the word *love*; I found difficulty in writing it for the first time, but, when I had once written it, I made use of it at all times and on all occasions afterwards. It is the same as with many other things which at first appear huge, terrible, or unattainable—once you become familiar with them you abandon yourself to them completely so as to make up for all your former hesitations and fears. This *spirituelle* observation does not appear to me to be very lucid, but I must expend my energy. I worked until seven, but as there is still some of it remaining, I must let it flow away from the point of my pen.

I am growing thin.   Well—God be merciful to me!

Sunday, December 23.—True artists can never be happy; they are conscious, in the first place, that the majority of people do not understand them; they know they are working for a hundred people or so, and that all the others follow their own bad taste, or the opinions of *Figaro*.

The ignorance that prevails among all classes respecting everything that pertains to art is frightful.

Those who speak understandingly of art, for the most part repeat the opinions which they have heard or read of those who are considered competent judges in the matter.

But I think there are days when one feels those things more acutely—days when nonsensical talk is especially insupportable; when foolish observations cause one actual suffering; and to hear people exchanging for hours silly remarks that have not even the merit of sprightliness or the varnish of fashion to recommend them, is a positive affliction.

And observe that I am not one of those superior beings who shed tears when they are compelled to listen to the hackneyed phrases of the drawing-room—its affectations, its stereotyped compliments, its remarks about the weather or the Italian opera. I am not foolish enough to require that all conversation should be interesting, and to hear the commonplace talk of society, lively, it is true, at times, but more often dull, does not disturb my tranquillity in the least. I can submit to it, occasionally, even, with pleasure; what I have reference to is real folly, real stupidity, a lack of—in short, the commonplace conversation of people who are not only worldly but stupid.

To listen to this is like being burned at a slow fire.

Monday, December 31.—The Marechale and Claire dined yesterday with the Princess Mathilde. and Claire tells me that Lefebvre said to her of me that I had undoubted talent, that I was a very uncommon person, that I went a great deal into society, and that. in addition to this, I was watched over and directed by a celebrated painter (this with a meaning look.)

Claire (looking at him fixedly): "What celebrated painter? Julian? Lefebvre?"

"No, Bastien-Lepage."

Claire: "Oh, you are entirely mistaken, monsieur; she works all the time, and goes out very little. As to Bastien-Lepage. she sees him nowhere except in her mother's drawing-room; he never goes up to her studio."

Claire is a love of a girl, and she said nothing but what is true, for God is my witness that this Jules gives me no assistance whatever. Lefebvre, however, looked as if he thought he did.

It is two o'clock in the morning; the new year has begun, and at midnight, at the theater, with my watch in my hand, I made a wish in one single word—a word that is grand, sonorous, beautiful, intoxicating, whether it be written or spoken—Fame!

1884.

My Aunt Helene, my father's sister, died a week ago. Paul telegraphed the news to us.

We received another telegraphic dispatch to-day : my Uucle Alexander has just died of apoplexy ; the news was a great shock to us ; he was devoted to his family, and loved his wife to distraction.   As he had never read Balzac, nor indeed any other novelist, perhaps, he knew but little about the romantic phrases employed by lovers to express their affection ; certain words of his, however, I remember, to recall which now makes me feel all the greater sorrow for his death.   On one occasion some one tried to make him believe that his wife was receiving the attentions of a neighbor, and I remember to have heard him say: " Well, suppose this infamous thing they tell me were true ! Is not my wife, whom I have lived with for fifteen years, flesh of my flesh, blood of my blood, soul of my soul ?   Are we not one ?   If I had committed a fault, would I not forgive myself for it ?   Why then should I not forgive my wife ?   Not to do so would be like plucking out one of my eyes, or cutting off an arm."

Friday, January 4.—It is true, then ; I have consumption, and the disease is far advanced.

I feel very ill ; I have said nothing about it, but I have fever every night.

Saturday, January 5.—The opening of the Manet Exhibition at the School of Fine Arts takes place to-day.

I am going there.

It is not quite a year since Manet died. I do not know a great deal about him. The collection, take it all in all, is a remarkable one.

It is at once childish, extravagant, and grand.

There are some absurd things among the pictures, but there are also some that are magnificent. A little more and Manet would have been a great painter. The pictures are, in general, repulsive ; some of them are altogether out of drawing ; but all are life-like. There are some splendid sketches among them ; and even in the most faulty of the pictures there is a something that rivets the attention, and almost calls forth admiration—they reveal so evident a self-confidence on the part of the artist, so profound a belief in his own powers, joined to an ignorance no less profound. They are such pictures as a great genius might have produced in his childhood. And then there are things copied almost exactly from Titian (the sketch of the female figure and the negro, for instance), Velasquez, Courbet, and Goya. But then all these painters stole from each other. And has not Moliere taken whole pages from other authors ?

Monday, January 14.—I feel as if I myself had been at Damvillers, Emile Bastien has told us so much about it—about the picture, his brother's manner of life, etc. According to him, if the artist has not invited us to see the studies painted by him at Concarneau, it is because he never invites any one to see his paintings. He even thinks it would be a mark of conceit on his part to ask any one to go look at a few unimportant studies made while he was resting in the country ; and finally, he says he thought from the friendliness we showed him that he might be dispensed from using ceremony ; that he would have been delighted to see us if we had gone there, etc. He says, that, even in the case of his more important paintings, he never invites any one to see them ; he merely requests his brother to let his intimate friends know when he has finished one.

But here is something more serious : when his brother spoke to him of my picture he said : " Why did you not tell me of it when I was in Paris ? I would have gone to see it."

" I told him nothing about it in Paris," his brother added, " because if he had gone to look at it, you would have hidden everything away, according to your custom ; he has never seen any of your pictures except those you exhibited at the *Salon.* Do you know that he will never care to look at your pictures if you continue to act in this way ? "

" He will, if I wish it—if I ask him to give me his advice."

" He will be always delighted to give you his advice," he said.

" But unfortunately I am not a pupil of his."

" And why are you not ? He would ask for nothing better ; he would feel very much flattered if you consulted him, and he would give you judicious advice—disinterested advice ; he has a correct judgment, and is not prejudiced in favor of any school, and he would be delighted to have so interesting a pupil. I assure you it would please and flatter him very much."

Wednesday, January 16.—The architect has told me that there is a painting of the "Shepherds at Bethlehem " among his brother's pictures. For the last two days my head has been filled with this subject ; so strong is the impression it has produced in my mind that I can compare it to nothing else than the feeling entertained by the shepherds them-selves—a blending of holy enthusiasm and profound adora-tion.

Can you not already imagine with what mystery, what tenderness, what sublime simplicity, he will invest this subject? One who is familiar with his paintings can do so, in some measure, by observing the mysterious and fantastic resemblance that exists between the " Jeanne d'Arc "and the "Soir au Village"—the effect of both which pictures will be in some sort reproduced in the " Shepherds." But perhaps you think it absurd of me to grow enthusiastic about a painting that I have never seen—that is not even yet in existence? Well, let us suppose that in the eyes of the majority of people I appear ridiculous by doing so, there will always be a few dreamers who will take my part ; and, if need were, I could do without even those.

" Jeanne d'Arc " has never been appreciated in France ; in America it was enthusiastically admired. The "Jeanne d'Arc," both in composition and in sentiment, is a masterpiece.

The reception it met with in Paris was a disgrace to the French people.

Are only the " Phædras " and the " Auroras," then, to meet with success? Neither Millet, Rousseau, nor Corot were admired by the public until after they had become famous.

What is most to be deplored, in our day, is the hypocrisy of the enlightened few who affect to see nothing either serious or elevated in modern art, and who exalt to the skies those painters who follow the traditions of the old masters. Is it necessary to point out and insist upon the fallacies involved in these views of art? What then is high art if it be not the art which, while it renders the flesh, the dress, and the landscapes with such perfection that we want to touch them, so to speak, to see if they be real, endows them at the same time with soul, with spirit, and with life. The "Jeanne d'Arc" they say is not high art because the artist depicts his subject, not clad in armor and with the white and delicate hands of a lady, but as a peasant girl and in the midst of homely surroundings.

Stupid or dishonest critics praise the "Amour au Village," which is inferior to the "Jeanne d'Arc," with the purpose of making it appear that the artist excels only in this style, indignant that a painter who has made peasant life a study should take it into his head to paint anything else—to paint a peasant famous in history, for instance, like the "Jeanne d'Arc."

Pharisees and hypocrites !

For, after all, any artist can paint flesh, but who can portray the soul within, the divine spark, as he has done? No one.   In the eyes of his characters I can read their lives ; I almost think I know them.   I have tried to feel this in looking at other paintings, but without success.

Who would prefer as a subject for a painting the execution of a Lady Jane Grey or a Bajizet to some little girl who looks at you with clear and animated glance as you pass her by in the street ?

This great artist possesses a quality which is to be met with only in the religious paintings of the Italians at a time when artists were also believers.

Has it never happened to you, on finding yourself alone of an evening in the country, under a clear and cloudless sky, to feel your being pervaded by a mysterious longing— a vague aspiration toward the Infinite ; to feel yourself, as it were, on the threshold of some great event, some supernatural occurrence?   Were you never, in your dreams, transported into unknown regions ?

If not you would seek in vain to understand Bastien-Lepage, and I advise you to buy an " Aurora" by Bouguereau or a historical picture by Cabanel.

And all this is in order to say that I worship the genius of Bastien-Lepage ?

Yes.

Sunday, January 20.—It is a sad confession to make, but I have no woman friend : there is no woman who loves me or whom I love.

I am well aware that if I have no such friend, it is because I allow it to be seen, without intending it, from what a height " I survey the crowd."

No one likes to be humiliated. I might console myself by the reflection that truly great natures are never loved. Such persons are surrounded by worshipers who bask in the sunshine of their fame, but who, at heart, hate them and disparage them when the opportunity to do so presents itself. They are talking just now of erecting a statue to Balzac, and the newspapers are filled with recollections of the great man contributed by his friends. Such friends are a disgrace to humanity.

They vie with one another to see which will be foremost in dragging before the public view his most secret faults and foibles. I would rather have such people as those for my enemies than for my friends. At least their slanders would in that case be less likely to be believed.

Saturday, February 23.—At about one o'clock the Mare-chale and Claire came to meet Madeleine Lemaire, who wished to see my picture. This lady, besides being a wo-man of society, is also a celebrated artist in water-colors, and obtains very good prices for her pictures. Of course she said only flattering things of my picture.

I think I must be going to die soon, for my whole life, with all its stupid details, rises before me—details that it makes me shed tears of rage to remember. It has never been my habit to go to balls, like other girls. I would go to one occasionally—three or four times a year perhaps. For the last two years, when I no longer cared to do so, I might have gone as often as I chose.

And is it I, you ask, whose ambition it is to become a

great artist, who regret not having been allowed to go to balls more often ? Indeed, yes. And what are my regrets for now ? Not for balls, but there are other reunions where one may meet thinkers, authors, artists, singers, men of science—all those who constitute the world of intellect, in short. The most rational, the most philosophical person in the world need not be ashamed of desiring to meet once a week, or once a fortnight, persons who are the flower of Parisian intellect. I have always been unfortunate in everything ! Through my own merits I have succeeded in becoming acquainted with the best people in Paris, and only to be humiliated.

I am too unhappy not to believe in a God who could take pity upon me if he would ; but if there were indeed a God, would He allow such injustice to exist ? What have I ever done that I should be as unhappy as I am ?

It is not in the God of the Bible that I can believe, however. The Bible is a narrative of primitive times, in which all that relates to God is treated from the point of view of a child. The only God I can believe in is the God of philosophy—an abstract being—the Great Mystery—earth, heaven, the universe, Pan.

But this is a God who can in no way help us ; this is a God on whom our thoughts may dwell in adoration as we look up to the stars at night, seeking to penetrate to the heart of the spiritual universe, *à la* Renan. But a God who sees everything that takes place, who interests Himself in our affairs, to whom we may pray for what we desire—I should indeed, like to believe in such a God, but if He existed, would He suffer things to be as they are ?

Tuesday, March 11.—It is raining. But it is not that alone that depresses me ; I am sick—Heaven has overwhelmed me with misfortunes.

But I am still at an age when one may find a certain ecstasy in everything, even in the thought of death.

I fancy there is no one who takes so intense a delight in *all things* as I do—art, music, painting, books, society, dress, luxury, gayety, solitude ; tears and laughter, sadness and rejoicing ; love, cold, heat ; the solemn plains of Russia and the mountains that surround Naples ; the snows of winter, the rains of autumn, spring with its intoxicating joys, the calm days and the glorious starlit nights of summer—I love them and delight in them all. Everything in nature presents itself to me under an aspect either interesting or sublime ; I long to see everything, to grasp everything, to embrace everything, to enter into the heart of everything, and to die—since die I must, whether in one year or in thirty years, I care not which—to die, exhaling my being in an ecstasy of joy at solving this last mystery of all, the end of all things, or the beginning of things divine.

And this sentiment of universal love is not the result of the fever that accompanies my malady. I have always felt it as strongly as I feel it now. Just ten years ago—in 1874, as I remember, after enumerating the pleasures of the different seasons—I wrote thus :

" In vain would I seek to choose ; all seasons of the year, all periods of life, are equally beautiful,"

The good Robert-Fleury dines with us this evening ; he says that my picture of the little *gamins* is greatly improved—that it is good, in fact, and that it will be accepted at the *Salon.*

I forgot to say that it is called " A Meeting."

Wednesday, March 12.—The portrait of Dina will not be finished in time, so that I shall send on the " Meeting."

There was a friendly gathering at Mme. Hochon's this evening. Among those present, besides ourselves, were the Duchess d'Uzes ; the Countess Cornet, and the Marechale ;

and a number of artists—Cabanel, Jalabert, Siebert, G. Ferrier, Boulanger, etc. There was music, and Salvayre played and sang some airs from his "Henri III." All these people, not excepting Cabanel, were very friendly to me.

Saturday, March 15.—Abbema came to see my picture this morning.

I thought the 15th would never come. The weather is glorious, and on Monday or Tuesday I am going into the country to work. I will no longer waste my admiration on Bastien-Lepage. Indeed I know but little of him, his disposition is so—reserved ; besides, it is better to spend one's energy on one's work than in worshiping at any one's shrine.

Sunday, March 16.—The pictures have been sent away.

I came home at about half-past six so exhausted with fatigue that the sensation was delicious. Perhaps you may not believe it, but for me every overpowering sensation, even the sensation of pain, is a joy.

I remember once when I had hurt my finger, some years ago, that for half an hour the pain was so acute that I took pleasure in it.

And so it was with the lassitude I felt this evening, lying in the bath, and afterward in bed, my limbs powerless, my head full of vague and confused ideas. I fell asleep repeating words as disconnected as the thoughts that passed through my head—Cabanel, varnishing-day, the Marechal, Breslau, art, Algeria, the line, Wolff.

Wednesday, March 19.—I have discovered an orchard for the scene of my picture, at Sevres ; I returned home very much fatigued. Some friends dined with us in the evening.

Yesterday the election of members to the club of Russian artists took place. I was unanimously elected.

Claire saw an acquaintance to-day who told her he had visited Bastien-Lepage not long ago, and that he had found him very ill ; he met Bastien's physician on the following day, who said to him : " The man is very ill, but I do not think his disease is rheumatism ; the trouble is here," and he tapped himself on the stomach. So, then, he is really ill ! He went to Blidah three or four days ago, accompanied by his mother.

Saturday, March 22.—I have not yet begun work at Sevres, but all my preparations are made.

Julian writes : " Your picture has been accepted and will receive a No. 3 at the very least."

What does this *at the very least* mean ?

God be thanked ! I had not the slightest doubt as to my pictures being accepted !

Monday, March 24.—For the past few days we have lived in an atmosphere of discord ; and this has kept me apart from the others and given me an opportunity to look into the depths of my inner self. No, everything is too sad to make it worth while to complain of any one thing in particular. I am overwhelmed by it all.

I have just re-read a book which I read some years ago but did not then like. I now admire it greatly. The style of the book, its *execution*, so to say, is perfect. But the question is not one of style alone.—The clouds that darken my mental horizon make me see the realities of life all the more clearly—realities so hard, so bitter that I could not keep from tears if I were to write them down. But I cannot even write them down. Where would be the use of doing so ? What is the use of anything ? I have spent six years working ten hours a day to gain what ? The knowledge of all I have yet to learn in my art—and a fatal disease. I went to see my doctor this morning, and I talked with so much animation that he said to me : " I see you have not yet lost your gayety."

If I still wish to cherish the hope that fame is to recompense me for all my sufferings, I must live, and in order to live I must take care of my health.

Here are dreams side by side with the frightful reality.

One never believes in any coming trouble until it comes. I remember once when I was very young I was traveling for the first time in a railway coach—for the first time I came in contact with strangers. I had just taken my seat and filled the two seats next to mine with all sorts of articles, when two passengers entered the coach. " These seats are taken," I said coolly. " Very well," answered the gentleman I addressed, " I will speak to the conductor."

I thought this was an unmeaning threat—as if we had been *en famille ;* and it would be impossible to describe the feeling of amazement that came over me when the conductor came and removed my things from the seat, which the passenger took immediately. This was my first *reality.*

For a long time now I have been saying to myself that I was going to be ill, without really believing it.—But enough of this, I should not have had the opportunity to give you all these insignificant details, if it were not that I have been waiting for my model, and I might as well spend the time grumbling as doing nothing.

There is a March wind blowing, and the sky is gray and lowering.

I began my picture—a rather large one—in the old orchard at Sevres yesterday. It is a young girl seated under an apple-tree in blossom, that stands, with other fruit-trees in blossom also, in a grassy field sown with violets and little yellow flowers, like stars. The girl sits with half-closed eyes, in a revery. She leans her head in the palm of her left hand, while her elbow rests upon her knee.

The treatment is to be simple, and the spectator must be made to share in the intoxication produced in the girl by the breath of Spring. The sunlight plays among the branches of the trees.

The picture is to be about five feet in width, and a little more in height.

So, then, my picture has only received a number 3 ; and it will not be even hung upon the line—not even that !

This has caused me a feeling of discouragement, hopeless and profound. No one is to blame, however, if I am not gifted with genius. And this feeling of discouragement shows me that if I ceased to have faith in my genius I could no longer live. Yes, if the hope of success should again fail me, as it did this evening, then, indeed, there would be nothing left me but to die.

Thursday.—My mind has been greatly preoccupied about my work. Why have I not yet succeeded in producing anything in painting equal to my pastel of three years ago ?

Monday, March 31.—I have done very little to-day. I fear that my picture will be badly hung and that I shall receive no medal.

I remained in a hot bath for nearly an hour, and this brought on a slight hemorrhage of the lungs.

This was very foolish on my part, you will say, very likely ; but I am no longer prudent about my health ; I am discouraged, and almost distracted, from having so many things to struggle against.

Well, there is nothing to be said—nothing to be done. If this state of things continues, I may live for a year or so, while if my mind were at rest I might live for twenty years longer.

Yes, this 3 is hard to swallow. Zilhardt and Breslau have both received a number 3. And why then did I not receive a number 2 ? There are forty members in the committee, and it seems that I received so many votes for a number 2 that every one thought I should get it. Suppose I had fifteen votes in my favor, and twenty-five against me ; the committee is composed of fifteen or twenty men of note, and twenty wretchedly poor artists who have obtained the positions they occupy through intrigue. This is well known ; but even so it is bad enough ; the blow is a crushing one. It has not blinded me to the truth of the matter, however, and I can see myself as I am. I begin to think that if my picture had been really good—

Ah, never, never, never, have I touched the lowest depths of despair as I have done to-day. So long as there is a lower depth to be reached there is still room for hope, but when one has set foot, as I have done, on the black and slimy bottom of the gulf itself ; when one says to one's-self as I have done, " It is neither circumstances, nor surroundings, nor the world, that is to blame, it is my own want of genius," then there is nothing further to be hoped for ; then there is no higher power, human or divine, to appeal to. I can no longer go on working. All is over.

Here, then, is an overpowering sensation. Well, according to my theories I ought to find enjoyment in it. I am caught in my own trap !

Never mind. I will take some bromide ; that will make me sleep. And then, God is good, and every great sorrow brings along with it some consolation.

And to think that I cannot even tell my griefs to any one ; that I cannot even have the consolation of talking them over with any one—no, there is no one, no one !

Happy are the simple-hearted ; happy are they who

believe in a God on whom they can call for consolation.—
What should I call on God to console me for? Because I
am not gifted with genius.

You see this is the very bottom of the gulf; I ought to
find enjoyment in it.

That might be the case if there were spectators to my
misery.

Those who become famous have their friends to tell their
sorrows to the world—for they have had friends to whom
they could confide their sorrows. I have none. Even if
I should utter my complaints to any one, if I should say,
" No, I will never paint again!" what then? No one is the
loser by it if I do not happen to be gifted with genius.

But of all the sorrows that I hide within my heart because
there is none to whom I can turn for sympathy, the deepest, the most humiliating is this : to feel, to know, that I
am nothing !

If this were to continue I could not live.

Wednesday, April 2.—I went to-day to Petit's (an exhibition of paintings in the Rue de Seze) ; I stayed for an
hour admiring the incomparable paintings of Bastien-Lepage and of Cazin.

Then I went to Robert-Fleury's and asked him with an
unconcerned air, "Well, how did things go at the committee ? "

" Oh, very well," he answered ; "when your picture was
inspected some of the members said—not one or two of
them, but several—'Stay, that is good ; it deserves a number 2.' "

" Oh, monsieur, is it possible? "

" Yes, and do not think I say this merely to please you ;
it was so. Then the votes were taken, and if the president
had been in his right mind that day, you would have had a
number 2,"

" But what fault do they find with the picture?"

" None."

" How, none; is it not bad, then?"

" It is good."

" And then?"

" Then it is a piece of ill-luck, that is all. Now, if you could find a member of the committee to ask to have it hung on the line, he would have it done, for the picture is good."

" And you—could you not have it done?"

" I am only a member of the bureau whose duty it is to see that the order of the numbers is not interfered with; But if any other member should ask to have it done, be sure I shall not oppose it."

Then I went to see Julian, who laughed a little at Robert-Fleury's advice, and said I might make my mind quite easy; that it would surprise him very much if I were not on the line, and that.—And then Robert-Fleury told me that he conscientiously thought I deserved a number 2, and that, morally speaking, I have received it. Morally speaking!— And then it would be only justice!

Oh, no; To ask as a favor that which is my due, that would be too much!

Friday, April 4.—The exhibition of Bastien-Lepage is no doubt a brilliant one, but the pictures are almost all old ones. They are: 1. A portrait of Mme. Drouet, of last year. 2. Another portrait of 1882. 3. A landscape with two women washing in the foreground, and an apple-tree in blossom, of 1882 also; 4. His picture for the *concours*, which was awarded the Prix de Rome (he received only the second Prix de Rome) of 1875; and then there is a little sketch made last year at Concarneau—five in all. " Le Mar de Damvillers," 6; " Les Bles ou les Faucheurs," in which only the back of one little mower is to be seen, 7;

an aged mendicant gathering wood in a forest, makes eight. "Le Mar de Damvillers," the mowers, and the mendicant are in the full sunlight. His landscapes are of equal merit with his figures, for a truly great artist has no specialty.

I saw an Andromeda in the studio of Bastien-Lepage which, although small, is a study of the nude such as few artists could make. Precision of outline, character, nobility of form, grace of attitude, fineness of tone,—it possesses all these, and in addition an execution at once broad in spirit and exquisite in detail. In short, it is nature itself, the living flesh. Among twilight scenes the "Soir au Village" is a masterpiece. In his poetic style, *a la* Millet, he has perhaps gone to the extreme. I say *a la* Millet so as to make my meaning understood, for Bastien is always himself; and because Millet has painted sunsets and moonlight scenes is no reason why others should not do the same if they choose.

The effect of this "Soir au Village" is wonderful; why did I not buy it?

He has also painted some English landscapes—views of the Thames, in which one can almost see the water flowing—that heavy, turbid water that moves onward in its bed with a snake-like motion. To conclude, nothing could be finer than his portraits in miniature; they are as fine as the portraits of the old masters. As for the portrait of his mother (life-size) the execution of it is wonderful; it is nature's self, and the illusion is preserved, however closely the picture be examined. The "Jeanne d'Arc" is an inspiration of genius.

Bastien-Lepage is thirty-five years old. Raphael died at thirty-seven, leaving behind him a greater number of works than Bastien has yet produced. But Raphael had been cradled, so to speak, in the lap of duchesses and of cardinals, who procured for him the instructions of the great Perugino; Raphael at the age of fifteen made copies of his master's

paintings that could scarcely be distinguished from the orig-
inals—at fifteen he was already a great artist. And then,
in those great paintings that we admire as much for the
time in which they were executed as for their merit, the
chief part of the work was done by the pupils; in many of
them, indeed, with the exception of the Cartoons, there is
nothing of Raphael's work.

Whereas Bastien-Lepage in his early years sorted letters
in the post-office in Paris to gain a livelihood. He exhibited, I believe, for the first time in 1869.

In this respect, however, he was no worse off than I, who
have always lived amid surroundings little favorable to art.
True, I took a few drawing lessons in my childhood, as all
children do, and fourteen or fifteen lessons afterward, for
a space of three or four years, still continuing to live in
the midst of these same surroundings. That would give me
six years and a few months of study, but then there were
travels and a serious illness to interfere. But, after all—
what have I accomplished?

Have I accomplished as much as Bastien had accomplished in 1874? This question is a piece of insanity.

If I were to repeat in public, even in the presence of
those who are artists themselves, what I have written here
of Bastien, people would declare me to be insane—some
from conviction, others on principle so that they might not
be compelled to admit the superior merit of so young an
artist.

Saturday, April 5.—Here are my plans:

First, I will finish the painting at Sevres. Then I will
take up seriously the study of sculpture in the mornings,
and of the nude in the afternoons—the sketch for to-day is
already done. That will take me into July. In July I
will begin a painting of "Evening," representing a meadow,
with a far-stretching treeless road fading into the sunset sky

in the distance.   On the road is to be a wagon, drawn by two oxen and filled with hay, on the top of which an old man is lying face downward, his chin resting in the palms of his hands.   The outlines stand in bold relief against the sunset sky.   The oxen are led by a country boy.

That would have a simple, grand, and poetic effect.

As soon as I shall have finished this and two or three little things I have in hand, I will set out for Jerusalem, where I shall spend the winter both for my health and on account of my picture.

And next winter Julian will call me a great artist.

I write all this here because it is interesting to see afterward how our plans turn out.

Sunday, April 6.—My aunt left for Russia this evening.

Saturday, April 12.—Julian has written to tell me that my picture is hung on the line.

Wednesday, April 16.—I go to Sevres every day.   My picture has taken complete possession of me.   The apple-tree is in blossom, the trees around are full of budding leaves, in which the sunlight falls, and little yellow flowers dot the grass; at the foot of the apple-tree the young girl is seated, "languid and intoxicated," as Andre Theuriet says, "by the balmy breath of Spring."   If I can only render the effect of the sunlight and of the budding life of spring, the picture will be beautiful.

Tuesday, April 29.—To-morrow is varnishing-day.   In the morning I shall see *Figaro* and the *Gaulois;* what will they say of me?   Will it be good, will it be bad, or will they say nothing at all?

Wednesday, April 30.—Things are not so bad, after all, for the *Gaulois* speaks very well of me; it gives me a sepa-

SPRING.

rate notice.   The article is very *chic*.   It is by Fourcaud,
the Wolff of the *Gaulois*.

The *Voltaire* treats me in the same fashion as the *Gaulois*.   Both notices are important ones.

The *Journal des Arts* also mentions me, and *L'Intransi-
géant* speaks of me in terms of praise.   The other journals
will notice the Exhibition from day to day.   It is only
Figaro, the *Gaulois*, and the *Voltaire* that give a general
mention of the pictures on varnishing-day.

Am I satisfied?   It is easy to answer that question; I am
neither satisfied nor dissatisfied.   My success is just enough
to keep me from being unhappy; that is all.

I have just returned from the *Salon*.   We did not go until
noon and we left at five—an hour before the exhibition
closes.—I have a headache.

We remained for a long time seated on a bench before
the picture.   It attracted a good deal of attention, and I
smiled to myself at the thought that no one would ever
imagine the elegantly dressed young girl seated before it,
showing the tips of her little boots, to be the artist.

Ah, all this is a great deal better than last year!

Have I achieved a success, in the true, serious meaning
of the word?   I almost think so.

Breslau has two portraits, only one of which I have seen,
and that surprised me greatly.   It is a copy of Manet—
which I do not like,—and is not so good as her previous
work.   Perhaps you will be shocked by the confession I am
going to make, but—this does not grieve me; neither am I
rejoiced at it, however; there is room for every one, but
I confess I am better pleased that the picture is not a
good one.   ·

Bastien-Lepage sends nothing but his little picture of last
year—"La Forge."   He is not yet well enough to go on working.   The poor architect looks very dejected and says he
is going to throw himself into the river.

I, too, am sad, and notwithstanding my painting, my sculpture, my music, my reading, I believe I am tired of life.

Saturday, May 3.—Emile Bastien came to-day at about half-past eleven. I went down to see him, very much surprised at his visit.

He had a great many pleasant things to tell me ; he says I have achieved a genuine success.

" I do not mean compared with your previous work, or with that of your fellow-pupils at the studio," he said, " but as compared with that of any artist. I saw Ollendorff yesterday, who said that if it were the work of a Frenchman, the State would have purchased it. " Yes, truly, M. Bashkirtseff paints well," he added. (The painting is signed M. Bashkirtseff.) " I told him that you were a young girl—and a pretty one, I added. He could not believe it. Every one has spoken to me of it as a great success."

Ah, I begin to believe in it a little, myself. I am always slow to believe in any piece of good fortune, lest I should be disappointed afterward.

In short, I shall be the last to believe that people believe in my genius. But it really seems as if they would, in the end.

" A genuine and great success," Emile Bastien says.

Is it then a success equal to that of Jules Bastien, in 1874 or 1875 ? Ah, if it only were ! I am not yet overjoyed, however, for I can scarcely believe that. I want to be overjoyed.

This very good friend of mine has asked me to sign a paper giving permission to Charles Baude, the engraver, and an intimate friend of his brother, to photograph and engrave my painting for the *Monde Illustré.* That will be of very great advantage to me,

He told me also that Friant (who is a man of talent) is enthusiastic about my picture.

People whom I have never seen talk about me are interested in me, discuss my merits. What happiness! Ah. I have waited for this and hoped for this so long that, now that it has come, I can scarcely believe it.

I received a letter from a stranger yesterday asking my permission to photograph my picture. I prefer that Baude should do it, however (the one Bastien-Lepage calls Charlot, and to whom he writes letters eight pages long).

I am going down to mamma's drawing-room now, to receive the congratulations of all the imbeciles who regard my pictures as the works of a woman of society, and who pay any little fool the same compliments as they pay me.

Rosalie, I think, is the one who takes the liveliest satisfaction in my success. She is wild with joy; when she speaks to me about it she shows the delight an old nurse might show at the success of her nursling; and she talks of it to everybody, with the garrulity of a portress. For her this is an event, a piece of good-fortune that has befallen her.

Monday, May 5.—Death is a thing we write and talk about lightly enough, but to think one is going to die soon, to *believe* it—that is another matter. Do I then believe that I am going to die soon? No, but I fear it.

The fact is not to be disguised; I have consumption. The right lung is far gone, and the left lung has been affected for a year past. Both lungs, then. If I were differently built, I should look almost thin. Not that I am much thinner than many other young girls are, but I am much more so than I was. A year ago my figure was perfect—neither too stout nor too thin. At present the flesh on my arms is no longer firm, and on the upper part of the arm, near the shoulder, where a smooth round surface was to be seen before, the bone is plainly visible. In short, my health is gone past recovery. " But, wretched creature," you will say, "why then will you not take more care of yourself?" But I take excessive care of myself. I have had my chest burned on both sides, so that I shall be unable to wear a low-necked dress for four months to come. And it will be necessary to continue the burnings from time to time so that I may be able to sleep. The question is no longer one of getting well. It may be thought that I exaggerate matters ; but no, I say only what is the truth. And besides the burnings there are so many other things to be done. I do them all ; I take cod-liver oil, arsenic, and goat's milk— they have bought me a goat.

I may linger on for a while, but I am doomed.

The trouble is that I have had too many things to contend against, and they are killing me ; this was only to be expected, but it is none the less horrible.

There are so many things to make life interesting ; reading alone would be enough.

I have just obtained the complete works of Zola and Renan, and some of Taine's works. I prefer Taine's " Revolution " to that of Michelet. Michelet is rambling, and wanting in precision of thought, and notwithstanding his sympathy with the heroic aspects of the Revolution, and Taine's evident purpose to depict it on its worst side, I like Taine's work best.

And what is to be said of art? Ah, if one could only believe in a beneficent God who interests himself in our affairs and arranges them to our satisfaction !

Tuesday, May 6.—I have been devoting all my time to reading ; I have read all Zola's works. He is an intellectual giant.

Here is another man of genius whom the French people evidently do not appreciate !

I have just received a letter from Dusseldorff, containing a request for permission to engrave and publish my picture, as well as some other things of mine. This is amusing. As for me I cannot believe in it yet. In short, I must acknowledge that I have achieved a success—every one tells me so. They did not tell me so last year, however. Last year I obtained some reputation as an artist, owing to the pastel; but it was nothing compared to the reputation this year's picture has given me. Of course it is not an astounding success; and my name, announced in any drawing-room to-night, would not create the slightest sensation. And to convince me of my success and make me perfectly happy, that would be necessary.

Yes, when my name is mentioned every voice must be hushed, every head turned in my direction, in order to satisfy me.

Since the opening of the *Salon* there is not a single journal that has not spoken of my picture; but that is not all; there was an article by Etincelle in the *Paris* of this morning. It is very *chic !* I come immediately after Claire and have as many lines devoted to me as she has! I am a Greuze! I am a blonde, with liquid eyes and the imperious brow of one destined to become famous; I dress with elegance; I have marked ability, and my pictures are good specimens of the realistic school, after the manner of Bastien-Lepage. But this is not all; I have the smile and the winning grace of a child. And I am not transported with delight? Well, no, not at all.

Thursday, May 8.—How is it that Wolff has made no mention of my picture ! It is possible, indeed, that he may not yet have seen it; his attention may have been diverted by something while he was making the tour of the room in which it is hung. It cannot be because I am unworthy of engaging the attention of so famous a man, for he has noticed persons—of even less importance than I.

What is it then? Is it a piece of ill-luck, like the number 3? I do not believe in making ill-luck an excuse for our want of success—that would be too easy a way of soothing one's wounded self-love; and, besides, it makes one look foolish. I attribute it rather to my want of merit.

And the most astounding thing is that this is the truth.

Friday, May 9.—I am reading Zola, and I admire him greatly. His criticisms and studies are admirable, and I am delighted with them. To gain the love of such a man, what would not a woman do? Do you suppose me, then, capable of love, as another woman might be? Oh, Heaven!

Well, the affection I felt for Bastien-Lepage was the same as that I now feel for Zola, whom I have never seen, who is forty-five years old, and corpulent, and who has a wife. I ask you if the men one meets in society—the men one is expected to marry—are not altogether absurd? What could I find to say to any one of those the whole day long?

Emile Bastien dined with us to-day, and told me he would bring M. Hayem, a well-known art-connoisseur, to see me next Thursday morning.

He possesses pictures of Delacroix, Corot, and Bastien-Lepage, and he has a special gift for discovering latent genius.

The day following the one in which the portrait of Bastien-Lepage's grandfather was exhibited, Hayem went to see the artist in his studio and gave him an order for a portrait of his father. It seems he has an astonishingly keen scent for genius; Emile Bastien saw him standing before my picture to-day, looking at it.

" What do you think of that? " he asked him.

"I think it very good," returned the connoisseur; "do you know the artist? Is she young?" and so on.

This Hayem has been *following me* since last year, when he looked at my pastel, as he did at my painting this year.

In short,.they are coming here on Thursday; he wishes to buy one of my pictures.

Monday, May 12.—After a period of intensely cold weather, the temperature for the last three days has risen to 28 or 29 degrees. This is overpowering.

While waiting for M. Hayem's visit, I have been finishing a study of a little girl, in the garden.

I forgot to mention that we met Hecht on the staircase of the Italiens. He spoke enthusiastically of my picture.

I have not yet achieved the success I desire, however. But neither had Bastien-Lepage achieved the success he desired, before he exhibited the portrait of his grandfather. True, but nevertheless—as I am fated to die soon, I want success to come quickly.

All the symptoms seem to indicate that Bastien-Lepage has a cancer in the stomach. It is all over with him, then. But perhaps they are mistaken. The poor fellow cannot sleep. It is atrocious. And his porter probably enjoys excellent health. It is atrocious.

Thursday, May 15.—E. Bastien came with M. Hayem this morning to see my pictures. Is it not absurd? I can scarcely believe it to be true: I am an artist. I have genius—and speaking seriously, not in jest. And a man of M. Hayem's reputation comes to see my paintings, and cares to look at what I have done. Can it be possible?

Emile Bastien is delighted at all this. The other day he said to me: "It seems to me as if it were I myself who was concerned." The poor fellow is very unhappy; I fear his brother will not get over this.

May 15.—I spent the whole afternoon walking up and down my room, very happy, with little shivers running up and down my back at the thought of the medal.

The medal is for the public ; as a matter of fact, I prefer such a success as mine, without a medal, to some kinds of medals.

Saturday, May 17.—I have just returned from the Bois, where I went with the demoiselles Staritsky, who are in Paris for a few days ; I met Bagnisky there, who told me they were discussing the Exhibition at Bogoluboff's the other day, and that some one remarked that my pictures resembled the paintings of Bastien-Lepage.

On the whole, I am flattered by the stir my picture has made. I am envied : I am slandered ; I am some one ; so that I may be allowed to put on airs if I choose.

Instead of doing this, however, I cry out in a heart-breaking tone, " Is it not horrible and enough to discourage any one ? I spend six years—the six best years of my life—working like a galley-slave, seeing no one, enjoying nothing ; at the end of that time I succeed in painting a good picture, and they dare to say I have received assistance in doing it ! The reward of all my efforts is to be vilely slandered ! "

This I say half-jestingly, half seriously, reclining on a bearskin with my arms hanging listlessly by my sides. Mamma takes it all seriously, however, and this drives me wild.

They give the medal of honor to X   , let us suppose ; naturally I cry out that it is an injustice, that it is a shame ; that I am furious, etc.

Mamma : " But, for Heaven's sake, do not get so excited ; they have not given it to him ; it is not true, they have not given it to him. And if they have done so, they have done it on purpose ; they know your disposition ; they know you

will fly into a rage about it. They have done it purposely,
and you allow yourself to be caught in the trap, like a
little fool!"

This is not an accusation, remember; it is only a supposition; but wait until X receives his medal, and you
shall see!

Another example: The novel of the pitiful creature Y,
who happens to be in fashion just now, has reached—I
don't know how many editions. Naturally, I am enraged.
"You see," I cry, "this is what the public like; this is
what their minds feed upon! *O tempora! O mores!*"
Would you believe that mamma begins the same tirade
over again, or almost the same as in the case of X. This
has already happened more than once. She is afraid I
shall break in pieces at the slightest shock; that it will kill
me; and she seeks to save me from this fate by such means
as cause me an attack of fever in the end.

Again: X, Y, or Z chances to say in the course of a
visit, "Do you know that the ball at Larochefoucauld's was
a very brilliant affair?"

I scowl at this. Mamma observes it, and five minutes
later says something, as if by chance, that is calculated to
disparage the ball in my eyes—if she does not try to prove
that it has not taken place at all.

It has come to this—inventions and childish subterfuges;
it makes me foam with rage to think that they should believe
me so easily imposed upon.

Tuesday, *May* 20.—I went to the *Salon* at ten o'clock
this morning with M. H   . He says my picture is so
good that people think I have received assistance in painting it.

This is outrageous.

He had the daring to say that Bastien has never composed a picture, that he is a portrait-painter; that his pic-

tures are only portraits, and that he has never done anything in the nude. The audacity of this Jew amazes me.

He spoke of the medal and said he would interest himself
about it ; he knows all the members of the committee.

We went from the *Salon* to Robert-Fleury's. I told him
very excitedly that I was accused of not having painted my
own picture.

He said he had heard nothing about it ; that such a thing
was not mentioned by any member of the committee ; that
if it had been mentioned, he was there to contradict it. He
thought me much more agitated than I really was, and
came home with me to breakfast, so as to soothe and console me. " How can you let everything agitate you in this
way ? " he said. " Such things should be treated with the
contempt they deserve."

" I only wish one of the committee would say such a
thing in my presence," he added, " I should be furious, I
would annihilate him on the spot."

" Ah, thank you, monsieur," I said.

" No," he returned, " you must not thank me ; the question is not one of friendship, it is one of justice ; and I
know what you can do better than any one else."

He repeated all these pleasant things to me again and
again, and also said that my chances of receiving the medal
were good ; one can never tell with certainty, of course,
but it appears that I have a good chance.

Saturday, May 24.—The medals of the first and second
classes are to be awarded to-day ; to-morrow those of the
third class.

To-day is warm and I feel tired. The *France Illustre* has
asked my permission to reproduce the painting. Some one
called Lecadre has written to me asking permission also.
I have granted it in both cases ; let them reproduce it as
much as they will.

And then medals are awarded to paintings that are not so good as mine. Oh, I am not at all uneasy ; true genius will make itself recognized under all circumstances ; only it is tiresome to be waiting for anything. It is better not to count upon it. The mention was promised as a certainty ; the medal is doubtful, but it will be unjust if I do not receive it.

Evidently.

Sunday, May 25.—What have I accomplished since the first of May ? Nothing. And why ? Ah, woe is me !

I have just come from Sevres ; it is frightful ; the landscape is so changed that it will never do ; it is Spring no longer. And then my apple-blossoms (in the painting) have turned yellow ; I had mixed in too much oil. I was an idiot, but I have altered it ; well, we shall see. But this picture must be finished. What with the *Salon*, the newspapers, the rain, H—— and other stupid things of the kind, I have lost twenty-five days ; this is maddening ; but there is an end to it all now.

The medal is to be awarded to-day, and it is now four o'clock. The rain is falling in torrents. Last year I was sure of receiving it, and all that troubled me was having to wait for the news. This year I am by no means sure of receiving it, and I am much more tranquil than I was then.

This year it is yes or no, without any doubt about the matter. If it is yes, I shall know it by eight o'clock this evening. Meantime I shall go recline in the easy-chair by the window, and amuse myself looking out at the passers-by while I am waiting for the news.

It is now twenty minutes past five, and I am not much more tired than if I had remained idle all this time without waiting for anything.

It vexes me to think of that oil that has turned my apple-blossoms yellow. When I looked at them for the first time

the perspiration broke out on my face.   Let us hope it will
not be very noticeable, however.—In two hours more I shall
know.   Perhaps you think I am very nervous about the
matter.   No, I assure you ; I am not much more nervous
than I have often been after spending an afternoon listless
and alone, doing nothing.

In any case I shall learn the result from to-morrow's
papers.

I am tired to death waiting ; I am feverish, and I have a
slight headache.

Ah, I shall not receive it, and it is the thought of what
mamma will say that most annoys me !   I do not wish my
affairs to be pried upon by others, my feelings to be commented upon by them.   It makes me turn hot, as if I had
committed some immodest action.   No matter what my
feelings are, I wish to be allowed to indulge them in peace.
Mamma will imagine that I am grieving, and that exasperates me.

The air is close and foggy ; I can scarcely breathe.

It is thirty-five minutes past seven ; I am called to dinner.
All is over.

Monday, May 26.—This is better ; instead of stupidly
waiting, I am now indignant, but indignation is a feeling
one need not conceal and is rather refreshing than otherwise.   Twenty-six medals were awarded yesterday ; there
are still six more to be awarded.   M—— has received a
medal for his portrait of Julian.

What can be the reason that I have received no medal ?
For certainly pictures no better than mine have received
medals.

Injustice ?   That is an excuse I am not very fond of.
It is one that any fool can claim.

They may admire my picture or not, as they choose, but
it is an undeniable fact that it contains seven figures, life-

size, grouped together, on a background that has some
merit also.   Every one whose opinion is worth having
thinks it very good, or at least good ; some persons have
even said that I received assistance in painting it.   Even
the elder Robert-Fleury, without knowing whose the picture was, thought it very good ; and Boulanger has said to
people who do not know me that he does not like that
style, it is true, but that the picture is well executed and
very interesting.

What can be the reason I have received no medal then ?

Paintings without any merit whatever have been awarded
medals ; I know very well that this is often the case.   But
on the other hand, there is no artist of merit who has not
received one or more medals.   What then ? what then ? I
also have eyes to see ; my picture is a composition.

Suppose I had painted those urchins in the costume of
the Middle Ages, and executed the work in a studio—which
is much easier than to work in the open air—against a
background of tapestry.

I should then have a historical picture which would be
very much admired in Russia.

What am I to believe ?

Here is another request for permission to reproduce my
picture ; it is from Barschet, the celebrated editor.

This is the fifth I have given.   And what then ?

Tuesday, May 27.—It is over.   I have received no
medal.

Oh, it is humiliating !   I had had hopes up to this morning.   And if you but knew the things that have received
medals !

Why am I not disheartened by this ?   I am very much
surprised at it, however.   If my picture is good, why has it
not received a prize ?

Intrigues, you will say.

But all the same, if my picture is good, why has it not received a prize ?   I have no wish to pose as an unsophisticated child who ignores that there are such things as intrigues, but it appears to me that if the painting really had merit—

Then the trouble is that the painting is bad ?   No, not that either.

I have eyes to see for myself—and then, others have praised it.   And how about the newspapers ?

Thursday, May 29.—I have had a fever all night, and my nerves are in a state of the most frightful irritation ; it is enough to make one mad.   This irritation of the nerves, however, is due as much to having passed a sleepless night as to my not having received a medal.

I am very unhappy.   I wish that I could believe in God. Is it not natural to look up to some power above when one is sick and miserable and unfortunate ?   One would fain believe in an Omnipotent Being, whose aid one has only to invoke in order to receive it ; to whom one can address one's-self without being slighted or humiliated, and to whom one has access at all times.   When physicians fail to help us, we ask that a miracle may be wrought ; the miracle is not wrought, but while we are waiting for it we are less miserable ; this is not much consolation.   If there be a God, He must be a just God ; and if He is just, how can He allow things to be as they are ?   Alas ? if we let thoughts like this enter into our minds, we can no longer believe in a God.   Why live ?   What purpose is served by dragging on longer this miserable existence ?   To die would have at least this advantage : One might then learn what this other life is that people talk so much about ; that is to say, if there be another life—which is what we shall learn when we are dead.

Friday, May 30.—I have been considering that it is very foolish on my part to take no thought of the only thing in life worth having—the one thing that can compensate for every want, that can make us forget every misery—love, in a word. Two beings who love each other believe each other to be morally and physically perfect,—morally so, especially. One who loves you must of necessity be just, loyal, generous, and ready to perform a heroic action with simplicity.

Two beings who love each other believe the universe to be what the philosophers, such as Aristotle and I, for instance, have dreamed it to be,—admirable and perfect, and this is, in my opinion, the chief attraction love possesses for the soul.

In our intercourse with our family, with our friends, with the world, some glimpse of the weaknesses of humanity is sure to be had ; here of avarice or of folly, there of envy, of meanness, or of injustice ; the friend we love most dearly has thoughts which he conceals from us, so that, as Maupassant says, man is always alone, for even in their most confidential moments there will still remain some thought hidden from him in the bosom of his friend.

Well, love works this miracle of blending two souls in one. It is only an illusion, it is true, but what matter ? *That which we believe to exist, exists.* Love makes the universe appear to us such as it ought to be. If I were God—

Well, what then ?

Saturday, May 31.—Villevielle has just told me that the reason I did not receive a medal was because I made a fuss about last year's mention, and spoke publicly of the committee as idiots. It is true that I did so.

My picture is not indeed a very large one, nor is it very bold in style ; if it were, the " Meeting " would be a masterpiece. But is it necessary that a painting should be a masterpiece to obtain an insignificant third-class medal? The engraving of Baude has appeared, accompanied by an article which says that the public are disappointed at my having received no medal. My painting is dry, it is said. But they say the same thing of Bastien's painting. .

Is there any one in the world who can say that the portrait of M   *has more merit than my picture has?

Bastien-Lepage received eight votes for his "Jeanne d'Arc." M—— received a medal for his portrait. And the great M—— received twenty-eight votes, exactly twenty more than I received. There is neither conscience nor justice in the world. Truly I know not what to think.

I went downstairs when H—— came, in order to show this Jew that I am not cast down.

I appeared so haughty and unconcerned while we chatted of photographs, engravings, patrons of art, etc., that this son of Israel finally made up his mind to transact some business with me—even though I have received no medal! "I will buy your pastel" ("Armandine"), he said, "and the Head of the Laughing Baby." Two! He arranged the matter of the purchase with Dina, but we referred him, as to the price, to Emile Bastien. I am very well satisfied.

Sunday, June 1.—For a month past I have done nothing! Yes, I began the works of Sully-Prudhomme yesterday morning and I have been reading them ever since. I have two of his books, and I like them extremely.

I trouble my head but little about verse; when it is bad it annoys me, but, otherwise, I think only of the idea expressed. If people like to make rhymes, let them do so, provided only that they do it in such a way as not to distract my attention from the thought. And the thought is what pleases me in Sully-Prudhomme. There is an elevation of style, a subtlety of reasoning, that is almost abstract in his works, which is in harmony with my own way of thinking.

I spent several hours, stretched on my divan or walking up and down on my balcony, reading the preface to "Lucretius," as well as the work itself—"De Natura Rerum." Those who have read the book will be able to appreciate this.

To understand this work great concentration of thought is necessary. Even those accustomed to deal with such subjects must find it difficult reading. I understood all I read, though the meaning would at times escape me ; but on such occasions I read the passage over and over again until I had grasped the thought. I ought to admire Sully-Prudhomme greatly for writing things which I find it difficult to understand.

He is as familiar with the management of thoughts as I am with the management of colors.

Then he ought to admire me greatly too, for with a few "muddy paints," as the antipathetic Theophile Gautier says, I can create a countenance that will express human emotions, landscapes that will reflect Nature in all her aspects— the sky, the trees, the atmosphere. Probably he thinks himself a thousand times superior to a painter, because he is able to ransack the secret recesses of the mind. But what does he or any one else learn from that ?

How mind works ? To give to the intellectual processes, swift and elusive as they are, names—it seem to me in my ignorance that this is an unprofitable occupation for the mind. It is an interesting and refined amusement, and one that requires the exercise of skill, but what end does it serve ? Is it by giving names to strange and abstract things that the great writers and thinkers of the world have been formed.

" Man," these metaphysicians say, " can take cognizance of an object only in so far as he comes into relations with it, etc." The greater number of my readers will be able to make nothing out of this. I will cite another passage: " Our knowledge, therefore, cannot exceed the knowledge expressed in our categories, as applied to our perceptions." Good : we can understand no more than we can understand. That is self-evident.

If I had received a thorough and systematic education, I should be a remarkable person. Everthing I know I have taught myself. I myself drew out the plan of my studies at Nice, with the professors of the Lyceum, who could not get over their amazement at the intelligence displayed in it. In forming it I was guided partly by my own ideas in the matter, partly by ideas gathered in the course of my reading. Since then I have read the Greek and Latin authors, the French and English classics, contemporary writers—everything I came across, in short.

But all this knowledge is in a chaotic state, notwithstanding the efforts I have made, through my natural love of harmony, to reduce it to order.

What is there in this writer, Sully-Prudhomme, to attract me ? I bought his works six months ago, and tried to read them then, but cast them aside, after a time, as agreeable verses, indeed, but nothing more. To-day I found thoughts in them that enchanted me and read on for hours, under the influence of Francois Coppee's visit. But neither Coppee nor any one else has ever spoken to me of him. In what then does his attraction for me consist, and how have I came to discover it only now ?

I might, by a great effort of the mind, succeed in making a philosophical analysis of this great achievement of the human intellect—" De Natura Rerum." But what purpose would it serve ? Would it make me alter a single one of my opinions ?

Thursday, June 5.—Prater is dead ; he had grown up with

me ; they bought him for me at Vienna in 1870; he was three weeks old at the time, and had a habit of hiding behind the trunks, among the papers in which parcels came wrapped from the shops.

He was my faithful and attached dog ; he would whine when I left the house, and pass whole hours at the window, waiting for my return. Afterward, in Rome, I had a fancy for another dog, and mamma took Prater, who was always jealous of his rival, however. Poor Prater, with his tawny hide, like a lion's, and his beautiful eyes ; I blush for myself when I think of my heartlessness !

My new dog, who was called Pincio, was stolen from me in Paris. Instead of taking back Prater, who had never been able to console himself for my abandonment of him, I was foolish enough to take Coco I. and afterward the real Coco. This was base, it was despicable. For four years these two animals were alway ready to devour each other, and finally it was necessary to shut Prater in an upper room, where he was kept a prisoner, while Coco walked over people and did as he chose. His death was due to old age. I spent a couple of hours with him yesterday ; he dragged himself to my side, and rested his head upon my knee.

Ah, I am a pretty wretch, with my affectionate sentiments. What a despicable character is mine ! I shed tears as I write, and I think the while that these tears will procure me, with those who read me, the reputation of having a good heart. I always intended to take back the poor brute, but never went beyond giving him a lump of sugar, or a caress, as I passed him by.

You should have seen his tail at such times ! It would turn round and round so fast that it looked like a wheel.

It seems, after all, that the poor creature is not yet dead : I had thought he was dead because I no longer saw him in his room ; he had hidden himself behind a trunk or a bathtub, as he used to do at Vienna, and I thought they had taken away his dead body, and were afraid to tell me of it. But his death must certainly take place either to-night or to-morrow.

Robert-Fleury found me crying to-day. I had written to him in regard to the reproduction of my picture, and he came in answer to my letter. It appears I had neglected to sign a little paper by means of which others were to be prevented from reproducing the picture, and thus, perhaps, involving me in a law-suit. You must know that I am very proud of all these requests for permission to reproduce my picture, and I should be proud even of a law-suit.

Friday, June 6.—I have been thinking a great deal about the soiree at the Embassy ; I only fear that something may occur to spoil it for me. I can never believe in the possibility of anything pleasant happening to me. Everything may seem to be propitious, but in the end something is always sure to occur, some obstacle to oppose itself to the realization of my hopes. This has been the case for a long time past.

We went to the *Salon* to-day—I, for the purpose of seeing the picture that had received the medal. We met Robert-Fleury there, and, as we were standing before one of the pictures that had been awarded a second-class medal, I asked him what he would say if I had shown him a picture like that.

" In the first place, I hope you will take good care not to paint pictures like that," he answered seriously.

" But how about the medal then ? " I asked.

" Oh, well," he answered, " he is a man who has been exhibiting for a long time, and then—you can understand how it is—"

Saturday, June 7.—We are preparing for this night's event in silence.

I am to wear a gown of white silk mull. The bodice is trimmed with two pieces of the mull, crossing each other in folds, in front, and fastened on the shoulders with knots of the material. The sleeves are short and trimmed in the same way. There is a wide, white sash with long ends falling behind. The skirt is made of the mull draped from left to right, and falling to the feet. In the back are two lengths of the material, the one touching the ground, the other a little shorter. My slippers are white and quite plain. The general effect is charming. My hair is dressed *à la Psyche*, and is without ornament. The drapery in the front is a dream. It is all so simple and elegant that I shall look very pretty. Mamma will wear a black damask gown covered with jet, with a long train, and diamonds.

Sunday, June 8.—I looked as well as I have ever looked in my life, or as it would be possible for me to look. The gown produced a charming effect, and my complexion was as fresh and blooming as in the old days at Nice or Rome.

People who only see me as I am every day looked at me with amazement.

We arrived a little late. Madame Fredericks was not with the Ambassadress, with whom mamma exchanged a few words. I was very calm and very much at my ease. We met many acquaintances. Madame d'A , whom I saw at the Gavinis, but who had not bowed to me, bowed to me last night very graciously. I took the arm of Gavini, who looked very well with his ribbons and stars ; he presented Menabrea, the Italian Minister, to me, and we discussed art together. Afterwards M. de Lesseps talked to me for a long time about his children and their nurses, and the share of the Suez Canal. Then Chevreau gave me his arm, and we took a turn through the rooms together.

As for the *chargés d'affaires* and the *attachés*, I neglected them in order to devote myself to the old men, with their decorations.   Later on, having duly burned incense at the shrine of fame, I chatted with some of the artists who were there ; they were very curious to know me, and asked to be presented to me.   But I was so pretty and well-dressed that they will be convinced that I did not paint my picture without assistance.   There were Cheremetieff, Lehman, a very amiable old man, of some talent, and Edelfeldt, who has a great deal of talent.

The latter is a handsome, though vulgar, young man—a Russian, from Finland.   Altogether I spent a very pleasant evening.   The chief thing, you see, is to be pretty ; everything depends upon that.

Tuesday, June 10.—How interesting it is to watch the passers-by in the street ; to note the expression on their faces, their peculiarities ; to obtain glimpses into the souls of those who are strangers to us ; and to endow all this with life, or rather to picture to ourselves the life, of each of these strangers !

One paints a combat of Roman gladiators, which one has never seen, from Parisian models.   Why not paint the gladiators of Paris from the Parisian populace, also ?   In five or six centuries this would be antiquity, and the fools of that time would regard it with veneration.

Saturday, June 14.—We had a great many visitors to-day, as it is mamma's birthday.   I wore a very handsome gown— gray taffeta, with a white mull vest in the style of Louis XVI.

Monday, June 16.—We went to-night to see Sarah Bernhardt in " Macbeth " (Richepin's translation).   The Gavinis were with us.   I so seldom go to the theater that I enjoyed it.   The declamatory style of the actors, however, offended my artistic sense.   How much more agreeable it would be if these people only spoke naturally !

Marais ("Macbeth ") was good at times ; his intonation was so theatrical, so artificial, that it was painful to listen to him. Sarah, however, is always admirable, though her voice is no longer the silvery voice it was.

Tuesday, June 17.—I am tormented by the thought of my picture, and the hands are still to be done ! It interests me no longer—this apple-tree in blossom, and these violets ; and this peasant girl half-asleep ! A canvas three feet in length would have been quite large enough for it, and I have made it life-size. It is good for nothing. Three months thrown away !

Wednesday, June 18.—I am still at Sevres ! What torments me is that I have an attack of fever every day. And then it seems impossible for me to grow fat. Yet I drink six or seven glasses of milk a day.

Friday, June 20.—The architect has written to me from Algiers. At the end of my letter to him I had drawn our three likenesses, with a medal around the neck of each. To Jules I had given the medal of honor, to myself a medal of the first, and to the architect a medal of the second class, for next year's *Salon.* I also sent him a photograph of "The Meeting." And he tells me he showed them both to his brother, who was delighted to be able to form some idea of the picture he had heard so much about, and which he thought very good.

" How stupid they are," he says his brother exclaimed, " not to have awarded a medal to this painting, which seems to me very good indeed ! "

He would like very much to have written to me, Emile adds, but it was not possible for him to do so. He still suffers greatly ; notwithstanding this, however, he has resolved to start for home a week from to-day. He charged the architect to give me his friendly regards, and to thank me for the embroidery.

A year ago this would have delighted me. He would like to have written to me ! I can only take a retrospective pleasure in this, for at present such things are almost indifferent to me.

At the end of the letter is my likeness, with the medal of honor for 1886 around the neck.

He must have been touched by the delicate manner in which I sought to console his brother in my letter. The letter began seriously, with comforting words, and· ended with pleasantries, according to my custom.

Wednesday, June 25.—I have just been reading my journal for the years 1875, 1876, and 1877. I find it full of vague aspirations toward some unknown goal. My evenings were spent in wild and despairing attempts to find some outlet for my powers. Should I go to Italy ? Remain in Paris ? Marry ? Paint ? What should I strive to become ? If I went to Italy, I should no longer be in Paris, and my desire was to be everywhere at once. What a waste of energy was there ?

If I had been born a man, I would have conquered Europe. As I was born a woman, I exhausted my energy in tirades against fate, and in eccentricities. There are moments when one believes one's-self capable of all things. " If I only had the time," I wrote, " I would be a sculptor, a writer, a musician ! "

I am consumed by an inward fire, but death is the inevitable end of all things, whether I indulge in these vain longings or not.

But if I am nothing, if I am to be nothing, why these dreams of fame, since the time I was first able to think ? Why these wild longings after a greatness that presented itself then to my imagination under the form of riches and honors?

Why, since I was first able to think, since the time when I was four years old, have I had longings, vague but intense, for glory, for grandeur, for splendor? How many characters have I been in turn, in my childish imagination! First, I was a dancer—a famous dancer—worshiped by all St. Petersburg. Every evening I would make them put a low-necked dress on me, and flowers in my hair, and I would dance, very gravely, in the drawing-room, while every one in the house looked on. Then I was the most famous prima donna in the world; I sang and accompanied myself on the harp, and I was carried in triumph, where or by whom I do not know. Then I electrified the people by my eloquence. The Emperor of Russia married me; that he might be able to maintain himself on his throne. I came into personal relations with my people; I explained my political views to them in my speeches, and both people and sovereign were moved to tears.

And then I was in love. The man I loved proved false, and was afterward killed by some accident, generally a fall from his horse, just at the moment when I felt that my love for him was beginning to decrease. When my lovers died I consoled myself, but when they proved false to me I fell into despair and finally died of grief.

In short, I have pictured every human feeling, every earthly pleasure to myself as superior to the reality, and if my dreams are to remain forever unrealized, it is better that I should die.

Why has not my picture been awarded a medal?

The medal! It must be because some of the committee thought I had received assistance. It has happened once or twice already that medals have been given to women who, as has afterward been discovered, had received assistance in their work; and when a medal has been once awarded the recipient has the right to exhibit on the following year, and may send the most worthless or insignificant picture if he chooses.

Yet I am young and elegant, and have been praised by the papers! But these people are all alike. Breslau, for instance, said to my model that I would paint a great deal better if I went less into society. They think I go out every evening. How deceitful appearances are! But to suspect that my picture is not all my own work is too serious a matter; thank Heaven, they have not publicly given utterance to their suspicions, however! Robert-Fleury told me he was surprised that I had not received a medal, for that every time he spoke of me to his colleagues of the committee, they responded, "*It is very good;* it is a very *interesting picture.*"

"What do you suppose they mean when they say that?" he asked me.

Then *it is* this suspicion.

Friday, June 27.—Just as we were going to take a drive in the Bois, who should appear beside the carriage but the Architect! They arrived in Paris this morning, and he came to tell us that Jules is a little better; that he bore the journey well, but that, unhappily, he cannot leave the house. It would give him so much pleasure, his brother added, to tell me himself how greatly my picture had been admired by every one to whom he had shown the photograph in Algiers.

"Then we will go to see him to-morrow," said mamma.

"You could not give him a greater pleasure," he answered; "he says your picture—but no, he will tell it to you himself to-morrow; that will be better."

Saturday, June 28.—We went, according to our promise, to the Rue Legendre.

He rose to receive us, and took a few steps forward to meet us; he seemed mortified at the change that had taken place in his appearance.

He is changed, indeed, very much changed; but his disease is not in the stomach; I am no doctor, but his looks are enough to tell me that.

In short, I find him so changed that all I could say was: "Well, so we have you here among us again." He was not at all reserved; on the contrary he was as cordial and friendly as possible. He spoke in the most flattering terms of my picture, telling me again and again not to trouble myself about the medal—that the success of the picture itself was sufficient.

I made him laugh, telling him his illness would do him good; that he was beginning to grow too stout. The Architect seemed enchanted to see his invalid so gay and so amiable. Thus encouraged, I grew talkative. He complimented me on my gown, and even on the handle of my parasol. He made me sit at his feet on his reclining chair. How thin he has grown! And his eyes look larger than they were and very bright, and his hair looks uncared-for.

But he looked very interesting, and since he has asked me to do so, I shall go to see him often.

The Architect, who accompanied us downstairs, asked us to do so also. "It makes Jules so happy," he said; "it is so great a pleasure for him to see you; I assure you he thinks you have a great deal of talent."

I write all these details about the reception I met with, because it made me very happy.

But the feeling I have for him is a maternal one, very calm and very tender, and one of which I feel proud, as if it conferred a new dignity upon me. He will recover from this, I am sure.

Monday, June 30.—I could scarcely keep from cutting

my painting to pieces to-day. There is not an inch of it painted to please me.

And one of the hands is still to be done! But when this hand is done there will be only so much the more to be undone! Ah, misery!

And it has cost me three months—three months!

I have been amusing myself painting a basket of straw-berries such as were never before seen. I gathered them myself, picking a few green ones also, for the sake of the color.

And such leaves! In short, wonderful strawberries, gathered by an artist, with the delicate touch and coquettish air of one engaged in an unaccustomed occupation.

And among them is a branch of red gooseberries.

I walked with them through the streets of Sevres, and in the railway coach I held the basket in my lap, taking care to keep it slightly raised, so that the air might pass beneath, and prevent the heat of my dress from spoiling the strawberries, not one of which had a speck or spot on it.

Rosalie laughed : " If any of those at home were only to see you now, mademoiselle ! " she said.

" Could this be possible ? " I thought.

" But then, it is for the sake of his painting, which deserves it, " not for his face, which does not. There is nothing however, which his painting does not deserve."

" Then it is his painting that will eat the strawberries? "

Tuesday, July 1.—Still at that odious Sevres ! But I got home in good time, before five o'clock. My picture is almost finished.   .

I am in the deepest dejection, however. Everything goes wrong with me. It would be necessary that some great event should take place in order to dispel this gloom.

And I, who do not believe in a God, have fixed my hopes upon God.

Formerly, after these fits of depression something would always occur to bring me back to an interest in life.

My God, why hast thou given me the power to reason? It would make me so happy if I could but believe blindly.

I believe and I do not believe. When I reason I no longer believe. But in moments of extreme joy or extreme wretchedness my first thought is always of that God who is so cruel to me.

Wednesday, July 2.—We went to see Jules Bastien to-day—this time to his studio. I really think he is growing better. His mother was there. She is a woman of about sixty, and she looks to be forty-five or fifty; she is much better looking than her picture. Her hair is of a pretty blonde color, with here and there a silver thread or two. Her smile reveals goodness of heart; and with her black and white gown she presents quite a pleasing appearance. She embroiders with skill from designs of her own.

The two upper front teeth of Bastien-Lepage are far apart like mine.

Thursday.—I went to see Potain this morning at about seven o'clock. He made a superficial examination and ordered me to Eaux-Bonnes. Afterward he will see, he says. But I have read the letter which he gave me for his colleague. In it he says that the upper part of the right lung is gone, and that I am the most unmanageable and imprudent patient he has ever had.

Afterward, as it was not yet eight o'clock, I went to see the little doctor of the Rue de la Echiquier. He impressed me as being a very serious person; he appeared disagreeably surprised by my condition, and insisted strongly that I should consult some of the shining lights in the profession, Bouchard or Grancher, for instance.

As I at first refused to do this, he offered to accompany me, and I at last consented.

Potain pretends that my lungs have been in worse condition than they are at present, but that an unexpected improvement took place in them, and that the old trouble has now returned, but will soon pass away again.

And Potain is such an optimist that when he speaks thus I must be in a very bad way indeed.

Little B——, however, is not of this opinion ; he says that my disease had indeed at one time assumed a more serious form than it now presents, but that the attack was an acute one which they thought would carry me off suddenly ; this did not happen, and that is the improvement that has taken place. The chronic trouble, however, has now become aggravated ; in short, he insists on my seeing **Grancher.**

I will do so.

So, then, I have consumption !

That, and everything else. The prospect is not very encouraging.

And nothing to console me in the least for all this.

Friday, July 4.—The Sevres picture is here in my studio. I might call it " April." The name is of little consequence, however, if the picture itself were only good, which it is not.

The green of the background is at once both bright and muddy, and the figure of the girl herself is not in the least like what I had intended it to be.

I have hurried through with it as it was, without waiting to make it better, but there is nothing of the sentiment I had intended in the picture—nothing at all. In short, it is three months thrown away.

Saturday, July 5.—I have a charming new gray linen

gown ; the waist is a blouse, without any trimming except
the lace around the neck and sleeves. The hat is an ideal
one ; it is trimmed with a large and coquettish-looking bow
of antique lace. It was so becoming to me that I thought
of going to the Rue Legendre ; only I feared it might seem
as if I went there too often. And yet why should I think
so? I go there simply as a fellow-artist, an admirer, to
help to make the time pass pleasantly for him while he is
so ill.

We went there, accordingly. His mother was delighted
to see us ; she patted me on the shoulder, and said I had
beautiful hair. The Architect is still downcast, but the
great painter is a little better.

He ate his soup and his egg before us. His mother runs
for whatever he wants, and waits on him herself so that the
servant may not have to come in. And he takes it all quite
naturally and accepts our services with the greatest *sang-
froid*, without manifesting the least surprise. Some one in
speaking of his appearance said that he ought to have his
hair cut, and mamma mentioned that she used to cut her
son's hair when he was a child, and her father's when he
was sick. " Would you like me to cut yours ?" she added ;
" I have a lucky hand."

We all laughed, but he consented immediately ; his
mother ran to bring a *peignoir* and mamma set to work at
once, and succeeded very creditably in her task.

I wanted to have a hand in it, also, but the stupid fellow
said I should be sure to commit some folly ; I revenged
myself by comparing him to Samson in the hands of Dalilah.
That will be my next picture !

He condescended to smile at this.

· His brother, emboldened by his good-humor, proposed to
cut his beard also, which he did slowly and solemnly, his
hands trembling slightly while he did it.

This altered the expression of his face completely; it took

away the sickly look it had before worn ; his mother gave little cries of joy when she saw him.   " Now I see my boy again," she said, " my dear little boy, my dear child ! "

She is an excellent woman—so amiable and unaffected ; and then she has the greatest admiration for her distinguished son.

They are very worthy people.

Monday, July 14.—I have commenced the treatment which is to cure me.   And I am perfectly tranquil concerning the result.

Even the prospects in regard to my painting seem better.

What opportunities for study does the Boulevard des Batignolles, or even the Avenue Wagram, present to the artist !

Have you ever watched the faces of the people who frequent those streets ?

With each one of the benches one may connect some tragedy or some romance.   See the social outcast, as he sits there, one arm leaning on the back of the seat, the other resting on his knee, looking around him with furtive glance; the woman with her child seated in her lap ; the busy, bustling woman, sitting down to take a moment's rest ; the grocer's boy reading his little newspaper, as if he had not a care in the world ; the workman fallen asleep in his seat ; the philosophic or the hopeless man silently smoking.   Perhaps I let my imagination run away with me, but look at all this any day at five or six o'clock in the evening, and judge for yourselves.

Yes, that is it !

I think I have found a subject for my picture.   ·

Yes, yes, yes !   I may not be able to execute it, but I am quite satisfied as to the subject.   I could dance for joy.

How differently do we feel at different times !

Sometimes life seems a void, and sometimes—I begin to take an interest in everything again—in all my surroundings.

It is as if a sudden flood of life had come into my soul.

And yet there is nothing to rejoice about.

So much the worse ; then I shall find something to cheer and please me even in the thought of my death.

Nature intended me to be happy, but,

> Pourquoi dans ton œuvre celeste
> Tant d' elements si peu d'accord ?

Tuesday, July 15.—Every time I see people sitting on the benches in the public parks or streets an old idea of mine occurs to me—that here are to be found splendid opportunities for the study of art. It is always better to paint scenes in which the characters are in repose, than scenes of action. Let it not be thought that I am opposed to action in painting, but in scenes where violent action is represented there can be neither illusion nor pleasure for persons of refined tastes. One is painfully impressed (though one may not be conscious of the fact) by this arm which is raised to strike, but which does not strike, by these legs depicted in the act of running, and which remain always in the same position. There are violent situations, however, in which one can imagine the actors as for an instant motionless, and for the purposes of art an instant is sufficient.

It is always preferable to seize the instant following a violent action rather than the one preceding it. The " Jeanne d'Arc " of Bastien-Lepage has heard mysterious voices ; she hurries forward, overturning her spinning-wheel in her haste, and stops suddenly to lean against a tree. But in scenes where the arm is raised to strike, in which *action* is portrayed, the artistic enjoyment is never complete.

Take the " Distribution of Flags by the Emperor at Versailles."

Every one is rushing forward with arms raised ; and yet the action does not shock the artistic sense, because the figures are depicted during a moment of expectation, and we are ourselves moved and carried away by the emotion of these men ; we share in their impatience. The spirit and force of the painting are prodigious, precisely because it is possible to imagine an instant during which the action is arrested—an instant during which we can tranquilly contemplate this scene, as if it were a real scene and not a painting.

But action, whether in sculpture or in painting, is never capable of the same sublimity of treatment as repose.

Compare the pictures of Millet with the most powerfully treated scenes of action you are acquainted with.

See the "Moses " of Michael Angelo ; he is motionless, but he is *alive.* His " Penseroso " neither moves nor speaks, but this is because he wills it to be so. He is a *living* man who is absorbed in his own reflections.

The " Pas-meche " of Bastien-Lepage looks at you and you listen as if he were going to speak, because he *lives.* In Lepage's " Foins " the man lying on his back, his face covered with his hat, sleeps ; but he is alive ! The woman sitting down is in a revery, and is motionless, but we feel that she is living.

No scene can satisfy the artistic sense completely but one in which the characters are in repose. This gives us time to grasp its beauties, to possess ourselves of its meaning, to endow it in our imagination with life.

Ignorant or stupid people think scenes of repose more easy to paint than scenes of action.

When I die my death will be caused by indignation at the stupidity of human nature, which, as Flaubert says, has no limit.

During the past twenty years Russia has produced admirable works in literature,

In reading Count Tolstoï's " Peace and War," I was so impressed by this fact as to exclaim involuntarily, " Why, this is equal to Zola ! "

And this is true. There is an article in the *Revue des Deux Mondes* to-day devoted to our Tolstoï, and my heart, as a Russian, leaped for joy when I read it. It is by M. de Vogue, who was Secretary of the French Embassy in Russia. He has made a study of our literature and manners, and has already published several remarkably just and profound articles on this great and wonderful country of mine.

And I, wretch that I am—I live in France ; I prefer to be a stranger in a strange land to living in my own country !

Since I love my country—the beautiful, the great, the glorious Russia—I ought to go there to live.

But I, too, labor for the glory of my country—though I may never become a celebrated genius like Tolstoï !

But if it were not for my painting, I would go there to live ; yes, I would go ! But my art absorbs all my faculties ; everything else is only an interlude, an amusement.

Monday, July 21.—I walked for more than four hours to-day in search of a background for my picture ; it is to be a street, but I have not yet fixed on the particular spot.

It is evident that a public seat on a boulevard on the outskirts of the city is very different from a seat in the Champs-Elysees, where porters, grooms, nurses, and idlers sit.

Here there is no field for the artist ; here there is no soul, no romance. With the exception of some particular case these people are nothing more than human machines.

But the outcast who sits on the edge of yonder bench, how he appeals to the imagination ! That is the real man— a man such as Shakspeare might have portrayed.

Now that I have discovered this treasure I am possessed by an unreasoning dread lest it should escape from me before I can fix it on canvas. What if the weather should not prove propitious, or if it should be beyond my powers of execution ?

Well, if I have no genius, then Heaven has chosen to mock me ; for it inflicts upon me all the tortures that a genius could suffer—Alas !

Wednesday, July 23.—My picture is sketched in,—my models have been found.   I have been running about since five o'clock this morning—to Villette and to Batignolles ; Rosalie spoke to the various people I pointed out to her.

The whole affair is neither very easy nor very pleasant.

Friday, August 1.—When I treat you to moving phrases you must not allow yourselves to be too much affected by them. . . .

Shall I ever know what it is to love ?

For my own part I think love—impossible—to one who looks at human nature through a microscope, as I do. They who see only what they wish to see in those around them are very fortunate.

Shall I tell you something ?   Well, I am neither an artist, nor a sculptor, nor a musician ; neither woman, girl, nor friend.   My only purpose in life is to observe, to reflect, and to analyze.

A glance, a face I see by chance, a sound, a pleasure, a pain, is at once weighed, examined, verified, classified, noted. And not until this is accomplished is my mind at rest.

Saturday, August 2.—Tuesday, Wednesday, Thursday, Friday—five days, and my picture is finished.   Claire and I commenced on the same day, with the same subject, on a canvas 3 ft. 4 x 3 ft. 3—a picture of some size, as you see—La Bievre, immortalized in his verse by Victor Hugo ; in the background is a farmhouse ; in the foreground a young girl sits by the river-side talking to a youth who stands on the opposite bank.

And is the picture a good one? There is something too hackneyed in the sentiment of the composition for this to be the case, and then I wished to finish it quickly. It is amusing to hear them criticise it; one says, "What a pretty scene!" Another says the picture has no merit whatever, and yet another, "It is very good indeed; a really pretty painting!" Claire has not yet finished hers.

Good heavens! how many things there are that shock me! Almost all true artists are like me in this respect.

I wonder at people who can eat great pieces of raw fat mutton.

I wonder at those fortunate people who can swallow raspberries whole, without minding the little insects that are almost always to be found in them.

As for me, I must first examine them closely, so that the pleasure of eating them does not pay me for the trouble.

I wonder at people who can eat all sorts of hashes and stews, without knowing what they are composed of.

I wonder at, or rather I envy, simple, healthy, common-place natures, in short.

Thursday, August 7.—We have sent a little ice-box to the Rue Legendre; he wished to have one that might stand near his bed.

I only hope he may not think we are paying him all these attentions in order to get one of his pictures for a mere song!

My picture is sketched in colors. But I do not feel very strong. I find it necessary to lie down and rest very frequently, and when I get up again I am so dizzy that for some moments I can scarcely see. At last, at about five o'clock I was obliged to leave my work, and go for a turn in the deserted walks of the Bois.

Monday, August 11.—I left the house at five this morning to make a sketch for my picture, but there were so many people in the streets already that I was compelled to return home furious. No less than twenty persons had gathered around the carriage, although it remained closed.

I drove through the streets again in the afternoon, but succeeded no better.

I went to the Bois.

Tuesday, Aug. 12.—In short, my friends, all this means that I am ill. I still struggle against the feeling, and try to drag myself about, but I thought this morning that I should at last have to succumb—that is to say, lie down and give up work. But suddenly I felt a little stronger, and I went out again in search of some hints for my picture. My weakness, and the preoccupation of my thoughts, keep me apart from the real world, which, however, I have never seen so clearly as I do now. All its baseness, all its meanness, stand out before my mind with saddening distinctness.

Foreigner though I be—not to speak of my youth and my ignorance—I find passages to criticise in the writings of the best authors and poets. As for the newspapers, I cannot read half a dozen lines in one of them without throwing it aside in disgust, not only because of the style, which is that of a scullion, but because of the sentiments expressed. There is no honesty in them. Every article is either written to serve a purpose, or is paid for.

There is neither good faith nor sincerity to be found anywhere.

And what is to be said of men, who call themselves men of honor, who will deliberately falsify the truth through party spirit?

It is disgusting.

We came home to dine after leaving Bastien, who is still in bed, though his eyes are bright and he seems to be free from pain. He has gray eyes, the exquisite charm of which vulgar souls cannot be expected to appreciate. Do you understand what I mean by this? Eyes that have looked into the eyes of Jeanne d'Arc.

We spoke of the picture, and he complained of not being sufficiently appreciated. I told him he was appreciated by those who had souls to understand him, and that "Jeanne d'Arc" was a work which people admired more than they dared say to his face.

Saturday, August 16.—This is the first day I have been really able to work in the *fiacre*, and I came home with such a pain in my back that I was obliged to have it bathed and rubbed.

But how well I feel now! The Architect put my painting in place this morning. His brother is better. He went for an airing to the Bois to-day. They carried him downstairs in an easy-chair. Felix told me this when he came for some milk this afternoon.

For a week past Bastien has been drinking goat's milk—the milk of our goat. Imagine the joy of our people. But this is not all. He condescends to be so friendly with us that he sends for it himself whenever he has a fancy for it. This is delightful.

He will soon be lost to us then, since he is growing better. Yes, our good times are coming to an end. One cannot go visit a man who is well enough to go out.

But I must not exaggerate things. He went to the Bois, but he was carried there in an easy-chair, and he went back to bed again on his return home. That does not mean that he is well enough to go out.

Tuesday, August 19.—I was so exhausted that I had scarcely strength enough to put on a linen gown and go to see Bastien. His mother received us with reproaches. Three days! she said, three days without coming to see him! It was dreadful! And when we were in his room Emile cried out: "All is ended, then? We are friends no longer?" "So, then, you have deserted me?" said *he himself*. Ah, I ought not to have stayed away so long.

My vanity tempts me to repeat here all his friendly reproaches, and his assurances that never, never, never could we come too often.

Thursday, August 21.—I do nothing but lounge about all day, except for a couple of hours in the morning—from five to seven—when I work out-of-doors in a carriage.

I have had a photograph taken of the scene I have chosen for my picture, so as to be able to copy with exactness the lines of the sidewalk.

This was done at seven this morning ; the Architect was there at six. Afterwards we all drove home, I, Rosalie, the Architect, Coco, and the photograph.

Not that the presence of the brother was at all necessary, but it was pleasant to have him with us. I always like to have a guard of honor around me.

All is over! He is doomed!

Baude, who spent the evening here with the Architect, told it to mamma.

Baude is his most intimate friend—the one to whom he wrote the letter from Algiers that I read.

All is over, then.

Can it be possible?

I cannot yet realize what will be the effect of this crushing news upon me.

This is a new sensation—to see a man who is under sentence of death.

Tuesday, August 26.—All the confused thoughts that have filled my brain and distracted my mind have now settled immovably around this new misfortune.

It is a new experience—to see a man, a great painter—to see *him*, in short—

Condemned to die !

This is something not to be lightly spoken of.

And every day, until the day arrives, I shall be thinking, "He is dying!"

It is horrible !

I have summoned all my courage, and now I stand, with head erect, ready to receive the blow.

Has it not been thus with me all my life?

When the blow comes I shall receive it without flinching.

At times I refuse to believe it, I rebel against it; I give way to lamentations, when I know that all is ended.

I cannot utter two sentences connectedly.

But do not imagine that I am overwhelmed; I am only profoundly engrossed by the thoughts of how it will be with me—afterward.

Saturday, August 30.—It seems that matters are growing worse. I am unable to do anything. I have done nothing since the Sevres picture was finished—nothing, that is to say, except two miserable panels.

I sleep for hours at a time in the broad daylight. I have finished the sketch for my picture, but it is laughable !

The canvas is there; everything is ready, I alone am wanting.

If I were to write here all I feel!—the terrible fears that assail me !—

September is here now, winter is not far distant.

The slightest cold might confine me to bed for a couple of months, and then, the convalescence—

And my picture! So that I should have sacrificed everything without—

Now is the moment to believe in God and to pray to Him.

Yes, the fear of falling ill is what paralyzes me; in the

state in which I am, a heavy cold would put an end to me in six weeks.

And that is how I shall die at last.

For I am resolved to work at my picture in any case— and, as the weather will be cold—and if I do not take cold working, I shall take cold walking; how many people there are who do not paint; and who die all the same—

Here it is at last, then, the end of all my miseries! So many aspirations, so many hopes, so many plans—to die at twenty-four, on the threshold of everything.

I knew that this would be so. Since God could not grant me all that was necessary to my life, without ceasing to be just, He will let me die. There are so many years in a lifetime, so many—and I have lived so few—and accomplished nothing!

Wednesday, September 3.—I am making the design for the *Figaro,* but I am obliged to leave off work from time to time, to rest for an hour or so. I have a constant fever. I can obtain no relief. I have never before been so ill as I am now, but I say nothing of it to any one; I go out, I paint. What need of further words? I am sick, let that suffice. Will talking about it do any good? But going out is another thing, you will say.

It is a disease that permits of doing that in the intervals of comparative ease.

Thursday, September 11.—On Tuesday I began a study in the nude, of a child. It might make a very good picture if well treated.

The Architect was here yesterday; his brother desires to know why we have neglected him for so many days. So we went to the Bois in the afternoon, hoping to see him, but we arrived late; he was taking his usual turn through the walks; we waited for him, and you should have seen the surprise of all three to find us there.   He grasped both my hands in his, and when we were going home he took a seat in our carriage, while my aunt returned with his mother. It is as well to get into this habit.

Saturday, September 13.—We are friends; he likes me; he esteems me; he finds me interesting.   He said yesterday that I was wrong to torment myself as I do; that I should consider myself very fortunate.   There is not another woman, he says, who has accomplished as much as I have done in as short a time.

"You have a name," he added; "every one knows who Mlle. Bashkirtseff is.   There is no doubt about your success.   But as for you, you would like to send a picture every six months to the Salon; you are impatient to reach the goal.   But that is quite natural, when one is ambitious; I have passed through all that myself."

And to-day he said: "They see me driving with you; it is fortunate that I am sick, or they might accuse me of painting your picture."

"They have done that already," responded the Architect.

"Not in the papers!"

"Oh, no."

Wednesday, September 17.—Few days pass in which I am not tormented by the recollection of my father.   I ought to have gone to him and nursed him during his last illness. He made no complaint, for his nature was like mine, but my neglect must have made him suffer cruelly.   Why did I not go?

It is since Bastien-Lepage has come back—since we have visited him so often and shown him so many little attentions, given him so many marks of our affection—that I feel this especially.

In mamma's case it was different, they had lived apart

for so many years—until within five of his death—but I, his daughter!

It is just, then, that God should punish me. But if we go to the root of the matter, we owe our parents no duty, if they have not protected us and cared for us from our entrance into the world.

But that does not prevent—but I have no time to analyze the question.—Bastien-Lepage causes me to feel remorse. This is a chastisement from God. But if I do not believe in God? I scarcely know whether I do or not, but even if I did not, I still have my conscience, and my conscience reproaches me for my neglect.

And one cannot say absolutely, "I do not believe in God." That depends on what we understand by the word God. If the God we desire to believe in, the God who loves us, existed, the world would not be what it is.

Though there be no God to hear my evening prayer, yet I pray to Him every night in despite of my reason.

> " Si le ciel est desert, nous n'offensons personne,
>   Si quelqu'un nous entend, qu'il nous prenne en pitie."

Yet how believe?

Bastien-Lepage continues very ill; we found him in the Bois, writhing with pain; none of the doctors have been able to relieve him; it would be well to bring Charcot to see him some day as if by chance. When we were alone Bastien said it was abominable to have neglected him for two whole days.

Thursday, September 18.—I have just seen Julian! I have missed him indeed, but it was so long since we had seen each other that we had but little to say. He thought I had a successful and contented look. There is nothing, after all, but art; nothing else is worth a thought.

The whole family are with Bastien-Lepage, his sisters as

well as his mother; they are to remain with him until the end; they seem to be good women, though garrulous.

That tyrant of a Bastien-Lepage will insist upon my taking care of myself: he wants me to be rid of my cold in a month; he buttons my jacket for me, and is always careful to see that I am warmly clad.

Once when they were all sitting on the left side of his bed, as usual, and I had seated myself on the right, he turned his back to the others, settled himself comfortably, and began to chat with me softly about art.

Yes, he certainly has a feeling of friendship for me—of selfish friendship, even. When I said to him that I was going to resume work again to-morrow, he answered:

"Oh, not yet, you must not desert me!"

Friday, September 19.—He continues to grow worse; we scarcely know what to do—whether to remain in the room while he is groaning with pain, or to go out.

To leave the room would look as if we thought him very ill; to remain would seem as if we wished to be spectators of his sufferings!

It seems shocking to speak in this way—as if I were wanting in feeling. It seems as if one might find words more—that is to say, less.—Poor fellow!

Wednesday, October 1.—Nothing but sorrow and annoyance!

But why write all this down?

My aunt left for Russia on Monday; she will arrive there at one in the morning.

Bastien-Lepage goes from bad to worse.

I am unable to work.

My picture will not be finished.

Here are misfortunes enough!

He is dying, and he suffers intensely. When I am with

him I feel as if he were no longer of this earth; he already soars above us; there are days when I feel as if I too soared above this earth. I see the people around me; they speak to me, I answer them, but I am no longer of them. I feel a passive indifference to everything—a sensation somewhat like that produced by opium.

At last he is dying; I still go to see him, but only from habit; it is only his shadow that is there: I myself am hardly more than a shadow.

He is scarcely conscious of my presence. I am of no use to him; his eyes do not brighten when he sees me; he likes me to be there, that is all.

Yes, he is dying, and the thought does not move me; I am indifferent to it; something is fading out of sight—that is all.

And then everything will be ended.

Everything will be ended.

I shall die with the dying year.

Thursday, October 9.—It is as you see—I do nothing. I am never without fever; my physicians are a pair of imbeciles. I have sent for Potain and put myself into his hands again. He cured me once before. He is kind, attentive, and conscientious. After all, it seems that my emaciation, and all the rest of it, do not come from the lungs, but from some malady I contracted without knowing when, and to which I paid no attention, thinking it would go away of itself; as for my lungs, they are no worse than before.

But it is not necessary for me to trouble you with my ailments; what is certain, however, is that I can do nothing.

Nothing!

Yesterday I went to dress myself to go to the Bois, and twice I was on the point of giving up, I was so overcome with weakness.

I succedeed at last; however.

Mme. Bastien-Lepage has been at Damvillers since Monday last, for the vintage, and, although there are women enough about him, he was glad to see us.

Sunday, October 12.—I have not been able to go out for the past few days. I am very ill, although I am not confined to bed.

Potain and his substitute come to see me on alternate days.

Ah, my God! and my picture, my picture, my picture!

Julian has come to see me. They have told him, then, that I was ill.

Alas! how could it be concealed? And how shall I be able to go see Bastien-Lepage?

Thursday, October 16.—I have a constant fever that is sapping my strength. I spend the whole day in the drawing-room, going from the easy-chair to the sofa and back again.

Dina reads novels to me. Potain came yesterday, and is to come again to-morrow. This man is no longer in need of money, and if he comes to see me so often, it must be because he takes some little interest in me.

I cannot leave the house at all, but poor Bastien-Lepage is still able to go out, so he had himself brought here and installed in an easy-chair, his feet supported by cushions. I was by his side, in another easy-chair, and so we remained until six o'clock.

I was dressed in a white plush morning-gown, trimmed with white lace, but of a different shade; Bastien-Lepage's eyes dilated with pleasure as they rested on me.

"Ah, if I could only paint!" he said.

And I!—

There is an end to this year's picture!

Saturday, October 18.—Bastien-Lepage comes almost every day. His mother has returned, and all three came to-day.

Potain came yesterday: I am no better.

Sunday, October 19.—Tony and Julian are to dine with us to-night.

Monday, October 20.—Although the weather is magnificient, Bastien-Lepage comes here instead of going to the Bois. He can scarcely walk at all now; his brother supports him under each arm; he almost carries him.

By the time he is seated in his easy-chair the poor fellow is exhausted. Woe is me! And how many porters there are who do not know what it is to be ill! Emile is an admirable brother. He it is who carries Jules on his shoulders up and down their three flights of stairs. Dina is equally devoted to me. For the last two days my bed has been in the drawing-room, but as this is very large, and divided by screens, *poufs*, and the piano, it is not noticed. I find it too difficult to go upstairs.

The journal stops here—Marie Bashkirtseff died eleven days afterward, on the 31st of October, 1884.

A VISIT TO MARIE BASHKIRTSEFF.*

BY FRANÇOIS COPPÉE.

LAST winter I went to pay my respects to a Russian lady of my acquaintance who was passing through Paris, and who was stopping with Madame Bashkirtseff at her hotel in the Rue Ampere.

I found there a very sympathetic company of middle-aged ladies and young girls, all speaking French perfectly, with that slight accent which gives to our language, when spoken by Russians, an indescribable softness.

In this charming circle, with its pleasant surroundings, I received a cordial welcome. But scarcely was I seated near the "samovar," a cup of tea in my hand, when my attention was arrested by a large portrait of one of the young ladies present—a perfect likeness, freely and boldly treated, with all the *fougue* of a master's brush. "It is my daughter Marie," said Madame Bashkirtseff to me, "who painted this portrait of her cousin."

I began by saying something complimentary. I could not go on. Another canvas, and another, and still another, attracted me, revealing to me an exceptional artist. I was charmed by one picture after the other. The drawing-room walls were covered with them, and at each one of my exclamations of delighted surprise, Madame Bashkirtseff repeated to me, with a tone in her voice of tenderness, rather than of pride, "It is by my daughter Marie"—or, "It is my daughter's."

---

* Printed in the catalogue of Marie Bashkirtseff's paintings exhibited in Paris in 1885, shortly after her death.

At this moment Mlle. Bashkirtseff appeared. I saw her but once. I saw her only for an hour. I shall never forget her. Twenty-three years old, but she appeared much younger. Rather short, but with a perfect figure, an oval face exquisitely modeled, golden hair, dark eyes kindling with intelligence—eyes consumed by the desire to see and to know everything—a firm mouth, tender and thoughtful, nostrils quivering like those of a wild horse of the Ukraine.

At the first glance Mlle. Bashkirtseff gave me the rare impression of being possessed of strength in gentleness, dignity in grace. Everything in this adorable young girl betrayed a superior mind. Beneath her womanly charms, she had a truly masculine will of iron, and one was reminded of the gift of Ulysses to the young Achilles—a sword hidden within the garments of a woman.

She replied to my congratulations in a frank and well-modulated voice—without false modesty acknowledging her high ambitions, and—poor child ! already with the finger of death upon her—her impatience for fame.

In order to see her other works we all went upstairs to her studio. There was this extraordinary young girl entirely "in her element."

The large hall was divided into two rooms. The studio proper, where the light streamed through the large sash, and a darker corner heaped up with papers and books. In the one she worked, in the other she read.

By instinct I went straight to the *chef-d'œuvre*—to that "Meeting" which at the last *Salon* had engrossed so much attention. A group of little Parisian street boys, talking seriously together, undoubtedly planning some mischief, before a wooden fence at the corner of a street. It *is a chef-d'œuvre* I maintain. The faces and the attitudes of the children are strikingly real. The glimpse of meager landscape expresses the sadness of the poorer neighborhoods.

At the Exhibition, before this charming picture, the public had with a unanimous voice bestowed the medal on Mlle. Bashkirtseff, who had been already "mentioned" the year before. Why was this verdict not confirmed by the jury? Because the artist was a foreigner? Who knows? Perhaps because of her wealth? This injustice made her suffer, and she endeavored—the noble child!—to avenge herself by redoubling her efforts.

In one hour I saw there twenty canvases commenced; a hundred designs—drawings, painted studies, the cast of a statue, portraits which suggested to me the name of Frans Hals, scenes made from life in the open streets; notably one large sketch of a landscape—the October mist on the shore, the trees half stripped, big yellow leaves strewing the ground. In a word, works in which is incessantly sought, or more often asserts itself, the sentiment of the sincerest and most original art, and of the most personal talent.

Notwithstanding this, a lively curiosity impelled me to the dark corner of the studio, where I saw numerous volumes on shelves, and scattered over a work-table. I went closer and looked at the titles. They were the great works of the greatest intellects. They were all there in their own languages—French, Italian, English, and German; Latin also, and even Greek, and they were not "library books," either, as the Philistines call them, "show books," but well-thumbed volumes, read, re-read, and pored over. A copy of Plato, open at a sublime passage, was on the desk.

Before my visible astonishment Mlle. Bashkirtseff lowered her eyes, as if confused at the fear that I might think her a "blue stocking," while her mother proudly kept on telling me of her daughter's encyclopedic learning, and pointed out to me manuscripts black with notes, and the open piano at which her beautiful hands interpreted all kinds of music.

Evidently annoyed by the expression of maternal pride,

the young girl laughingly interrupted the conversation. It was time for me to leave, and moreover for a moment I experienced a vague apprehension, a sort of alarm—I can scarcely call it a presentiment.

Before that pale and ardent young girl I thought of some extraordinary hot-house plant, beautiful and fragrant beyond words, and in my heart of hearts a sweet voice murmured, " It is too much ! "

Alas ! it was indeed too much. A few months after my one visit to the Rue Ampere I received the sinister notice bordered with black, informing me that Mlle. Bashkirtseff was no more. She had died at twenty-three years of age, having taken a cold while making a sketch in the open air. Once again I visited the now desolate house. The stricken mother, a prey to a devouring and arid grief, unable to shed tears, showed me, for the second time, in their old places, the pictures and the books. She spoke to me for a long time of her poor dead child, revealing the tenderness of her heart, which her intellect had not extinguished. She led me, convulsed by sobs, even to the bed-chamber, before the little iron bedstead, the bed of a soldier, upon which the heroic child had fallen asleep forever. . . .

But why try to influence the public ? In the presence of the works of Marie Bashkirtseff, before that harvest of hopes wilted by the breath of death, every one would surely experience, with an emotion deep as my own, the same profound melancholy as would be inspired by edifices crumbling before their completion, or new ruins scarcely risen from the ground, which flowers and ivy have not yet covered. . . .

Uni
s

Printed in Great Britain
by Amazon